Anna,
The Voice of the
Magdalenes

A Sequel to Anna, Grandmother of Jesus

Dedicated to

You in Oneness

"Anna as Rosa Mystica" by Claire Heartsong

Anna,
The Voice of the
Magdalenes

*A Sequel to Anna,
Grandmother of Jesus*

CLAIRE HEARTSONG

In Co-Creation with

Catherine Ann Clemett

S.E.E. Publishing Company, USA
www.claireheartsong.com

Copyright © 2010 Laura Anne Duffy-Gipson
aka Claire Heartsong
and Catherine Ann Clemett

All rights reserved. No part of this book may be reproduced without written permission from the publisher, except by a reviewer who may quote brief passages or reproduce illustrations in a review; nor may any part of this book be reproduced, stored in a retrieval system, or transmitted in any form or by any means electronic, mechanical, photocopying, recording or other, without written permission from the publisher.

This book is manufactured in the United States of America.

Cover Design: Lightbourne

ISBN # 978-0-9844863-0-4

Library of Congress Control Number: 2010903229

Spiritual Education Endeavors Publishing Company
www.claireheartsong.com

Anna,
The Voice of the Magdalenes

Laying the Foundation

TABLE OF CONTENTS

INVOCATION

ASPIRATIONS

INTRODUCTIONS

BLESSINGS

"THE BREATH OF ONENESS"

"THE OPENING OF THE MOUTH"

THE MAGDALENES

MAPS

*Chalice Well Gardens, Glastonbury, England
Photo by Claire Heartsong*

*My beloved friend,
We await you at the Garden's Gate.
Arm in arm,
we leave all fear behind
and pass through the mists of time
to Avalon's farther luminous shore.*

- Anna and the Magdalenes

TABLE OF CONTENTS

FOREWORD

Archangel Gabriel's Invocation	FOREWORD – 1
Aspirations	FOREWORD – 2
Claire's Introduction	FOREWORD – 3
Catherine Ann's Introduction	FOREWORD – 9
Anna's Introduction to Claire	FOREWORD– 13
Anna's Introduction	FOREWORD– 15
Mother Mary's (Mary Anna's) Blessing	FOREWORD– 18
Jesus (Yeshua's) Blessing Yeshua Offers a Guided Meditation "The Breath of Oneness"	FOREWORD– 19
The Three Marys' Blessing	FOREWORD– 26
Myriam of Tyana Speaks Lifting the Suppressed Feminine Voice A Note from the Authors	FOREWORD– 29
Map of the Magdalene's World	FOREWORD– 34
Map of the Great Sea	FOREWORD– 35
Map of Roman Gaul	FOREWORD– 36
Map of Britain	FOREWORD– 37
Introducing the Magdalenes	FOREWORD– 38

PART I: The Voice of the Magdalenes
Anna's Historical & Geographical Overview   2

  1. ANNA: A New Life Begins   4
    Saintes-Maries-de-la-Mer, 32 AD

2. ANNA: Our Journey to the New Mount Carmel ... 11
   "TRANSITIONAL NOTES" ... 19
3. ANNA: The New Mount Carmel ... 21
   Anna Reveals the Two Marys and Yeshua's Children
4. ANNA: Yeshua Comes for a Visit ... 34
5. GALEA, 14 AD ... 40
   The Wedding of Yeshua and Myriam of Tyana
6. MYRIAM OF TYANA, 25 AD ... 54
7. MARY OF BETHANY ... 63
   Discourse on Spiritual Lineages
   Discourse on "Past Life" as "Mary Magdalene"
   Discourse on Relationship with Yeshua and Myriam
   Discourse on Egyptian Sepulcher Initiation
8. NATHANIEL OF MOUNT CARMEL ... 89
9. MARIAM OF MOUNT CARMEL ... 105
10. SARA OF MOUNT BUGURACH ... 118
11. LIZBETT (ELIZABETH HANNAH) (Age 3) ... 125
    (Daughter of Yeshua and Mary of Bethany) 36 AD
    Mount Bugarach, Early Summer, 38 AD (Age 5)
    Brittany, Late Fall, 38 AD (Age – Almost 6)
12. LAZARUS OF BETHANY ... 135
13. JOSEPH OF ARIMATHEA ... 148

PART II: The Suppression of the Magdalene Voice ... 153

14. MOTHER MARY (MARY ANNA) ... 154
    Rome, Italy, 39 AD
15. SARA OF MOUNT BUGURACH ... 165
    (Continuation of Chapter 10)
16. PHILLIP OF BETHSAIDA ... 171
    Ephesus, Turkey, 40 AD
    Mount Bugarach, 49 AD

Mount Bugarach, Early Spring, 55 AD

17. JOHANNES (Age 22)   182
(Youngest Son of Yeshua and Myriam of Tyana)
Cappadocia, Turkey, 48 AD

PART III: The Voices of Avalon   189
The Druid-Magdalene Voice Emerges

18. MARTHA OF BETHANY   190

19. LIZBETT (Continuation of Chapter 11)   211
Avalon, 41 AD (Age 7)
Avalon, 47 AD (Age 13)
Avalon, 48 AD (Age 14)

20. ANNA AND JOHN   225

21. DANCING WIND   234
Dancing Wind's *Guided Meditation*

22. NOAH   250
Mona (Anglesey, Wales) 47 AD

23. SAR'H (Age 18)   263
(Daughter of Yeshua and Mary of Bethany)

24. JOHANNES (Continuation of Chapter 17)   273
Stonehenge, 53 AD (Age 28)

PART IV: The Great Gathering & The Dispersion of the Seeds of Light

25. LIZBETT (Continuation of Chapter 17)   281
Glamorgan, Wales, 55 AD (Age 21)

26. SAR'H SPEAKS (Continuation of Chapter 23)   285
"The Great Gathering"
Fortingall, Scotland, Summer Solstice, 55 AD

27. MARIAM AND ANNA, 57 AD   291
Anna Speaks: Ambush on the Way to Mona, 55 AD
Mariam, A Wisdom Teaching on Consciousness
Mariam, A Teaching on Physical Immortality

28. **ANNA** 316
   The Dispersion of Anna's Family from Avalon

29. **MARIAM** 321
   Mariam Heals Martyr Consciousness, India, 62 AD

THE MAGDALENE VOICE WITHDRAWS INTO SILENCE

30. **MOTHER MARY (MARY ANNA)** 325
   Ephesus, Turkey, 61 AD

31. **SAR'H ON THE ISLAND OF IBIZA** 330
   Ibiza, Spain, 63 AD (Continuation of Chapter 26)

32. **ANNA'S LAST YEARS** 338
   Avalon, Winter Solstice, 80 AD
   The Seeding of the Lineage of Light

30. **BROTHER GEOFFREY** 348
   Avalon, (Glastonbury, England) 186 AD

ANNA'S LAST WORDS 361

APPENDIX 363

Timeline 365
The Seeding of Light Chart 374
Anna's Descendent Chart 378
Joseph of Arimathea's Descendent Chart 379
Yeshua's Descendent Chart 380
Bibliography 381
Acknowledgments 382
About the Authors 384
Books by the Authors 386

FOREWORD

Archangel Gabriel's
INVOCATION

I bring you glad tidings from the realms of Light. I am the one you know as Gabriel. I come from on High as an over-lighting presence to assist you in the delivery of this work unto the Earthplane. I come forth into this space to assist the minds and hearts of many beings so that these words and awakening energies may be received in a manner that truly uplifts and empowers. I also bring greetings, as is appropriate from time to time, from the archangelic Councils of Light and all other hosts, who bring support to the continued unfolding of this work. I walk with you, in this your day, as I have walked with you in seasons past.

May all beings remember the way of love and Oneness.

I am Gabriel. I bid you fond farewell.

LAYING THE FOUNDATION

Aspirations

May the shroud covering and silencing the
Christ and Magdalene
Be gently, but surely, removed in the ripeness of time
– From both Husband and Bride –
– Historical, mythical and essential Being –
May all who have safeguarded the
Christ-Magdalene legacy find sweet rest;
And relax the sore tension of holding
secret oaths and martyrs' deaths.
May the Magdalene mysteries shared herein
Awaken and liberate the Christ entombed within every breast.
May her/his voice be clearly received;
And dissolve boundaries of gender and creed.
May wars fought in their name end and fade
forever from memory.
S/He and their coded DNA live on in every incarnation –
Humanity is their bloodline.
May we awaken to the equanimity and truth of the
Oneness we all share,
Embracing and nurturing the living
Christ-Magdalene in self and "other."
Let us be awake in our dream;
May all suffering cease.
May we hear the Voice within the voices
of those who proclaim the Great Peace.
May this book serve as a portal into
the Beloved's infinite embrace.
In mystical union beyond Avalon's farther shore,
let us be graced.

Amen and Amen.

FOREWORD

Claire's Introduction
January 2010

Twelve years have passed since first receiving Anna's messages which evolved into the book, "*Anna, Grandmother of Jesus,*" published in the fall of 2002. A promise was made then to bring forth a sequel. I am choosing to make good on that promise. Although I originally thought this material would manifest in the same way as with the first book, it has taken a different course. My intention is that these words of introduction assist you to come to this offering with a fresh perspective and with perhaps fewer expectations because of your previous experiences with Anna.

My journey with Anna has involved experiences in which I have felt as if I were "in her skin": seeing, hearing, feeling, smelling, tasting, thinking and emoting as she might have in her time and space. Those experiences of Oneness were both rapturously blissful and intensely demanding. This has also been true in my experiences as I have brought forth this sequel material.

In the physical sense, my earlier very intimate journey with Anna was a solitary process. That is, if you were the proverbial fly on the wall you would have seen me alone typing at my computer. If you had ears to hear beyond the physical plane you may have heard Anna and her team of interdimensional beings (*I call them my Council of Light*) in telepathic communication among themselves and with me. You might also have discerned a kind of holographic energy grid enveloping me, which made it possible to fulfill my work as Anna's scribe. In order to utilize the holographic grid effectively the Councils carefully instructed me in how to align my frequency and consciousness through conscious breathing, visualization and mantra practices. This assisted me to receive the messages and energy transmissions in clarity.

With practice I began to trust my capacity to fulfill my assignment. I trusted Anna to support me through the process of healing and clearing the karmic cellular and soul memory which was profoundly activated by her story. Acknowledging my humanity, I was and still am willing to be accountable for any unintentional errors and misinformation that may occur because of my many ego filters and limited view.

Inseparable from trusting myself, I found Anna, as my information Source, to consistently possess not only a great lucid wisdom but also a comforting unconditional compassion toward all beings. This same level of higher awareness and intention extends throughout this book. It is also to be noted here that Anna no longer is my primary information source in the sequel; however, the Source remains the same.

Once *"Anna, the Grandmother of Jesus"* was published I knew I had had enough of feeling like a sequestered monk in a monastic cell. I very firmly requested Anna and my Council of Light to send me a physical support team. I'll always remember the blessed day when I received emails from CW (*who wishes to remain anonymous*) and Catherine Ann Clemett in response to my website plea for assistants. As it turned out, it was not just for the purpose of assuaging my loneliness that they left their homes and came to my aid. It soon became abundantly clear that their active involvement in the actual transmission process was required.

One morning in early June 2006, I sat before my computer. A blank document awaited my first keystroke. I prepared myself with the usual alignment protocol. I enjoyed a sense of confidence; albeit I also felt a concomitant feeling of intimidation, overwhelm and self-doubt at being able to accomplish what was being asked of me. With a sense of deep devotional commitment to what feels to be a "Calling from on High," and with the palpable presence of my physical support team waiting just outside the closed door, I felt sufficiently supported to commence.

The writing began. The first two chapters called "A New Life" and "Our Journey to the New Mount Carmel" took days to write. I was disappointed to find the words feeling flat and labored. In spite of the alignment process, there seemed to be too much of my discursive mind present, as if I were writing a historical novel. There wasn't enough of Anna's consciousness piercing my intellectual veil, as I had grown accustomed to in my past experiences as her scribe. What was I to do?

Then I heard Anna telling me I would find the answer to the dilemma just beyond the closed door. Following her guidance, I asked Catherine Ann, a certified hypnotherapist, if she would be willing to facilitate as a "past-life regression coach." Although I knew I didn't require her to take me into a more expanded brain state, it became apparent that Anna had something in mind that involved our three-fold group synergy. Without hesitation, we entered into the process. I found it easy to relax on the couch as soon as I was reassured that the tape recorder would provide accurate transcriptions. What a relief to not be typing at the computer!

Lying back on my comfortable couch, Catherine Ann took her place beside me. She asked inspired questions and operated the recording equipment. CW "held space" at my feet and transcribed voluminous audiocassettes. Everything came together for a very effective and dynamic interactive process. Within a very short time it became possible to expand Anna's narrative by directly dialoguing with nineteen different men and women (*including Anna*), all intimately involved in the Christ drama. We witnessed and heard voices that had been silenced for millennia!

I had known for years that other characters in the Anna story wanted to share their personal messages. I also knew there were readers who would feel a resonance with certain of these characters, and that by reading the Magdalenes' stories, the reader could potentially experience healing and a greater awakening in this lifetime. As if on cue, within days of Anna introducing herself through this new protocol, numerous friends and members of Anna's family began stepping through the veil of time.

As we met both familiar and new personalities, heard their words and felt their often emotionally charged vocal intonations, we realized that the sequel messages could put a light on new information that had been overlooked by many researchers (*historical and psychic*). Not only would it serve to "fill in some sizeable blanks," but it would bring suppressed material, thought to be heretical by orthodoxy, forward to be consciously contemplated. We immediately realized that if I had insisted on accessing the messages in the way I had done previously, we would have missed a great deal of hidden treasure.

We were stunned by the exquisite beauty and pathos; the palpable energy and the magnitude of the startling secrets that were revealed. Our work poured forth in torrents for almost six weeks and then it abruptly stopped. For reasons that will become obvious to you, as you read the forthcoming chapters, I felt deeply conflicted about making the heretical revelations public. Whether fact or fiction, I personally cannot prove or disprove the accuracy of the stories that were presented through me.[1] I simply had the experiences and was a witness to the process. It was not my intention to compose fiction and I do not believe that was the case with the Magdalenes, whose stories you will read. It will be for each reader to decide what rings true for them – whether the details can ever be proved correct or not is another matter. As always, the Anna material is multi-leveled, and I believe its real purpose serves the awakening of consciousness, rather than merely serving as conjectured "history" or as merely entertainment.

It took two more years to finally come to a place of sufficient internal equilibrium and clarity to pick up "The Voice of the Magdalenes" transcripts and determine if the content had any real value as a spiritual teaching vehicle. I asked myself if the material was in sufficient alignment with authentic spiritual realms of higher consciousness, so as to actually transmit life-enhancing wisdom and quickening energies. (*I know this is true with the first Anna book.*)

---

[1] Anna encouraged me to do research concerning the Roman occupation of Gaul and the Roman invasion of Britain. I have cited these references at the end of this book. Over many years I have read about and visited the places in France and Britain which are referred to in this material. During the course of developing the original transcriptions into this sequel, I did not actively read books about the Holy Family or the Grail Bloodline in France and Britain. I acknowledge that whatever had been integrated earlier into my frame of reference (filter) concerning these topics does influence the content of the Magdalene "voices."

Although the sequel material was different, I determined there was enough alignment with higher consciousness to proceed. I then looked deeply within to see if I were up to the task of publishing another book; if I were up to dealing with the consequences of making this controversial material available to a public audience. The answers to this self-inquiry were in the affirmative. Catherine Ann and I have devoted many hours during 2009 to bringing the fragmented contents of the original transcripts to a level in which it might be read with a degree of ease and lucidity. It might be noted here that the sequence of the sequel chapters is not in the order in which the characters originally spoke.

Anna continues to be our principal guide through this material. She understands that you will likely have many questions along the way. She desires you to know that you are not alone, and that she is readily accessible, once you attune to her frequency in a space of love and gratitude. With her expansive view, she can assist you in your personal journey traversing what may be a confusing and mystifying terrain. Anna speaks with a clarion voice for the Divine Mother and the Councils of Light, whose unified consciousness extends beyond all time and space. Besides the Magdalene accounts which span many lands over a rather long period of time, Anna's personal story takes us to her experiences in southern France and her beloved Avalon in Britain, where she reveals her last years on the Earthplane.

Anna has asked me to act as a present-day interpreter, who, while acknowledging my human limitations, bridges and weaves the numerous voices and settings of then and now. You will find throughout, that I have provided contextual information for your contemplation. Anecdotal accounts of personal events that occurred during this remarkable process are also shared. Charts and maps are enclosed with the intention that they provide you with a way to organize and make sense of the complex array of "voices" – interrelated beings speaking across a considerable timeline and geography.

In order to expedite this material getting to you, I have intentionally chosen to not give the same amount of time to the

LAYING THE FOUNDATION

writing process, as I did the first book. Please forgive omissions and editorial errors. Catherine Ann and I have done our best to bring many disjointed fragments together into as cohesive a presentation as possible. We believe what is given, although perhaps still incomplete in many ways, is still a sufficient catalyst which may serve you and your personal purpose for taking this journey with Anna and the Magdalenes.

We continue to contemplate and question the information you are about to read. We encourage you to do likewise. Test it within your own mind and heart. There are controversial aspects of the stories that will likely be misunderstood. This gives me concern. So I breathe and I let go. I continue to trust in the ultimate outcome which I have stated in the affirmations preceding my introduction. We humbly and gratefully lay it all at your feet, affirming you will transform anything that is potentially harmful into the light of wisdom, within the stillness of a clear mind and open heart. Perhaps much that is offered is best left to simply abide in the mysterious realm – "don't know." And for all that has been given; may we rest in gratitude.

"Anna, the Voice of the Magdalenes" ushers us across yet another threshold of understanding into a greater awakening. There is an urgency to make the most of the time given to us while in this precious human birth. May we meet beyond all fears, and walk together arm in arm through the mists of Avalon. May we meet in the Pureland where polarity and paradox embrace as the Infinite One. May we joyfully dance emptiness and intrinsic awareness!

FOREWORD

Catherine Ann's Introduction
January 2010

I feel most honored and am most grateful for the privilege to have been so intimately involved in the unfolding of this sequel. It is not a place that I ever imagined I would be. What is ours to do in life sometimes comes completely out of left field as was the case with me.

I first heard about the book, *Anna, Grandmother of Jesus*, in the summer of 2004 from a teacher of an advanced DNA healing workshop I was taking in Coeur D'Alene, Idaho. This teacher, who never had mentioned any particular books before, told us how Claire's book was the best book she'd read in a long time. When I returned to Portland, OR after the workshop, I bought the book and read it that summer. Like many of you, I had a strong resonance with the book. Anna's story, and her version of the Christ drama, definitely rang true for me unlike anything I'd ever read before. What really piqued my interest however was Claire's account, in the last chapter, of her meeting with the master St. Germain. I had had a similar experience with a master in the spring of 1982, whom I later discovered, was also St. Germain. After reading the Anna book, I emailed Claire asking her if she'd be willing to share with me, in more detail, the story of her encounter with him. At that time, in 2004, I did not hear back from Claire – not that I necessarily expected that I would. However the connection had been made.

Through an unbelievably synchronistic series of events over the next almost two years which I go into more detail about in my own book, *Soulweaving: Keys That Unlock the Treasure of Your Soul*, Anna and the Councils of Light from the other side of the veil orchestrated my friend, CW, and I coming together with Claire to support her in bringing forth the sequel. CW and I suddenly found ourselves relocating from Portland to the Zion National Park area in southern Utah to assist Claire. We thought what we were to do was to take care of Claire's business and personal needs (*cooking, cleaning, errands and such*) so that she would be freed up to concentrate on writing the sequel. As Claire has already shared, it turned into much more of a collaborative effort of us working together in accessing the records of these characters' lives and teachings. Sometimes in the sessions, we were completely taken by surprise by who chose to come through and speak to us. As you will notice, it often took a little bit of communication back and forth with the character before their identity was revealed.

Working with Anna and the Councils, we were instructed on the protocol for the sessions; how to set the field for the greatest safety, greatest clarity of information to come through, greatest healing, and highest good for all involved. All of our roles became clear, including that of Theo, Claire's Maine Coon cat. Theo was an important member of the team holding space for whatever was happening. During the regressions he usually perched himself on Claire's body either on her stomach, heart area, or thighs. We knew we could not start a session without Theo. He always showed up when we were ready to start. There was a time or two when we had to call him to come thinking that we were ready to start. Inevitably the phone would ring, or something else would happen, that would delay the start of our session a few minutes. Theo would then nonchalantly come waltzing in right on cue, always in the perfect timing. Sometimes I think Theo was the most tuned-in one of us all!

As the sessions progressed, a curious thing started happening. Before starting any kind of regression with clients, I always have them empty their bladder so there would be no bodily interference that could potentially bring someone out of the altered state. After our first few sessions, despite having emptied her bladder, Claire would always have to go to the bathroom within about ten minutes. Not wanting to bring her up out of the deep state she was in, I would help her up from the couch, take her by the shoulders and guide her – with her eyes still closed – through the master bedroom to the bathroom. After assisting her I would stand in the doorway to make sure that nothing happened to her while in this state. I am sure this need to go to the bathroom was because of many reasons; deep cellular releasing in her body, as well as clearing on a soul level; however we began to have an inkling that something else was going on as well. What began to happen on these bathroom excursions is that whatever character had come through in the session and was still somewhat present in Claire's body would start making comments about this bathroom experience. They (*through Claire's body*) would marvel at things like the toilet paper, stroking it and examining it, for this was not something they had in their time. We finally figured out that word was spreading through the ranks of particularly the female characters coming through. They all wanted to have this experience of the excursion to the bathroom in Claire's world.

My favorite was when Martha came through. She squealed with delight as she walked across Claire's oriental carpet in the bedroom – letting me know that it was a familiar sensation to her as they had those in her time as well. She proceeded with a detailed account (*unfortunately not recorded*) about the chamber pots they used and her adventures and duties in taking care of them. The cycle of the bathroom visits finally ended when the first man, Nathaniel, came through. Like usual I led Claire to the bathroom. This time, however, Claire-Nathaniel just sort of reluctantly stood there not knowing what to do. Finally, in a strong authoritative voice, I commanded Nathaniel to sit down, as standing up which was his usual way was certainly not going to work in this situation.

Through these bathroom excursions, and other times when the buzzer on Claire's dryer would go off, or the answering machine for the phone would come on, I would often have to either explain to, or reassure, the character coming through that it was just some normal occurrence in Claire's world that they didn't have to be concerned with. What became evident through all of these sessions, and all of these experiences, was that these weren't just characters in a book, but real beings and personalities that we were having an exchange with. In some cases we were not only interacting with them, but helping them to rewrite aspects of their lives. Likewise they, in turn, are helping us to heal deep soul wounds and expand our beings in a profound way.

LAYING THE FOUNDATION

Two years after the initial material was brought through the regression sessions we did in Utah in the summer of 2006, Claire revisited the material and expanded upon the foundation of what had come through at that time. With so many different characters, different time periods, and different points of view being presented, we wondered at the purpose of this format and why the writing of the sequel was such a different process than the first book. We wondered how all of these accounts from the different characters were going to come together. Claire and I started to co-creatively tune-in, ask questions and brainstorm about this. I am reminded of our beloved Yeshua's teaching, "When two or more are gathered, there I AM."

Once we started tuning-in in a co-creative manner, a greater level of understanding and the macrocosmic picture about the Magdalene's voice and the seeding that was taking place for future generations on all levels, including the physical, started emerging. Through this co-creative process the deeper mysteries also began emerging bringing much insight and greater understanding for both Claire and me about our own personal journeys and initiatory experiences in this, our current lifetime. All I can say is that I am most awed and humbled by what has come through.

Many of you reading this, although you may not be aware of it, are also part of the Magdalene Order. We are the future generation that was held in sacredness and seeded by these characters and others long ago. We are those seeds now reaching maturity. In this maturity we now awaken, once again, to our path of service. We no longer need to be bound by lifetimes and layers of vows of silence and secrecy. We, now, are the collective voice of the Magdalenes who have come to be set free and to fly, now in this time.

FOREWORD

Anna's Introduction to Claire

For you, Claire, I suggest the following: Prepare this space to be a sanctuary of serenity. A space dedicated to the purpose of birthing the book that is about to commence; a sanctuary from the world and those vibrations that pull you down and obscure your light – the Truth of that whom you BE. You have traveled long on this path and it is unseemly to miss the mark that is plainly before you. Look not outwardly for excuses, for there are none to be found. Now that you have set your affairs in order and the means are splendidly provided for the work to go forward, it is for you to simply choose to take affirmative and humble action.

You have done well in accomplishing this and the research you have done concerning the Romans in Gaul and Britain has placed you in an advantageous position to receive the impressions that will arise within your mind. These can now be translated into word pictures and energy transmissions appropriate for this advanced undertaking. It shall be a work in many ways unlike that which was its precedent. But it shall also be an instrument of awakening and a clarion missal sent unto those with ears to hear this added portion.

I have long held the memories of my life in France and Britain close to my heart. I have long awaited this turning of the ages for my story's dispersal to my posterity and the family of mankind. It is time to begin the writing process. You are well aware that there are forces of resistance to this message. These resistive forces reside within and all about you. Intrinsic within this work are potent transformational and empowering energies that will stir deep cellular and soul memory for every reader. Memory that has long been suppressed shall arise and be given a voice.

For some, the voice most clearly heard will be the cry of the abandoned feminine, held in abeyance and subservience to the unbalanced masculine. In truth, however, the uniting voice of the Christ-Magdalene takes a stand for the ultimate freedom of both men and women to embrace one another in equanimity. For others,

LAYING THE FOUNDATION

the resounding echoes of "holy war," clashing in mutinous betrayal of the divinity of life, will grind against still bitter and grieving hearts. A wellspring of forgiveness and compassion may arise to dissolve all cause for war within self and perceived other. Some will come seeking Mary Magdalene and her children. And for these, a new way of seeing and feeling is required in order to enter her mystery. On a more subtle level, Christ-Magdalene initiates may hear the Voice of the Beloved and receive a further quickening of their very blood in order to transmute deeper regions of fear – the source of separation. And then beyond the stories and words themselves, it is also possible for those with eyes to see and ears to hear, to receive the pervading Infinite Light frequencies.

Many there shall be who will remember who they are and why they are here at this very time when so much is astir. This work will facilitate preparedness and allowance of inevitable planetary change, as the watchword "All is One!" is given utterance by the souls choosing to establish an ascended reality of peace and harmony – excluding no form of life from its natural birthright. This message is being created inter-dimensionally in order to empower synchronistic moments of realization for every soul, within all lands, who is calling forth the Divine Mother's comforting words and loving presence.

As with the previous book, this is an initiatory process of internal and external alchemy. And so it is that there is the necessity for the various dynamics of polarity within duality to be acknowledged and appropriately balanced into empowered expression. In this way, the energy of transformation may be felt first within your self, as you integrate our communication through the veils, and then the empowerment may extend to all who would likewise choose the peace that passeth understanding. I am with you continually. And though there will be interruptions from time to time in the course of the writing, we shall easily pick up the story line with its attendant multi-dimensional energies and perspectives.

May you, dear Claire, find deep peace, joy and liberation as your soul heals through all space and time. May all beings likewise benefit from your accumulated merit and committed devotion to bringing forth a greater light. So be it!

FOREWORD

Anna's Introduction

Greetings, my beloved friend, I am Anna. Once again I am with you. As you have asked of me, so I freely give. You may have already read of my life that leads to this sharing. And it is alright if you are not familiar with me or my long life's journey. The story I am about to tell can stand on its own, if you wish. However, in order to acquaint yourself with my manner of speaking and to have a context for the characters' lives that continue in this telling, I encourage you to partake of the substance of the published book, *"Anna, Grandmother of Jesus."* Within this book I weave a tapestry of energy and details about my experiences as a physical immortal from the time of my birth in Judea in 612 BC to my arrival in southern France three years after my grandson, Yeshua's crucifixion and resurrection. This sequel shall take you to my last years in Britain.

I am mindful that you have been stretched by the many revelations I have shared with you about my self-mastery initiations. For it was through these experiences that I was prepared to be the mother of Mary Anna (*Mother Mary*) and the grandmother of Yeshua (*Jesus*). I have also shared detailed accounts of my family and our community of Essenes who supported and enacted the Christ drama in what is termed the Holy Land. As I share my remaining story you will realize that what began, long ago, continues uninterrupted, although it has assumed other labels and taken other venues.

A few among us who walked in Palestine, Britain and France demonstrated how to transmute the cycles of human suffering and thus escape humanity's self-imposed prison. I come forth now so that you may hear the suppressed voices of the Magdalenes – the women and men who walked with Yeshua, who know of the way of resurrection and eternal life. For this purpose I now reveal what has long been hidden.

My words are multi-faceted in their design. They are sourced from cosmic realms. Interdimensional energies are couched within and between the phrases I communicate to your mind. I am an

LAYING THE FOUNDATION

emissary of the Mother Divine and I am closer than you may think. For purposes as yet unknown by the majority of humankind I have come because **you** have called me forth to walk at your side. In the course of hearing these words and the love frequencies within them, you are invited to take the steps that may bring you closer to your Mother/Father Creator – your Beloved on High – who patiently awaits you, within this moment, beyond the illusion of time and mental concepts.

Know this, my friend, what I share with you is to be discerned through your own spirit's knowing, supported by your rational mind. Question what is given, weigh it within your mind and heart. Nurture only those seeds which increase joy and peace in the living of your life. My intent is to expand consciousness through wisdom born of clarity and love. Though filtered through my scribe, you may use the frequencies and the multi-leveled messages pervading my words as a key to open your own Book of Life. If you choose to enter the Hall of Records – the Akasha of Mother Earth, you may meet me as one of your guides. While this is the more direct path into wisdom's sure knowing, let it be known that I honor and respect those who are led to the inarguable physical remnants we sealed up to be found in the ripeness of time.

Please attend to your own soul's awakening to greater loving-kindness by whatever methods work for you within your relationships and daily life. Doing so is far more important than getting lost in the rambling details of my story or laboring with doubt over the controversial secrets we cautiously reveal. What is shared is a heresy that goes against the grain of unquestioned tradition and the "truths" held within conditioned mind. Find the liberating essence of love and wisdom woven through my words. To prove or disprove – to argue and contend is a waste of precious time. Contention is not my way – awakening to our Infinite Nature is. There is more to be accomplished than to fabricate another history or Grail romance, whether based in truth or fiction, which distracts you from the true enlightenment of your mind.

FOREWORD

May the shroud of silence be lifted!

The voice of the Magdalenes rises from the dust –

Listen, beloveds.

Listen! Be!

Hear the Voice in the Silence!

LAYING THE FOUNDATION

Mother Mary's (Mary Anna's) Blessing

MOTHER MARY (*Mary Anna***):** I bid you welcome. I am called Mary Anna by my Essene family.

The voice of the Great Mother of Life shall be very much present throughout our co-creation, my children. It is not just me, who, in most minds, represent her. I speak as her child, and yet I am also that Mother. You are my sisters and my brothers; you are my fathers, my sons and daughters. We share in the mysteries, in the awakenings, in the drinking of the sacred cup of union. We are remembering together for the benefit of all. Some of you walked with me across these lands. You labored in the vineyard of souls and you toiled much. Indeed, you gave all that you could give.

We have given to life so that there might be more abundant life for all. This work is our chosen destiny. We take it into our hearts as a gift and a treasure which we cherish above all else upon this plane. We do not see it as a burden. It is as if we lift up a thirsty lamb upon our shoulders and carry it cheerfully across the wilderness to a place where it can receive nurturance and rest. It is our offering to the Father-Mother of Life. It is our devotional offering laid out upon the altar of our hearts for the upliftment of all who thirst and hunger for the Living Light. This has always been my way, and you know that, and I thank you for entering into this way once again.

My son is so very close at hand. Others of the family are close as well. We are indeed gathering. For this I rejoice. There are precious ones coming from all quadrants of this earth. They are gathering into the high places and into the low places; into the places of wilderness and into the places that are heavily populated. There is no place on this earth that is not being reached by the Christ-Magdalene Voice. Within this clarion call is an invitation to awaken and enter into the embrace of the Mother Divine and the Beloved Father who sent her. She has come to bring her children Home into the Infinite Light of Oneness. Within her silent heart is the Great Peace known beyond the understanding of words.

FOREWORD

I am your mother, you are my children. I bid you adieu....

Jesus' (Yeshua's) Blessing

"Yeshua with Lamb" by Claire Heartsong

LAYING THE FOUNDATION

JESUS (*Yeshua*): I am your brother and beloved friend. I am called by my family in the Aramaic language, *Yeshua*.

I am gathering myself for this meeting, as I gathered levels of my consciousness in the years after passing through the portal of crucifixion and resurrection. I do this in order to appear unto my brethren and my sisters on every land across all timelines and dimensions.

There are many mysteries and many misunderstandings concerning my life, my work and my relationships. For the purpose of this story, I blend my voice with the voices of those with whom I walked 2,000 years ago. Among these, there were those who knew me in my body of flesh and those who knew me in my transmuted body of immortal light. For it was after my crucifixion that I attained a full enlightenment of my physical and subtle bodies. I became what may be called "Light anointed" – or Christed – I realized myself as a Christ – a Teacher of Righteousness among my Essene family; just as Gautama realized himself as a Buddha within his culture. I tarried upon the Earthplane for forty more years, continuing the work I had begun earlier. During the time referred to in this sequel story, however, my service to humanity was accomplished in more subtle ways.

When I came forth after the resurrection I presented myself in a variety of forms so as to be able to walk unhindered amongst humanity. For the most part, I brought little attention to myself. Even now, as in those days, I move unnoticed amongst my brothers and my sisters. For souls who are ready to behold me, whether in or out of form, my frequency is recognized, and together we have communion. I often present myself in the fashion in which I have been known: as son, brother, uncle, husband, or father; or as a guide and friend. Sometimes I appear a bit older, sometimes quite young, and sometimes even as a child. I am known for my sense of lightness and humor. There are times I present myself in a tangible body, yet a body that, indeed, exudes a good deal of energy and light. In equanimity with all forms of life, I have also come forth in more subtle forms such as the wind or a body of water; as various animals, birds or insects; or the essence of trees and flowers.

FOREWORD

Sometimes I come forth as a beam or orb of light. Most often I simply bring my presence as a vibration, which quickens the heart in the manner in which the Holy Spirit is known; being neither male nor female, being both, unified and whole.

For anyone who has the capacity to behold me fully, who can withstand and merge with my intense energy field, there is an exquisite blending, in which we may know the rapture of divine Union beyond time and form. In deep communion, we exalt and glorify the Father/Mother Birther of Life. It was in this way of Tantric alchemy that I came unto my beloveds, the Magdalenes, who knew me as their husband.

I spent many years, while my beloveds were yet in flesh; walking in the areas you call Britain, France and Eastern Europe. Often we removed ourselves from the world and resided in caves where we deepened our alchemical practices and ascended our frequencies. It was within such womb-like caves in Europe, and in the Middle and Far East, where most of my children were Light-conceived. Although we would take journeys in our bodies of light to other places and planes of existence, the choice was to have our presence anchored in these particular areas of the earth for quite a long season.

When all was accomplished, I departed to the Himalayas which became my primary focus for attaining further cosmic levels of ascension. My beloveds joined me there at the end of my days. In extended retreat, we together entered the deepest levels of High Alchemy for the benefit of all beings existing in all the times and realms.

I retained a measure of physicality right up to the moment in which my last conscious breath left my etherealized lungs. While sitting in the posture of equipoise, with omniscient Awareness, my immortal body of Light rose through the crown of my skull and merged with the All – the Great Emptiness – beyond the Central Sun. With my Magdalenes as witnesses, I let go my earthly tabernacle. My residual, elemental form was laid to rest within a remote mountain cave where a radiation of cosmic Light continues.

Did I assist in the conception of children? I say to you, yea, this is true. It is also true that my intention was never to establish a dynastic lineage to rule the sons and daughters of men. Neither was this the intention of the beloveds who bore my seed in their wombs. Indeed the whole of humanity is my family seeded with my Father's Light. You are remembering that within your blood is hidden the light codes of the Christ, which when awakened, may guide your way Home. Kneeling before the Father-Mother who birthed you, you may receive the anointing elixirs and awaken to your True Nature — realizing yourself as a Son/Sun of God — the Light of the world.

My signature vibration permeates my grandmother's first book and there shall be an added measure in this sequel. This may be felt as a comforting presence for those who call me forth. And I say to you, my beloved, do call me forth.

Again, I say, I invite you to call me forth as your beloved Friend.

You have thought me to be separate and distant from you. I say unto you, I am here and you can come into my arms. If you wish, at any time of your choosing, we can enter into a meditative space where we can meet and know the presence of Love.

Yeshua Offers a Guided Meditation: "The Breath of Oneness"

Imagine me as a dear friend (or as an orb of golden light) coming to meet you face to face. A radiant golden sphere of light surrounds us. Within this calm and illumined space we breathe The Breath of Life.

I invite you to slowly and gently breathe with me. Join your breath with mine. Simply breathe....

Exhale. Send any tension and weariness into a light or a flame, as you may imagine it, inside my heart. See my heart-flame growing brighter with every breath you breathe.

FOREWORD

Audibly sigh…Ahh!

Inhale. Breathe in my eternal light. Breathe in my eternal love. Breathe in my peace.

Exhale. I breathe in any pain you may be feeling…it's alright…audibly sigh. Ahh!

Inhale. Feel the warmth of my love expanding your heart – igniting your heart-flame. I send you my love and my peace upon the wings of my breath. Breathe in peace.

Exhale – I breathe in your pain; all the suffering of your body, mind and spirit. Ahh! Give me your burdens and I shall make them light.

Inhale – My Peace I give unto you.

Exhale – Imagine your sufferings, like a moth; flying into the crucible of my heart. See your grief, anger and fear transmute into golden light – a new dawn rises!

Inhale – I AM the Resurrection and the Life.

Breathe with me again… Remember the Christ within. We breathe the Breath of Life, my beloved friend.

Softly breathe. Rest in the stillness of the Great Silence – simply be aware of your breathing, nothing to do but follow your breath. Just come back to your gentle breathing.

Become aware of the Breath within the breath, flowing freely with each deep inhalation and exhalation. Breathe in the infinite light and love. Receive me into your sacred heart.

Relax…allow your heart to smile…Ahh!

LAYING THE FOUNDATION

The stone of separation rolls back from your heart. The Son of God calls forth the entombed Christ lying within. Come forth! Awaken and arise!

I say unto you, peace. Peace. PEACE... Allow the quickening of Light within every cell. Allow the falling away of what no longer serves you. Breathe sweet peace into every cell. Come into the light. Come away from the tomb of ignorance. Come with me to the purelands and forgive that which dies and is dead.

Gather up your fragmented self and place it all within the comforting womb of your Christ-Magdalene heart – the infinite heart of compassion. Let the Christ child grow within you. With each breath receive renewed vitality; every cell resurrecting.

Deeply breathe... Become aware of the golden orb of light that surrounds us. Allow the form of your human body to BE the Son/Sun of God. Be the Infinite Light!

Come home to the Father/Mother of your being. Let go of your identity in flesh and merge with me into a greater light; beyond all light, beyond all forms.

Breathe.... Relax...Simply BE....

My breath is your breath. The beating of my heart is the beating of your heart. My body is your body. Self and "other" are merged in divine Union: Bridegroom and Bride – Christ and Magdalene – One Life.

Now, knowing the Oneness, feeling compassion for all life, breathe awake your awareness of the suffering of others as being no different from your own. Gently breathe out your gift of love's pure light into your brothers' and sisters' hearts...gently breathe in and receive their pain as a "ball of darkness." Place the black or dark grey ball of suffering gently inside your Christed heart. Watch as the darkness melts into the light….Every heart glowing… Every heart is calmly at peace.

    Be not in expectation of change or reward; simply allow what is, to be, as it is – this is infinite love. Just know "other" IS your "self" – the Great Perfection. As I know your heart is mine; so it is that the One beyond names continues to breathe the Breath of Life.

    Regardless of how many times you may choose to experience this union of souls and hearts; this marriage of spirit, let it serve you well, my beloved brother/sister, my beloved Magdalene.

    Peace be unto you, now – within this breath, and unto the end of the world. Be not concerned about the form I may take when next we embrace, for you shall know me as I Am, beyond all forms and names. It is for you to choose, and in this way, know yourself as the Christ-Magdalene you seek.

    Lo, I AM with you always.

The Three Marys' Blessing
MYRIAM OF TYANA
MARY OF BETHANY
MARIAM OF MOUNT CARMEL

Together, as one trinity, we fulfill and reveal what has been held in abeyance for many eons of time. With us comes a company of Magdalenes who also bear witness of the Great Mother and the empowerment of the feminine in men and women. Together we shall lift up that which has been buried and hidden, suppressed underfoot. We shall raise, indeed, our voices as one voice in harmonious unison and exude from the center of our collective heart the fragrance of ascension.

Our voice is as one – the Voice of the Magdalenes. Each of us speaks for one another.

Our merged desire is the healing of the feminine heart and the flowering of this earth – the healing of deserts and the wastelands within souls. Therefore, our vision encompasses men and women walking together as equals, where families, communities and nations honor differences and similarities, allowing and encouraging everyone to express their infinite potential. We see every soul capable of expressing their intrinsic light and bringing forth the highest forms of creativity, each according to their nature and karmic conditions. We also honor and accept choices of limitation. Although these choices may cause suffering, we also know suffering is a divine expression of the Great Perfection. Limitation, as an expression of contrast and choice, has within it the infinite potential to be a catalyst for awakening, compassionate healing and wisdom. Our merged desire is to catalyze and witness the cessation of all forms of suffering while incarnated within our shared human condition.

FOREWORD

So we come forth as emissaries of the Mother Divine, manifesting as the Christ-Magdalenes, the physical vessels through which she expresses her power on earth. At this time in your day and age there is great need to bring the masculine and feminine into balanced union. By this statement let it be understood that it is never our intention to overpower or cause any aspect of consciousness to become subservient. Ours, at this time of great planetary crisis, is to restore balance to the technologically based mind, which we see as unbalanced masculine energy – for example, the clear evidence that Mother Earth and her creations are dying from all manner of escalating violence, insensitivity, greed and pollution. We experience the masculine mind as bereft and devoid of the feminine heart – the ability, for example, to holistically experience the interconnectedness of all life.

We see that a greater percentage of the Divine Feminine is required. This is why you are hearing so many messages and appearances from the Divine Mother, such as those of Mother Mary. This is the reason books are coming forth, such as the one you are now reading. Because a greater expression of the Divine Feminine is what will bring balance and harmony, we come forth as a female trinity with our beloved Yeshua.

Together we represent the Divine Feminine and Divine Masculine in harmonious union. As a trinity of three women, we exponentially expand the energy of the Divine Feminine within ourselves. Then when we are joined with Yeshua's focusing of the Divine Masculine at the center, there is the co-creation of an encompassing sphere, or an alchemical Grail Cup, in which Mother Earth and humanity may be held. With Yeshua joining us as a fourth force, we also co-create the strong base of a pyramid, by which we "square the circle," and stabilize the unbalanced energies presently multiplying at an exponential rate.

What I have described as "our" stabilizing effort is a microcosm of a universal quantum process, which for this sharing, will not be described in further detail as it is not our intended focus here. Impermanence, expressing as planetary change, is inevitable. Our desire is to awaken individual choice, based on infinite, intrinsic

LAYING THE FOUNDATION

potential, so that this time of great change may be utilized as an unprecedented catalyst and opportunity for awakening to our individual and collective Infinite Nature. We are choosing to act as a stabilizing agent for this cyclical, birthing/dying process.

We have shared with you the Greater Part of our spiritual work within the Order of the Magdalene; which, whether great or small in its effect, is done on behalf of humanity. Our work is multi-leveled and not easily understood by the ordinary mind. Already it may be dawning within your mind that there was not just one Magdalene but, in fact, many Magdalenes; not just one Mary Magdalene with Yeshua, but three. We know you have questions regarding our personal relationships with each other, our children and Yeshua – a mystery and secret that is in the process of being partially unveiled and told. There is the ripeness now for bringing to light portions of what has been veiled in oaths of secrecy. Even so, for many, what shall be presented will be difficult to hear, much less to integrate. Therefore, we shall bring forth our stories with great mindfulness.

Be at peace, my brothers and sisters. We are the Magdalenes; we carry the gene of Isis to regenerate and bring forth a new genesis, a new creation, and a new "Adam and Eve" – a new generation, a new world and a new heaven. And so it is.

Myriam of Tyana Speaks:

Lifting the Suppressed Feminine Voice

MYRIAM OF TYANA: I know that you have many questions to ask of me. I understand that I have been quite a mystery package. I am one whose time has come to emerge out of obscurity and to bring light to so much that has been confusing and unnecessarily compromising.

I will bring forth my understandings and my perceptions, as best I can, through the octaves of light and through this instrument. However, know this, my dears, this one who is speaking cannot be limited by name or feature of presence in one singular embodiment, for I am much more.

I shall introduce you to my relationship with my beloved Yeshua and my function therein. My children shall be introduced. I will also speak of my spiritual work with the Magdalenes – both women and men – and how we create an alchemical cup with Yeshua, in which to transmute fear-based consciousness and assist the liberated energy to express as harmony and loving-kindness.

I join with the others who will speak of those times when we removed ourselves from the world. How we sealed ourselves up in caves and climbed to the high places where we practiced the resurrection and conception practices known to the Magdalene Order – we, who are the daughters and sons of Isis – a name for the Great Mother. We will share a portion of that which has been hidden and allow the remainder to rest as seeds in the ground of consciousness until there is a readiness for more. This is wisdom. There is so much conditioned fear; it is best to give more light only when there is true receptivity and benefit.

I say to you again, it is time now for the fear that has closed our voices to be laid to rest – for those who have been silenced, to speak at last.

LAYING THE FOUNDATION

May all beings hear the Mother's gentle voice before she is required to use a much louder one! May all beings experience the ultimate liberation within and beyond form! May all beings know peace! May all suffering cease! Amen and amen!

Now for the benefit of all beings:

"The Opening of the Mouth"

"In Oneness with our Christ-Magdalene sisters and brothers and with the Councils of Light under the auspices of the Divine Mother-Father, we wish to initiate what the Egyptian alchemists call: The Opening of the Mouth.

*"It is time for what has been silenced to be heard.
It is enough! It is enough!!
IT IS ENOUGH!!!"*
{Spoken with great emphasis and passion}

A Note from the Authors

CLAIRE: So that you may know the power behind Myriam of Tyana's words, I would like to share the experience I had following her initiating *"The Opening of the Mouth."*

Inseparable from the need for awakening and healing consciousness of its wound of separation, I have come to believe that there is a collective "wound" that involves feeling verbal restraint and not feeling heard. This wound abides on personal and universal levels. The basic, personal core wound, no doubt, has its origin in not feeling met and heard as a child. But this "inner child" wound can be exacerbated, as an adult, when a more collectively agreed silencing occurs. On the personal level, as an adult, this communication wound involves being silenced either by personal choice or by an outer authority: on the one hand, choosing to take vows of silence and perhaps not being able to relinquish the vows for any number of reasons; and on the other hand, being externally forced to be silent.

FOREWORD

On a more universal level the communication wound may appear as the silencing of "the still voice" – the Voice of the Great Mother or the Divine Feminine. This wound shows up for everyone deafened by ordinary, conditioned consciousness, because the veil of perceived separation makes subtle, spiritual frequencies very difficult to hear. It also shows up in patriarchal and male-dominated cultures which censor women; societies which are indifferent, belittling or hostile toward females generally and toward all kinds of feminine expression specifically, in both women and men.

In Myriam's facilitation of *"The Opening of the Mouth,"* she is initiating the opening of all voices on a personal level, giving everyone the freedom to speak, if they choose to do so. On an universal level, Myriam, in concert with the Great Mother, transmits an energy that opens closed inner ears so that the Mother's Voice can be heard – a Voice which carries the frequency of universal awakening and healing into wholeness/Oneness.

In my case, immediately and abruptly, after Myriam's presence departed, as I was lying on the couch in the process of returning to ordinary consciousness, I suddenly became aware of a very large energy-field seeming to approach me from behind. I sensed this energy; what I have come to understand as a spontaneous rising of Kundalini, to be the magnitude of a tidal wave. Instantly, the energy ascended from the base of my spine to the crown of my head. Its force lifted me very quickly into a sitting position, causing my neck to whiplash. Before I could consciously censor it, a shattering scream came out of my throat. It seemed to express the collective anguish, grief and rage of all beings whose voices (*Beingness*) have been silenced through time.

To say that I was acting as a proxy for all beings may be an exaggeration. But, nevertheless, the force that flowed through me was very real and very intense. It was as if an ancient gag had been removed from my mouth and a dammed (*damned*) energy was released. I fell back on the couch, stunned. The pain in my neck was severe and the injury took a full year to heal. It has been explained that my body and chakras were requiring further clearing and that the degree of resistance on the physical and etheric levels, in relation to the force of the rising Kundalini, resulted in the severe muscle and ligament tears and strain.

Myriam's words became very real and accessible in Catherine Ann's and my immediate daily experiences. We looked deeply into how we were holding on to ancient vows of silence. We became increasingly aware of how we have misinterpreted current life experiences which still trigger fear about expressing our truth – all the ways in which, we, especially as women, feel silenced by internal and external suggestions and conditions. This opening of my throat chakra, the seat of empowered communication and creativity, has provided me with greater clarity and power in speaking and listening. This has been true in bringing through and completing Anna's sequel, as well as enhancing mindful, open communication in my personal life and relationships.

CATHERINE ANN: Claire's sudden and forceful bolting upright and the ensuing scream that emerged through her was profoundly unnerving. Of course I was very concerned and bewildered at this as I thought she had pretty much returned to her waking consciousness state and had come out of the session. Usually when I work with clients if there is any agitation during a session, I assist the person and their energy to come to a harmonious resolution as best it can be before completing the session. In this case, there was no indication of any strong, overwhelming emotion during the session (*albeit when Myriam of Tyana spoke, "It is enough!" three times, it was expressed with great intensity*). The scream seemed to come out of nowhere.

Later we gained a greater perspective in terms of a synchronistic event in Anna's life that came to light in later sessions and the understanding that Claire, in a sense, was being the conduit through which the collective, locked Magdalene voice was finally breaking free of its long history of persecution and need for secrecy. This was a contract that Claire (*and no doubt others*) had made on a soul level. Although Anna later communicated to her that it needn't necessarily have been to the degree of injury which occurred, it was how the resistance unfolded in her body. This occurrence from a larger perspective, I think, helped create an opening in the fields of consciousness not only for the voices of the Magdalene in this sequel to come forth more powerfully, but for the voice of the Divine Feminine to be felt, heard, honored, and expressed more fully now, in our time, in both men and women.

LAYING THE FOUNDATION

Map of the Magdalene's World

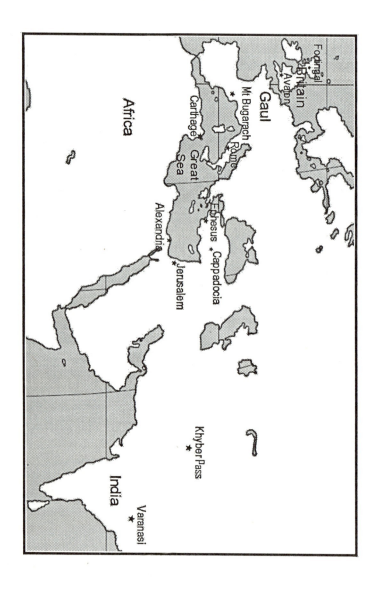

Map of the Great Sea

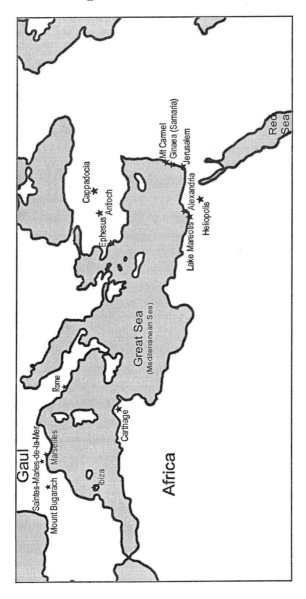

LAYING THE FOUNDATION

Map of Roman Gaul

Map of Britain

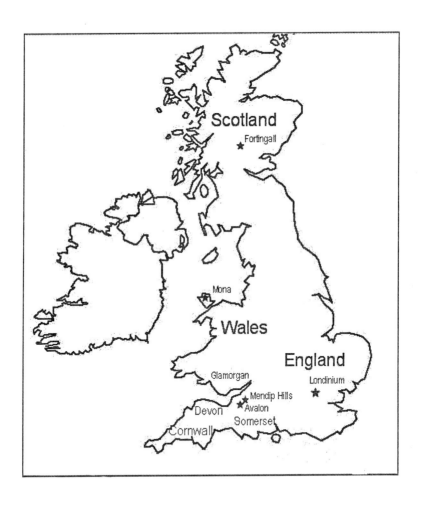

LAYING THE FOUNDATION

Introducing the Magdalenes

You are about to meet nineteen different "Magdalenes" who carry the Voice of the Christ-Magdalene, including Anna. Many of these are family members and friends connected with the Christ drama depicted in *"Anna, Grandmother of Jesus."* There are others who are entirely new. They will all provide glimpses into their personal lives as they relate to specific experiences, times and locations. Many also offer spiritual teachings that transcend time and place.

As you become acquainted with these individuals, you may note that there are unique personalities who share from their various perspectives and levels of awareness. With some, you may experience more of the human dimension than you did with the earlier Anna material. Likewise, the energy frequency may be experienced as heavier and more mundane – the higher frequencies, which are also present, more subtly accessed. You are encouraged to look deeply into this phenomenon, should you experience it, and, in your own mind, question why this is so.

After the first two introductory Anna chapters, the format will shift from a singular narrative to a "question and answer" dialogue. The chapters are named after the specific Magdalene (*either gender*) who is speaking. You will find the content grouped into four parts. These parts correspond loosely with chronological time and with three distinct geographical locations: Southern France, Britain (*before and after the family dispersion*) and the Middle East. At certain key points, we will introduce personal anecdotes. It is hoped that these "asides" may assist you to better understand what Catherine Ann and I were experiencing at the time the Magdalenes were presenting their messages. And, if you choose, you can use these notes as a way to also enter more fully into the energies and messages. Brief historical accounts are also footnoted in order to provide contextual information.

FOREWORD

You may also notice that many of the accounts are incomplete. It is our hope that you will use what is provided as a springboard for further exploration, as you feel guided. It is our deeper intention that this material will bring illumination to your path so that you may realize your own Christ-Magdalene voice and your intrinsic, luminous nature.

LAYING THE FOUNDATION

Mount Bugarach, France

Photo by Catherine Ann Clemett

PART I

THE MAGDALENES SPEAK

Lifting the Vow of Silence: Secrets Revealed

FRANCE, SAMARIA, INDIA, EGYPT

14–38 AD

ANNA, the Voice of the Magdalenes: Historical & Geographical Overview

Now I shall give you a brief historical and geographical overview so that you may orient yourself and relax into my story's telling. In the fair lands of France and Britain I walked with my grandson, Yeshua, his mother, Mary Anna, his beloved Magdalenes, and others of the family. These precious souls shall speak of things withheld through time. Their voices can now be heard by those of you who are prepared to awaken and demonstrate the power of the Grail seeded deeply within you. For it is that we partook of initiation mysteries in which a higher order of ascension was realized and recorded into the stones of these holy lands and into the genetics of the generations that followed. So it is that my words are far more than just the telling of my sojourn's last remaining years.

We will take up the thread of my tale's weaving with the telling of my brief sojourn in France (*then called Roman Gaul*), my journey across her breadth to a northerly port village, and then setting sail to Britain's hoped for haven. Subsequent years unfolded with short respites of leisurely repose, punctuated by times of challenging human drama. With family and friends, I warmed chilled bones with the telling of wisdom stories beside hearth fires. Across the lands of Gaul and Britain we consecrated our life-force within sacred groves, caves and standing stone circles, which have stood witness to the divinity in all life from "time before time." Sad to say, tranquil peace within our cottages, orchards and Essene way of life was constantly overshadowed by the haunting presence of Rome which had earlier made Gaul its colonial state. And in 55 and 54 BC Julius Caesar's territorial stake had also been driven into the tribal lands of southeastern Britain.

Fortunately Caesar's armies retreated back to the Continent soon after their landing and Britain's fair lands remained untouched by Roman legions for many years. When I first arrived in Avalon in

HISTOTRICAL & GEOGRAPHICAL OVERVIEW

late 38 AD we were free of their influence for almost five years. Yet, during that time there was always a foreboding sense that my virginal haven amidst the British Celts would not last forever. My peaceful refuge ceased to be, when, in 43 AD, the Emperor Claudius took Britain as a provincial prize. Soon the island's lowlands and highlands were crisscrossed with well-engineered roads and bridges; rustic Celtic timbered hill-forts were replaced with fortresses; tribal king's mud and wattle strongholds gave way to stone villas; and sacred springs fed lavish baths for sophisticated, urbane patrons. I witnessed the first forty of what was to total over three hundred years of Roman occupation. Within a decade of Claudius' coming, the thread of my story continued to twist torturously through nightmarish terrain. *grandauhaft / alphrauinlay*

Now let us begin at the beginning of this story's full telling, by returning to the estuary of the Rhone River where our boat without sail or oars found refuge from the Great Sea. Where, if, in your day, you were to visit the village called Saintes-Maries-de-la-Mer, you would encounter the annual gathering of Gypsies who remember and honor through time the coming of the Two Marys (*actually more, if the truth be known*) and a veiled girl-child they call Sar'h.

3

— Chapter 1 —

ANNA: A New Life Begins

The Family Arrives in Southern Gaul

I am glad that you are here, my beloved friend. The cloak that has concealed my life has grown heavy. It is time to share and lighten the load my family and I have carried. You are ready to hear what has long been kept hidden. Yea, indeed, there is a deep soreness etched into our bones from the oaths of secrecy we have taken to protect what we know from those who would be harmed or bring harm to others.

What has come to be called Christianity, and, indeed, we ourselves, have purposely obscured our footsteps and our simple path. During my time, our Essene and Gnostic ways were held suspect by those in power in Rome. Among the splintered factions that never knew Yeshua personally — a powerful mythos and religious doctrine began to be formed which was based on his little understood life and the true basis of his teachings. Secreted truths that couldn't be entirely suppressed became increasingly threatening to the growing Church of Rome. Its patriarchal hierarchy merged church and state in order to gain an empire of great wealth and influence. As more years passed, we who safeguarded these secrets were branded heretics, and in the name of God, the fruit of our family tree was burned at the stake.

Sadly, like all spiritual lineages, that come to be the unifying light within the dance of duality, ours is a lineage of light-bearers familiar with threats of torture and loss of life. Yet, what darkened our days was not so much the grieving of personal loss of life, as much as the trampling of those ways we freely shared in which any sincere heart could know a greater liberation. It was the twisting of the message of love's power that caused us distress. Yet, paradoxically, it was within our suffering that our hearts of compassion opened still wider, for we knew in a season yet to come the suffering borne by those who oppressed us would be far greater than ours – what is sown must be harvested.

It is for all these reasons that I am glad that you and I may meet through these pages. Let us walk together arm in arm across the shadowy terrain of my remaining years. Along the way, I shall reveal secrets which I have held close to my heart in order to protect the truth of my family's legacy. But first I must take you aside and request that you ask yourself these questions: "Once you hear what I am about to tell; what will you do with any expanded understanding? What will you do with what might be considered heresy? Will being exposed to another possible truth make your heart lighter and more loving? Will you live your life in a way that will be of greater benefit to others?" Please pause. Contemplate deeply what you find in your mind and heart – then we shall go on.

Saintes-Maries-de-la-Mer, 32 AD

We are met now upon the shore where the mighty Rhone delta meets the Great Sea. This land is called Gaul by the emperors of Rome who have claimed it by force, wresting it from the ancient Celtic tribes who now pay heavy tribute to those who call themselves gods. As it was in Galilee and Judea, so the yoke of oppression is also felt here. We remain a family in exile.

Memory of our arrival and the beginning of a new life rises as do the early morning mists that hover softly above our new homeland. Out of these ethereal threads a tapestry of myriad impressions coalesces around my mind and heart. A balmy haze gathers upon the shore where now we walk. Warm, languid waters lap at our bare feet as we stroll between grassy dunes and sea swept beaches laden with dark silt carried by the river from the uplands. Off in the distance to the north there is evidence of a small fishing village with its moored skiffs and children at play. Fishermen cast their nets for the day's catch as they bob upon the gentle current. Climbing a small hillock covered with dune grass and dense scrub, we can gaze seaward where large wind-driven freighting

ANNA, THE VOICE OF THE MAGDALENES

boats sport colorful sails. These are familiar to me for my son, Joseph of Arimathea, made his business trade upon the seas. Just weeks earlier in Alexandria, it had been one of Joseph's boats stripped of its sails and oars, by order of an offended Roman Centurion, that had carried us miraculously undetected, against all odds, to this gentle haven. Underscoring our recent trauma, a large slave-driven, Roman warship looms now into view. As quickly as it appears slicing the water with skilled precision, it fades into the hazy horizon.

Not far from us, where the main body of the Rhone spreads wide, there is a Roman stronghold you call Marseilles. Its history as a citadel of trade and war stretches far back in time. Its strategic position served the ancient seafaring Phoenicians and Greeks before Rome came to power. I was also aware that just upriver from us there was a newer burgeoning city, called Arles, that catered to the tastes of the aristocracy. It was said to be modeled after the Imperial City.

About such things, I learned much during the lively talks we shared with our generous hosts, after breaking bread in the evenings. Many stories were told about the suffering of the local people and how similar their lives were to ours during those last years Yeshua walked with us in Mount Carmel and Jerusalem. My body involuntarily contracts as I recall the accumulated stress and tension we all had to master in those days. Like the sea plowed by a man-of-war disappearing into a gathering fog, unsettling thoughts rise up to disturb the otherwise tranquil waters of my mind. I breathe. And my body easily relaxes into the gifts of the now.

Although there are moments of anxiety, these are soon replaced with abundant feelings of gratitude that so many of my family are here with me. At another telling, when more is in place, I will share as openly as I can about these family members. Meanwhile, let us patiently set the stage.

This is a rich and fertile land. We are given sufficient provisions day by day for our needs. The children who came with us on the harrowing journey from Alexandria were made strong through our initiation of faith. This will prepare them for the challenges they are

ANNA: A NEW LIFE BEGINS

sure to face. In these days of much needed rest we instill calm in one another, as well as vigilance. We must be continually watchful, ready to move at a moment's notice. We are relaxed, yet eager for our new life before us.

Though we limped into the estuary of the Rhone, we regained our strength quickly with the help of the villagers who took us into their humble homes and treated us as honored guests. We refrained from telling all that could be said that might identify us as fugitives. However, we did share about the miracles at sea when Creator heard our unified prayers and set our listing boat on a northwesterly current that eventually washed us upon this blessed shore. They delighted to hear how our bellies were fed by fish aplenty and our parched throats were quenched by gentle rain. They marveled at our faith and our vibrant health and cheery dispositions.

Shortly upon our arrival, my eldest son, Joseph (*of Arimathea*), who knew a great deal about the Mediterranean coastline, and thus our whereabouts, immediately sent word by messenger to a friend in commerce who lived nearby in Marseilles. He was a well-trusted merchant who had for many years been an undercover liaison for Joseph when he had brought initiates, manuscripts and supplies to various Essene communities throughout southern Gaul. In various stages, word was carried by boat and rider to the Essene sanctuary at the foot of the Pyrenees where my sons, Isaac and Jacob, live in seclusion. This compound, fashioned after Mount Carmel, was one of its most important outreaches. It was here that I came shortly after I had conceived Mary Anna (*Mother Mary*) in Britain. It was here that she and I were destined to return.

In 18 BC Isaac and Jacob had moved permanently to this region of the Languedoc where the mystical Mt. Bugarach dominates the landscape. With dedicated industry and devotion they contributed much to expanding this Essene monastic outpost. They also gave freely of their time and energy to the physical and spiritual welfare of the families who lived in the surrounding small rural villages. For those who came from abroad and those living nearby who wished to deepen their capacity for joyful, simple living, the school they established taught how to maintain physical and

7

emotional well-being, good farming and husbandry practices, and how to live in greater harmony with one another and nature.

Those with sufficient interest and discipline were also taught how to memorize and recite oral arcane teachings as well as how to read and write. They could then make good use of the library I initiated many years earlier. Among these were also men and women who sought a deeper contemplative life removed from worldly distractions. As in Mount Carmel, it was possible to sustain a consistent practice of the ancient methods for attaining various levels of enlightenment.

It has been over thirty years since I last saw Isaac who is now 79 years of age. I am eager to embrace him and hope his Essene practices of meditation and diet have served his body well. Likewise, I have not seen his beautiful Egyptian wife, Tabitha, in many years and hope she also has benefited from our wisdom teachings and way of life. Jacob, who never married, is now 77. Fortunately I had the opportunity to have Jacob close to me for a year in Mount Carmel after he fulfilled his duties as Yeshua, James and Joseph the Younger's chaperone to and from India. (*My grandson, Joseph, remained in India.*) Nevertheless, it has been far too many years since being with this son who reminds me so much of his father, my beloved Joachim. As I attune to Jacob, I sense his robust energy. I know that once he receives word of our place of arrival he will make haste and escort us to his Languedoc home, our new Mount Carmel.

A Month after Arriving in Gaul and Two Weeks Before the Journey to Mount Bugarach

And indeed, it was my energetic Jacob who first arrived at the abode where Mary Anna (*Mother Mary*), her younger children and I have received refuge. Mary Anna's youngest boy child, Matteas, who had just turned eight, saw his uncle in a dream the previous night and knew he was close. This precocious child had a sense of this man called Jacob, for he was always one of the children closest to my knee when I told stories about the adventures of his stepbrothers, Yeshua, James and Joseph the Younger in India. He remembered that it was his Uncle Jacob who took these older brothers to the Orient where they learned many great things from many great teachers. Matteas knew this mysterious uncle lived in the mountains to the west, where we would soon travel, and that it would be this uncle who would help us find a safe haven.

Keeping his dream to himself, Matteas was the first to see Jacob's approach from his favorite lookout. Perched high in the limbs of a great sycamore tree, he watched a lone horseman coming at a trot. Mounted on a large black draft horse common to Gaul, his uncle was easy to recognize, even from a distance. Responding to Matteas' waving of a white cloth, Jacob urged his horse to a gallop, stopping just in time to gather the laughing lad into his arms – setting him astride in front of him. Hearing the clattering of hoofs and merry voices, the rest of the children in the household turned away from their chores to run out the thatched gate. Thankfully their much talked about uncle had safely arrived. Though at first a stranger, he was soon embraced and plied with a hundred questions before he could even think of coming inside. Needless to say his sister, Mary Anna, and I were among the throng to greet him.

What a delight to behold my son, who indeed, looked younger than his years. He appeared to look so much like his father that I had to suppress a startled sigh. Jacob explained that he had ridden several hours ahead of Isaac and Tabitha who were coming with a small caravan of wagons which would transport us comfortably to our new home. During the short time that Jacob required to wash him self, as was our custom, the children ran to the other households to spread the good news. In no time, we were all gathered around a large hand-hewn table in our host's great room. Jacob was given goat's milk and new wine, breads and cheeses, dried figs and nut meats, and the season's first crop of apples and pears. It was difficult to hold our customary silence as he mindfully ate each bite. As soon as my son was finished eating and before he could rinse his hands, we began peppering him with a steady stream of questions. He loved every moment of it!

Jacob, like many of his siblings, was a great storyteller. He enthusiastically responded to our requests for news about the family scattered here and there and those who lived in the community from whence he had come.

While Jacob was still elaborating on various topics of interest, the village children ran out to meet Isaac and Tabitha's caravan. Once spotted, the children and their parents escorted the whole lot to our door. In spite of all the clamor and milling around, I ran through the crowd to my son and daughter-in-law's wagon. A teary-eyed Tabitha jumped immediately to the ground and was soon enveloped in her daughter, Sara's exuberant arms. Isaac, smiling from ear to ear, was slower to climb down and limped toward me with the aid of a cane. Once getting his land legs, he picked me up in his bear-like arms, as if I were a child. I could not hold back the tears of joy and remembrance of those days, when, as now, any of my family members returned from a long absence.

Introductions were made all around and soon the great room and outer porch were filled to overflowing. Knowing there would be many beloved mouths to feed, we women had for days been busy preparing a feast. As soon as everyone was made ready and the ritual candles were lit, great platters and bowls were heaped high with all manner of savory foods. The bounty was placed on the table and in laps for all to enjoy. Festivities went on into the late hours. It had been a long time since we had celebrated with so much good food, singing and dancing. Those who had come to take us to our new Mount Carmel home stayed on for several more days in order to rest the animals and gather supplies for our journey to the mountains. I will long cherish these memories of care-free merriment, after so many years of hardship.

When next we meet, dear friend, we will take our departure from Saintes-Maries-de-la-Mer and I shall describe how it was that we finally arrived at the little valley nestled close to the mysterious mountain called Bugarach. Soon thereafter, we shall hear from those family members and friends who also desire to share their voices

— Chapter 2 —
ANNA:
Our Journey to the New Mount Carmel

Mount Bugarach of the Languedoc
Early autumn, 32 AD

During the weeks we were waiting for Isaac and Jacob's arrival, Joseph of Arimathea made connections, in person and by messenger, with his network of confidantes who lived in the Provence region of southern Gaul. These trusted merchants had overseen his commerce and wealth for many years. Through his skillful resourcefulness we were able to secure funds and supplies for our journey. As soon as everything was in order our caravan of wagons began its long trek. It felt good to be moving in unison toward our destination that lay at the foot of the Pyrenees.

Once we had finally passed through the estuary marshlands of the Camargue with its more primitive tracks, we were glad for the Romans' extraordinary road building skills that made our journey much easier. This was brilliantly exemplified by the Via Domitia, the primary east-west cobblestone road, which makes the journey from Rome to the Iberian Peninsula far swifter than it had been for the Celts and earlier invaders stretching back into prehistory.

Of the same construction as the roads which supported the military occupation of Palestine, I was thankful it now served our passage to freedom. Jacob explained the amazing construction which utilized the labor of many soldiers and slaves under the direction of Imperial engineers. Trenches, often as much as 8 feet deep, were filled with layers of rock, sand, cement and broken tile. The surface was finished with closely fitted paving stones. These roads were meant to endure the ravages of time and were almost maintenance free. It was this amazing network that defined and extended Augustus' and Julius Caesar's envisioned empire, which, in time, spanned the known world.

It was hoped that by acquiring provincial control over foreign lands, Rome would prosper and know relative peace. Retired, contentious and idle military leaders were moved from the overcrowded capitol to the outlying regions where they were granted large estates and villas as a reward for their foreign campaigns. With the advantages of greater autonomy, they could take command and oversee the taxation of the provincial peoples. These retired and ambitious Tribunes and Centurions ensured the popularity of the emperor within the capitol city. This in turn aided their own political prospects, because it was the vanquished that paid the heavy toll of Roman excess, and not the citizens of Rome.

We traveled the Via Domitia without incident. The children counted the milestones that distanced us from the tiny village where we had found refuge during the past weeks. Each marker seemed to give us a welcoming salute as we passed by. On occasion, rural way-stations welcomed us for the night. Most often we found rest in an open field near a grove of sheltering trees. Passing through the open markets of village forums gave us the opportunity to purchase fresh produce which we later ate for a roadside respite or evening meal. All in all, it was a pleasant adventure – a time to enjoy family camaraderie and renewed vitality.

On the estuary of the Aude River where the first Roman provincial port city called Narbo Martius or Narbonesis is sited on the northwest coast of the Great Sea, we gladly accepted an invitation to rest for several days. One of Joseph's trusted liaisons, a wealthy man who held a high position in the provincial government, opened his large home to us. He was of Gallic and Roman descent and had assisted Joseph through the years in gaining the appropriate papers needed for the passage and portage of his boats.

Most importantly, he understood and supported Joseph's greater purpose which was to bring initiates and supplies to the several Essene communities located in the Languedoc region. He was also adept at gathering intelligence about the movements and agendas of the Roman military so that we could move forward with greater confidence and with fewer obstacles. In order to be better informed about our coming days' travel, several women and all the men in our party met privily with our generous host to discuss the state of affairs in Gaul and Britain. I excused myself and chose a time for quiet contemplation, knowing that I would be given the necessary details later.

The second leg of our journey meant leaving the Via Domitia and embarking on the Via Aquitania that bridges the Great Sea and Atlantic Ocean. With each mile we traveled, I felt an uplifting energy expanding my heart. I had not realized how the past years' stresses had burdened my body and soul. As we followed the beautiful Aude River, which was home to all manner of fish, waterfowl and flora, I found my breath deepening. Buried tension dissolved into the laughing waters flowing by. My mind became as crystal clear as the blue sky after the morning haze burns away.

Each mile took us deeper into the interior of the Roman province of Gallia Narbonesis, which you now call the Languedoc.[2] We joyfully passed through hillside vales that had been cultivated to grow vegetables, grapes, fruit trees and grains. I could see that this was a plentiful year and that the crops were nearing their final harvest. Laborers – men, women and children, could be seen gathering, shocking and winnowing the fruits of the fields. I greeted their steady gazes with a smile, and often smiles were returned, especially from the children who stopped to curiously watch us as we passed by. In the distance the snow-capped spires of the Pyrenees could be seen. With the counting of each additional milestone, these majestic mountains grew in size. I knew our new Mount Carmel sanctuary lay at their forested feet.

I could feel an increasing sense of homecoming as I sent an aspect of my energy body ahead to await my physical arrival in a few more days. My soul soared and I rediscovered childlike wonderment and awe within every breath. All my senses were heightened.

---

[2] Languedoc means the language of the Occident derived from the Gallic languages and the Roman soldiers' vernacular Latin.

ANNA, THE VOICE OF THE MAGDALENES

Nostalgic memories of my beloved Mount Carmel and similar Galilean pastoral scenes spread like a transparent overlay. Then, as if reading my mind, Mary Anna, who sat beside me in the wagon, gently took my hand and held it to her heart. We both sighed deeply. Each of us allowed ourselves to linger with cherished memories, while also retaining mindfulness of all that was arising in each present moment.

Instantly, visions arose into my awareness of those blessed weeks before Mary Anna was fully conceived in Ephesus. Preliminary conception initiations had occurred in Britain and also within a cave near the now not far distant Mount Bugarach. Well over fifty years have passed since my beloved Joachim had been here with me. Also our sons Andrew, Josephus and Noah had come with us on that important journey, though, once we arrived in Britain, they chose to remain on the isles of Avalon. They saw that their souls' work could be accomplished better there with the Druids and they were eager to assist in the development of an Essene-Druid community and mystery school.

Remembering the remarkable bliss I had known with my beloved, as we drew down the Immaculate Light, I was suddenly overtaken with pangs of emotion surging through my breast. Flashes of longing for Joachim's physical touch and his soothing voice collided with a growing joyful anticipation of what was coming. I realized I was now much closer to revisiting Britain's verdant lands and feeling my beloved sons' embraces.

Stepping more fully into these holographic visions, I was returned to the twelve initiatory experiences in which I was prepared for Mary Anna's Light Conception. Seven long years had been dedicated to developing my capacity to support the Divine Mother's cosmic frequencies on every level, as Her Presence was stepped down into form – for she would express as a living Incarnate. If I were to avoid a miscarriage, this deep inner work was required. With these remembrances, a greater awareness began to dawn, which was held within the unfolding present. I knew with increasing conviction there was more important work for us to do on the Earthplane. There was more for those of us who wore the mantle of the

ANNA: OUR JOURNEY TO THE NEW MOUNT CARMEL

Magdalene to bring forth for the benefit of humanity. As I energetically revisited the powerful energy vortexes of Avalon and Mount Bugarach, I realized how important it was that we bring our physical presence to these places of power at this time.

All of a sudden the wagon wheels fell in and out of an unusually deep rut. I was jolted more fully back into present time. Breathing with greater conscious awareness, my body/mind realigned and I could feel Mary Anna's great loving warmth and gentle strength supporting me. Smiling, we nodded a consenting "Yes!" as we allowed our consciousness to expand and lift upward through our crowns. Our energy bodies flew together over the landscape, as if we were eagles whose overview oriented us to this land and her people. We were happy to find a resonance and deep nurturing to our souls as we attuned to all we surveyed. We knew that somehow the work that lay ahead would be supported in every way.

Regardless of the inconveniences that at times slowed our progress; I felt an expanding buoyancy and lightness of heart. Nothing dampened my growing passion for this fertile land and our life's new beginning. Even as we approached the bustling fortified town of Carcasum, now called Carcassonne, my spirits remained high. That is, until we began to see a cloud of dust rising on the horizon and heard a gathering dull rumble. We realized we were seeing the bristling advance of a large Roman legion marching toward us.

Knowing we would be ordered to pull off the roadway, we carefully found a safe place to withdraw, where an intersecting path crossed the Via Aquitania. If we had ever entertained the thought that this road had been built for our convenience, there was now no mistaking the original purpose for such mighty highways. The adage, "All roads lead to Rome" took on expanded meaning. Our friend in Narbo had said that a legion was about to muster in Carcasum, but he thought it would not leave for another day or two. Although surprised, we chose to embrace this oncoming tidal wave of military might rather than resist it.

I watched the children's various reactions to the relentless passing of legionary cohorts: infantry, cavalry and baggage carriers led by an imperious general and a number of tribunes. Although they had seen small companies of soldiers before on the Via Domitia, this display of brute force aroused the all too recent memory of the centurion in Alexandria who sentenced us to die aboard our floating "mystery school." There were also the lingering memories of the soldiers' earlier hostility toward us and many others in Galilee and Judea before and after Yeshua's crucifixion. It was a sharp reminder, that although we were free to travel – Joseph of Arimathea had made sure that we had the necessary papers – we might be falsely recognized as fugitives.

So it was that I observed some of the boys, wide-eyed, as they scrutinized the general's grim face as he rode by on his proud horse; his white and purple toga flowing and his molded breastplate displaying exaggerated muscles. Rank upon rank of infantry soldiers marched by, their tightly fitted armor glinting in the sunlight. Most of the weary men looked doggedly ahead, while some glanced at us with disdain. A few foot soldiers, mostly Gallic slaves forced to fight for the emperor, offered us feeble smiles. The younger girls among us withdrew, peeking out from the adults' protective huddle. We wanted to shield them from the reality that the haven we sought was marred by potential hazards. We all attempted to be strong and unaffected, but we couldn't help but put hands over our ears to lessen the deafening sounds. The clattering staccato of shod horses' hooves and thousands of soldiers' hobnailed shoes rose and fell in thundering waves upon our tender hearts.

The legion seemed like an unstoppable war machine parading its might before us. Then, as if to further convince us that we best not resist the power of Rome, we endured the cacophony of each cohort's wagons and carts pulled mostly by mules. All kinds of camping equipment, timbers, grain and metal objects of war filled every conveyance. A few wagons carried wounded soldiers that had survived a recent campaign to the north. Following in the dust were shackled men, women and children soon to be sold at the slave market in Narbo Martius. We couldn't help flinching as the drivers and equestrian guards snapped their whips over humans and beasts alike, shouting endless obscenities, as they goaded tender shoulders and flanks. Stopped short, we always find it startling to realize to what degree the economy of the Romans and Celts, alike, was built upon the backs of slaves and human trafficking. Oh, the suffering of humanity! Would it ever end?

Finally the rear guard passed and we were left alone in the deafening silence. Slowly we gathered ourselves and pressed on to Carcasum. Not wanting to linger, we moved as quickly as possible through the forum and followed the Aude River south toward its source in the foothills of the Pyrenees. We gladly left the Via Aquitania with its busy concourse of commerce and military presence.

Because some of the wagons required repair and the animals were weary, it was agreed that a full day's rest in the thriving village of Limoux was in order. We found grazing for the animals near the blacksmith's shop. The farrier and wheel-wright were glad to get our business. While the horses requiring shoeing were shod and the wagons requiring repairs were repaired, we enjoyed taking the children through the colorful market where we took in the additional supplies Isaac had been asked to bring to our mountain community. After the wagons were made ready, we heaped them as full as room allowed and continued south through a deepening canyon.

Our night's destination was the Roman bath fed by the hot mineral springs flowing through the limestone grottos of the Aude River at Alet le Bains. The baths had been made into an elaborate affair that served all manner of recreational and healing purposes for the Roman gentry who took excursions here from Narbo Martius. Except for those who were of Roman descent, or those who had adopted Roman ways, we noticed that we were among more and more descendants of the ancient Celts and other tribal peoples. These rustic folk wore the plain garb they had known for centuries. Those who served the nearby shrines and grotto springs dedicated to Minerva and Mithras wore Roman dress, except, of course, when clothing was laid aside for bathing. I could not help smiling to myself, as I contemplated our common humanity, once outer pretense is removed.

We were told that there had been a party of revelers just a few days earlier, which had prospered the local merchants and brothels. This particular afternoon we had the good fortune of having the healing waters to ourselves. How good the refreshing warm waters felt to our bone-tired bodies which had endured so much these many months since leaving Palestine. We gave thanks to the Mother/Father of Life and to the healing angels who carried away our cares and pains, as we soaked for hours. Most of the children had never experienced such luxuriant delight. Their playful squeals of laughter ignited levity in us all.

We were even more delighted when, at sunset, a rider, whom Jacob, Isaac and Tabitha hailed as Brother Tobias, sought us out. He was broad of shoulder and stocky of frame. His deeply tanned and smiling face bore a full beard that compensated for the sparse black hair which barely covered his ears and nape. He announced, after greeting everyone with a warm hug, that he had sent a runner earlier to secure rooms for us at a nearby inn, which was stewarded by an Essene family, whose service it was to look after the needs of fellow pilgrims. How lovely to be taken in and fed a wholesome meal. Then there was the joyful singing of sacred psalms and rounds of folk songs. For those who could stay awake, Joseph and Jacob rendered a brief accounting of our long trek and news of the conditions we had last encountered in Jerusalem and Alexandria. For myself, I once again begged my leave and followed other nodding heads. How wonderful it was to slip into a clean bed!

Even though it meant our journey would become more challenging, we were glad to press on to our final destination. The Roman road that now followed the river was more primitive, a mixture of cobblestone, worn logs and rutted earth which had been recently washed out in places. Several times we were forced to make a detour after a sudden thunderstorm made muddy lakes out of a number of low-lying sections of dirt track. We knew it would not be long before this road would be brought up to the standards we had enjoyed earlier.

ANNA: OUR JOURNEY TO THE NEW MOUNT CARMEL

We were aware by now that we had covered most of the distance and it would not be long before arriving at our new home within the fertile valleys nestled below the great mountains. As we approached Mount Bugarach, we drew welcoming attention from the local farmers who were expecting us. Some of these kind-hearted people had made ready to join us to our final destination. They desired to know, first hand, Jacob, Isaac and Tabitha's relatives, whom they had heard so much about. And likewise, we delighted to feel once again the joy of kindred souls bound together in a community led by Spirit.

Our ancient narrow track followed the contours of the rising slopes of Bugarach's forested south side until we crossed its gentle pass. A beautiful vista of snow-capped peaks, just off in the distance, welcomed us, as did a spring-fed glen. Perched on an outcropping of weathered stone were the gated walls of our new Mount Carmel sanctuary. Those who call it home ran out to meet us. Our tired bodies were assisted to dismount and make ready for a welcoming feast. Blessed were we all to gather in a circle, arm in arm, as the sun's late afternoon rays shone golden on the mountain snow. Purple shadows streaked across the beautiful sunlit meadows and pasture lands. Sheep and goats bleated a chorus of welcome. Though our bodies were thoroughly worn, our souls soared with grateful Hosannas. We had arrived at our haven of peace, at last!

"TRANSITIONAL NOTES"

Transitional Notes (segues) will appear between "{}" marks.

{*We are now at the point in the next chapters where Anna's narrative shifts to a "Question and Answer" format, in which Catherine Ann is in co-creation with Claire. Catherine Ann facilitates Claire by joining her in the deeper consciousness (imaginal realm) of the Akashic Records[3] and "holds*

---

[3] The Akashic Records or Hall of Records are the holographically recorded "Book of Life realities" of the collective consciousness or The Mind

19

space," while asking questions and operating the recording equipment. Claire holographically "embodies" each character's Akashic record and brings forth each "voice." *"There is also an instance where Claire and Catherine Ann reverse roles where Claire assists Catherine Ann in bringing forth a particular Magdalene "voice."* For the sake of clarity for the reader, the identity of the "voice" that is speaking is designated oftentimes before that identity is actually revealed in the dialogue process.

Anna continues her story within the Essene monastery at Mount Bugarach, France. Mount Bugarach is located in the Languedoc region of southern France near the Pyrenees Mountains and the presently well-known community of Rennes-le-Chateau. The area is steeped in the legends and mysteries of Mary Magdalene.

Anna reveals long-held secrets of the Magdalenes.}

---

wherein all emanated lifetimes are held. Each soul's physical incarnation is recorded and can be accessed and "read." In this instance the "virtual reality" process is interactive. Omniscient consciousness, in Oneness, knows the All by being simultaneously aware of the content of the Akasha, as both real and illusory. A Christ or Buddha has merged Awareness with Emptiness; form and formlessness, existing and non-existing Beingness.

— Chapter 3 —
ANNA: The New Mount Carmel
Anna Reveals the Two Marys & Yeshua's Children
Mount Bugarach, 33 AD

ANNA: I am walking on a path that passes through a field of green grasses and wild flowers. The path is narrow and well worn. I hear water off in the distance. There is no one around, but I sense that there are others not too far away.

CATHERINE ANN (*Henceforth: CA*): Look down at your feet – what are you wearing?

ANNA: My sandals are made of fairly thick, worn leather. I am a woman who appears to be about 50 years of age. There is a shawl on my head that covers my hair which is a dark chestnut brown mixed with some grey. There is no jewelry or ornamentation. I am also wearing a shawl that is slung over my left shoulder which is used to carry a bundle on my right hip. The bundle holds root vegetables; carrots and turnips. My clothing is made of course homespun fabric. There is a long, unbleached linen skirt that serves as an apron. Underneath the apron I am wearing a robe-like dress that is light brown and blue in color with fastenings made of bone at the neck and wrists to keep the chill out. It is fashioned in the manner of local women's clothing.

I am returning home from one of the large community orchards and gardens. I have been picking late apples, digging edible roots and gathering leafy-green vegetables for our evening meal. It is a little later in the season and we have been harvesting a plentiful crop for some time. I live near the lofty mountains that divide Gaul from Iberia. There are mountains all around and I am in a small valley. It is quite lovely and peaceful. I can hear a bell in the distance.

ANNA, THE VOICE OF THE MAGDALENES

Our rather large communal home is reminiscent of what we had in Carmel. There is a wooden fence, somewhat like a stockade, that surrounds a cluster of buildings made of stone and wood that share common walls. There are also structures which are made of heavy, woven fabric and others that are made of mud and wattle. The enclosures serve various purposes. The gate I am passing through is woven of willows. It is the one we use most often because it is easy to open and close. There is another gate that is made of heavier wood. My family lives here.

I am glad that you and I can be here now. (*Tears*) I have wanted to bring you to this beautiful place for a long time. We have lived in this valley by the great mountain almost a year. One winter has passed and we are approaching the end of the hot season. We are very happy being here. It has been such a long time since we have felt the kind of peace we have come to know from day to day.

My family calls me Anna.

CA: Welcome, Anna. Move forward to a meal, where do you eat?

ANNA: We have a communal kitchen with a large adjoining dining room. In the middle of the kitchen there is a big table used for preparing meals. Jacob made it from thick timbers, planed smooth. It shows lots of use. There is a carved wooden bucket that holds peelings and other refuse which we take out to the goats, chickens and other fowl. I have a sharp knife which I use to cut the turnips and carrots into small pieces. There is a large hearth with an iron grate and a hook from which to hang a large kettle. There are flat irons for grilling food and making flat bread. The vegetables will go into the water which is getting hot. I scrape the turnips and carrots into the kettle to cook and then they will be made into a mush, which I will season later. Most of our foods are eaten raw but we also prepare some cooked foods like the local people eat.

CA: Are there other people in the kitchen?

ANNA: Two of my great-granddaughters and my granddaughter Mariam are here helping me with the food preparation. I am looking to see if there is anyone else. I can hear the sound of spinning in the corner. It is Tabitha sitting at a simple

ANNA: THE NEW MOUNT CARMEL

spinning wheel making wool yarn. She has also been preparing flax fibers for spinning. There are spindles full of yarn and a simple loom near the window. It is being used to weave a heavy winter blanket. A baby is down on the floor by her feet. Tabitha is Isaac's wife and the baby is one of her great-grandchildren.

CA: And who are Tabitha's parents?

ANNA: They are no longer living. But when they were living, they resided in Egypt – some of the time in Alexandria and some of the time in Heliopolis. They were of Egyptian and Jewish descent and they were fairly wealthy. One of their homes was by the Great Sea and the other was located upriver on the Nile at Heliopolis. There are large Jewish communities in both cities. Many of their descendants continue to live there.

CA: Who are Isaac's parents?

ANNA: Oh, that would be Joachim and me. But Joachim is not with us in the physical any longer. He is always near me, and I miss him sometimes, especially in this place where it is so peaceful. It would be lovely to share this peace and beauty with him. He is working with Yeshua very closely from the spirit planes. Sometimes he gives me reports about how Yeshua is doing in his further mastery. With Yeshua, I have to tune in and go deeper to know where he is. He is not here. He is still living, but he is not in this place in the mountains.

CA: Move ahead now. The meal is cooked and everyone is gathering to eat. Tell me, is there a blessing?

ANNA: Yes, we all stand together before we sit. We acknowledge all the angels and their hand in the creation of this bounty that keeps us strong. We offer psalms of thanksgiving that there is so much to enjoy and share. Before every meal we always prepare one or more special bowls and baskets, filled full, as an offering to those who do not have as we have. Usually someone from the village comes to take our offering to a family in need. That is something we always do.

CA: Who is gathering?

ANNA: We have a fairly large gathering room. It is not nearly as big as the one in Mount Carmel. There are four very long wooden dining tables with benches and chairs, which Jacob made in our carpentry shop. Jacob is at the head of one of the tables and I am seated opposite him at the other end. On my side to the left are Mariam and Nathaniel. Next is Mary of Bethany, also called the Magdalene, who has a child on her lap. Beside her is one of the boys she and Yeshua adopted, and next to him are two little girls. We have lots of children *(laughter)*. There's another boy, he is another of the children that Yeshua and Mary of Bethany adopted. He is sitting right here to my right and beside him is a young girl that we brought with us from Egypt, her name is pronounced Sar'h. Next to her sits Miriam, the girl child that Yeshua and Mary adopted.

At the table next to me are Isaac, Tabitha and their oldest daughter, Sara, who is quite pregnant. She is sitting next to her husband, Philip. It is lovely to see. She's wanted this child for a long time. We have been praying her pregnancy will go well. *(Tears)* It's unusual for me to feel so emotional, but this is a great occasion to have you here. Next to Sara is Mary Salome and then there are Mary Anna's three younger children. Mary Anna usually sits to Isaac's left but she is not here now. Seated at another table are Joseph of Arimathea and his children, Lois Salome, Martha and Lazarus. There are also Mary Anna's oldest daughter, Ruth and other members of the family who came with us. Other members of the monastic community are interspersed among us and at the remaining table. That is all for now. I can see that Jacob is going to have to make another table! *(Laughter)*

CA: Take a look again at Mary Magdalene and the baby sitting on her lap. Is that her baby?

(Claire: I am feeling my throat constrict and my heart beating faster. There is a great reluctance to speak. I feel deeply conflicted on a cellular level; on the one hand, knowing it time to openly share about Yeshua's children, and, on the other hand, feeling a profound constraint. The feeling of constraint seems like a gag restricting what Anna desires to bring forth at this time. As we proceed, I am aware that a clearing and healing of a deep cellular obscuration is occurring.)

ANNA: I hesitate to answer that. I know what it is that you desire to know, but I hesitate to answer.

ANNA: THE NEW MOUNT CARMEL

CA: Share it if you like. If you are not ready, that's an OK choice.

ANNA: We have to keep so much secrecy.

CA: Know that you are totally safe in this moment and nothing is going to jeopardize anything that is appropriate to share. Please share only that which is to be shared at this time.

ANNA: *(very softly)* ... Yes, the child is hers.

CA: Is Yeshua the father?

ANNA: Yes.

CA: Is this the only child they have together?

ANNA: No.

CA: Does this child have older brothers and sisters?

ANNA: Yes. The little one beside me....

CA: What is that older child's name?

ANNA: Sar'h.

CA: What is the baby's name?

ANNA: We call her little Lizbett. Her full name is Elizabeth Hannah. You may be wondering why Mary Anna (*Mother Mary*) is not with us.

CA: Yes, I was wondering that.

ANNA: She has gone to be with Yeshua. You may wonder why Mary of Bethany is not with him and Mary Anna is. More often than not it is Mary of Bethany who goes away with him. They have – again, it's so difficult to bring these things out *(Tears)*.... we have to be so careful.

CA: You have done an incredible job of being careful and helping each other to be careful.

ANNA: Sometimes it is Mary Salome or Mariam who go with him. Occasionally Philip goes and sometimes it is Joseph of Arimathea, Lazarus, Nathaniel, Jacob or Isaac.

CA: When one of the Marys or one of the men go with Yeshua, where do they go?

ANNA: More often than not they go to the nearby mountain called Bugarach. Sometimes they go deeper into the Pyrenees. Sometimes they go quite a ways to the east into the foothills of the Alps. Occasionally they will go with Yeshua far to the north and to

Britain. What I am sharing here about these journeys did not all happen in this past year, but I am looking into quite a few years into the future.

CA: What do they do when they go to these places?

ANNA: They take themselves into seclusion so that they can connect with Great Beings from the other side. They go to many places on the etheric planes. On several occasions I have gone as well. Often we go into caves, just as in the old country where we used to live. When we are in retreat we bilocate ourselves to meet with many, many peoples. It is quite wonderful! Yeshua has introduced me to many lands and people that I could not have imagined without having seen it all for myself.

I taught Yeshua how to refine this practice when he was a lad. Now when we do it, he invites me to join my mind with his mind while he projects a scene and almost materializes it. In this way he introduces me to other cultures and people that are foreign to my mind. Since his resurrection, Yeshua has progressed more in his ability to hold subtle frequencies and now we can hold them better, too. His body is not the same as before the crucifixion. He can go in and out of this dimension very easily. His body becomes a vapor and disappears and then it manifests again in a vapor... just like that.... *(Claire snaps her fingers.)*

During the resurrection process he became aware of much more of the Earth and humanity. He realized there was much work to do among Mother Earth's peoples who are very ripe and receptive to his Presence and teachings; far more receptive than our Jewish people had been. After coming back from these journeys he expresses so much joy. *(Joyful tears)* It gives him so much pleasure when hearts are open to the teaching stories he tells them. He is especially joyful when more awake souls recognize the Infinite Light in him and do not just fall on their faces. He does not want to be adored or worshipped. He assists those who have difficulty seeing beyond his outer manifestation, so that they can give their adoration and love to their Creator, instead of to him. He tells them, "I am here to bring you closer to your Father-Mother Creator and to that Heaven which is within you."

ANNA: THE NEW MOUNT CARMEL

CA: How much time has passed since the crucifixion?
ANNA: It's been three and a half years.
CA: And Sar'h. Was she conceived the night of the last supper?
ANNA: Yes.
CA: And was that a Light Conception?
ANNA: Yes, it was. We all held the space for that.
CA: And where was Sar'h born?
ANNA: Just south of Alexandria within an Essene community on the shore of Lake Mareotis. We felt she would be safe there. There is much more to be shared about all of that, but perhaps another time.
CA: So the place where you are now, what is that called?
ANNA: Let's call it Mount Bugarach. This great mystical mountain is south of the village called Rennes la Chateau that has been made famous through the legends told about Mary Magdalene in your day. In my time, the Romans have taken this old Gallic hill fort and use its strategic vantage point for surveillance, as needed from time to time. Mount Bugarach is a predominant landmark. This area used to be covered by water so there are many limestone caves, which we use for a variety of purposes; just as we did in Mount Carmel.
CA: What is the focus, now, after the drama of the crucifixion?
ANNA: We desire very much to finish the anchoring of cosmic energies into the Earth, to attain as much cosmic consciousness ourselves, and to safeguard all the children – all my grandchildren's offspring, who live here now. As we look into the immediate future, we see that our efforts will be, as you say, coming up against a brick wall. We know that often when there is a bursting forth of light in the night sky, it subsides, and then the night appears to be darker than it was before. We know that the pendulum will swing and it will be like a whiplash. We don't know how it will dramatize, but we are doing everything that we can to hold the higher cosmic energies in our own bodies.

Our choice is to stay on the Earthplane as long as we can benefit others. When there isn't any more we can do, then we will let go of our physical forms and remain close to the Earthplane in our light bodies. We do much of our work from the subtle realms until it is time to incarnate again. Having taken vows of compassion, we return to the physical plane as often as necessary. We have all gained some measure of enlightenment. Of course, Mary Anna and Yeshua, as avatars, were born awake. Their mastery and compassionate service, in healing humanity's collective karma, has been a source of inspiration for us all. But for most of us, there always seems to be some measure of personal karma to clear and infinite levels of consciousness to realize.

CA: You mentioned that Yeshua would come in and out of form. Tell us more about the times when Yeshua visits.

ANNA: Sometimes he appears, as if out of thin air. When he appears there is so much light – it is amazing! Not amazing, really; we have more or less become accustomed to his radiant presence – not accustomed in a complacent way, however. We always feel great joy and reverence when he comes. *(Deep feeling)* At first he was quite tangible. When we reached out and embraced, we could feel of one another's flesh in almost the same way as before the resurrection. It seems that his body is becoming more ethereal. His visits are becoming briefer and less frequent. In order to experience and be with him, it is required of us to meet him more and more in the Light.

CA: He came in this form with Mary of Bethany, and they experienced a Light Conception in order to bring forth Lizbett?

ANNA: Yes

CA: How many years was it after the crucifixion until he stopped appearing in the way you have described?

ANNA: It was another 40 years in which we experienced him in a form that could be seen with the physical eyes. But as I have said, during these years his form became increasingly subtle – unless he chose to present himself more tangibly, which was rare. He was on the Earthplane for quite some time, but we saw him less and less over the years.

CA: Did Mary of Bethany go with him often?

ANNA: A fair amount, yes. Her lot is to be more of the Earth vibration, while Yeshua held more of the cosmic frequencies.

Sometimes this was difficult for her, but she accepted it, because she deeply understood the work of the Goddess.

CA: Were Mary of Bethany and Yeshua married?

ANNA: They were betrothed, but they did not take the final rite of marriage in the Jewish tradition. They didn't feel that was necessary.

CA: Did Yeshua have a betrothal and marriage with anyone else?

(Claire: I felt considerable contraction and hesitancy to respond to this question. The revelation that Yeshua was married to another woman startled me – that is, the Claire consciousness witnessing what Anna was saying. I had had a sense that Yeshua may have had more than one consort with whom to practice high Tantric alchemy (as have other Masters, such as Padmasambhava in Tibetan Buddhism.). But I felt very troubled by the idea of polygamy, as it is commonly practiced, with all its attendant abuses and suffering. I felt even more troubled about making this revelation about Yeshua practicing polygamy public because I knew – and still know – it will likely be misunderstood in ways that can overshadow Yeshua's actual intentions and practices. But ultimately, trusting the process I had entered into with Anna, I chose to breathe into my fears and was able to relax my mind sufficiently so as to allow Anna a voice.)

ANNA: Yes. She is another Mary. We call her Mary Salome or Myriam. She is also known as Myriam of Tyana. She is a distant cousin of Apollonius of Tyana who is rather well-known as an extraordinary being, much like Yeshua.

CA: Is this Mary a member of the Magdalene Order?

ANNA: Oh, yes. All we women are Magdalenes. All of us have taken oaths and initiations within this particular order of Isis. We all know the mysteries of resurrection. That is our life's work.

CA: Did Yeshua have children with this other Mary?

ANNA: He had two boys and one girl.

CA: Was that after the time of Sar'h and Lizbett?

ANNA: Before.

CA: Before the time of the crucifixion?

ANNA: Yes

CA: How old were they at the time of the crucifixion?

ANNA: They were approaching fourteen, ten and eight.

CA: What were their names?

ANNA: Joses Simeon, Miriam and Johannes.

CA: Did they leave Palestine and travel with the family across the sea?

ANNA: Joses and Miriam were born in India during the six years that Yeshua lived there as a young man. Johannes was born later in India during the time that Yeshua made his second journey to the Orient, just before the public ministry. It was decided that Johannes stay with Yeshua's brother, Joseph, until he is an adult. He is there now. When he is an adult he will have the option of choosing whether to remain in India or come to Gaul or perhaps go on to Britain. You may recall Yeshua and Mary of Bethany had three adopted children who came with us on the boat: Joses, Judas and Miriam. Judas was adopted, but Joses and Miriam are Yeshua and Myriam's children. Myriam will explain more fully.

In my earlier story there were many things that I could have said, but I chose not to reveal. You recall how profoundly Claire was affected in her emotional body when I began to reveal these secrets. This news about Yeshua's relationships will likely be difficult for others to hear, as well. Although we didn't have the same cultural stigma you currently have about polygamy, we had good reason to be very judicious and secretive about the children and our comings and goings. We felt very protective of all the children, and especially Yeshua's. There has been much misunderstanding that has arisen because of our efforts to protect Yeshua's children and the true nature of his relationships and teachings. More readers of my story are now ready to hear what has been secreted away, though it will still be a big stretch for most.

CA: What happened to that marriage?

ANNA: As I look into the future, it continued through the remainder of Yeshua's life, but it was kept a secret, especially from the Romans in Palestine, Alexandria and now here. They publicly shun having more than one wife, though this does not stop many from having extramarital affairs. There are very few people who can understand the deeper purposes of these two marriages. Let me assure you our revelation of it now is certainly not to proselytize polygamy! Far too much suffering has occurred within this ancient patriarchal tradition, which has oppressed women for thousands of years. And certainly, speaking openly about Yeshua's multiple partners is not about condoning licentious sexual activity or any sexual practice where love is absent, for that matter.

Very few are able to look at the fact that we, as more liberal Essenes, practice conscious sexuality, whether as celibates or as married couples. For those who have been conditioned with fictitious stories that Yeshua was celibate and that sex is sinful, it is very difficult to envision Yeshua as a married man and conceiving children. Some people feel that because Yeshua is an avatar, he is somehow "above" being sexual, as sexuality seems to make him more human. But these people do not understand the esoteric practices of Tantric alchemy, which include the conscious cultivation, retention and channeling of life-force energy through the body, with or without a partner, for the attainment of spiritual enlightenment. Some people, at the other extreme, might think, because Yeshua "did it" – not knowing what "it" is – they have a license to practice any manner of lust-based, genitally focused sexuality.

Great karmic harm has come to many individuals and many generations because of this ignorance – either erring in the way of extreme austerities or blatantly indulging harmful self-gratification, promiscuity and all manner of human bondage. I assure you once again, what Yeshua and we Magdalenes practice does not in any way indulge lust. We transmute life-force energy, or what you would term sexual passion, by respecting its creative and destructive power. We bring loving mindfulness and deep care for one another's well-being, not just in the moment of mutual pleasure, but for our beloved's entire lifetime and for lifetimes to come. We utilize our sexual energy in disciplined ways to attain enlightenment of body and mind. We consciously conceive children in such a way as to lessen the obscurations that they might otherwise have at birth. We do this so that they might have more favorable conditions for awakening in this lifetime. We do this not only for ourselves, but we dedicate our joyful, healing sexual energy to the awakening and happiness of all beings.

Let me say further, our preferred expression of matrimony is a mutual commitment to monogamous fidelity to each other, and a mutual devotion to the Beloved on High, unless it is revealed to us that there is a greater purpose to be served through polygamous fidelity. Generally speaking, we find monogamy promotes the greatest spiritual awakening, harmony and well-being within couples, families and communities. Among us, you will find few who practice polygamy; and of these, there are only advanced adepts. As we proceed with my story more understanding may come.

It is with some reluctance that I share these revelations with you. It is only because a deeper spiritual awareness is beginning to dawn at this time, that I offer this controversial information for you to consider and weigh in your own heart.

CA: I have a question now about the Yeshua and Magdalene Bloodline. Does it carry through to this time and is it important because it carries the vibration of the Light Conception?

ANNA: Yes. But it is also to be understood that the bloodline is not just Yeshua's descendants. It includes other Light conceived children born to my other children who were conscious enough to participate in the initiations that prepared them for Light conception. It is also to understand that there were other awakened families throughout the Earth who have conceived and are conceiving children in the Light.

With regard to my children and grandchildren, I have descendants who cover the earth in your time. What we did through Light conception was to set an expanded, more unifying cosmic pattern or matrix into the earth. This has been done by enlightened beings through the cycles of time. All beings are born of the elements of the earth. These Light frequencies impregnate the elements and genetics of all forms. They hold coherent matrixes or patterns of Light that facilitate consciousness to be aware of Oneness. Although we live in one of the darkest of Earth's cosmic cycles, nevertheless, it may be that this is the most auspicious opportunity for awakening these intrinsic, coherent patterns or codes of light/Oneness.

I leave you now to deeply contemplate my words.

— Chapter 4 —
ANNA: Yeshua Comes for a Visit
Mount Bugarach, 32–33 AD

CATHERINE ANN (*Henceforth:* CA): Where are you now?

ANNA: I am on a hillside. From my point of view I can see a portion of Mt Bugarach and other mountains which are farther away.

CA: What time of year is it?

ANNA: A few weeks have passed since we were last together. It is now definitely the autumn season. There is a chill in the air and leaves are falling from the trees.

CA: What are you doing in this moment on the hillside?

ANNA: I am looking down unto the valley floor. There is a cart pulled by one of our oxen. It is followed by another wagon, bigger than the cart. The men and children have been out harvesting some of the last fields of grasses which will be used for fodder. They are coming home now.

CA: Are you going home?

ANNA: Yes. I have been gathering mushrooms and a few medicinal and cooking herbs. These things are very light and I have them all in a basket. I am taking them down the hillside to our sanctuary. Some of the children are with me, as usual. We have been on a pleasant afternoon outing.

CA: How many children are with you?

ANNA: There are three. Coming up the hill, to meet us, is one of the girls, and behind her, Mariam is carrying Lizbett on her hip. They are waving to us. Gesturing, I can hear them say, "Hurry Nana, get a hustle on!" (*Pause*) We are moving ahead in years. (*Pause*)

CA: Where are you now?

beeil dich!

ANNA: YESHUA COMES FOR A VISIT

ANNA: I am at the same monastery. It has been expanded because there are more people living here now. I am aware that my son, Joseph, is expected. We have been preparing for his arrival. We have an idea when he will be arriving, but the exact day is not exactly known.

CA: In these years that have passed, has your life been a normal routine?

ANNA: Yes, in many ways; but there have been a few momentous or significant moments.

CA: Tell me about one of those.

ANNA: One that stands out right now is when Yeshua came for a visit about six weeks after we had first arrived in Bugarach. It was so wonderful to have him in our midst again. (*Tears*) There is something about his eyes that is like no other's eyes – the way he takes you in and engages you. He has always had this ability from the time he was a small lad. It is like being taken into the most brilliant light; like how you might imagine it would be going into the sun.

Some of the older boys saw him coming up the pathway. He looked like an ordinary traveler...but as he got closer, they recognized him. Of course Joses and Jude had known their father for years. The other children who have lived here all their lives had not experienced him until now. The younger ones all grabbed his hands and arms and tugged at his traveling cloak. Squealing, they all broke out into a trot. (*Laughter*) He gave some of the younger children turns riding on his shoulders. Others he whirled around just like he used to do with the children at Mount Carmel. It did not take long before everyone in our community knew he was here and we all poured out the doors and gates to give him our fond embrace. Such rejoicing and merriment!

As we approached the main entrance to the sanctuary, he asked us all to be very still. It wasn't that he was discounting all of the frivolity up to that point; it was simply time to gather our energy and prepare for whatever he was bringing to us. We immediately gathered everyone into the great room. There was a great hushed silence.

We gathered in the large dining room. The benches were arranged in a circle. There were a few cushions and blankets spread out on the floor. As I speak, I am recalling this beautiful experience as if it is happening right now .... Yeshua stands in our midst. He raises his hands. We all stand up in prayer and the singing of psalms. Now we sit down. Mary of Bethany sits beside him. Myriam is at his feet. All of us are weeping as she washes his feet and anoints them with oil.

CA: What is it that Yeshua is sharing with you?

ANNA: He is asking us to make a feast ready; a simple feast of all of the fruits of harvest time. My mind immediately goes to our storehouse. We have roots, cheeses, fresh pressed juices and new wine to bring up from the cooling cellar. There are dried fruits, honeycombs, fresh apples and pears. Grains and seeds will be ground and made into bread. Legumes will be soaked and sprouted. There is plenty of olive oil and the granary is very full. It has been a good season. It will be a wonderful feast and celebration!

Yeshua tells us that he will be with us for a fortnight. We are overjoyed to have him with us for so long. He says we will have our celebration feast in two more days. There are two smaller Essene communities not too far away. He desires that runners be sent right away to invite these brothers and sisters to join us. He says, "I could have appeared there, but why make it too simple?" (*Laughter*)

CA: Was this a surprise?

ANNA: Yes, it was. We had no idea! (*Laughter*) But that is his way! He loves to surprise us and see our faces light up. He loves to spread joy and light-heartedness all around. Often he does not tell us his plans because he might be delayed for any number of reasons. Something could come up. He was needed for this, he was needed for that. He always responded at a moment's notice to any need. Rather than disappoint us by creating an expectation that he would be coming at a certain time, he often said, "Expect me when you see me." (*Laughter*) It wasn't to make things difficult for us that he said this, but rather, he was encouraging us to be childlike, enjoying the miracle of the moment. He would tell us, "Be the child who is faithful and diligent and happy with whatever is in the moment."

ANNA: YESHUA COMES FOR A VISIT

CA: Is it different being with him now compared to being with him before the crucifixion?

ANNA: Oh, yes. Yeshua's skin looks very different. He used to be quite tanned. Now there is a translucent milky-whiteness about his skin. It doesn't look sickly. It exudes a soft, lovely light. He was always very – what you would say – beautiful, in a manly way. He has a beautiful countenance and a noble, gentle gracefulness in the way he carries himself. He used to be quite tangible, but now there is more of his light body present. After a number of weeks passed after his resurrection, we could feel his flesh when we touched him. He allowed us to feel his body. He had merged enough with his higher frequency energy bodies so that he could easily allow this. He is still quite tangible; but there is more of an ethereal quality about him.

To be with him feels like being seen through every pore of his skin. It is as if every pore is an eye that can see and know everything about you on every level of consciousness. Every part of him is very awake and alive – all seeing – all-knowing. There can be no secrets. It is beautiful. We don't worry or try to hide from his ability to see us completely. We want to be naked like an innocent child with him. It is this quality of gentle, open innocence that he evokes with us. It is beautiful to feel so safe while being so vulnerable. We are greatly strengthened and inspired to be as he is.

CA: Have you ever felt that way with anyone else?

ANNA: Yes. I especially felt a deep transparency and radiation of energy during and after my rejuvenation processes. I noticed this was especially true when I was more out of my body than in my body. But in this instance, with Yeshua, I am in my body and I am experiencing the Infinite Light very profoundly. It is far easier to hold such intense energy in the body when you are with someone of great mastery, and it also easier to transmute any obscuration that arises – whether it is of the body, emotions or mind.

I am recalling two of Yeshua's beloved expressions. (*Tears*) "Where two or more are gathered, there I AM." "All that you see me do, you can do also." When there is sufficient faith beyond belief, the True Self witnesses these truths.

CA: So that which you experienced on the inner planes, out of your body, you could bring home into your body?

ANNA: Yes. If the experiences on the inner planes are not brought fully into the body, it has little merit. If such journeys into the subtle realms enhance being more awake, mindful and compassionate in every moment of one's life in physicality, no matter how mundane or how much suffering may be present, then this expanded awareness serves. Otherwise, to have access to the subtle planes can be a form of escape and self-created fantasy which leads to greater self-delusion.

We all treasure these moments when Yeshua's presence is close. It feels as though Heaven and Earth are merged in us. These experiences feel so natural; we sometimes catch ourselves becoming complacent. But then we stop short when we remember we might not have him with us for long. We never knew how long it would be before we'd see him again. We do not know how tangible his body might be next time. When such thoughts arise, we recognize our attachment to his physical form.

Times like this are always teaching moments to remind ourselves about the impermanence of all things — that what has a beginning has an ending. It is important to remain calmly present in the midst of this world's constant change. We remember the changeless, clear Awareness and Peace we always feel when we attune to Yeshua, whether he is physically present or not. We gently remind ourselves, "Let's stay awake within this precious sacred moment. Let's relish our true treasure which is the Infinite Love we feel right now and always."

This visit with Yeshua was a very powerful turning point for our community. His coming supported our resolve to be more mindful and kind. It fortified us is a way that lets us know our gentle way of transparent vulnerability is our greatest strength. It focused us in an extraordinary way.

Would that the world communities of your day know the truth of what I am witnessing, and anchor it in your daily living. Would that more individuals, who desire to awaken and be of greater service to others, harvest the frequencies of Light — the Christ

ANNA: YESHUA COMES FOR A VISIT

Presence within every cell. Your bodies can be like a granary [Silo] full of wheat, oats, barley and millet. Within every cell and every atom, there is room for entertaining and welcoming your own True Self as your precious guest. When this Guest comes, it is like a feast – enlivening your very soul. Yes, bring honor and reverence to the externalized Christ, the one we call Yeshua. When he invites you to sup with him, he will reflect you and show you who you truly are. That is truly a feast beyond words.

CA: Is there anything more that was significant in that visit?

ANNA: Yes. Yeshua turned to Mary of Bethany at the end of his visit and asked if she were willing to come with him on a little journey. And of course, (*Laughter*) she was very willing! When she came back, she announced that she was with child. It was this child who was sitting on her lap when I first took you into our new Mount Carmel sanctuary.

CA: Lizbett?

ANNA: Yes.

CA: Is there more to share?

ANNA: No. Not at this time. We shall hear now from the other Magdalenes who wish to speak.

{*Anna and the Councils have assessed that the previous readers of "Anna, Grandmother of Jesus" are now ready to hear the secrets that had been held back concerning the Magdalenes and Yeshua's relationship to them. In order to proceed, it is now necessary to retrace Yeshua's earlier experiences and tell about his marriage with Myriam of Tyana, a Magdalene priestess.*

We are taken to the area where Galilee and Samaria border one another near Mt. Gilboa. It is here where Yeshua meets Myriam at a well, and shortly thereafter, marries her. This chapter provides a first-witness account of their wedding celebration.}

— Chapter 5 —

GALEAH

The Wedding of Yeshua & Myriam of Tyana
Ginaea, Samaria, 14 AD
{East of Caesarea near Mt Gilboa}

GALEAH: First of all, I'd like to report that I am hearing the sound of musical instruments: cymbals, tambourines, drums, flutes, horns and stringed instruments. It is a celebration of great happiness and joy. There are joyful sounds of music, clapping, laughter and much singing.

As I look down at my feet, they are unshod and tanned. My soles are calloused. I can move freely on the sandy ground and the flagstone paving without any sense of discomfort. I am dancing now and my garment is gracefully sweeping over the flat stones. I am raising my skirt up a bit to expose my ankles and calves. With great joy I whirl around and around. My black hair hangs in thick lustrous strands below my waist. The crown of my head is covered with a long, red silk scarf, which I wrap in such a way that it is knotted at the nape of my neck; the fringed loose ends flow among my wavy locks. My full bosom is accented by my red robe, which is gathered tightly around my waist with a scarf of many colors and intricate patterns. My arms are deeply tanned and mostly bare.

CATHERINE ANN (*Henceforth: CA*): Do you have any kind of ornamentation?

GALEAH: Just a bangle here on my left wrist and some earrings. I hope someday to wear the serpent of the Goddess on my arm.

CA: Are you carrying anything?

GALEAH: I am holding a tambourine. It has a tight skin on one side. When I shake and strike it, the bells and drum make rhythmic sounds. There are other girls and women dancing with tambourines and cymbals.

CA: How old are you?
GALEAH: Fifteen.
CA: What are you called?
GALEAH: One name my family and friends like to call me is Galeah.
CA: What is the celebration?
GALEAH: Yeshua is getting married.
CA: Who is his bride?
GALEAH: Oh, that is the beautiful one, Myriam. There are many guests and it is very lovely. There is so much joy. I am very happy she and Yeshua ben Joseph are honoring their love under the wedding canopy.
CA: Where does the wedding take place?
GALEAH: It is taking place in Uncle Eleazar of Tyana's home. We live in the land called Samaria northwest of Jerusalem. Not too far away, to the west, there is a Roman city called Caesarea that lies beside the Great Sea. To the north and northeast are the beautiful hills which climb up to Mount Carmel and Mount Tabor. To the east are Mount Gilboa and the gentle River Jordan. The Galilean road from Sepphoris and Nazareth runs through our valley plain and pasturelands, where many sheep, goats and cattle feed. My uncle's large home is near the village of Ginaea. I live with my family in the village, but my father is not so rich in land and animals. My father is a tradesman who buys and sells many things. Our home is smaller and cannot support such an occasion as this. Myriam is my aunt; the youngest of my father's many sisters. Uncle Eleazar is proud to host so many people.
CA: Please tell me more about the celebration. You have shared there is music. Tell me about the ceremony, the food, and how long this wedding will be.
GALEAH: It will go on for days. Most of the guests will be here for three days. Others who have traveled a long distance will stay for a week or so. Yeshua's uncle, called Joseph of Arimathea, has land he inherited from his father-in-law, south of here, in the Samaritan village of Arimathea. I am told he also owns houses in Bethany and Jerusalem, and boats that make voyages on the Great

Sea. He is very rich. It is he who is making it possible for all of Yeshua's relatives to come here from Mount Carmel, Cana and Nazareth.

As I said, my Uncle Eleazar is wealthy in land and many herds of animals. He and my father, Achim and their wives joined cousins who have lived in Samaria and Galilee for generations. My family came here before I was born. They and all their ancestors came from a land far to the north in a region called Cappadocia. My family came from a village called Tyana. I have heard our forefathers, who are mostly of the tribe of Benjamin, came from this land, where we now live, many, many generations ago. But they were taken captive and forced to live in Assyria and Babylon. There was a great dispersion of the tribes of Israel at that time. We feel that we have returned to our original homeland.

Tyana is where Myriam used to live. She came to live with us several years ago. My father brought her for a visit when he returned from one of his journeys to Cilicia and Cappadocia gathering goods to sell. She enjoyed being here and chose to stay. My family talks about Yeshua's and Myriam's marriage being an important liaison. My father and uncle are very happy for this reconnection of the family tree.

Several generations ago there was an uncomfortable estrangement between both paternal and maternal lineages, from which Yeshua also comes. They feel Yeshua's connection to the royal house of David through both his parents is good for them politically, since most Jews despise the people of Samaria for the Assyrian blood that runs in our veins. There are many among us who see the Jews corrupt bigots and it is we who better live the original teachings of our fathers, Abraham and Moses. I think this is especially true in the way many of my family honor the Great Mother of life. I experience these quarrels as petty distractions and the poisonous source of unnecessary suffering. I, like my elders, am glad for the healing that may come of this union.

CA: Has the wedding ceremony begun?

GALEAH: This is the day we prepare for the actual marriage ceremony.

CA: How do you prepare?

GALEAH: We prepare with lots of dancing and feasting! *(Laughter)*

CA: That sounds fun! *(Big laugh)*

GALEAH: I am Myriam's favorite niece and I love her very much. Actually I think my other cousins also feel like they are Myriam's favorite. She has a way of making everyone feel seen and special.

CA: How do you feel about her and Yeshua getting married?

GALEAH: I am very happy for them. I hope I can have a husband like Yeshua. His brothers are here and I am going to look at them and see if they are as handsome and kind as he is.[4] His parents and other aunts and uncles are visiting, too. I like his family. They dress very simply and their robes mostly look the same. They carry a peace within them that I enjoy very much. His mother is beautiful. She is different from the other women, not only because she has lighter skin and hair, but there is something so gentle about her, like a turtledove. She took me right into her arms when we first met. I felt like I never wanted to leave her embrace – it was so still, so comforting.

His mother, Mary Anna, introduced me to her mother, Anna of Mount Carmel, who also embraced me, but she felt different – like someone who is mysterious and rather distant. Like I feel when I go with my mother to the shrine of the Goddess. I don't have words to describe exactly how I felt. They both made my heart feel huge, but if I had to choose between them, it would be Mary Anna I would choose for my mother.

CA: Did you meet Yeshua before or at the time of the wedding?

GALEAH: I first met him almost six months ago, shortly after he found Myriam at the well. She had been gathering water for the household and animals late in the afternoon. He was on his way

---

[4] Galeah did meet Yeshua's brother Jude, and in the course of time they married and raised a large family near Nazareth on the land that belonged to Anna's son, Nathan.

to Arimathea from Nazareth with his Uncle Joseph who had invited Yeshua to travel with him. The purpose of the journey was to assess his uncle's holdings in Samaria and then visit the temple in Jerusalem and stay for a time in Joseph's home in Bethany. When Yeshua asked Myriam for water and he looked deeply into her eyes, they were stunned with deep recognition and a great love swept over them. Myriam persuaded her new acquaintances to come to my uncle's home to have sup and rest for the night. Yeshua continued his journey after several days, but shortened his stay in Bethany so that he might return to our village to court Myriam.

After several weeks of deep communion and meeting family members, my father escorted Myriam to Nazareth so that Yeshua's parents might meet her and give their blessing for a betrothal. That celebration occurred there two weeks ago. Now we are celebrating their formal wedding. We have been told that Yeshua and his brother James are going with an uncle named Jacob to his grandfather Joachim's ancestral lands near the great mountain[5] not far from Tyana. Now that Myriam is his bride, she will introduce her new husband to our extended family remaining in that region.

Then they will travel to the Orient, a very mysterious land, so I have been told. One of the main reasons for traveling such a distance is to meet many great teachers – greater even than Yeshua's mother and grandmother. I can hardly imagine such ones, because in the few moments I was in Anna and Mary Anna's embrace my mind began to expand without me doing anything. Even I, with little experience, can sense these women can lead anyone who is ready, to know and see what the Goddess knows and sees.

CA: What is your favorite part of the wedding week?

GALEAH: Besides the dancing, there are special foods that we usually don't eat except for occasions like this. Some of the ingredients are rare. They come from long distances, like Egypt and Persia. There are also spices that come from even further away. The caravans bring them here from the Orient where Yeshua and

---

[5] Mount Ararat, in present day Turkey.

Myriam are going. My favorite foods are the ones that are sweet. I like anything that is sweet.

CA: Are there many sweet things?

GALEAH: Oh, yes! There are all manner of sweets made with honey and date paste. All the food is a feast for the eyes and it's been in preparation for weeks. I feel like a child who can barely wait to sample everything. Imagining how it might taste, and smelling the exotic spices, brings great pleasure to my senses. To taste it, though, is far better than eager anticipation and fond memory, because so much love and happiness is put into everything. And sharing it with everyone, in seemingly unending courses, is a crescendo of expanding delights!

CA: Tell me about the ceremony. What are Yeshua and Myriam wearing?

GALEAH: There has not been much time to prepare our usual elaborate wedding garments. But there are special fabrics that have been purchased and woven over the years. They are set aside for occasions like this. My women relatives have been busy sewing ever since the betrothal. Myriam's skirt is mostly woven of diaphanous white cotton from Egypt. It drapes beautifully over her hips, where it is gathered under a fitted girdle of knotted linen threads. There are wonderful little bells, shells, stones and silver pieces tied to it. These are sewn and strung in such a way as to emphasize her feminine qualities. Her shapely breasts and arms are adorned with a short blouse with long draping sleeves. It is worn over the flowing skirt. When she raises her arms her slender belly is exposed. The long sleeves flow in the breeze when she stands and spread like wings when she dances. On her chest hangs a beautiful heirloom medallion made of silver, gold and small jewels. She wears the golden serpent of the Goddess on her left arm, signifying she is an initiate of the Magdalene mysteries. Her breasts are full and lovely, like mine. Her long, wavy and very thick hair is quite a rich dark brown, almost black, highlighted with mahogany henna dye that glints like specks of fire in the sun.

CA: Does she wear anything on her head?

GALEAH: She is wearing a long, shawl-like scarf made of the same gauzy fabric as her skirt. It is embroidered with intricate designs that portray floral garlands, doves, pomegranates and other symbols of fertility. The threads are made of red and white silk. A simple band of gold that fits tightly over the crown of her head holds it in place. There are garlands of sweet roses and jasmine entwined around the band. When it is time, part of the shawl will come forward and hang down over her face. She has lovely henna designs on her hands, arms and feet. A silver crescent moon hangs from her head band over her forehead. Her full lips are painted red and her wide-set, almond shaped golden-brown eyes are heavily outlined with black kohl.

When you look into Myriam's eyes there is a gentle softness and there is also a passionate fire. On the one hand, you want to lay still forever in her arms, and, on the other, you want to dance with her, arm in arm, flying into the sun. You can tell her any secret and know it is safe with her. She's not that much older than me, but I look up to her almost like an elder. She seems so wise, way beyond her years. I am told she is two years older than Yeshua who recently turned seventeen, though it is difficult to tell how old he is. Sometimes he seems very young and at other times he has the look of a wise sage. There is a peculiar quality about him. He remains a mystery to me.

CA: What do you find peculiar about Yeshua?

GALEAH: He is mysterious like Myriam. There's a mystery in their eyes that you can't quite fathom. One minute you think you have them figured out, and then the next thing you know, they say or do something unpredictable. There's an energy that I feel when I am with them I cannot find words to describe in my mind. It feels like quicksand, not in a bad way; it just means that I am constantly letting go of any ideas I might think about them. Without saying anything, I feel like they invite me to be with them moment by moment.

It's fun – like when I was a child. Sometimes we just sit still, and when I look into their eyes, it's as if they are somewhere else, while their bodies are here. There's a feeling of letting go of any thoughts about being separate from each other, from the sky, the sun, the earth, the ants and the flies moving about us. And then in another breath we are none of these things – just pure space like the deep, cobalt blue sky. Then in the blink of an eye we are in cheerful conversation again. *(Pause)* Being with them gives me much to contemplate.

It's like your body is here, but where are you? Who are you? Who is looking? When I look into their eyes it is like looking into a deep, deep well or looking into the blinding sun. I notice there are only a few people in our village who linger, gazing eye to eye with Yeshua and Myriam. Most feel uncomfortable looking into their eyes. They cast their eyes to the earth and turn away. But with me, it's like I don't want Yeshua or Myriam to ever blink. I never want their eyes taken off me.

Yeshua is so easy to love. Even though I am only a girl, I know what I feel in my heart is a love coming from him that is pure, like a mother's love for her child. The energy that comes out of his eyes is like the scintillating rays of the sun, which clears away all the darkness in my mind. Usually you can feel a powerful energy around him and you know when he is somewhere nearby. But sometimes he pulls his energy in close, and then when you least expect it, he will come up from behind and gently tickle your ribs, take your hands, turn you around, dance with you - laughing like there is no tomorrow! Yeshua can be very playful and he has the most wonderful laugh. Myriam does, too. *(Sigh)* I wish I were Myriam.

CA: She is very happy to be marrying Yeshua, isn't she?

GALEAH: Yes, very. Her smiling face is glowing. It is as though a rapturous song sings through her entire body. He is happy, too. They are beautiful together. The kind of couple every girl dreams of for herself.

CA: What is Yeshua wearing?

GALEAH: His family members are Essenes from Mount Carmel, where everyone dresses very simply. Our way is more elaborate. His mother made him a simple robe of very fine linen. It has a wide neckline, which he can pull easily over his head. Part of his chest is exposed. There is a little fine hair showing. His luminous skin is very tanned and beautiful. His wavy hair is a dark auburn brown that hangs below his shoulders. There are locks that grow from his temples and crown that have never been cut. They are twisted into a small knot at the top of his head, which is held in place with a slender ivory hair pick.

We have an ancient love poem among our scriptures passed down to us from Solomon the Wise and Queen Sheba. Myriam has taught a number of us how to understand it on levels beyond the ordinary mind. Much of it requires a different way of seeing. It ignites passion for the beloved, as God incarnate – the Beloved. It sets the stage for conceiving a child in a space of love and light. As I look at Yeshua and Myriam, it's as if *"The Song of Songs"* was written just for them.

CA: Is Yeshua taller than Myriam?

GALEAH: Myriam's head is just slightly above his shoulder.

CA: Does he have a beard?

GALEAH: Right now, he is mostly clean shaven. He had the beginnings of a beard before the ceremony. I am not sure why it's been shaved. I'm sure he will soon have a beard again, as is the custom of the Nazarite Essenes.

CA: What color are his eyes?

GALEAH: Oh, they are a deep warm hazel brown with lots of blue-grey specks. They seem to change like quicksilver. Sometimes they look more blue-grey and sometimes a little more golden brown. They have a clear watery look to them. His eyes dance, like sunlight on water. They are very lively, and yet, they are like a very still, deep well. As I said, he's a walking enigma – a lovable mystery.

CA: What else would you like to share about this celebration?

GALEAH: This wedding is an enactment of *"The Song of Songs."* It is an ancient ritual of the Goddess Mother mating with Father Creator. It is the anointing of the Bridegroom to prepare him to enter the Bride's sacred chamber where they will open to one another. In union, they bring Heaven's great light into the Earth Mother's body. It is a sacred blessing upon all life, in all its myriad forms, so all beings may be abundantly fertile and happy.

After we have had our feast and more dancing, Myriam will be brought out of a dark room and led to a special place that has been prepared. There is a platform under a red silk canopy that is tied in such a way as to reveal a bed of richly upholstered cushions covered with cloths, sheepskins and even a leopard skin. It is used by Egyptian priests who officiate in the conception and resurrection rites of Isis, Osiris and Horus. When night draws nigh the canopy veils will be untied and the heavy red silks will be unfurled. The wedding bed will then be hidden from our view.

Now we are ready for the actual ceremony. At the foot of the canopy is a long bench upon which Yeshua is sitting in calm repose. Myriam is brought to stand a distance in front of him. Yeshua silently beckons Myriam to come close. She kneels at his feet. His entire body was washed earlier in a special ritual that is done among the men. This is also true for Myriam with the assistance of the women. She bends low. Slowly and gently she kisses his feet, her long hair cascading all around, veiling her sacred supplication. Yeshua places a hand on her head, indicating it is time to rise.

Standing before him, she removes a sealed alabaster vial of expensive spikenard oil from her girdle. The heat of her body has made its thick syrupy texture into anointing oil that is easy to pour and apply. All is very hushed until she breaks the wax seal from the head of the vial. As she pours some of the pungent spikenard upon Yeshua's head, we, who are in attendance, offer a soft collective sigh. Then she places both hands upon his crown. His hair, which was previously knotted, hangs long and limp down his back. A quickening energy begins to rise as Myriam's belly quivers and her hips begin an almost imperceptible undulation. Yeshua's head falls back, his eyes closed, his hands resting in equipoise on his thighs. Myriam kneels once more at her beloved's feet and begins to pour oil upon them. Some of the string instruments begin a slow drone and the percussion a very soft, quivering rhythm. A chorus of voices begins a slow vibrato.

A male cantor now starts reciting the entire *"Song of Songs"* – the way of opening to the Beloved on High. Myriam tenderly lifts each anointed foot into her lap and massages it in a very sensual way.

Slowly, she massages the soles of his feet, each toe and between the toes. Ever so slowly, she anoints and massages his calves. She rises up on bended knees and reaches under his robe to anoint and massage his thighs which are like smooth, white, marble pillars. The music becomes more ardent and the harmonies more complex. Our voices make the cooing sound of doves. Among us, a solo female voice joins the male cantor with melodious and increasingly ecstatic refrains. She weaves her beautiful voice through the entire tapestry of sound.

The voice of the Divine Feminine, the Queen of heaven and earth, calls forth the King of kings to make his descent. She calls forth the winds from their four directions. She calls forth the angels of earth, fire, water and air to bear witness. She weaves the sounds of all creation and infinite space to come and be present here. Myriam anoints Yeshua's head once more, now massaging every orifice and plane of his face, neck, shoulders, back and arms. She takes his hands and lifts them to her mouth and kisses them. Placing his hands upon her hips, she pulls his head to her breasts. Her breasts are like pomegranates, rich and full and nurturing. She continues to coax the energy to rise up Yeshua's spine, one hand upon his crown and the other behind his heart.

Our bodies begin to undulate, our eyes, wet with tears. We are all feeling the serpent power rising in our spines. Tears stream from Myriam's eyes. Her body quivers. The male and female cantor alternate between singing in unison and reciting in response to each other. The beloved song of ecstasy awakens passion within our hearts and loins. Myriam bends low and places her mouth above Yeshua's head. A ram's horn is raised to the sky. Myriam blows the breath of life into her beloved's crown and the horn ushers forth a quickening tone – clear and fervent. We feel an awakening shudder through our bodies. It is as if what Myriam is doing to Yeshua, she is also doing to us. She, representing the Great Mother, anoints and awakens her children.

Yeshua raises himself from the bench. His diaphanous robe clings to his anointed body. He takes Myriam's hands and beckons her to take his place upon the bench. It is the Bride's turn to be honored and anointed. The male cantor's tenor notes and the woman's contralto passages weave into each other, soothing and coaxing an ever rising flow of energy. The ancient, primordial marriage of "The Dying and Risen King with the Queen of Heaven and Earth" – the consecration of their bodies to bring forth a covenant child – is enacted before our eyes.

As Yeshua anoints his beloved, it is as if we can feel a life-giving fountain offering up her waters, freely spreading her greening wetness upon the earth's dry wastelands. We can feel the Great Mother quenching all beings' thirst. As his hands anoint Myriam's hands, heart and belly, we also feel a fiery energy rising up from the earth's center. It penetrates our bodies, as if the flame of a cosmic fire is surging upward to merge with the light of the stars, sun and moon.

Then he blows the breath of life into her crown – the horn resounds! Once again we are quickened. There are no dry eyes.

A large cushion is placed between them and they kneel upon it facing each other. A small glass bowl is handed first to Myriam. In it is a red paste made of ground minerals and olive oil. She gathers the paste upon the middle finger of her right hand and draws a red stripe down Yeshua's forehead, nose, lips, chin, throat, and then she stops at his heart. Yeshua takes the bowl and does likewise with Myriam. All the while they are looking deeply into each other's eyes. It makes me want to swoon! Myriam is quivering. Yeshua is quivering. Then he raises his hands and she takes the red paste and presses it deeply into his palms and wrists. Yeshua does likewise with Myriam's palms and wrists. They bring there hands and wrists toward each other until they are pressed together. Slowly they bring their bodies close as their hands and forearms extend out to the side. At last they rest together heart to heart, thigh to thigh, forehead to forehead and mouth to mouth.

For those able to see, way up above their heads, there is bright golden-white light swirling around. It descends and gathers like a pillar around them. In perfect unison, they stand up within the pillar of light. There is a weaving of multi-hued energy, penetrating and weaving their bodies into one entwined body. There is an extended hush. In the deafening silence we feel like we are being lifted up into the canopy of the heavens.

(Pause)

Then, all of a sudden, someone strikes cymbals faster and faster. *(Fast clapping)* Some of the men rush in and gather Yeshua up. James and Jude bend down, their arms held fast around each other's waists. The men place Yeshua on his brothers' strong shoulders. *(Excitedly)* There are other men who rush in and gather up Myriam. They place her on Uncle Eleazar's broad shoulder. The music starts up, and it builds and builds, as we begin to dance in a big circle around them. We are in joyous ecstasy – dancing, dancing, dancing, dancing, dancing, and dancing....whirling like sunlit clouds of glory! We spin the light! We weave the light into and through ourselves. *(An elevated sense of being permeates Galeah's words.)*

There is laughter. There is drinking. There is more eating and more sweetcakes. *(Excited and happy)*

It is dark outside now. The stars are shining brightly. Oh my!! They are taking Yeshua and Myriam to the bridal chamber. Its thick veils are down and drawn close. The other girls and I, who are still virgins, can't help but giggle a little. It is all so lovely. The scent of burning sandalwood and frankincense fills the air. I breathe in the sweet and pungent aroma of spikenard, lotus flowers and other oils. Oh, it all smells so good! *(Sigh)* It is so intoxicating! I pray that I shall have such a blessing when it is my time to marry my true beloved. *(Big sigh)*

I am Galeah and I am happy we could experience this beautiful ceremony together today.

CA: I am happy, too. Thank you for sharing all the beauty and excitement.

GALEAH: Oh! The next thing I want to say is *(emphatically)*; several weeks after the wedding Myriam announced she is with child! We are feeling very happy about this good news. And we are also feeling some sadness. Myriam will be leaving us soon to begin the long journey to the great mountains of the East. We will miss her. We pour out blessings upon her, Yeshua, and their unborn child.

It is good. We are all happy Yeshua's and Myriam's marriage ceremony has been shared. Now those who live in your day can know about it. This is enough for now.

CA: Thank you for coming and sharing with us.

— Chapter 6 —
MYRIAM OF TYANA, 25 AD[6]
Myriam Reveals Her Meeting with Yeshua at the Well
{Near the Kyber Pass, 14 AD}

{*The Khyber Pass is on the border between present-day Afghanistan and Pakistan. Myriam meets Yeshua at the well in Samaria.*}

MYRIAM: I am pouring water into a basin into which I am placing my beloved Yeshua's tired feet. I cleanse away the dust of the road and then gently massage olive and essential oils into his dry, cracked skin. There are others of the brothers and sisters whose feet I also gladly wash before we enter the dining area. A wonderful meal has been laid out for us. Our hosts have been expecting us and preparing for our arrival for days. We have been away for a long time. It has been more than the passing of one full moon since we left my parents' home in Tyana, which is located in Cappadocia, Turkey. We are not far from the Khyber Pass. Once through the high mountain pass, the last portion of our long journey will take us to my brother-in-law, Joseph *(the Younger's)* home in Varanasi *(Benares)*, near the source of the sacred Ganges River at the foot of the high Himalayas.

Shortly after our marriage eleven years ago, when we first traveled to India, Yeshua and I had found lodging in this same large home. This family has given refuge to such pilgrims traversing the road that connects the Middle and Far East for many generations.

---

[6] This journey to India is Yeshua's and Myriam's second trip, which occurred several years before the public ministry began in 28 AD. See *"Anna, Grandmother of Jesus"* for more details.

Mariam and I are glad to be able to assist the women of this household in exchange for a comfortable place to rest.

I am now helping with the clearing away of our meal. Our hosts and the other men, Mary of Bethany, and several of the other sisters who chose to travel with us, are gathered around Yeshua to hear from his mouth any glad tidings. His sharing is brief because we are weary from our travels. We excuse ourselves early and go to our appointed chambers. I am particularly glad for our very comfortable quarters because I am heavy with child.

CATHERINE ANN (*Henceforth: CA*): Is this your first baby?

MYRIAM: This is my first child since giving birth to Joses and Miriam. Joses was born shortly after we arrived in India in 14 AD. Miriam was born four years later. I have been barren seven years. I rejoice in the opening of my womb. I rejoice in this child who will have the blessing of being born, as were his siblings, within the household of Yeshua's brother, Joseph, who has become a renowned physician in this region.

CA: How close are you to giving birth?

MYRIAM: If all bodes well, I have another three months.

CA: How does Yeshua feel about this child?

MYRIAM: He is very happy. He loves to put his hand on my swollen belly and feel the wonder of the child moving. Sometimes he cups my swollen breasts as he kisses me on each cheek, my forehead and then lingers at my mouth. He likes that I am with child. We sense that it is a boy-child. We shall call him Johannes.

CA: How old are you and how old is Yeshua at this time?

MYRIAM: He is in his 29th year and I am in my 31st.

CA: What else would you like to share?

MYRIAM: I know there is much that has been hidden regarding me and my place in the life of Yeshua. When I look into the future, into your time, I know that my presence, my ways, my wisdom, my children and my experiences with Yeshua may be of benefit to others who love Yeshua and feel a resonance with "Mary Magdalene." There is so much that I could share about my life, but I am going to refrain so that other family members and friends may have an opportunity to speak. I am pleased that I may utter a few words and bare my heart to those who wish to know me and all that I represent.

CA: Thank you for coming and clarifying some of the misunderstandings many people have about Mary Magdalene and her relationship with Yeshua. In Anna's earlier book, Yeshua reveals that he had a Tantric lover during the years he was first in India. Did you meet her? Can you tell us about this woman?

MYRIAM: Yes, I knew this beautiful woman who became one of my closest friends and confidants. She was also my Tantric sister, who trained with Yeshua and me in the mysteries of lifting and transmuting lust-based sexuality and channeling this life-force energy for the purpose of attaining enlightenment. She was named after Krishna's consort, Radha. Her father was a powerful, Tantric yogi. She was highly skilled in all manner of spiritual practices and she was an extraordinarily gentle and compassionate woman. I did not feel threatened by Radha or Yeshua's love for her. I am thankful for the grace and unconditional love that expressed so naturally for us; which made our harmonious and empowering journey together possible. Several years before we were to leave India, we were greatly saddened by Radha's death which occurred while giving birth to Yeshua's son, Jude. I gladly adopted him as my own child.

CA: Can you share more about how you and Yeshua met and what it is like being his wife and Tantric partner?

MYRIAM: My family is of the tribes of Benjamin and Manasseh and most of them have lived in the region of Cappadocia in Turkey for many generations. Before that, my ancestors were held captive in northern Babylonia. Before the time of King Nebuchadnezzar, they lived in Israel, and prior to that, Egypt. Our forefather is Abraham and our great matriarch is Sarah, who went to Egypt and Mt Sinai from Ur of the Chaldees. My blood is seeded not only with this auspicious lineage, but also with that of the pharaohs of Egypt, Queen Sheba of Ethiopia and the Assyrian royalty. Some of my relatives left Cappadocia and took up residence in what used to be known as Israel, but is now called Samaria and Galilee near Mt Tabor. Many of the tribes of Judah and Ephraim spurn us, calling us Samaritans, saying our bloodline is tainted and our worship of the Goddess is blasphemous. I used to find their condescension and bigoted attachment to the letter of the law bothersome, now I feel compassion toward anyone who is bound by such ignorance.

My immediate family is considered affluent and well-educated. We do not keep slaves and we abhor sacrifice of any kind. Many of us, including my father, ascribe to the teachings of Zoroaster, in addition to the writings within the Torah and other mystical oral traditions passed down from Moses, the Egyptian alchemists and the Greek philosophers. I have especially enjoyed being taught by Oriental teachers, who, in private audience, have shared the Hindu Vedas and the sayings of Buddha with me. We are aware of the many gods and goddesses and how all is of an interconnected Oneness.

My mother was particularly fond of the mythic hero and heroine stories. She seemed to understand these very well; having memorized some of the epics. She had a keen interest in sharing her understanding with me. She knew various ways of contacting these mythic realms, as parts of herself, which assisted her ability to be fertile. Demonstrating her mastery, fourteen healthy children came forth from her womb, I being the youngest.

Mama demonstrated an unusual generosity of heart while cultivating harmony and patience during the more recent years that she lived with my father's two younger wives. She had a highly developed intuition; what you would call psychic abilities. She was very wise and very astute. Her cheerful, earthy laughter and gentle voice calmed every troubled heart. Nurturing her family, which she considered her greatest treasure, was her supreme joy. Mama was highly respected in our community. She was often looked to for guidance and match-making. I am still grieving the loss of her, my dearest of my mothers, who recently passed beyond the veil. Unfortunately, I did not have the opportunity to sit with her soul as it passed from her body.

My father's other two wives have given him twelve children all together. These women, my two other mothers, are still living with Papa in Tyana. I rejoiced in our reunion with my large family and the many days of feasting and dancing which we all enjoyed before we joined this caravan. It has taken us to these mountains so far away from familiar faces and customs. But, lest I forget, there is family to embrace on the other side of the mountain pass. ... But, I am getting ahead of my story....

It was my older brothers, Eleazar and Achim, after I joined my relatives in the fertile valleys below Mt Carmel, Mt Tabor and Mt Gilboa; who invited me to come live with them when I had reached the age of sixteen. Although I missed my parental home and my extended family, I found my new home in Samaria and Galilee very agreeable.

As I speak, my memories rise up as if what I am sharing is in the present moment. So I shall speak about my experiences. What most attracted me to this land was the nearby Mount Carmel Essene mystery school, which I briefly visited several times before finally meeting the great matriarch and teacher, Anna. She invited me to return when I felt the calling to begin my initiations. And so it was that within a year of my arrival, I entered into the Essene Way; which I find very compatible with my earlier esoteric training in Tyana. During the year that I was at the monastery at Mt Carmel I heard stories about a young man called Yeshua ben Joseph, Anna's grandson, who had recently returned from taking initiations in Britain. He was visiting his family in Nazareth at the time. Even though I was mildly curious about him, I was much more intrigued and mystified by the energies that seemed to quicken and spread warmth through my heart when I heard mention of his name.

I had already returned home to my brother's home in Ginaea before Yeshua came to Mount Carmel for an extended visit. Once engaged in my busy family life and absorbed in my meditation practices, I promptly forgot about the boy from Nazareth – thinking of him as a boy somehow made it easier to concentrate on what was at hand, rather than the quickening in my heart.

Then one day, a month or so later, I was at one of Eleazar's wells. My hard-working brother had a large estate with many sheep, goats, horses and camels which grazed the grassland where the Judean desert rises to meet the green mountains and valleys of

Galilee. Many wells dotted the land where his animals watered. Ponds ringed by date palms held the winter run-off from Mt Gilboa. The precious water from the wells and ponds flowed through a network of ditches to orchards and gardens. On this particular day I came to sit and contemplate beside one of the nearby wells which provided water for our primary household. While I was lingering there in solitude, enjoying the birdsong amidst the scuffling whispers of the palm fronds, I glimpsed a small group of a dozen or more men. They were making their way down from the higher country which borders my uncle's pastures to the northeast.

As they drew closer I recognized by their manner and clothing, that they were Nazarite Essenes, most likely from the Mount Carmel monastery. They wore plain, unadorned robes of unbleached linen. Their long hair which they all wore in a similar fashion, and their exceedingly calm, mindful bearing and movement, set them apart from the native lay-people of Galilee and Samaria. And of course they could not be mistaken for the Romans who occupied our lands.

As they approached, I could see that they were of varying ages; from adolescent boys to aged elders. My attention was drawn to one of the younger men. When my eyes looked upon him, I was startled by a profound energy that began to race through my heart. Though different in appearance from what I had imagined, I instantly knew him to be Yeshua ben Joseph – and he certainly was not a mere boy! To discreetly gaze upon him was impossible. I felt as though I was being repeatedly struck by lightning. Our eyes locked in an eternal embrace, as if recognizing one another from a distant time beyond this world. But here we were, now, in this world, in these bodies, in this tumultuous time. And then, time seemed to stand still, as any vestige of propriety melted away into the river of energy coursing between us.

I stood up, leaning against the well for support. Tears welled up and ran down both our cheeks. Yeshua dismounted his donkey and came over to me, gently placing his hand on my shoulder. I almost fainted. Loosing my balance, I nearly fell back into the well, but his strong arm gathered me to him. It was as if we were instantly one.

Seeing what was happening between us, Yeshua's oldest uncle, Joseph of Arimathea, known near and far as the wealthy mediator of the law from Samaria, immediately turned to his companions and announced that he would inquire of the householder who owned these wells – my eldest brother, if they might find lodging here for the night.

After drawing up water for men and animals, I eagerly led my new acquaintances to my brother's large house which was adjoined by a number of commodious tents. Upon meeting these new acquaintances, Eleazar, who grandly enjoyed hosting people, set forth making accommodations for our guests. After the evening meal and much camaraderie, our new friends decided to delay their journey to Arimathea and Jerusalem by several days. Both Eleazar and Joseph, sensing a good match and that a marriage between the two families might prove equitably beneficial, agreed to Yeshua's request to court me.

During this short time together, Yeshua and I bonded in an extraordinary way. We felt over-lit by the energies and blessings of the great angels of heaven. There was no question that marriage was our destiny. During the short time we spent together before vows were shared, Yeshua explained to me that he had very strong guidance to go to India where he could meet with numerous enlightened masters and the awakened saints who lived in that faraway land. Yeshua's brother James would be going and they would also have the protection of their uncle, Jacob, one of Anna's older sons, who lived in an Essene monastery in southern Gaul. Jacob was exceedingly glad to be invited to be his nephews' protector. (*As it later unfolded, just as we were about to leave Yeshua's family in Nazareth, his younger brother, Joseph, was given permission to come with us.*)

All was in preparation. Joseph of Arimathea gathered provisions and their departure was set to take place in a few short months. Joseph, who would soon be taking his regular freighting voyage to various destinations along the northern coastline of the Great Sea, would bring Uncle Jacob back with him from Gaul. Yeshua asked me if I would be willing and able to join him in India for an as yet undetermined length of time. I did not find his announcement a hindrance at all. Instantly, I took Yeshua's hands and told him about my love of the Masters and their teachings. I shared with him how thrilled I was to be able to be with my beloved in this land that offered so many opportunities for devotional practice. With that settled, we all agreed that arrangements for our betrothal and wedding be started immediately.

After Yeshua's trip to Jerusalem, we spent a blessed week together before he returned to Nazareth and Mount Carmel to announce our marriage to his parents and relatives. Meanwhile, my two brothers' wives and families began gathering my dowry and all that would make our betrothal and wedding ceremonies a source of joy for Yeshua's Galilean and Judean relatives, as well as a memorable time of festive celebration for my family and friends. Because of the time constraints created by our forthcoming journey to India, it was decided that the nuptial rituals would be celebrated within two weeks of each other instead of the usual time of nine months or more.

My niece, Galeah has shared about her experience and the excitement and joy she felt at our wedding. I hope that you too might joyfully celebrate our union.

CA: In The Holy Bible there is a story about a Samaritan woman whom Yeshua meets at a well. She gives Yeshua a drink and he offers to give her water, which if she drinks it, she will never thirst again. Are you the woman spoken of in this story?

MYRIAM: This story is a composite of several stories about different women he met at different wells. I am one of these women.

On a different day, shortly following our initial meeting, we shared water from one cup. Yeshua spoke of the difference between the unquenchable thirst of ordinary human desire and the Great Desire of, and for, the Beloved which consumes and satisfies all human desires. Human desires, he explained, are attached to getting and keeping what is ultimately impermanent; even if satisfied for a moment, there is never ongoing satisfaction – just unending thirst. This causes much suffering. I knew, within every cell of my body and beyond all bodies, what he meant. The Great Desire for

Oneness is satisfied by the living waters of the Beloved, which when drunk, the Divine Union is realized. During the course of our life's journey together, Yeshua and I drank from Love's Infinite Well, which never dries up. We are always deeply fulfilled.

Over the course of our years together, it became apparent to us that he could not do what was his to do without me. I knew for certain that I couldn't be liberated fully without him. So we embarked on the mystery of Mystical Union together. We gave to each other from our cups, holding nothing back, ever.

— Chapter 7 —
MARY OF BETHANY[7]

Discourses on Spirituality & Relationship with Yeshua and Sar'h
Lake Mareotis, Egypt, 30 AD

{*The setting for this chapter is near Alexandria, Egypt shortly after Yeshua's resurrection. Mary is with child.*}

CATHERINE ANN (*Henceforth: CA*): What is the first impression you have?

MARY OF BETHANY: Yeshua is kneeling before me. My hands are upon his head.

CA: What are you doing at this moment with your hands on his head?

MARY OF BETHANY: We are being still. I am placing his head against my belly that is filled with child. His arms are around me, pulling me close. I stroke his long, fine textured hair. I am happy he is here and that I now have the blessing of motherhood.

CA: Is this Mary of Bethany?

MARY OF BETHANY: It is. You called me forth. I am feeling somewhat weak. I have been ill with what you call morning sickness. The child is beginning to move and my belly is starting to swell with this ripeness, with this joy. I am in Egypt now.

CA: Has Yeshua been with you the whole time or only occasionally?

---

[7] Mary of Bethany is the Light-conceived daughter of Joseph of Arimathea and Mary of Magdala. She is Yeshua's cousin. See the *"Anna's Descendants"* charts and *"Anna, Grandmother of Jesus"* for more information about Mary of Bethany.

MARY OF BETHANY: We have had relatively lengthy visits. He is not always with me because he has much to do. It is quite hot now. I stay in the shadows where it is somewhat cooler. I have cloths that are dampened with water which I place upon my head. I hear the nearby reassuring sounds of families and the soft voices of those who are cloistered at this monastery of the Essenes and Therapeutae. It is a place of safety. We live on the shore of Lake Mareotis, which is located south of Alexandria where the Nile makes many branches, as does a tree. Except instead of stretching skyward, her limbs spread out and empty into the blue waters of the Great Sea. She brings fertile soil and abundant water to this region where we are abiding.

CA: Are there others of the family with you?

MARY OF BETHANY: My father, Joseph of Arimathea, brought me and Myriam of Tyana and her children a few weeks ago from Alexandria. We had found refuge in the city for almost two months, but now that I am beginning to be swollen with child, it was decided that we come to a place of greater safety. Father will be leaving soon. He has much concern for the many family members left in Judea and Galilee. I am glad that Yeshua is here with me, Myriam and the children. Yeshua is still recovering from his great ordeal. We all need much rest. Our constitutions have been stretched thin. I am thankful for our safe passage to Alexandria and the serenity that abides here in this Essene sanctuary. I know those who live in this community can keep our very guarded secret from those who would bring us harm.

CA: Who would bring you harm?

MARY OF BETHANY: There are people of the Jewish priesthood who hold much fear and anger toward us. They misperceive our purposes and our work. Their eyes are blinded. They see not what is before them that could make their way easier and their path smoother. Their ears are closed. They hear not how they can better fulfill the higher law of love spoken of by the great teachers and prophets. They, in their pride, prefer strife and conflict rather than claim a way of life in which they can enjoy a grander harmony within their souls and a greater peace within their homes and families.

Then there are also the Romans who insist that the people who live in the lands they occupy pay tribute to Emperor Tiberius and render obedience to the Roman gods. They encourage peace, but it is a controlled peace ruled with a closed fist. Yeshua was arrested by the Pharisees and judged worthy of crucifixion by Pontius Pilate. Word has spread that my beloved did not die. We are considered fugitives from both Roman and Jewish law. There are ruthless men who would gladly exchange our lives for bounty. We must take great precautions. It is a harrowing time with much unrest. Souls are goaded by fear. Many people barely subsist on the little that is their lot. They have turned to us begging for relief. Few of them know how to sustain any measure of peace within their hearts and lives.

Even though I am not able to see the effects for good, as yet, I feel that we have succeeded quite well in our mission to bring a greater light to humanity. We have held up a mirror in which to behold the innate beauty and perfection abiding within every heart. We have left sayings that, if contemplated and practiced, will enable the seeker of Heaven's treasures the ability to find immeasurable gifts of peace and equanimity within the stillness of their own mind and breast. It is wise for us not expect much positive change in this, our lifetime, though I believe a goodly harvest of the seeds we planted will be enjoyed by all who choose to partake of their fruits in the generations to come.

It takes a great faith to rest in the simple comfort that we gave our all to the way of loving-kindness in the years we toiled upon the plains, deserts and mountains. We take comfort, not pride, in the fact that our vow to end humanity's suffering did not stop with only the crowds who came to us for healing. Our vow of eternal love and our assurance in the truth that death has no sting found victory in the life-giving garden sepulcher. We came to know the liberating truth beyond the shadows that still darken the killing field of Golgotha.

We do not know how our beloved planet and the coming generations of humanity will receive the intense energies we anchored before and during the week of Passover in Jerusalem. We are still too close to the events and the energies that were poured out during those days in which we fulfilled our promised destiny, as we understood it. However, I can say that even though it has only been a few short months since Gethsemane, I feel a different vibration when I walk upon the Earth Mother. Our brothers and sisters of space and those of the angelic realms whom we had come to dearly know and honor through our deep inner work, assisted us to anchor cosmic frequencies. They are continuing to hold their positions. These wonderful beings of light are monitoring the grids and assisting the Earth to stabilize her axis. Though this long cosmic era will likely continue to see much darkness, we hold a different view in which a peace-loving society may come forth in the midst of great adversity to be true gardeners and stewards of life. We hold forth a vision of men, women and children wisely and compassionately holding the scale of balance and harmony for the benefit of all in seamless Oneness.

Thankfully, we are here, on the shore of a lovely lake near Alexandria, where we can enjoy a time of rest and turning inward, a place dedicated to living quietly and simply. We can now give our attention to a different purpose. Instead of ministering to the masses, we must make sure Yeshua's children, and all the children conceived by those of us in our generation, live long enough to be able to awaken the cosmic Light that is genetically encoded within them. We must teach this next generation how to live and demonstrate the way of love and liberation that was the same purpose for which we took birth.

Yeshua has spoken of eleven other male avatars and their wise consorts who abide upon the earth at this pivotal time. Each has endowed the world with the gift of enlightened teachings. Some of them also have children. These children are being brought up by families dedicated to sharing love's fruits equally with all. We must do our best to prepare receptive fields where all our children can disperse love's quickening light to the entire world so that suffering, caused by perceived separation from the source of love, might someday cease.

Discourse on the Light-Seeded Children & Spiritual Awakening

I wish to clarify some misunderstandings I experience that many people have about us and their possible relationship to us; which are, in truth, often their own ego projections seeking aggrandizement. Speaking more directly about our children, some people think of our posterity as a special lineage endowed with exceptional abilities and with preordained authority, simply because they are descended directly from Yeshua. Some place a lot of misguided energy into seeking out their possible bloodline connection or a past life spent with us or they claim to be a future incarnation of one of us. This does not mean that there is no truth to authentic spiritual lineages or that a very real soul connection is not possible; rather I am encouraging such a seeker to look clearly into what motivates them to believe and seek such information. Then I encourage them to question the authenticity, relevancy and benefit of what they find with their unfolding understanding of their present life's purpose; which is ultimately to awaken from separation's dream, regardless of lineages and past-life connections – though these auspicious conditions, when wisely directed, may indeed assist.

When I talk about our children, who are special in our eyes, I do not mean to say that our children are superior to other children. All beings are uniquely special. We are all collectively divine. All life is cosmically endowed with Light, not just our children. The skillful means to fully express that Light is given freely to every heart that humbly knocks and asks our heavenly Father-Mother for the grace of remembrance. For most human beings, their intrinsic radiance – their essential being – is obscured by their ceaseless mental ruminations on the past and future, accompanied by all manner of emotional suffering. For others who are more awake, their True Nature – the Infinite Light – is more easily accessed, and they are more willing to acknowledge their obscurations so that they can skillfully be "removed." With such awakened individuals, a spontaneously arising, self-luminous presence can be seen and felt, as is the case with Yeshua – especially now that he has attained his immortal body of light.

We understand, from a larger perspective, it is karmically appropriate and agreed by the collective souls of humanity that wise, compassionate teachers – some, who are fully enlightened, take incarnation during the cycles of time in order to be of service to the interconnected web of life. Such ones vow to remain close to the Earth and to take repeated conscious births in order to assist all beings whose lives endure endless deaths and rebirths so that we may all collectively awaken from our dream of suffering. The children I speak of are some of these more awakened and compassionate souls. They consciously choose to incarnate in order to be a light to humanity during times of great darkness.

They are often birthed within favorable conditions – such as supportive families, communities, teachers and teachings – everything that is required to provide stability and skillful means for remembering who they are. I have observed that when children are conceived and reared by couples whose consciousness and example is more awake, they are more interested in opening their minds and hearts to the way of mindfulness and loving-kindness. They are aware of each present moment and the naked "suchness" of everything that arises within it; recognizing each transient breath as a fleeting opportunity to feel intrinsic joy, and each heartbeat a brief chance to express kindness, knowing that this precious human birth offers a most auspicious opportunity for awakening. Once their minds and hearts are opened to acknowledging and understanding the existence of suffering; its causes, conditions and cessation – rather than deny, judge and reject it, they know their transitory experiences of pain are opportunities to bring compassionate awareness to their own humanity and to other people in such a way as to lessen the suffering we all experience.

The children who are born into more conscious families are made aware that they are not immune from working out and healing their own personal karmas, or from directly experiencing the karma we all share – that of basic ignorance which, beginning with unconscious birth trauma, often results in the perception of being a separate "I" in a separate body; divided within self, left to grieve our heart's immense loss when we perceive ourselves disconnected and alone.

A false, pretentious self; what you call a persona – an ego, forms out of this core grief and terror. An immense need to be in control of life's uncertainties arises; an unquenchable thirst for more of whatever can, even briefly, assuage an ever deepening despair, becomes a constant preoccupation. The false self tries to preserve its existence and unmet desires with great tenacity. Attachment and addiction to unrequited desires obscures the True Self in the same way the sun becomes obscured by clouds. But it is also the sun's light that reveals the clouds that obscure it. So it is, likewise, that the intrinsic Light, which is the True Self, reveals the "false self" and its obscuring masquerade of fleeting and fickle desires.

If training is given in how to observe these ego desires: in understanding how clinging to selfish desires causes anxiety, anger and grief; how trying to make the illusory nature of life – solid, and the impermanent state of the material world – everlasting, which only causes them to feel more and more insecure, frustrated, confused and confined; then they can grow beyond the limited self. As their awareness increases, they see that humanity has locked itself in a self-made prison. And with this awareness comes a deep-seated desire – the Great Desire – that extends beyond the ego's need to escape suffering; that extends beyond liberation for the sake of oneself only.

With the Great Desire comes an innate compassion for all beings. As the compassionate initiate seeks liberation for all forms of life, not just for themselves, they begin to experience a consistent, joyful motivation to investigate spiritual teachings and to be disciplined in the practices. Through this process comes the ability to embrace and love all beings as oneself - the True Self – inseparable from the Beloved, loving as the Beloved loves.

However, just being born into favorable conditions does not guarantee this liberation. I have also known many great souls born into the most grievous and adverse of circumstances; knowing abuses of all kinds, who, knowing they are either working out their personal karmas or are serving the greater whole, humbly open their hearts and awaken, as the Beloved. I have also known enlightened masters born awake, who consciously chose to be born as a light in the midst of the greatest darkness. Unfortunately, there are also children, born into the best of circumstances, who later become complacent or who are overtaken by the poisons of their minds. Sadly these souls forfeit the purpose of their human incarnation – an opportunity for awakening in this lifetime.

Although Yeshua's children may be extraordinarily gifted in the ways I have shared, I wish it to be understood when I speak of our conscious conception and protection of them, that we are not motivated by any thought of establishing and guarding a political dynasty, much less an ecclesiastical lineage. We do not feel entitled to, nor have any intention, to presume we have the right and authority to govern and lead others. We do not require or seek such powers for our children, although we are dedicated to teaching and learning the necessary skills which make it possible to take on the responsibilities of leadership, when it is clearly indicated that others will truly benefit from our guidance or intervention. Our purpose is to freely offer loving-kindness to all we meet and to set an example that may awaken wise and compassionate self-governance and a unified harmony among all beings, as we all progress step by step on our shared journey.

In the 2,000 years since we, and the other eleven avatars and their consorts, walked the earth many generations have been born – billions of souls call this planet home. With each succeeding generation, the cosmic Light, which we anchored into our DNA and into the elements of the earth, during our time, has been passed biologically and etherically on to all of you through the multiple lineages of our descendants.[8] That same liberating illumination,

---

[8] The descendants referred to here are not only Yeshua's and the Magdalenes but also Light-conceived children of Anna's genetic lineage. Although not discussed in detail, this also includes the descendants of the other avatars on the Earthplane who conceived children at the same time as did Yeshua; and perhaps unknown others Light-conceived, as well.

which avatars (*both male and female*) have brought to the Earthplane through all times, abides within the living cells of humanity and all living things. There are no "special" descendants or a privileged lineage to seek; we are already what we are seeking.

Searching for the historical Jesus Christ, Mary Magdalene and our children is best done with a willingness to discern one's motivation with clarity and honesty. Once engaged in this rather intriguing search, a generous dose of common sense and a sense of humor is needed to keep the purpose of the self-chosen "destination" in clear perspective. Yes, it is important to know that we lived, that we loved dearly, and that we had children. It is however even more important that you also consciously live and love and bring forth children who know the ways of loving-kindness, in this, your day. Rather than be distracted by our story, it is more important that you open to your own encoded "Christ-Magdalene" nature – your essential Light-anointed nature – in every precious moment. In this simple way, we can all reach the same destination – and once arriving, know we have never left Home.

Discourse on Spiritual Lineages

CA: You said you and Yeshua never intended to create a family dynasty or an ecclesiastical lineage; what about a spiritual lineage? Did you create a spiritual lineage and does it still exist?

MARY OF BETHANY: In a sense we created a new spiritual lineage, in that Yeshua as an avatar, and Myriam and I, as his anointed consorts,[9] were the first to present a distinct spiritual teaching not previously offered publicly in exactly the same way in which we had been trained in the ancient wisdom traditions. These ancient lineages that have held our ancient wisdom traditions are tributaries of a commonly shared Wisdom Source which extends into the cosmos and subtle realms beyond this planet; ultimately having their origin in the Absolute beyond the conceptual mind.

---

[9] Yeshua's cousin, Mariam, later became one of Yeshua's spiritual consorts forming a trinity with Myriam & Mary known as "The Three Marys."

ANNA, THE VOICE OF THE MAGDALENES

The basis of our external teachings, if they are to be clearly understood, can be found within the context of the Mount Carmel Essenes, who practice a deep mysticism which draws directly upon this ancient multi-dimensional wisdom. Within our Essene Order are master teachers who know how to receive authentic empowerments, and who, having the authority to transmit the sacred oral teachings and awakening energies, still give these to initiates who are ready to receive them. We could not have done our work had it not been for the master teachers at Mount Carmel, such as Grandmother Anna, who set the stage and gathered a community of resonant souls – a spiritual lineage if you will – with whom we could effectively play our roles.

The essential wisdom and empowerments we espouse and embody are never used for the purpose of creating a religious doctrine and church, such as Christianity – which, by the way is not a spiritual lineage. This is not to say masters and initiates of an authentic spiritual lineage do not participate in all manner of religious, spiritual, philosophical and scientific groups. Such ones work to bring benefit within and outside the doors of organized religion. In most cases, a thread of truth that benefits the lives of many is to be found in all doctrines and churches. Our way, however, is a lineage of Light – beyond names and creed – that carries and transmits the necessary authentic empowerments for anyone who wishes to awaken to her or his True Nature – the infinite Light and Love of the Beloved, regardless of having or not having a particular religious or group affiliation.

Our sayings and demonstrations are given to the seeker as an invitation to do as we do and turn inward where "the Peace that passes understanding" is to be found. We offer practical skills for investigating how it is that our divisive minds and grieving hearts cause confusion, self-doubt and all manner of suffering. In stillness, following the breath, we suggest how to witness the transient process of our minds and senses – calmly resting in the great unmoving, unifying spaciousness; simply watching passing thoughts, feelings and sensations as naked "suchness" – without conceptualizing, without grasping the pleasurable or avoiding the painful, noting the impermanent and empty nature of our mind's contents and our body's sensations.

Our way is to embrace the afflictive emotions of fear, anger and grief – the poisons of the mind and heart – the obscurations that distort the self-luminous light, that dam the flow of eternal love. We encourage getting acquainted with these unacknowledged and rejected parts of self, which are poisonous by nature; using the poisons skillfully as alchemical antidotes to heal back into wholeness. Once free of emotional blockages and mental distortions, an ever-present, infinite well-spring of abiding calm and joy is realized – the Great Peace – always present and comforting.

It is true that the deeper, transformational and often paradoxical meaning beyond Yeshua's words cannot be grasped by the ordinary mind. It is also true that those who listen with a lesser understanding – identifying with their impermanent physical bodies, seeking to lessen the burden of their fearful, guilt-ridden and grief-stricken lives – often take Yeshua's metaphysical and metaphorical sayings literally.

Among these people are those who feel inadequate and powerless, who assume that an intellectual, literal interpretation is enough to qualify them to teach and lead others; who, not realizing the consequences of abusing their positions of influence, see an opportunity to wield power over others – the "wolves in sheep's clothing" – who take advantage of the "sheep" who ignorantly give their power away. These "wolves and sheep" create man-made dogmas and religions; enacting, rationalizing and justifying "holy wars" against projected evils – their own disowned darkness, in the name of their professed saviors and gods – the "One God" divided against itself.

Such ones are to be embraced and forgiven, for they know not what they do. They are the blind who take themselves, and those who follow them, into the ditch.

There are also the unquestioning, anxious orthodoxy, fearing a man-made, jealous and angry god – (*again the blind trying to lead the blind*) – who distrust Yeshua's unorthodox methods; such as honoring women as being equal to men; inviting the beggar and prostitute, the prince and ascetic to equally enjoy his company and sayings – seeing the uncircumcised as worthy as the sons of Abraham – finding them all sons and daughters of a loving Mother-Father Creator. Yeshua also teaches us how to embrace the mystical union of polar opposites instead of fostering the dualistic conflict of good against evil. And, perhaps most threatening, is his teaching that God's presence is directly available to all without an intercessory "savior/god/goddess" or an ordained priesthood. It is agreed that though such mediators may grandly assist, they are not absolutely required in the actual moment of enlightenment – the existential, experiential instant of at-one-ment.

For those able to hear and comprehend the subtlest of his teachings; which are ungraspable by the ordinary mind, the empowerments come through an unbroken lineage of returning avatars, such as Yeshua. The enlightened ones orally transmit the awakening energies and practices to adepts who then pass on the quickening energies and teachings to initiates from generation to generation. Some of these teachings are recorded in sacred texts. What cannot be conveyed through spoken concepts and written symbols is transmitted orally as pure sound syllables and ultrasonic frequencies. With the coming of a master there is also the gathering of disciples and the organization of the teachings; out of convenience, these are usually collectively known by their enlightened teacher's name. But the label is not the content – merely calling yourself a Christian does not make you Light-Anointed.

You, like all initiates on the path of awakening, when all is in a ripeness, may also, as we did, receive, practice and Know for yourself the existence and fruit of the spiritual lineage of Light beyond names. We encourage those who walk with us, who sincerely ask to know the Infinite Way, to investigate, question and experiment with our teachings and practices. Intend that the dormant light-codes passed down to you through your genetics be activated. Have your own personal and direct experiences of the truths we share – come alone to the Beloved and know the Oneness.

MARY OF BETHANY

In my years with Yeshua and Myriam in India, before we began our public ministry, I had many experiences with masters and saints – experiences that could fill books. Besides the beautiful teachings of Ram, Krishna and Babaji; we feel a great affinity with the copious words of wisdom and alchemical practices given by Shakyamuni Buddha to his disciples. His teachings have been passed on orally these past five hundred years. Buddha's Dharma is only now being carefully recorded – and even so, there are differences of opinion regarding its translation.

We continue to give the ancient scriptures from India and other texts, especially those which were translated and preserved in our Mount Carmel library, much study and contemplation. There are some among us whose responsibility it is to commit Yeshua's sayings to writing, even though we realize our words may be distorted and destroyed by those who hold fear-based power now and in the future. Grandmother Anna has encouraged us to write our stories, nevertheless.

Some of Yeshua's, and his closest disciples', esoteric meaning is clearly given in our records for those with ears to hear, but most of the deeper meaning is intentionally obscured so that a novice without sufficient training is not harmed and cannot bring harm to others. The remainder of the teachings and practices, which are quite vast and powerful, are given orally to anyone who is ready to take on the increased responsibility of bringing no harm to any form of life – bringing only benefit to all beings.

Yes, this spiritual lineage exists in your day. But the ones, both male and female master teachers, capable of transmitting the authentic empowerments are not necessarily affiliated with any particular religion. Although there are some masters who definitely hold influential positions and are known publicly, there are others who choose to remain incognito.

Should you be led through synchronous events to "find" such a teacher, be patient, take time and really get acquainted with them. Get to know the devotees, the teachings and their fruits. Carefully observe and question. Do not be gullible; your soul is ultimately your responsibility – not your teacher's. Until you know with absolute certainty that you can place your life in their hands and that they are willing and capable of joining you completely in the transmutation of your karma, refrain from giving your power away.

One key to recognizing an authentic teacher is to assess how you feel in their presence. Is your heart and mind expanded with love? Is their luminosity and behavior consistent and stable? Do they present themselves with humility and a lightness of being? Some teachers may be very unorthodox and outrageous in their methods. Others may be quite stern and disciplined, but none take themselves or this illusory world too seriously. After a time with your teacher, are you finding the hard edges of your persona and mind softening, the boundaries that confine your heart dissolving, your actions less reactive and your embrace of life more kind, gentle, patient and spacious?

The adage, "When the student is ready, the teacher appears," is the appropriate view – perhaps frustrating and mysterious to the naïve seeker, but understood by the ripe soul. (*Pause*)

Discourse on "Past Life" as "Mary Magdalene"

CA: I know quite a few women who sincerely feel they had a past-life as Mary Magdalene. What would you say to these women?

MARY OF BETHANY: I could say much about this is delicate topic. But I am guided to speak only a few words to these beloved sisters. First of all, Yeshua's consorts, including myself, Myriam of Tyana, and later my cousin, Mariam – "the legendary three Marys" – left a very powerful holographic record within the ethers of Mother Earth. This "living" record can be easily accessed. The Mary Magdalene "imprint" is influenced by many filtering variables: such as soul resonance; clarity of spiritual view; cultural, psychological and mythic stereotypes and religious biases; and motivation and emotional stability. Each woman who accesses her own experience of "Mary Magdalene" will do so in a way that feels very real and uniquely personal to her. The women who were close to us; those who were trained in the Magdalene Order, all "embodied" the Magdalene frequencies and experiences in extraordinary ways – ways unique to each of us. We, as a sister-brotherhood, experienced such Oneness, that it was possible to support each other and "The Work" with Yeshua almost seamlessly. The point I am making here, is there are many influencing variables to be questioned.

I would say to these dear sisters; those of you, who have "tapped into" the experiences of "The Three Marys," as if our experiences were your own – you did have one or more lifetimes as a Magdalene priestess or priest. In other words, you were initiated into the mysteries of Isis, Osiris and Horus. Most likely you knew and served with Yeshua as a Magdalene – you may have been one of the women who walked with him. These experiences were so impactful, that you, no doubt, feel extremely close to him, even today. You likely experience a high resonance with his mystical teachings, whether found in The Holy Bible or The Apocrypha, in translations of the recently discovered Gnostic and Essene scrolls, in the arcane literature of the Western wisdom schools, in ascended master channelings or in your own revelatory meditations. It is also possible that you might have found, or may yet find, Yeshua's teachings within Hinduism, Buddhism or among the mystical Kabbalists and Sufis. You may find him in the teaching stories handed down by indigenous tribes around the world. Regardless, of how you become connected, you feel Yeshua in your heart, as do all Magdalenes.

For those who feel that you were "Mary Magdalene," it is also highly possible that you are descended from our bloodline. Because of this genetic coding it is easier to access our holographic or Akashic records. But, as I have already shared, this does not make you special, or designate you the "Mary Magdalene," then or now. As has already been shared, the Mary Magdalene you are familiar with is actually a composite of Myriam of Tyana, Mary of Bethany, and Mariam of Mount Carmel. There are many millions who are our literal descendants, and every form of life – animate and inanimate – carries the encoded higher frequencies of Cosmic Consciousness we anchored into the elements and ethers of the Earth Mother as well as being encoded in our DNA and carried forth through our descendant's DNA. Therefore, it is possible for anyone with the appropriate attunement and resonance to "experience" aspects or portions of the life of "Mary Magdalene" – though it is important to be aware that your experience is more or less filtered by your present-day consciousness.

It is very unlikely that you actually had a past-life incarnation as one of "The Three Marys." If you did, whether as a full incarnation or as a holographic soul aspect, you would know it through irrefutable means. You would not speak idly of it, nor draw attention to yourself in an ego-aggrandizing or defensive way. Our presence is close and very accessible anytime you wish to receive loving assistance from us as you walk your path as a present-day Magdalene initiate. But refrain, please, from calling yourself Mary Magdalene, for you will be misleading yourself and others.

I wish to also speak to the many women who feel sexual guilt and shame because of their painful sexual experiences. They identify with Mary Magdalene, the Penitent, as portrayed by the Roman Catholic Church – an insecure and angry patriarchal priesthood that has felt threatened by the real understanding of the Magdalene for two millennia. For those women who suffer, it is somehow comforting to think of the absolved Saint Mary Magdalene as a woman who also knew suffering because of her "sinful" sexuality; and who, because she was forgiven by Yeshua (*Jesus*) – that is, the Church's version of Yeshua as "The Savior archetype" – she was able to heal her "fallen" nature. But this wanton, hysterical caricature of Mary Magdalene is not the true Mary Magdalene, any more than being cast as "the Dying and Resurrected King archetype," is the true Yeshua ben Joseph – though in the understanding of the Osirian resurrection mysteries, Yeshua, in fact, did play that role.

The libel was cast and perpetuated by a man-made church many years after the last of us walked the earth. The mythical "Mary Magdalene" is none other than the derided archetypal "fallen woman, the seductress and the prostitute" – she who is put in her "lesser place" and gagged by those who fear her power. In this case, it is the power of a Magdalene priestess that is feared. She, who in

MARY OF BETHANY

the Osirian mysteries, acts as Isis, who resurrects her beloved Osiris' consciousness from its dream of death (*separation*) and lifts him up and places him in the alchemical Grail Cup of Divine Union. Merged in Oneness, they together conceive the Grail child, Horus. From the sanctified "Royal Blood – the Holy Grail" the Light returns and pours out a blessing upon the Earth and all beings. Just as Yeshua played the role of Osiris during the Week of Passover, so did Myriam (*of Tyana*), Mariam and I; and the other female Magdalenes, enact his beloved, Isis, the resurrecting Mother of Life.

The truth is, none of "The Three Marys" are whores, nor do we suffer because of our sexuality. We are empowered women, Tantric Dakinis – adepts, highly skilled, as are most trained Magdalenes, in the esoteric energy practices which channel sexual/life-force energy throughout the physical and subtle bodies in order to attain enlightened consciousness and to Light-conceive children. It is also true that, we, as Magdalene priestesses, have been called harlots throughout time – as has the Great Mother been called The Great Whore. Such is the way of ignorance and distrust of the Divine Feminine and her union with the Divine Masculine – for true alchemical union of the Divine Feminine and the Divine Masculine would mean the cessation of the "dramatic play" of duality and separation.

CA: Thank you. Your words are very helpful. Now return back once again to Egypt, to the room you are in, with Yeshua by your side. What is happening?

MARY OF BETHANY: It's getting dark outside. We are inside our small room which is humbly appointed. We have lit a little oil lamp which rests on a simple wooden table beside our pallet where we sleep. My beloved assists me to lie down beside him. He spoons me very gently in his arms. Breathing together, he helps my energy to stabilize and my weary mind to find deep rest. We feel the sweet presence of the babe within my womb. I feel certain that the heart beating softly beneath our hands is that of a girl-child and that she will be a vessel for the Great Mother's love.

CA: What do you know about this child, anything in particular?

MARY OF BETHANY: I see an expansive pink-hued light around her. I feel that she will be very delicate and yet quite strong. She will be a great gift to many. I don't think Yeshua will be disappointed that this is a girl-child. She carries a very powerful consciousness, what you would call a Great One. She will be named Sarah – Sar'h, as the Egyptians call her. I feel honored to be her mother. God is good to me and to us. (*Emotion*)

Discourse on Relationship with Yeshua & Myriam

CA: Would you tell me what it was like for you when you learned that Yeshua married Myriam of Tyana? How has your journey been with Myriam and Yeshua?

MARY OF BETHANY: If I were to tell you everything it would be quite a voluminous book, would it not? But I can give you some highlights that may provide some perspective and insight.

In our youth Mariam (*Yeshua's cousin*) and I went to Egypt to receive higher Magdalene initiations in the temples of Isis, Osiris and Horus. We felt honored that we were chosen to have these experiences at such a young age, which together with our training at Mount Carmel became the foundation of our future ministry with Yeshua. We did not know then how that future would play out, but we were always motivated by a deep sense of destiny. Any time there was an opportunity for growth, we took it, no questions asked. I was increasingly able to tame the rebellious tendencies of my earlier youth and by the time I went to Egypt it was easier for me to go through the necessary disciplines.

The initiations we went through in the temples were often very arduous; not the romantic quest the uninitiated might imagine. We did see progress, as measured by our increasing spiritual powers. Following the strong encouragement of our teachers, we undertook more advanced levels of Egyptian high alchemy and we both became initiated priestesses of Isis. We proudly wore her golden serpent upon our left arms, representing the raising of the resurrecting life-force energy – Kundalini or Sekhem, up the spine or the djed. We were looked to with respect and never spared the rigorous disciplines required of every initiate.

But none of these trainings prepared us for the initiation we went through when we learned Yeshua had met, married and gone to India with Myriam of Tyana. We felt devastated and betrayed that Yeshua actually chose to follow through with the strong suggestions of family members to seal an alliance through marriage with Myriam's family, deridingly referred to as Samaritans by the orthodox Jews.

Because the ancient temple injunction, "Know Thy Self and Be Free!" is our constant password, we were introduced to aspects of our inner darkness we could not have previously imagined existed within us. We were so beside ourselves. Judgment lashed out and the weight of self-doubt burdened us. Surprised and humbled by the intensity of our reactions, we feared we had lost our station as initiates. It was like a beast was dragging us around by its teeth. We were in a state of bewildered shock.

We thought we had been cast completely out of Yeshua's life. We did not know for certain if he would ever return. The youthful visions of growing up and being at his side seemed to disappear like an elusive desert mirage. We were left to despair in the dust of crumbling dreams. We were faced with the humbling realization that a goodly measure of our desire for taking initiations in the temples of Egypt was to become prepared to marry Yeshua. Bereft of Yeshua, our motivation for the hard inner-work began to wane. It became more and more difficult to concentrate. This was a dangerous thing, because a constant vigilance against serious injury or loss of life is required of any initiate in the midst of experiencing intense energies. Before an unfortunate incident happened, we were wisely and mercifully invited to return to our homes.

Once home, it took a great deal of work on both our parts to heal from the wounding stories we kept telling our hearts, convincing ourselves of the terrible loss of Yeshua. In spite of realizing I was keeping a fictitious story alive, I still continued to feel that my soul was inextricably woven with his. Letting him go seemed impossible. Mariam had the same feelings of deep connection and desire for marriage, but somehow, all my life, I knew the prize – Yeshua, was to be mine and no one else's. I had so convinced myself in my youth that I would be his only bride; I lost all sense of my moorings. I floundered in a sea of genuine grief. But more important for my eventual healing was the realization that I was drinking a poisonous brew of bitter jealousy mixed with generous doses of nauseating self-pity.

With the passing of time, I realized my wound was self-inflicted, for every soul is free to choose a path which is their own. How could I begrudge Yeshua his path in which to give and receive love, if my love for him be true? And the truth was, Yeshua had never promised to marry me and I knew he would never intentionally bring me harm. Might the antidote for the poisons of jealousy and self-pity, which were eating me alive, be found in rejoicing in his happiness? Of all the initiations I went through as a young woman, none were more difficult than this one. I believe I can say this was true for Mariam as well.

CA: Did you see it as an initiation at the time?

MARY OF BETHANY: I grew to see it as a karmic initiation that my soul would pass through on many levels for years to come.

Time slowly passed before Yeshua returned. In the beginning, in order to endure the loneliness and grief, I sought solace in the silent hillsides of Bethany. I took refuge from time to time with the Essenes at Qumran. There, I enjoyed the companionship of John, who later became known as The Baptist, and Judas, later known as Judas Iscariot. Drawing on profound inner strength, within the depth of my being, made it possible to rejoice in Yeshua's and Myriam's happiness; and with my mother's and father's encouragement, I finally emerged out of the shadows of self-pity and jealousy.

I joined my mother and my siblings, Lazarus and Martha, in their hospice work and the care of the homeless and diseased. I began to find solace and joy in my native gifts of healing. I found that by losing my self in the ministering to others, whose suffering was greater than my own, a sure path to my own heart's healing was opening. I redefined my sense of self and my life's purpose. I began to ask deeply probing questions. I could not settle for any answer that did not come directly from the Self who knew The Answers beyond my mind's relative concepts and my emotions' fickle desires.

As for Mariam, it was not long after our return that she and her long-time friend, Nathaniel, were married. Her painful loss of Yeshua was salved by Nathaniel's gentle love and the birth of their son, Benjamin.

CA: Did you ever consider any other men?

MARY OF BETHANY: How could I? There was no one else. I couldn't see anyone in my heart but Yeshua.

CA: Please share more about how you spent the years while Yeshua was away.

MARY OF BETHANY: As I was saying, my mother and father encouraged my healing gifts. Under my mother's guidance and prompting, my father expanded our home in Bethany in order to provide shelter and healing for battered women and pregnant mothers, orphans, the mentally and physically infirm and those who were dying. Mother's activities were so inspiring and successful that Father bought other properties which served the same purpose.

After my return from Egypt I slowly found renewed enthusiasm for life, as I tended all who came to us – from infants being born to elders taking their last breath. It was during this time that I realized how my own self-absorption had blinded me to the suffering that had always been around me. I had not allowed it into my heart until my heart broke with the grief of "losing" my beloved Yeshua. By allowing my selfish heart to break, I found an infinite love gushing up from an eternal wellspring; an endless flow of love sourced from deep within my Soul. I saw and felt how many people grieve losses far greater than mine. As I embraced each one entrusted into my care, we would join our in-breaths and out-breaths. Breathing in, I felt my grief lessen as I welcomed another's loss into my light-filled heart. I rejoiced as our merged grief flew into the Light beyond form. As I breathed love, gratitude and peace into their heart, we both experienced healing.

I began to know what it means to be a priestess in service to the Great Mother – to be her heart and hands. I had received the healing serpent of the Goddess upon my arm; now it was time to wear the mantle of a Magdalene – the same mantle my beloved mother wore with so much humility and devotion. Letting go of selfish desires that wanted to avoid suffering, I could feel every heart as if it were my own. Every broken body and tormented mind and anguished heart found a resonance within my own body and soul. I and "other" melted into one self. My view expanded. In selflessness I found my true Self and my true Beloved.

Discourse on Egyptian Sepulcher Initiation

I did not realize, however, until I returned to Egypt for more advanced initiations that within my self-identification as a healer was a more subtle form of selfish willfulness. This did not reveal itself until I undertook the more intense experiences of facing death headlong and the more advanced processes of dying which are consciously engaged in the Rites of the Sepulcher. It was during these initiations that I was introduced to the hell realms.

In my vow to alleviate suffering, there began to be a great force which welled up inside me. It felt like the protective fierceness of a great mother tigress or lioness. I was resolutely determined to heal and remove suffering from as many beings as possible. I was particularly resolved to find a way to remove the suffering from those who were deeply tormented within their souls – those you would call demented – twisted of mind and body. I could see and feel the immensity of what they were carrying. I could see the energies of attached disembodied spirits. I found that I could assist these spirits to let go of their hosts and move on in their journey. I wanted to learn more skillful and effective ways of doing this kind of healing.

As in my earlier Egyptian initiations, I went down again into dark cavernous temple chambers where I was sealed up in small spaces, such as sarcophagi. When I was in Egypt earlier, I had learned some of the basic skills used for stilling my vital signs. I thought I was now sufficiently prepared to practice the more advanced aspects of the Rites of the Sepulcher. While receiving this training I was introduced to the warrior goddesses – "the Dark Mothers" – Sekhmet, Durga, Kali, Demeter and many others. There was something about the energy of the "dark" Mother; the unconditionally loving presence who is willing to descend into the hell realms where she finds her lost and suffering children and returns them to the Light. It was this capacity to love this much that I wanted to embody and practice. I wanted to destroy the illusion of death and extinguish the causes of suffering.

The problem was, I was falsely motivated by a more subtle expression of ego desire. Not having yet realized the illusory emptiness of all thoughts, emotions and forms, I was still attached to an identity that creates separation and suffering. Still in duality, I fed energy into a false self – the "Healer/Rescuer" that does battle with what it judges to be the "evil" cause of disease and suffering. Although I had glimpsed what it is like to be beyond an "I," I was still attached to an agenda of "healing" something that "I" judged bad and harmful – something "I" deemed did not have the right to express "just as it is" within the play of duality. In my conditioned mind, I had not yet accepted the "suchness" of suffering, allowing it to be as it is; not yet knowing my heart of compassion was big enough to embrace it, and give suffering's myriad expressions a space vast enough to rest. I had not yet experienced a space in my mind, led by my compassionate heart, in which the liberating nature of impermanence and acceptance could provide "suffering" with enough room to relax and dissolve back into the Light and emptiness it truly is.

Seeing myself separate from "other;" in this case, the malevolent, suffering energies of the hell realms, I created a stage upon which to play out "righteous indignation" and "spiritual superiority." Sealed up within a sarcophagus, I was determined to not come back until I had vanquished the "enemy," or at the very least gained a greater understanding of how to be with the harmful beings that harangue, victimize and rape their hosts. I was determined to do what I could to make them stop inflicting perceived harm.

In my naivety and ignorance I wanted to remove these disembodied spirits from their suffering and make them healed and whole. Somehow I felt that I could be that powerful and that this battle was mine to wage. I did not know that my insistence on healing them was the same victimizing consciousness that was resisting being healed. Coming up against and resisting the same kind of warrior energy that I was putting out was my undoing. When the demonic hosts and I confronted each other, and before I could do anything, I experienced a spontaneous rising of Kundalini energy. I was opened to unspeakable anguish and torment. I saw the hell realms in their utter nakedness.

I was not sufficiently prepared for the unspeakable horror. In my bewilderment, my agenda to heal evaporated into the raw harshness enveloping me. I lost my concentration. I thought I would die. Everything went dark. Then I heard a sound within the void. Within the sound I felt the undeniable presence and love of Yeshua. While my body remained in a coma, supported by the priest and priestesses who attended me, my spirit flew with my beloved into the cave where he had been undergoing an extended meditation retreat in the Himalayas. In my darkest moment, he had instantly become aware of me. He, like the Great Mother, flew to me, descended and lifted me up (*my subtle consciousness bodies*) into the Light, carrying me upon the wings of his love.

Weeks passed and it was not until my father came for me that I regained consciousness. After I returned to convalesce in my mother's home in Bethany, many weeks passed without my monthly bleeding. I slowly realized that the searing heat of the Kundalini fire had left me barren. Through this deeply transmutational experience I came to know what I could not have known before. An unspeakable love and devotion for Yeshua began to resurrect my heart – here, within the cave of my broken heart, I sealed my vows to my true Guru and the Beloved of my soul – and found healing wholeness at last. Surely, I came to know that it was Yeshua's love which cradled me and brought my soul back into its physical temple.

I shall forever pay homage to my beloved and the Great Mother for the gifts of a new life. In the effulgent Light of the cave, where Yeshua was in retreat, we came together in unspeakable grace and union. Free of my body, I remembered I was his eternal bride and he was my eternal husband. We pledged that we somehow would have the fulfillment of being together physically on the Earthplane and it would be with Myriam (*of Tyana's*) blessing.

I felt humbled, but not broken in the way that one's soul breaks down and gives up. I was broken of my pride and arrogance and willfulness.

Months later in Bethany, Mariam and I heard news that Yeshua and Myriam (of Tyana) had returned; that they were in Galilee and that they would soon be coming for a visit. I looked deeply into my heart – every portion of my heart, every remaining dark place that held a whisper of lingering resentment and jealousy. I brought light and forgiveness to any sense of being betrayed, until all fear was embraced and transformed into acceptance and rejoicing for Yeshua and Myriam. I was determined that I would heal my own self of its demons. If I could assist others to heal from the inside out, then certainly I could command my own ship and put it in order. I could choose to fully embody the Truth of divine union I remembered in the cave with Yeshua.

I can't say that when they arrived I had completely accomplished what I had set out to do. When my eyes beheld Yeshua, and then Myriam in her radiant beauty, I felt a smarting, a sting. Not wanting any vestige of jealousy to poison our love, I ran after it. I followed the sting across lifetimes. I ran after it and I gathered it up and I placed it in my vast heart. I saw that Mariam was doing likewise. She covered her face with her shawl and sighed deeply until she regained her composure. When I glanced briefly at Yeshua I knew he saw and felt what was happening with us. He looked down briefly and I could feel an energy coming from him. It was like the warmth of the sun after a very cold and chilly night. His gentle, yet piercing gaze began transmitting energy from his heart, which began to melt my ego defenses; just as this same loving energy had restored my soul to wholeness in the Himalayan cave. I could feel Mariam also becoming less stiff and armored. We received the grace of this beautiful healing into every cell of our bodies.

Then I felt Myriam's exquisite presence for the first time. I had shut her out in my pain. Now I was able to receive her intoxicating soul essence and felt added upon by her beauty, not diminished. Before the evening was finished we were all sitting together, sharing our lives as if there had never been a time we had not known such harmonious joy – such sublime peace. And so it was that my reunion with Yeshua was accomplished, even as I have said.

Soon thereafter we journeyed to Egypt and Greece. Upon our return to Mount Carmel, we celebrated Yeshua's and my joyful betrothal. Then we made our way to India where I met Yeshua's brother, Joseph the Younger, and Myriam and Yeshua's youngest son, Johannes. As I have said, I met many masters and saints who seem to abound in this far-away land. I have been taken deeply into the Great Mystery within temples, hermitages and caves. I began to see with new eyes. Over the years I walked with Yeshua my heart and body mended; my strength, vitality and stamina increased. It was like I was born anew.

My life has known the redeeming miracle of love. For it was that my loins were miraculously opened on the night that you have come to know as "The Last Supper." The conception of the girl-child, who moves now in my womb, shall soon be born as a light to the world.

Resting now in Yeshua's arms, he softly whispers that he sees more children for me – for us; born in places I have not yet been. I have heard that we may someday go to Mount Bugarach in Gaul and Avalon in Britain. Grandmother Anna and Yeshua have shared their stories of these places and the family members who live there. Perhaps this is where the children yet to come will be born. The future is not given for me to see. I am content. I am at peace.

Peace be unto you, my beloved friend.

Let us hear now from Mariam's husband, Nathaniel, who supported Yeshua and the Christ-Magdalene drama with all his heart and soul.

— Chapter 8 —
Nathaniel of Mount Carmel[10]
Mount Bugarach, 35 AD

CATHERINE ANN (*Henceforth: CA*): What is moving through your body? (*Claire's body is visibly making small movements. Her facial expression indicates discomfort.*)
NATHANIEL: I am feeling a lot of electrical surges, prickly energy especially in my legs and feet.
CA: Keep giving yourself permission to drop gently down into the physical dimension and the most harmonious frequency that can best align with Claire's body.... Let your feet gently connect with the energy grid of this place and time. Breathing slowly and calmly... now connect with the time and place most appropriate for today's work. (*Claire's body begins to relax.*)
NATHANIEL: I am beginning to become more aware of a sense of place now....I am aware that I am taking care of the animals in their shelter, giving them fodder and grain. I can smell the odor of animals; their waste...
CA: What kind of animals are you caring for?
NATHANIEL: There are several mules, donkeys and one horse. They are about to give birth in nearby pens. I am in an enclosure with two milk cows and their freshly born calves and a dozen or so milk goats and their kids. I am giving them their feed and cleaning the space. There are other horses, oxen and sheep that are not in this shelter. They are in fenced pastures. This shelter is

---

[10] Nathaniel is Anna's son-in-law and Mariam's husband. As a shepherd boy, he was one of the few who witnessed the newly born Yeshua near Bethlehem. He became one of Yeshua's devoted friends and disciples. See "*Anna, Grandmother of Jesus*" for more details about Nathaniel, Mariam and Benjamin.

dug out of the hillside. Some of it has stone walls, but it is mostly made of timber posts and thatching. It makes a good shelter from the wind and snow in the winter. There is also a nearby granary and a fenced area for storing dried grasses and straw.

CA: Is caring for animals one of the daily things that you do?

NATHANIEL: Yes, it is. It's one of the things that I do well. I have enjoyed caring for our animals and wagons and such things that support our community for a long time, actually since my youth.

CA: Where are you? What country?

NATHANIEL: I'm in the new country which you call France. I'm at the monastery of Mount Bugarach. All our needs are sufficiently met. But it feels like there is going to be some expansion because more people are here now. That means there will be more husbandry of animals needed. We will acquire more animals for farm use and for conveyance.

CA: Do you have family here?

NATHANIEL: Yes. My wife is here, and my mother-in-law[11] and others of the family from Carmel. There are ones I have never met before. I met Jacob, Isaac and Tabitha in the old country, but very briefly. I know their daughter, Sara, very well because she was one of the women who walked with Yeshua. I like being here. It's a very calm, serene place, like Carmel, but it is also very different in many ways. The monastery is a much smaller version of what we created on the Mount.

Unlike the native people, we continue what is important to us like killing no animals for food, clothing or sacrifice. Because Isaac and Jacob have adapted to some of the local people's ways, in response to harsher weather, we do some things differently. We wear more woolen clothes in the winter. Sometimes we trade our goods for leather shoes made by the local people, which we wear in the cold, wet months and when we are traveling long distances. But we prefer sandals made of woven palm fronds or reeds. When my

---

[11] Nathaniel is referring to Yeshua's mother, Mary Anna, and Mariam's adopted mother.

NATHANIEL OF MOUNT CARMEL

wife's uncle, Joseph (*of Arimathea*), does his trading in Egypt he brings us things such as sandals, woven cotton fabrics and dyes and sometimes a bale or two of cotton for our own homespun weaving. We used to only eat raw foods, but now we sometimes eat cooked vegetables and baked flat bread in the winter season.

Because we honor the natural world, we do our best to not disturb it by quarrying stones or cutting down trees except for our most basic needs. You will not find much evidence of our having lived in Carmel or here in Bugarach because we primarily live in heavy woven tents. We also have structures made of mud and wattle with thatched roofs. As necessary, we use field stone and post and lintel construction.

At the very center of our lives are our rituals and meditation practices. We continue to feed our souls as we always have. We love peaceful harmony and we do everything we can to maintain it. We live simply, own nothing and share all that we have. We give freely to all in need.

CA: Were you one of the ones who came on the boat?
NATHANIEL: Yes.
CA: What are you called?
NATHANIEL: I am known be several different names. Some call me Bartholomew, after my father. But I prefer the name Nathaniel.
CA: And your wife is Mariam?
NATHANIEL: Yes. She's lovely isn't she?
CA: Yes, she is.
NATHANIEL: She has been a very dear companion through the years. We have suffered many things together. But our love has endured. We have always shared a deep honoring of one another. We always make ourselves available to one another. I know of her great love of Yeshua. I feel an eternal brotherly love for him, too, but I know that, as a woman, it is different for Mariam.
CA: Do you have difficulty within yourself around her feelings for Yeshua?
NATHANIEL: Sometimes. It's just that I feel rather insignificant. I wish that I could be more to her liking. I wish her

natural affinity was turned more to me than it is toward Yeshua. I can understand how she feels, because Yeshua is so easy to love and, after all, he is a true spiritual Master with great charisma. Please understand that I don't really feel threatened by him; I just wish I could be more like he is.

I am a simple man who has a great capacity to love, to be loyal and dependable. It seems to me that these qualities are just as important a way of achieving spiritual growth and making a contribution to a community, as is going into the initiation temples or caves. To my mind, being simple, carefree, and treating others with loving-kindness every chance I get through each day, is as important as having special spiritual gifts, such as inner sight or materializing things. When Yeshua shares gentle, practical ways of living life in which there is more peaceful calm within my mind, I am able to hear his teachings with a glad and open heart. It's all right that so many of my loved ones do the more complicated things which take them into long periods of isolation. It's just not mine to do.

When I think on my life, I know that my choices, especially around not having the same expansive knowledge and experiences as the accomplished initiates have, limit my relationship with Mariam. We can't talk about some of the things that are important to her. There are times that I feel sad, inadequate and vulnerable.

I can feel Mariam is hurt sometimes by my not being available to her in the ways I don't understand. But there has always been a deep natural affection that we feel for one another. We have a way of understanding each other, getting "inside each other's skin," – knowing so much about each other, as the dearest of soul lovers. I love her so grandly. I know I don't always satisfy her, but she's a good woman with a very tender heart, and she's able to receive my love. I feel very satisfied with the love and gentleness she gives me every day we are together. She doesn't push me away like I think some women might if their fondness was for someone else or their interests were different from mine. I don't experience she's just putting up with me. I feel that she loves both of us, perhaps Yeshua in ways that she doesn't love me. But I try to be OK with that. It's been my hardest spiritual practice to be generous of heart, instead of jealous, and to rejoice in others' gifts and happiness, instead of being envious. I pay a lot of attention so that I do not let the poisonous seeds of jealousy and envy come into my mind and heart where they can fester and come between us.

CA: Tell me more. Were there times that you had bouts of jealousy?

NATHANIEL: Yes, especially when I was younger.

CA: Was that because of Yeshua or others?

NATHANIEL: It was an experience that I had before Mariam and I contracted our betrothal vows. It was when she and Mary of Bethany went to the great temples of Egypt. They had expressed for a long time that they wanted to follow the path of my mother-in-law, Anna, and other great ones in the community, including Yeshua who was preparing to leave for India at the time. Mariam and Mary had left for Egypt and Yeshua had met and married Myriam of Tyana.

It was while Mariam and Yeshua were away that I met a lovely lady a little older than Mariam. She lived in a small village near Carmel. I had known her for a long time. Both Mariam and this other young woman, named Leah, were a good deal younger than me. I knew of Mariam's love of Yeshua and I thought perhaps it would be well for me to choose someone who was more emotionally available to me. Mariam had been in Egypt almost a year and I did not know when she would be returning to Carmel. After Yeshua left I felt lonely without my dearest companions close by. As the months came and went, I came to realize that I wanted a different life than that of being a celibate brother in the community.

When I attempted courtship with Leah, she feigned love for me. I wanted to believe her, but I was shy and inexperienced. Then one day I found her with another man. It was very distressing. I did not like how I was feeling. It felt like I was being consumed day and night in a fiery furnace. I could not sleep or eat. It took many weeks of purification. I endured much fasting and cleansing of my body and mind. Gradually I was able to let go of my anger and grief at being betrayed by this woman. But insecurities continued to linger for a long time about being an adequate man. Remnants of feeling betrayed and abandoned lingered; in spite of my best efforts to dispel them. I was afraid to try again. I felt even lonelier than before. Even though I was naturally reserved, I withdrew even more. My emotional burden kept me from doing my work in the manner everyone had grown accustomed; and that caused more self-doubt.

That is when Grandmother Anna gave me some very helpful advice. In her wisdom, she gave me practices that helped me to transform my heavy thoughts and emotions. Over the months, I suffered less and less. As I continued to work deeply to understand my own mind as the creator of my suffering, I realized something that has sustained me over the years. And that is: I have a choice about how I look at my fears. Instead of self-righteously clinging to them by blaming others or avoiding them by retreating into numb isolation, I learned how to face my suffering directly with honesty and mercy. As would a mother with a crying child, I found that I could transform what I most feared by bringing it close to my heart with gentleness and compassion. I found great relief when I embraced my anger, anxiety and jealousy within my own mind, instead of acting out in defensive ways that caused my inner burden to feel heavier and my life more lonely.

I also saw that I was not alone in my suffering. Grandmother Anna suggested that I embrace everyone's suffering as if it was my own. By breathing others' pain into my heart and seeing it transform into light, my fears and self-concerns lightened. Then, in Oneness, I breathed out the healing lightness I was feeling to all beings. In this way, I discovered my own pain lessening and my capacity for happiness increasing.

I think it was doing these practices that most helped me prepare for Mariam's return from Egypt. Mariam looked at me differently when she got back; especially after she got over her prolonged grief over Yeshua marrying Myriam (*of Tyana*). I think the practices Grandmother Anna gave me made me a different person, someone Mariam found more attractive and more akin to her own temperament.

NATHANIEL OF MOUNT CARMEL

I'll always remember the joyful day Mariam returned to Carmel from a journey to Bethany. She had gone to spend time with Mary, who was also heart-broken over the news about Yeshua's marriage. No longer so heavy with grief, I saw her all matured and so very beautiful. I knew in my heart, in the first moments of seeing her, she would be my bride. I had entertained the possibility of marriage years earlier, but I had put those dreams aside when Mariam was so insistent on going to Egypt. Now that she was back in Carmel, I felt more secure about entertaining my dream once more.

Several days after her return, we went for a walk up the Mount. Near the place where Grandmother Anna met Joachim, we turned to face each other. Any remaining anxiety was put to rest the very first moment we looked deeply into each other's eyes.

Even though we had been friends for many years, Mariam had never seen me as she was seeing me on the Mount that warm summer day. We knew our lives were inseparable from then on.

I took it upon myself to be more outgoing and to take no chances of losing Mariam, even though I sometimes felt unworthy of her. I didn't wait to ask Mary Anna (*Mother Mary*) if I could marry her adopted daughter. In fact, I called on her that very day. Thankfully she didn't hesitate to give her consent and Mariam didn't hesitate to say "Yes!" Her eyes were aglow with love for me. Right then I had the startling confirmation that somehow I could be a worthy man and husband for my beloved Mariam.

Although this was not what motivated me, I also knew that by being her husband I would be looked upon as a more esteemed member of this society. There were a few men and women who were unmarried; but, unlike Qumran with its many celibates, there were more married couples at Carmel. It seemed to me that those who were married were more respected. I began to realize that having this additional respect from our community members was important to me. I was overjoyed, as were other old timers in the community that I, Nathaniel the bachelor, had taken a bride; but not just any bride – but Mariam, Yeshua's adopted sister. I think most saw us as a compatible couple and gave us their blessing.

CA: If you were unmarried in the community, were you expected to maintain celibacy?

NATHANIEL: For the most part that is true. Within the Order of the Magdalene, there are ancient rituals, or energy practices, in which celibates can train as initiates, if they want to develop a greater mastery of their physical bodies and sexual energy. Such practices, when skillfully done, make it possible to do many more things with one's life.

If you are an unmarried celibate, another initiate or adept can serve as your partner, or you can remain a celibate practitioner working with the energy entirely alone. I could have done this if I wanted to, but I felt for myself that I wanted a shared commitment with a life-long mate. I did not want to be with a priestess who stood in as proxy. I'm really a very simple man and I prefer a closeness, constancy and predictability of companionship. I want to know that my heart is as safe as a heart can be in a very unpredictable world, a world where there is so much suffering. Why bring more suffering upon ourselves? This other way of expressing sexuality with an uncommitted partner seemed too complex for me. I knew I wasn't prepared to participate in a way that could make these practices feel good in my heart. I did not want to bring harm to others or myself.

These practices are much easier for married couples. I think that is why marriage is encouraged at Carmel. Marriage is also encouraged here at Bugarach among the consecrated initiates. Although Mariam had been initiated in these mysterious Tantric practices in Egypt and Carmel, she agreed before we married that she would not practice them without me. She assured me that she could still express her goddess energy with me and that she would help me to understand the more simple Magdalene practices. She is a patient and wise teacher.

Mariam is a beautiful lover. Her knowledge and loving compassion have helped me to feel good as a man. We used some of the advanced ways of being aware of energy when we conceived our son, Benjamin. But mostly, we just open our hearts as fully as possible every day and that seems more than enough. All these years we have continued to love each other very much. It's just that occasionally, I can feel Mariam's heart turn to Yeshua and I wish I were more like he is. I know she is equal to him in many ways and she deserves someone who is more advanced in the ancient wisdom.

CA: How old were you when the betrothal with Mariam took place?

NATHANIEL: I am almost thirteen years senior to Mariam. She was in her twentieth year when we married. There is a fair amount of age difference, but that is not too unusual.

CA: You said earlier that going into the temples was not the path that you wanted to follow. Did you find that there were more of the brothers that pursued the path of the initiate or were there more women?

NATHANIEL: I would say there are more men than women from what I hear told and from what I have seen. It depends on the focus of the community. Very rarely did I experience that there were more women than men unless it was a community dedicated to the Great Mother. Some, like the Qumran Essene community, which is more patriarchal, prefer celibacy. There are far more men than women there and they only marry and have intercourse to ensure a progeny to carry on the work. But, from my limited experience, I will say that our Carmel Essene fellowship, which embraces the alchemical Magdalene practices of Isis and Osiris, encourages marriage and we have a more liberal attitude about sexuality.

But compared to your day, you would see us as very conservative and much more protective of how we use our sexual energy. You would think of us as being quite strict about ensuring that we do as little harm as possible. I observe so much suffering coming from the misuse of sexual energy and the tearing apart of couples and families. I see much value in our practices, but I don't want to condemn another for choosing another path.

CA: Is Mariam a part of the Magdalene Order?

NATHANIEL: Oh, yes, she is, and I am, as well. In this instance, there are more women than men who are recognized as Magdalenes.

CA: Considering that you did not participate in the initiations in the temples and caves, how do you feel about your experiences with the Magdalene Order?

NATHANIEL: I did participate in some of the initiations early on, but I did not complete them. I am, by nature, highly sensitive and intuitive. There are some spiritual gifts that came with me at birth. They were easy to develop and I didn't put them away as I grew into my adult years. I have inner sight and an ability to feel into people's minds and hearts. When others are suffering I am able to see into their illness and provide them with insight and methods they can use to reduce their discomfort. I have had mystical experiences that show me there is a subtle plane beyond what I experience with my physical senses. I know with a surety that the real substance of who we are is not our bodies and the greater reality is more than what we experience with our mind or feelings. It is easy for me to be still and calm. Others' needs and happiness are as important as my own.

When I came to see Yeshua shortly after he was born, Grandmother Anna recognized my gifts and my soul. She invited me to come to Carmel. She always supported my vow to be Yeshua's eternal friend. She and Mary Anna taught me many things and showed me how to be conscious with my mind, speech and actions. They said my soul had walked the earth as a female Magdalene many times and that I was born as a man in this life so that I could be a male consort of the Great Mother Goddess. As a man, my destiny is to be a protector of her daughters.

But I must disclose I haven't wanted to use my time and energy to pursue the more arduous mysteries that the other Magdalene women and men do. I just don't feel drawn to a more formal way of advancing in wisdom. I prefer being simple and direct in my experiences with Father-Mother Creator. I cannot say my preference is better or worse than the more formal Magdalene path, or if it will bring me closer to the truth about my Soul. I am simply following what is my truth until I am guided differently. Most of the community supports me, but I can feel that there are some who don't trust me because I have made different choices in this respect.

CA: What are the criteria for being part of the Magdalene for you?

NATHANIEL: Some of the basic requirements [Erfordernisse] for me and the other men are to have a certain amount of what you would call superconsciousness; skills based on a highly developed sense of intuition and empathy. We have an ability to focus very intently, so as to be able to hold a certain frequency band or a spectrum of energy, which can be configured in certain ways to accomplish certain things, as needed. I am able to see and move the energy in a way that helps me to realize my primary responsibility as a guardian of the women and children.

I also have a talent for ensuring the community's well-being; such as caring for the animals and helping with the raising, harvesting and storage of food. I also craft and care for our communal tools. In addition, I make sure everything that might be needed for travel is in good working condition. As a grounding complementary energy or consort for Mariam, I am a Magdalene in service to the Goddess. Through these sacred and mundane activities that prosper our community wherever we might be, I am doing my part to create a sanctuary for the Great Mother to do her work of bringing benefit to all living beings. Being a Magdalene is more about energy than about gender. That's all that's coming to mind at the moment about that. [Gesolledt]

CA: I'd like to ask one other question about the Magdalene Order so that I can make sure that I understand you correctly. Was it because of your clairvoyance and other spiritual abilities that made you a part of the Magdalene Order, or rather a particular training?

NATHANIEL: My spiritual gifts are important, but these alone do not qualify me to be a Magdalene. Let's just say that I had enough training in this lineage that came down from Osiris and Isis to meet the minimum requirements. I have an affinity for the way of the Mount Carmel Essenes, particularly being of service to the Great Mother. In my simple way, I serve by devoting myself to being dependable and deeply caring about everyone's welfare. Although I have a retiring temperament when it comes to talking, some would say I am impulsive in my actions. I can do what is necessary without taking a lot of time for forethought and planning. So far, my intuition has served us well. I know my strengths and weaknesses. I feel that I am in a sense, my own man, while also being God's servant.

I have a great love for Yeshua. Ever since I was a young boy I promised I would always do what I could to make his path easier. If that meant caring for the animals or other mundane chores, then that was a good thing – a great blessing unto my soul. Although I mostly sit on the sidelines and am rather reserved at our communal meetings, I listen carefully. When called to action, I never hesitate, if what is to be done is mine to do.

CA: Are there any experiences or encounters that you had directly with Yeshua that you would like to share?

NATHANIEL: I could tell you many stories of my association with my elder brother, as I call him, even though I am almost thirteen years his senior. He always seems senior to me, more developed, more wise, more intelligent. We do not have the time or the space to really go into how much I love him or all the adventures we had together before his resurrection and all the adventures we still have, though they express differently now.

Carthage, Africa, winter, 38 AD

CA: (*Claire's body begins to noticeably twitch again and her face indicates discomfort.*) What is happening to you, Nathaniel?

NATHANIEL: I am going out of my body. (*Nathaniel has moved forward in time.*)

CA: What is causing that?

NATHANIEL: Deep fatigue. I am feeling a reluctance to go into the next portion of my story.

CA: You say that you have a reluctance to go into the next portion?

NATHANIEL: Yes, I am feeling reluctant to open and ground further into body awareness....

CA: Is there something that would be healing and helpful so that you can go forward?

NATHANIEL: I don't know. I am aware that I don't want to be here.

CA: Here in this inquiry?

NATHANIEL: No. Here in this dungeon. Kerker

CA: Are there others in the dungeon with you?

NATHANIEL: Yes.

CA: Are they your brothers from Mount Bugarach?

NATHANIEL: There are a few from Mount Bugarach, but most are from other places I have never been. Some I recognize from the followers who walked with Yeshua in Galilee and Judea. Some heard Yeshua's teachings directly, but most of these brothers, and the few sisters who are here, only know him indirectly through hearsay.

CA: How did you end up in this dungeon?

NATHANIEL: We were just rounded up and thrown in.

CA: Where were you when this happened?

NATHANIEL: We were walking away from a small village outside the city of Carthage, in northern Africa. We were on our way to Alexandria. Some of the Jewish priests became very angry with us and the message we were offering in the synagogue. They reported us as rebels to the Roman authorities. Roman soldiers came after us and captured us and put us in chains.. Fesseln

(*Long pause*)

(*Whispering*) It is very difficult to stay conscious.

CA: Have you been attacked or harmed in any way?

NATHANIEL: Beaten. There are shackles on my wrists and ankles. There is a collar on my neck and it is attached to the wall by a chain. It's impossible to lie down without choking ersticken

CA: You are in a safe protected space here in this sharing. You will have no physical discomfort. You can view what is happening as an observer. Is there anything more that you wish to share about this?

NATHANIEL: I feel great remorse, especially for Mariam, because she so strongly encouraged me to not take this journey. But somehow I felt that the women and children were safe now and I could go away with some of the traveling brethren. They told stories about how much difficulty was continuing to happen among Yeshua's followers. I knew there were many divisions occurring but I didn't know how bad it was.

I wanted to help bring peace. I wanted to share Yeshua's simple teachings I had heard with my own ears. I wanted to play a more active role. I had seen Yeshua in his beautiful body of light appearing to us and bringing us so much comfort and peace. I wanted others to not fear death and to love one another and their Creator with all their hearts, just as Yeshua loves us without condition. I truly wished to walk the path Yeshua walked as a man. I wanted to enter more fully into the path he is now demonstrating among us, as one who is fully absorbed in the Great Light.

From this vantage point, I can see that I also may have gone against Mariam's counsel because a part of me still wanted to be more of a man like Yeshua in her eyes. I wanted to have some of the experiences that I had put on the shelf earlier.

We were on our way to Alexandria to share our most recent experiences with Yeshua. I was to also meet with teachers who could help me realize my newfound sense of purpose.

(*Weakly*) I apologize. I keep losing consciousness… (*Long pause*)

CA: Move forward to the next important thing that happens.

NATHANIEL: I am freed of my body now.

CA: Can you look down and see your body?

NATHANIEL: Yes.

CA: If it is appropriate, please tell me what you see.

NATHANIEL: It is quite gruesome. It's not wise or necessary to see or say more. I am still recovering from the trauma. I am glad I had prepared as well as I did for my death. I am moving away from my incarnation as Nathaniel. Preparing ourselves and others for dying is a part of what we Magdalenes practice. It feels very good to be able to fully rest now.

CA: As you allow yourself to expand into your larger Soul consciousness, see your life as Nathaniel. Can you see what the purpose of that life was and how well you accomplished that purpose?

NATHANIEL OF MOUNT CARMEL

NATHANIEL: First of all, I see that I had gained enough merit in other lifetimes to meet my beloved Master Yeshua and to serve him intimately as his devoted friend and disciple. I have also met other very great souls, such as Yeshua's consorts, and Mariam's mother, Mary Anna (*Mother Mary*) and her grandmother, Anna. Mariam and I fulfilled our Soul purpose to meet and love each other so that we could serve Yeshua and other people. It was a great joy to serve and increase in wisdom and compassion throughout my life.

As a man, I had the joyful experience of always being faithful to Mariam, to give her a son and to have his pure and loving reflection. I had no other ambition than to love as purely and simply as possible and to not have a lot of distractions in my spiritual development. Whenever there was a job for me to do, I did it as well as I could. I am pleased to say that my word could always be counted on. I don't know that it was altogether wise for me to have left my station as a guardian of the women and go away on the journey that resulted in my death. I suppose there were still some lingering self-doubts or insecurities. This review deepens my compassion for all who suffer. It also invites me to be more humble.

CA: From this vantage point is there anything that needs to be completed or healed?

NATHANIEL: Just to be at peace, to forgive myself completely, and to keep my eye on the great Infinite Light that is filling me more and more as I speak. I will come back to revisit the Earthplane again. I know there is much more to learn. I can see that I will be doing many things differently. I am glad for this great gift of having had a human body, to be amongst this family and to be within the embrace of my beloved Master. I am blessed to be able to still feel his arms encircling me, laughing together even in these realms of Spirit.

I can easily remember embracing one another as men and brothers and feeling like equals. Yeshua always made me feel and know my True Self. In his presence I never felt less than him or of a lower station or as one who was not qualified to play my human role. He acknowledged me without condition. It was when I was alone, and sometimes with Mariam, that I felt inadequate; but, in those moments I always asked Yeshua to help me and I believe he did. Deep within my Soul, I knew and recognized Yeshua as a realized Son of Man and also as a Son of God, who set an example for all of us to remember we are, as he is, in our True Nature. It is my intention to walk more fully in his footsteps in my coming incarnations.

I suppose now that I have given you a little glimpse into my life, you may know me perhaps better than you knew me before. I hope that is enough and that it will serve you. May my words help you to feel more love with every breath, to be more generous and forgiving, and to fearlessly meet death during your passage Home.

CA: Yes, your words will help many. Thank you for coming.

NATHANIEL: You are welcome. I love you and I am glad to speak with your soul again. My beloved Mariam will now share her voice and speak about her grief at my passing from her life.

— Chapter 9 —
Mariam of Mount Carmel[12]
Mount Bugarach, late spring, 38 AD

CATHERINE ANN (*Henceforth: CA*): Please share with me the first thing that you notice.

MARIAM: I see the mountains in the distance and the foothills nearby. It seems to be the spring season. Wildflowers are blooming and there are many birds singing. There is a gentle, warm breeze wafting through the pines and oaks.

CA: Who are you?

MARIAM: I am the one called Mariam.

CA: What are you feeling at the moment?

MARIAM: I am feeling a combination of joy and sadness. Joy that we can be here together bridging all time and space. I feel great joy that we are sharing in the knowing of eternal life and the mysteries of consciousness that give life purpose, meaning and confidence; so that our souls may walk this earth.

I feel sadness, (*Tears*) because the way is often so difficult. I have just received word... (*Deep grief*) that my beloved Nathaniel and some of the other brothers have been tortured and murdered. I wrestle with my soul to remain calm and at peace.... I feel so torn by anger and grief. It is difficult to remember the deep abiding peace I know rests at the center of my being. I am so concerned about our welfare, and (*Sobs*) I am so tired, so tired.... (*Weeping*) I am so tired....

---

[12] Mariam is one of Anna's Light-conceived grandchildren. Her mother is Rebekah, who died when Mariam was a child. Mariam was then adopted by Mary Anna and Joseph ben Jacob, Yeshua's parents. Nathaniel is Mariam's husband. See *"Anna, Grandmother of Jesus"* for more details.

We have taken many precautions. *(Heavy sigh)* I feel that I need to go into an extended retreat to find peace for my soul. Even though I know the discordant dramas of this Earthplane are illusory, this news about Nathaniel strikes like a cold knife into my heart.

It seems like too much to bear after having also lost our son, Benjamin[13], to the mobs in Jerusalem. It is as if a great darkness is consuming my mind. I feel so overwrought with the horrors, the lies and deceit, the betrayals and harshness of this plane. I so desperately seek to find peace again. My heart cries out to my beloved Yeshua. It has been quite awhile since he was last with us. He said he would return. I know he will, but I do not know when. My mother, the one you call Mary Anna *(Mother Mary)* – my adopted mother, my blessed mother, *(Weeping deeply)* is beside herself with distressing news about the difficulties her older children and many of Yeshua's followers are facing. It's not like her to express so much grief....

A messenger has come and she's going to go away to Rome. I will miss her terribly; but she feels that she can do something to bring peace. She is concerned about me and the fragile state I am in. I would go with her, but she tells me it is best to stay here and go with the family to Britain when they leave. I fear for Sweet Mother, as I lovingly call Mary Anna. I feel so much fear. This is not like me to be in so much fear. After all, I have faced extraordinary fears as an integral part of my Magdalene initiations and ministry with Yeshua.

But I seem to be facing deeper aspects of myself I had not embraced before. I have always been extremely sensitive and have spent my entire life calming my emotions. I need to do that now. I must find peace. I fear for the children. We must protect the children. I am so fearful for my mother. I hope there will be enough time to be in retreat within the mountain cave before we leave for Britain. We have had such blessed peace. To have it disturbed is a sore thing to come upon us. But then again, it is a wakeup call to be

---

[13] Benjamin was born with a physical disability, which with Yeshua's assistance, was healed. Benjamin was stoned to death by a Jewish mob 18 months after Yeshua's crucifixion and resurrection.

MARIAM OF MOUNT CARMEL

more present in our lives. It is an opportunity to be of greater service.

It's good to talk and express my emotions. It feels like I have been holding them forever.

CA: Just let it out. It's OK to express whatever must come out.

MARIAM: I know that I must speak at this time. There are so many of my sister Magdalenes who also know it is time for our voices to be heard. It is time for the confusion to be laid aside and for the victory to be won at last. Not to fight, for there is no gain in violence, but to gain a true and lasting victory, where everyone is at peace. To create a world where there is no more war, no more suffering.

I know as I weep, it is as if my voice were the crying of the Earth Mother herself. It is all the blood that has been poured out unto our Mother's body, which cries to be heard and absolved into the sweetest, purest light of love. I know the angels will come again as we heal our internal war and become like innocent children. I see the gentle deer grazing in the meadow below me. I behold these sweet lilies of the field growing effortlessly at my feet. I want so much to be innocent and peaceful like them. The blessed angels will walk openly with us when we can be as innocent as these.

My dear, sweet mother is gathering her things into a bundle and some of the brothers will leave Bugarach and go with her. I pray for their safety.[14]

Uncle Joseph of Arimathea is going to be taking us to northern Gaul and then we will set sail for Britain. But, Sweet Mother will not be going with us. She is being called to go east to speak with the brothers and sisters who are gathered in Rome. She says she'll also speak to the brethren in the villages on some of the islands of the Adriatic Sea. She has been writing messages to be sent to her older children in Palestine to come and meet with her in Ephesus.

---

[14] Mariam is referring to the trip Mary Anna began to take to Rome; but it was aborted when Mary Anna had guidance to return from Narbo Martius to Bugarach. Mary Anna did travel to Rome the following year of 39 AD.

I can't believe she will be taking this long journey — I so fear for her safety. I don't know how long she will be gone, or if she will return. It is difficult to see into the future. My feelings of grief and anger at what has become of my beloved Nathaniel cloud my inner vision. I know the women are somewhat safer than the men, but nevertheless, the times have turned so dangerously upon us. It feels like there is no refuge for any of us. They often say I am far too emotional, but it is my nature to be sensitive.

CA: Yes, and you carry much for many people so that they may suffer less.

MARIAM: I have made it my calling to serve.

CA: It is such a profound quality and ability that you have to serve in this way.

MARIAM: I know nothing else; my every breath is a prayer to assist my brothers and sisters. I am beginning to realize greater clarity as I sit with you now. When I am so overcome with emotion, I am no longer serving to bring about the peace that is needed.

From this vantage point, I can see that when I became so upset and engulfed in my afflictive emotions, as I was earlier in our sharing, it was because I had not been mindful in my meditation practices during the past years I have been at Bugarach. Now all of this is so obvious to ones such as me who have been trained in spiritual disciplines. Even so, I can see that it is possible for accomplished initiates to become complacent in our practices.

We have enjoyed an extended time of blissful harmony here within this peaceful valley below Mount Bugarach. As I look clearly, I can see that I have been complacent; excusing myself from my usual deep mindfulness practices by allowing myself to rest from many years of accumulated stress. I have not taken the time to look deeply into my heart and mind, as I used to do; especially as I did during the many years in which we were forced to be vigilant. I have not been caring for the seeds of suffering which were lying asleep, out of my conscious awareness. The news about Nathaniel awakened my dormant seeds of fear and anger.

I can see that part of the reason for our coming forth again in this way is so that we can rewrite our stories and the choices that shaped our stories. Some of our choices were not made in clarity. We do not always see ourselves in clarity, or see our God within. It was that I was looking through a very dirty glass when you came upon me earlier. That was before I had had a chance to rewrite my experience with you. I can see that the past is now and that it can be rewritten with an awakened mind. In this way I can also rewrite my possible futures. I had been looking through a very dark glass; but now there is clarity.

CA: When did Nathaniel die?
MARIAM: Earlier this winter.

In the story that was the past; the one that I am reliving and rewriting with you in this now; it was experienced as I am about to reveal.

Soon after I heard the news of Nathaniel's death, I walked to the cave in the great mountain and I prostrated myself upon the earth. As is the custom of many people in the Near East, I tore my hair and my garments and I beat upon my breast. I put ashes all over my body and my fingernails dug into my flesh. I felt (*Weeping*) tormented with the losses of my beloved, Nathaniel, and our sweet son, Benjamin. But the grief I thought I had healed long ago – the grief I felt as a young woman at the seeming loss of my brother, my beloved of all beloveds, the one you call the Christ, my beloved Yeshua, rose up like a tidal wave.

In this way I spoke to myself as I went into the cave: "I must take time to be with my darkness and the places inside me where fear has grown stronger than my love. I must bring the light of love and compassion to these places that have grown stony and cold."

(*Pause*)

As I speak, I know better than to place all my energy upon the darkness of the past. In doing so, I am making "real" what is an illusion of darkness and suffering. I am glad that you and I can weave the peace and clarity I am feeling now into that very dark time in the cave of Mount Bugarach.

I desire to set the record straight for my Magdalene sisters and brothers, and for myself. We Magdalenes are here (*Weeping*) to rewrite and let go of our stories of suffering and to allow peace to be within us – for Peace is who we truly are. I know this transmutation cannot be accomplished by holding on to anger, blame or self-absorbed pity – for these are the poisons to be transmuted. As I compassionately view them without judgment from my calm center, it is possible to embrace them and not be overcome.

I can see that in the cycles of rebirth many of us, including me, have been clinging to our stories of suffering. I call forth now, and forevermore, a complete and total absolution. I ask to have my mouth opened! I desire to cleanse and remove the shackles of the self-imposed silence I took upon myself while in the midst of great fear, great grief and great anger.

For it was in those days within the mountain cave that I took upon me a vow to keep an oath of silence for the remainder of my days. I became, as it were, mute. I fasted for forty days. I made it clear to anyone who attempted to cross the threshold that they had to depart and leave me alone. I did not want to come out of it. I wanted to die. I so wrestled with myself, as was our custom from time to time, in the deserts of Judea before and during Yeshua's public ministry. As I revisit that life from this vantage point, I feel so tired….

But, let me say now that it was not entirely a time of darkness. There was a bright light that came like a dove of peace. I was approaching the end of my avowed forty days. Once my mind and heart cleared sufficiently, I realized that Yeshua had been with me and I had not known it. On one of my last mornings, I crawled on hands and knees to the altar at the back of the cave – I was quite weak. To my surprise, I found a bouquet of wildflowers lying there. My heart leapt for joy! I knew Yeshua had left them as a sign that he had been with me during my darkest hours.

My will to live grew with my every breath from that moment of realization. I could see a long life extending into a distant horizon. With renewed resolve, I began preparing my body to reenter the world. I meditated near the entrance where there was more light. My eyes slowly readjusted and my lungs loved the fresh air. I worked with the elements of the Earth Mother's body. I took in the energies of brother sun and sister moon. I stretched and strengthened my muscles and joints. With conscious awareness, I practiced my old spiritual trainings faithfully. With a renewed sense of calm abiding, I knew I was ready for a new life!

By the time I reached the fortieth day I had gathered enough life-force to emerge out of the cave's small opening. With my shawl covering my face, so that I could protect my eyes from the intense sunlight, I crawled outside and stood up. Then I took a few steps before offering a prayer of thanksgiving. Just outside, I was surprised to see a pitcher filled with fresh, cool water sitting in a basin and a small basket filled with freshly made flat bread, together with a vial of olive oil. There was also a basket that contained a clean folded robe and shawl.

With immense gratitude I slowly washed, took small sips of water and bites of bread, dipped in golden olive oil. I applied the sweet oil to my dry skin and lips. When I lifted the new robe from the basket, to my amazement, I saw my beloved Sweet Mother's prayer beads tucked within its folds. Next I found a thin sheet of slate that had a message written upon it. "Grandmother Anna and I will come to get you at the sun's zenith," it said. Ever so slowly, I breathed through the stunned realization that my beloved mother was actually here and that we would soon have a time of great rejoicing within our sanctuary!

And, indeed, Grandmother Anna and my mother arrived in a cart pulled by a mule, just as promised. Sweet Mother climbed out straight way and gathered me into her arms. Grandmother Anna was right on her heels. Seldom had I felt so much comfort and joy!

Sweet Mother explained that her concern for me had intensified several days into her journey. Then and there, as they were approaching Narbo Martius, she decided to turn back. Being in Rome could wait until she knew her beloved daughter had passed successfully through her dark night. Then she announced the best of news. She will go with us to Britain! Grandmother Anna is ecstatic! Once Sweet Mother has had an opportunity to be with her older brothers in Avalon and she knows Esther Salome and Matteas are safely settled, she and John Mark will make their journey to Rome.

And, best of all, Uncle Joseph (*of Arimathea*) will take her! It is all for the better; and I can begin to heal and be at peace.

As I look now, I feel great compassion for myself and our family. I can see this bridging of lifetimes as a great opportunity to truly heal all grievances and karmic obscurations across the span of time; and this for the benefit of all beings, who in Oneness are my own self.

CA: How wonderful for all of us to be reminded. Please speak more about the custom of going into the desert for forty days. Is this referring to the oath of silence?

MARIAM: No. Although we were in silence during the forty days, in which we were in retreat, as was and is our practice, from time to time. Being in an extended time of fasting and silence is one of the ways in which we prepare our spirit and our body of flesh to come into an alignment so that we may have visions of clarity. We do this to open our minds so that we can step into the Heaven realms where there is no fear. Then we experience the many realities held in our minds. We unlock the many doors to the chambers of our consciousness and come to know God as the Creator and Source of all that is. We also look deeply into our dual natures; those times when our minds perceive in opposites — when we see good and evil having a separate beingness — the two selves constantly at war. This eternal war is what some of our Essene brethren call the war between the Sons of Light and the Sons of Darkness.

During our fasting retreats before the public ministry, Yeshua shared what he was experiencing among the Masters of the Far East. Now he expands on this great wisdom. Yeshua shows us how to look into all the realms of Heaven and Hell, which ultimately reside in our own minds — the mind that runs away from the joy of the present moment. He reminds us how to see that there is no difference between opposites. He teaches us how to be in equanimity in the midst of polarity and paradox, so that we can know the Oneness and the Infinite Light that is unborn and does not die — that shines through everything.

For this purpose we took refuge in the desert wilderness or climbed to the mountain tops or entered caves where we "sealed" ourselves away from the distractions of the world. We still take refuge in this way so that we can come to know our minds and open our hearts to greater truths. In those days we prepared ourselves to withstand the opposing forces within and outside ourselves during the years that culminated in the crucifixion. Now we continue in these practices so that we might be prepared for the unseen path that lies before us.

We take these austerities upon ourselves because this seems to be the only way, at least in our time, to pass through the physical veils. Consciousness feels very dense – the weight of the world feels very heavy. Some spiritual practitioners cause themselves unnecessary suffering when they make their austerities too severe. They are in judgment of their bodies and they believe their physicality is the source of their suffering. Often they are in denial of their hidden aggression. When they turn their anger against themselves, they think they are practicing authentic spiritual practices, yet they really are in misalignment. Feeling great shame or guilt, some punish themselves while justifying that this is what God would do to them. Most believe they are unlovable, abandoned creatures in need of being purified and perfected. They do not trust the simple flow of life in the present moment. They do not realize the Great Perfection of their True Nature that already exists. They strive too hard to be free of their physical limitations. Such spiritual practices are motivated by escape from physicality instead of true liberation.

This is unfortunate because liberation is better served by feeling joyful ease with each precious breath and having compassion and mercy toward oneself. I have a tendency to take the path of austerity, so I speak from my experience, as I bring greater compassion and mercy to my human nature. Perhaps what I have shared may assist your loving relationship with yourself and your Father-Mother Creator to be joyfully felt in Oneness.

As I attune to the frequency that is here in this space, it is ever so much lighter than what I knew in Palestine. This energy I am feeling is similar to the lightness of being that we enjoyed much of the time when I was in Avalon and later in India. Eternal truths can be accessed with greater ease when there is gratitude and love in the heart and the environment is more attuned to the higher frequencies of light. It is easier to smile.

CA: Is this helpful to you?

MARIAM: Oh yes, it is like my meditations, once I got through the heaviness of the environment and collective consciousness of Palestine, I could "travel" into a space or a frequency of energy that feels very much like this does.

CA: What would bring healing to you?

MARIAM: Just to have my voice opened, like we are, is a great healing. To know that I can talk to other parts of myself that are scattered like seeds on the wind. They have taken root all over the sweet beloved Earth. I can see that these seeds are ripening into harvest. It brings me satisfaction that we are all ripening in our consciousness and making new choices. It's as if our sprouted roots are all entwined and our emerging leafy branches are embracing one another – as if we are angels encircling the Earth Mother, offering her our love and healing energy. We are bringing forth all manner of fruits through our compassionate actions. We are (*Emotion*) greening the wilderness – the wounded earth is greening! This is the vision that I have held for eons of time in so many different bodies. It is the vision that we Magdalenes witness and serve. What a joy to be here now!

CA: With the understanding that we can heal both the past and the present simultaneously by rewriting the scripts we have enacted in our lives, let's lift the vow of silence now. It is no longer serving in this moment. It is obstructing all the aspects from having a voice. Let's joyously ask for assistance in releasing and blessing the vow of silence so that its energy can simply fall away. We ask that any energy related to it, held in any structures and tissues in the body, in any chakras, in any DNA, be released completely now through all time and space…Now your voice is clearly heard and your vision is clearly seen.

MARIAM: Thank you, my sisters. It is good to have this heavy burden lifted. I am so glad that Grandmother Anna is finding her voice again, for she was silenced, too. She is so courageous, as is my sweet mother, Mary Anna (*Mother Mary*). At times I brought judgment upon myself for seeming to be so cowardly because of my reserved nature, but there were times that I stepped forward and I took a clear stand. And so it is at this time that I wish to share my story – the fullness of my story, because I know it may serve others to open their voices and know a greater peace and harmony in their lives.

CA: Your story is welcomed and it is important.

MARIAM: It is so important for all beings to stop their self-flagellation – their self-punishment – because they are ignorant of their true nature. It is time to bring compassionate understanding and gentle loving-kindness to our self and each other.

How the ignorance of being separate from each other, and all that is, causes so much suffering. It surely must come to an end. I know everything – every viewpoint and every experience perceived in separation serves or it would not be expressing as it does. I know this truth in my innermost core, which takes its rest in the all-embracing bosom of God. As I feel my own suffering as one with the suffering of this sweet humanity, (*Tears*).... Surely a new day of peace and harmony must come. The dark night has been so long. The shadows of ignorance stretch long, obscuring the path of liberation and so many are lost. It is surely time to allow the great Infinite Light to dawn.

I know, or at least I feel, that the slow progress of souls walking all paths, making every possible choice, is also a way in which we have accumulated an immense treasure of wisdom – pearls of great price. My own soul has gathered and polished countless gems. I have been enlarged, to be sure, by my life's journeys in all manner of forms through time and space. So I come condemning not the seemingly endless round of dying and rebirth that causes so much suffering. Yet, as I feel of my weariness, as I feel the suffering of the world, my soul cries out for the Beloved's Light and that all beings awaken and come Home together.

I admit that my impatience obscures my ability to let go and rest in the knowing that the Divine is expressing perfectly just as it is – no matter how something unfolds or what drama is playing out. I admit that I feel invested in what we did as a family of initiates to support our beloved Master and brother, Yeshua. Even to the pouring out of our blood – as did my beloved Nathaniel, and my son, Benjamin, and my beloved Yeshua, himself. There are others who have died. There will be many more who will pour out their sweet offering unto the earth. In my weariness and grief, I pray that our offering will bear fruit soon and that no more of our family will be required to give their lives… *(Deep sighs)*….

I can see from this vantage point that while it has been long in coming, and untold numbers have given their lives, the seeds we planted are scattered and ripening throughout the Earth. The harvest time is near. As I look more deeply and with greater clarity, I do not know what expanse of time "near" is. I see that I must let go of expectation in outcome and timing. I must see and rejoice in the perfection of love's fruit already existing in all its myriad forms, no matter how obscured its inner light may be. As I unconditionally embrace the seeds of peace and harmony hidden in everyone, they can find a space to ripen from the inside out and reveal their self-luminous nature in their own perfect way and season. Meanwhile, I can tend my own garden and bring forth the flowering of my own True Self who loves to touch all I see with kindness.

CA: And if it still appears to come out as impatience and judgment?

MARIAM: Perhaps in telling our stories we will unravel and let go of our martyr identities which seem to water the seeds of impatience and judgment. I see that our tendency to cling to victim stories and perceptions of renunciation, sacrifice and suffering is a big obstacle to our awakening over the course of lifetimes. Perhaps your generation will clearly see the source of their repetitive patterns of self-flagellation and seemingly justified prejudice. Then we may come home to our true hearts of love by letting go of our various addictions to suffering in all its many forms.

We must release the bondage of sacrifice as a way to atone or absolve perceived causes of pain. Blood atonement has been the cause of so much suffering; not its absolution. Within everyone is the savior who has the compassion to turn self-imposed afflictions and errors of perception into well-being and gentle kindness toward all life. To project that self-redeeming savior outside or to place our collective grievances onto a scapegoat is truly a misguided practice. Even though blood sacrifice has been practiced by almost every culture across the eons, it is a grievous error and a stumbling block.

I also see that it is time for the misplaced worship of saints to cease. Often one is not called a saint unless he or she is martyred. A saint is often seen as the necessary sacrificial lamb. Somehow being murdered makes us worthy of adoration and makes us more capable of mediating between a soul and its Creator. But I say it was how we lived our lives, not how we died, that matters. It serves better to look into how we loved without condition and expressed patience, devotional discipline, or some other exemplary trait that may be a source of inspiration. With study and much soul-searching, our very human lives may inspire a fellow seeker's path to enlightenment. My wish is that those who have looked to us as saints, renunciates and ascetics, will find that a more loving and empowering path connects them directly with their Creator. This will bear more fruit than to supplicate us in the misguided ways that are taught.

CA: Thank you for your wisdom. Now go to the next significant event in your life.

{Mariam continues her story in PART 4, Chapter 27}

– Chapter 10 –
SARA OF MOUNT BUGARACH[15]
(The Daughter of Isaac & Tabitha)
Mount Bugarach, 19 AD

{*This chapter introduces us to Yeshua's Light-conceived cousin, Sara, as a young girl*}

SARA: Greetings, my name is Sara, the daughter of Isaac and Tabitha the Egyptian. I am glad we have this opportunity to share. I would like you to know more about me. Perhaps you could use verbiage like you did with my grandmother, such as asking about what I am wearing, the appearance of my body, and so on....

CA: Welcome, Sara. Look down at your feet. Is there anything on them?

SARA: I am wearing sandals that are made in my motherland that you call Egypt. My feet are small and my ankles are shapely and fine boned. My skin is naturally dark, not black, but a lovely deep golden brown. My hair is black with glints of fire from henna dye. When it's loose, it hangs in thick waves down to my waist. As I look at my hands, they are small, and my fingers are long and slender. My fingernails are trimmed quite short. There is a little garden soil under the nails. My eyes are dark brown and I have a mole on my left cheek. My breasts are small and my waist and thighs are slender. I can feel the bones of my pelvis, which is narrow because I have never birthed a child. I would say that I am approximately 5'3" tall

---

[15] Sara is one of Anna's Light-conceived grandchildren. She married Phillip and both of them were close disciples of Yeshua during his public ministry. See *"Anna, Grandmother of Jesus"* for more details.

in your way of measuring. I experience my body to be clean and sweet smelling.

CA: What you are wearing?

SARA: Besides my homespun linen robe, which is tied at my waist with a colorful scarf, I am wearing a beaded necklace. It is made of several strands that have strung upon them turquoise, lapis, carnelian, red coral, and some silver beads. I have on both wrists several beaded bangles. There is a narrow band of gold on my right wrist. On my left arm, beginning at the elbow, and then spiraling around my upper arm is a golden serpent.[16] I have simple gold rings

---

[16] The serpent referred to represents the subtle, erectile and resurrecting, serpentine energy seated at the base of the spine, also called Kundalini by Hindu yogis, which when activated through advanced energetic or Tantric practices, can facilitate the opening and expansion of consciousness beyond ordinary mind into Cosmic Awareness. Kundalini is usually depicted as various goddesses and as the Serpent of Wisdom. Women, such as Sara, who are members of the Order of the Magdalene (and other Divine Feminine orders), often wore this symbol of resurrection, indicating that they had been initiated into the mysteries of Isis (or other similar goddess deities) and serve the Great Mother's creation and its awakening from "spiritual death" or separation consciousness. The electro (masculine)-magnetic (feminine) energy of the Earth also flows in a serpentine fashion, called ley lines. This energy can be harnessed and directed by adepts for benevolent purposes. The statuary of Mother Mary (the Roman Catholic representation of the "pagan" Great Mother) is often seen at sacred grottos and wells. She is depicted standing upon a serpent. One esoteric meaning is that the electro-magnetic energy of the Earth Mother is harnessed and directed under the auspices of the Divine Feminine to ensure the earth's fertility. There are other meanings and representations of the serpent energy, which is usually perceived by the conditioned mind as the embodiment of evil or Satan. But the serpent in these cases most often represents ignorance/duality/separation consciousness, the lower frequency sine wave out of which the material world assumes and releases form, and *"e-veil"* meaning an energy veil composed of the mental and emotional obscurations that veil one's True Nature – the Absolute, which abides within and beyond time and space. The Divine Mother standing upon the serpent, in these cases, represents the Divine Love within us that vanquishes and transmutes "evil" into the Wisdom of Unity Consciousness and births us as the Son/Sun of God, a Light-anointed Christ or Buddha, etc.

on both hands. My earlobes have a number of ear piercings. My earrings are rather large gold bangles from which hang little silver bells. They make a joyful tinkling sound when I move my head. As I lift my arms, I can smell the sweet fragrance of essential oils which come from my motherland. On my head I also have a long narrow scarf woven of bright colors, which I have folded lengthwise. My hair is entwined with the scarf and then it is wrapped around my head. I allow a portion of the scarf, which is beaded, to flow down over my left shoulder.

I care about my appearance and I am glad that most people find me attractive. I am not terribly attached to it, but, at the same time, keeping my body healthy is important to me and being attractive brings me pleasure. I do not feel it to be a vain pleasure, but the kind of pleasure that I feel birds experience when they sing and display their beautiful feathers, or the joy water must feel as sunlight sparkles upon its dancing surface, or the happiness of the gentle breezes as they caress palm fronds and jasmine vines. It is my nature to care about the things I take inside my body. I strictly follow the Essene laws of rejuvenation which I have done since my youth.

The Essene way that includes diet, and cleanliness of body and mind, have been followed for many generations by my family. I find people, who do not follow these rules of diet, suffering all manner of afflictions, which I feel could be avoided if they knew better. Some lack discipline and love for their physical temple. Some are simply ignorant, having never been taught another way. Other souls are too impoverished and can only survive as best they can. There is so much suffering in this world. My family and I do what we can to help alleviate the pain around us.

I see having a healthy body as one of the important ways to prevent unnecessary suffering. We all pass through sickness, aging and death, but we can meet each day of life with greater joy by being fully present in our physical temples and by having gratitude for all our lessons as they come to us. We can have greater peace if we take simple measures to be mindful and caring. What we take into our mouths and especially what comes out of our mouths determines our happiness.

It is important to ingest and cultivate good thoughts in the garden of our mind so that we may grow kind actions. By gratefully witnessing the beauty and goodness of all things that support us, we nurture our seeds of loving-kindness and allow the weeds to wither. When we speak words which nurture our loved ones and neighbors, we encourage greater harmony at home and in our communities. When we mindfully eat food rich in the nutrients of the Earth Mother we are more prosperous in our lives. When we eat living foods pulsing with the light of Brother Sun, who pours out his love upon all without condition, we, too, can be more generous with our abundance. In turn, we may add many more years to our lives in which to grow in wisdom. Then there are many more opportunities to give service to others in ways that benefit all.

We own nothing. We are stewards of all that is freely given. What comes to us blesses us during the few moments we may merge with it and have the increase of its reflection. But we suffer if we try to hold on to that which by its nature must change and return to that place from whence it came. We are as free as the wind that brings the clouds with their welcome rain and shade. How can the wind and clouds be imprisoned by our will? Though our physical world appears solid, it, too, as the air that coalesces into rain, does eventually evaporate. We, and all that comes and goes, are but visitors passing through countless guises. We and all things that appear are best allowed to be free to pass on in life's journey to fulfill a greater purpose. For all life has its season and its intrinsic wisdom, as does the sea her ebb and flow.

CA: Thank you for sharing your wisdom. How old are you?

SARA: I have almost reached my 23rd year. My mother, who was born in Egypt, is called Tabitha and she is quite lovely. She is much younger than my father. She is very intelligent and industrious. It seems that my mother accomplishes so much that benefits so many in our community. My father is called Isaac. He is the son of Grandmother Anna who lives in Mount Carmel on the far side of the Great Sea.

CA: Where are you living now?

SARA: I am living with my parents in an ancient Essene monastery that my father and Uncle Jacob moved to years ago, after they left the great wisdom school of Mount Carmel. With their skills, they have expanded it over the years into a lovely sanctuary, which is smaller, but in many ways similar to, the one they came from in Carmel. I have only been there once, but I was quite young and I do not remember it very well or my Uncle Joseph (*of Arimathea's*) home in Jerusalem.

CA: Are you in France now?

SARA: Yes. Near the great mountain called Bugarach.

CA: Do you have brothers and sisters?

SARA: Yes, I have other siblings; five brothers and two sisters. I am the youngest. It seems that my mother loved getting pregnant! She loves having a full household and keeping busy with the care of many people.

I have had a number of journeys to my motherland to visit with my cousins, aunts, uncles and my mother's parents who all live there. They do not come to visit us here. On occasion my Uncle Joseph of Arimathea comes and takes us in his wonderful boats. We go first to the great city on the sea named after the Greek general, Alexander, and then we take another boat with many oarsmen up the great river that you call the Nile to Heliopolis. I find it quite beautiful. There are many date groves and lush gardens and green fields with dazzling white sand dunes just beyond the narrow strip of fertile land. There are the most amazing ancient structures built by the Pharaohs over the course of thousands of years. Now the Romans are there and they are changing the way the temples look. They have adopted some of the Egyptian ways of honoring the deities, especially Mother Isis.

For months at a time, through my years, I have stayed there and have been taught in the ways of the Great Mother. I am proud that I may be her handmaiden, and that she has taken me under her all-encompassing wings and all-seeing eyes, so that I may come to know her mysteries. I have been introduced, as well, to my other cousins who are my father's nieces and nephews. We have a

SARA MOUNT BUGARACH

wonderful time together. Once, when my cousin, Yeshua, was a boy he visited us on his way to, and from, Britain. I love to hear Uncle Joseph tell stories about him. He travels many places. I have been told he is now in a very exotic faraway land you call India. I have also heard interesting stories about Yeshua's mother, Mary Anna and my Grandmother Anna. I feel them to be very wise. I hope to see them someday, now that I am an adult.

CA: What are you doing today?

SARA: I am doing some sewing for my mother and family. She does wonderful weaving with the cotton that we bring from the motherland, flax from the fields, wool from the sheep and the hair of the goats. She weaves tight and very durable cloth. It does not hold much dirt in its fibers. Instead, the dirt is repelled quite nicely. She has taught me how to cut and piece the cloth she makes into different garments for different purposes. Those that are worn next to the body are made of soft cotton and flax fibers. Depending on the season, if it is cold, we use animal fibers for our outer garments. I am sewing now and daydreaming. Sharing with you feels like a dream that I am having with my eyes open.

CA: You shared very beautifully about the necklace that you have on and the bracelet on your upper arm. Is it customary to wear these ornaments or is this a special occasion?

SARA: I simply like to wear these beautiful things. They are from Egypt. I like to think of myself like my mother, who is Egyptian. Don't misunderstand, I love my father very much; I simply have more of an affinity for things that are Egyptian. My relatives gave these ornaments to me. They are worn by the women there. There are some Essenes in Egypt who come from Palestine who do not wear jewelry or dyed fabric. They, in fact, are rather in judgment of them, preferring absolute simplicity and communal sameness. Some of the initiates who come here from Palestine often frown at me when they first see my colorful clothing and bangles.

When I was younger I was very reluctant to take my Egyptian things off. But then it was explained we could make our passages through the seaports and roadways with greater safety if I did not bring attention to myself. Then I gladly put my adornments out of sight, under my outer robes. I wrapped them tightly in a silk scarf, which I placed under a girdle against my body.

My mother also wears similar ornaments, but not as many as I do, and then only on rare occasions. When I am here in our little community I share these things with my little nephews and nieces who also take delight in them. I do not feel this is vanity and I am not trying to be different or better than others. If I find this is ever the case, I will gladly give these things away. I cannot change the color of my skin, which the native people find exotic. I suppose we are all different and unique; and it is best to celebrate our differences instead of being fearful.

CA: Are you married?

SARA: No, I do not yet have a mate. I am looking forward to that time. Sometimes I feel lonely and rather pensive without a beloved husband. Some of the brothers here and in Egypt have shown interest in me. That makes me glad for my beauty, but somehow I don't feel that I am to be with any of the men I have met. Thankfully, my parents honor me by not arranging a marriage. Experiencing a deep love remains a mystery I often ponder in my heart.

I have been opened to my sexual energy and the flowering of my womanhood in ceremonies I experienced in Egypt. But I have not had my womb opened to bear a child. I have not had a prolonged relationship. I do desire that very much. I look at my mother and my father. They are so content and so tender with one another. They set me and my siblings a good example. Mama and Papa are so devoted to all the souls in our little community. And so is my Uncle Jacob. His is such a tender soul. I have a lovely family and I am very proud of them.

Now I can hear my Grandma Anna, on the inner planes, saying, "It is time, Sara, to move forward in time."

CA: Yes, Sara, please move forward to the next important event in your life.

{Sara continues her story in PART 2, Chapter 15}

— Chapter 11 —

LIZBETT (Elizabeth Hannah)[17]

(Daughter of Yeshua & Mary of Bethany)
Mount Bugarach, 36 AD

{*Claire is functioning as the facilitator of this session by asking questions of Catherine Ann who responds as "Lizbett." When first learning about Lizbett during an early session with Anna, Catherine Ann expressed a desire to be Lizbett's Akashic Record proxy because she sensed a strong affinity with her. Lizbett begins her remarkable story as a three-year old child.*}

LIZBETT: You asked me to focus on a lifetime I had with Yeshua. He is standing at the foot of my cradle, which I have almost outgrown. I am around two or three years old. As I look, he's really, really tall and I am pretty small. He's looking down and he's smiling at me. I'm supposed to be going to sleep but I would rather be playing with him. He's my daddy. I don't see him a lot.

CLAIRE: How do you feel about that?
LIZBETT: I like it when he's here. He's really fun.
CLAIRE: Who takes care of you when he's not with you?
LIZBETT: Nana, my grandmother.
CLAIRE: Is that Anna? (Great Grandmother to Lizbett)
LIZBETT: Yes.
CLAIRE: Who is your mother?
LIZBETT: Her name is Mary (*Mary of Bethany*). I know my mother's around, but she's not the one who is around me the most.
CLAIRE: So there is Nana who cares for you. Who else?

---

[17] Lizbett was conceived at Winter Solstice of 32 AD and was born in the sign of Virgo the following September of 33 AD.

LIZBETT: Nana and Mariam (*Yeshua's cousin*) care for me the most. Then there are other little girls who are older than me, like my big sister, Sar'h – they play with me a lot. There are other relatives, too.

CLAIRE: Are there any boys who play with you?

LIZBETT: There are some boys, but they are older. They are not around me so much. They have other things they like to do. They prefer to leave the care of the young ones to the women. I know they are around. From my cradle I am aware that Nana is reading and writing. She's more in the background. Daddy has moved to the other side of the room where Mama is sitting on a large pillow on the floor. He puts his arm around her and she puts her head on his shoulder. They just sit quietly. I can tell they love each other a lot.

CLAIRE: What is the place like where you live? What is the light like?

LIZBETT: It's quite dim. There is a little fire that is dying down and there is a candle by Nana. There is a little lamp that burns some kind of oil. There is not a lot of light, it is pretty dim.

There are others around. Mariam and Martha (*Lizbett's aunt*) are over by one of the lamps working with their sewing. Everybody has their projects.

CLAIRE: Do you hear any sounds?

LIZBETT: I hear the others speaking very softly, but they are mostly quiet. I hear an owl and I hear the wind. It's cold outside.

CLAIRE: What time of year is it?

LIZBETT: I am hearing the word February.

CLAIRE: Is this one of Yeshua's visits – as he comes and goes?

LIZBETT: Yes.

CLAIRE: Will he get to be with you very long on this visit?

LIZBETT: No. I don't think so.

CLAIRE: I ask you to go forward now to another time during this visit with your father. Tell me about another experience you had with him.

LIZBETT: He is playing with all of us children. There are lots of children and he's laughing with us – running and jumping. He can be pretty silly sometimes. He likes playing with the children. He's fun. He's not so stern and stand-offish like some of the adults. He just gets right down and makes mud-pies with us. He tickles us and we all laugh. I love his laugh.

CLAIRE: What is your daddy (*Yeshua*) wearing?

LIZBETT: It's warmer now. The sun is out. He is wearing a very plain long tunic over some leggings. He is dressed like the other men who live here. The cloth is woven out of linen. It feels sort of rough.

CLAIRE: What are you wearing?

LIZBETT: I have a little tunic of similar material. But it's not so scratchy against my bare skin. It goes down almost to my ankles.

CLAIRE: Is there anything on your feet?

LIZBETT: No. Sometimes I have little leather sandals, but I always take them off. I like going barefoot. Even when the ground isn't warm yet, I still take my shoes off and go barefoot. Sometimes, when it is really warm, I take my tunic off. Some of the grown-ups try to put it back on me – but most of them don't really care.

CLAIRE: Who tries to put it back on you?

LIZBETT: Mariam. She doesn't like me running around without my tunic.

CLAIRE: Why doesn't she like you to do that?

LIZBETT: She's afraid I will catch a cold.

CLAIRE: She doesn't particularly care that you are naked?

LIZBETT: Hmmm...

CLAIRE: She's more concerned that you might be sick?

LIZBETT: Yes, she feels responsible for me and for making sure that nothing bad happens to me.

CLAIRE: Tell me about her. What does she look like when you are looking into her face?

LIZBETT: She has long, dark brown hair – it's almost black. It's really thick and a little bit frizzy. When it isn't tied back, it really sticks out. I like to run my fingers through it. Her skin is light, kind of golden with some freckles. She has a very nice face.

CLAIRE: A kind face?

LIZBETT: Yes, a very nice and kind face. She has light brownish-grey-green eyes. It depends on if she is in the sunlight. When the sun glints in them, then they are more of a pretty green. I like her eyes when she smiles; but sometimes she can be stern and then she frowns. Sometimes she's really sad and she cries.

CLAIRE: Is there anyone else you would like to tell me about?

LIZBETT: There's a little baby.

CLAIRE: Who's baby?

LIZBETT: She is Sara's. She is crawling. She is maybe eight months old. I like the baby. I get to play with her. It's fun.

CLAIRE: Do you teach the baby things?

LIZBETT: I show the baby things.

CLAIRE: What do you show her?

LIZBETT: I have some little toys. There's a little cloth dolly stuffed with lamb's wool and there are other things made out of carved bone and wood. There is one that I like best. It's shaped like this – (*Catherine Ann's fingers form a triangle*).

CLAIRE: What do you do with it?

LIZBETT: I play with it. I make believe it's a big house like the one I saw when we went to the town by the big river. Sometimes I get flowers and put them on my triangle. Sometimes I put it in the dirt and pretend it grows grass and other pretty things. Sometimes I hold it up to the sky and I block the sun out and watch the light dance all around it. Sometimes I run with it. Sometimes I show it to the baby. And sometimes when I pick little yellow flowers, the baby tries to grab them. When the yellow flowers get all white, the baby and I blow the white fluff and we watch the wind carry the seeds away.

CLAIRE: Thank you for sharing, Lizbett. Go forward in time to another experience you would like to share.

Mount Bugarach, early autumn, 38 AD

LIZBETT: There are soldiers marching – Roman soldiers.

CLAIRE: How old are you now?

LIZBETT: I'm five years old.

CLAIRE: Where are you? Who is with you?

LIZBETT: I am still in my home by the big mountain. The Roman soldiers are marching down a road that's not too far from the place where we live. Everybody is worried. Even though we dress like the other people who live nearby; and we have a kind of magic that we use so that our community doesn't attract too much attention, there is still concern that we will be found out.

CLAIRE: Why are you worried about being found out?

LIZBETT: Because of the way we live. Our customs are different than the soldiers' ways. We are afraid that they will disturb our way of life. Some of the other children and I climbed a nearby hill this morning where we can look through the thick trees down into the valley. We can see them off in the distance. There are lots of them. They have horses and carts and they make the dust rise. Long lines of them are walking. We can hear them. There's lots of dust and noise.

CLAIRE: What is the season now?

LIZBETT: It is early fall. The leaves are beginning to turn yellow. There is something going on – like something important that makes us feel uneasy.

CLAIRE: Have you heard the grownups talking?

LIZBETT: Yes. The local farmers and villagers are complaining a lot about how the Romans are making everyone give them more of our grain and animals. There are more Roman soldiers coming to the village these days. Just yesterday a small group of them rode horses right up to our gate. They did not show any respect. They just walked up to our big house where we gather for meals and sharing. While we were eating, they banged on the door. They didn't wait for us to open it. They just came in and looked all around. Isaac, Joseph and Nana talked to them and gave them something to eat. They went away with extra food.

The grown-ups talked late into the night. They are saying it is time for those of us who came here from the Old Country to go with Uncle Joseph (*of Arimathea*) to a far away island called Avalon. Uncle Joseph is very old. He is rich and he has boats. I haven't seen them; but I have heard lots of stories. He comes and goes like my daddy and my two mothers.

CLAIRE: Two mothers? Who is your other mother?

LIZBETT: Myriam (*of Tyana*). She looks different from my mother. She's taller and bigger and she has darker skin. She's very beautiful. Mama's very pretty, but I think Myriam is beautiful like Queen Esther. She comes and goes, too. But most of the time she and my mother are here. She is fun like my daddy. She laughs a lot and sometimes I like to be with her more than my mother. Mama seems more far away, even when she is here. I know she loves me and my big sister, Sar'h. I think Sar'h is more like her than me.

CLAIRE: Do you feel safe when your daddy is with you?

LIZBETT: I feel better, but right now nobody is feeling really safe. It's like they have been through this before. The others have said that. They tire of it because there are many times in different places when they have been through this concern. They used to be concerned about other Jews, who are different from us; who don't like us. They say in the Old Country both the Jews and the Romans gave us trouble. Here, it is the Romans who give us concern. I heard the grown-ups talking about how Nathaniel was arrested by the Jews and killed by the Romans in a far-away place. I have heard stories of how my daddy had this happen to him, except he didn't die – he is still alive. I am so glad Daddy is still here, though I don't get to see him much. I don't know very much about how Nathaniel died. I just know it has been very hard for Mariam. She cries more than she used to cry. Before it was like if she felt tender about a beautiful flower or sunset, or about a new-born baby or lamb, she would cry...but she was smiling when she cried. Now she cries and she's sad. She doesn't talk anymore. We find other ways to talk. I wish I understood better because I love Mariam very much. I just know that everyone is concerned that what happened to Nathaniel could happen to us.

CLAIRE: That must be difficult for everyone. Tell me, Lizbett, about your grandmother, Mary Anna, your daddy's mommy. Is she here?

LIZBETT: I love my Grand Mama, Mary Anna (*Mother Mary*). She is so nice and so kind and she likes me so much. Yes, she is here at the moment, but she's not here all the time. She comes and goes, too.

CLAIRE: Do you hear stories about where she goes and what she does?

LIZBETT: Sometimes she goes off with my daddy. Sometimes she goes off to other villages where there are others like us. She loves taking care of people when they are sick. Everyone feels better when she is around and when she tells her lovely stories about my daddy. She has a way of showing people how to be happy and how to be kind to each other. I miss her when she is away. She is like another mother. Daddy's younger brothers and his sisters are here, too. I like them a lot. I have a very large and loving family.

CLAIRE: What are the names of Grandmother Mary Anna's children who are living with you?

LIZBETT: The oldest sister is Aunt Ruth and then there's a big girl named Esther Salome. They also like to take care of me. The boys are John Mark and Matteas.

CLAIRE: Does she take other people with her?

LIZBETT: Some of the men go with her to give her protection. Often Nana, Ruth, Esther Salome, Myriam and Sara go with her. Sometimes my mother goes and Sar'h and I get to go, too, if it's not too far away.

CLAIRE: Tell me about Tabitha's daughter, Sara, and her husband, Philip. Does she have other children besides the baby?

LIZBETT: Besides the baby she has a boy that is older. Justus was born not long after me.

CLAIRE: Tell me about Philip. What is he like?

LIZBETT: He has black hair and a bushy beard and brown eyes with bushy eyebrows. He's nice, but he can be very serious at times. He seems a lot older than Sara. He is good with the animals. He is good with the horses, the mules and the donkeys. He knows how to train them to be good for riding and pulling wagons and plows. He is very handsome riding our big, new stallion that has glistening brown hair and a long, flowing black tail. Sometimes he lets me ride behind him, my arms wrapped around his skinny waist. He likes to tell us stories about my daddy. I like it when he sits me down in front of him and takes my hands in his and tells me special stories about my daddy and my mother. He knows that I miss Daddy and he wants me to know I am loved very much.

CLAIRE: What is Phillip like when he is with your daddy?

LIZBETT: He makes sure that everything is taken care of when Daddy travels with any of the grown-ups. He takes care of the animals and makes sure there are enough provisions for everyone. He feels very responsible. He makes sure everything works right.

CLAIRE: Tell me about Sara. Do you like to be with her?

LIZBETT: She's very sweet and she has a beautiful face like Mama Myriam. They both have dark golden skin in the summertime. But Sara's skin is darker, like her mother's, and sometimes she has very rosy cheeks. She likes to pick little berries that grow wild on the hillsides. When she takes us with her to help her pick, she sometimes puts berries in our mouths. Her baby (*little laugh*) makes a funny face. The berry must not be sweet enough – and she spits it out. She collects herbs with Nana. Nana has taught her about herbs. I like to go herb gathering with them.

CLAIRE: What does she do with the herbs?

LIZBETT: The herbs are for when you are sick. Sometimes they make a paste or salve out of the herbs. If you get a rash or something, they put the herbs on the rash.

CLAIRE: Have you had that done to you?

LIZBETT: Yes. I had it put on my leg when it was hurt a few weeks ago. It itched a lot. They put it on the sores and told me I wasn't supposed to touch it or scratch it. It made my leg better in a couple of days. Actually, it felt better right away, but it took a couple of days for the rash to disappear.

CLAIRE: I would like you to go forward now to another important time in your life.

Brittany, Late Fall, 38 AD

LIZBETT: We are traveling. We are wearing thick, warm travel garments that are kind of rough, like burlap. They are dark brown so that we blend into the countryside. We travel mostly at night when we're not so visible. We are going to a place where the Druids live. We are friends with the Druids. It is a place where we can be safe while the Romans are marching around the countryside. We're not settling there, we're just going to take refuge for a time. We have visited other Druids on our journey. They help us a lot.

CLAIRE: Are you still in Gaul (*France*) or are you in Avalon (*Britain*) now? What time of year is it?

LIZBETT: We are still in Gaul. We are traveling to a place where we can cross the ocean in boats. We have already come close to the great ocean several times. I could see it shining far off in the distance. It went on forever into the misty blue sky. Uncle Joseph (*of Arimathea*) knows the way. He has everything arranged. Nothing bad has happened to us. Sometimes it's really cold and rainy. That slows us down, but our Druid friends give us shelter. Most of the leaves are off the trees now.

CLAIRE: Please go on to the next thing that happens on your journey.

LIZBETT: We are at the place where the boats are being prepared for sailing. It's pretty here. I like to see the foamy waves splashing on the big stones. I like the smells and the many sea birds. Everything is windswept and wild. Inland a little ways, there is a village where Uncle Joseph's friends live. I like the children who live here. I don't quite understand their words; but we find a way to share our stories and play games. They like to take the other children and me to the places where there are standing stones and groves of old trees. There are fairies here. There are lots of fairies and little people called elves. The people who live here and do their magic can see the little people and talk to them.

CLAIRE: How do you feel about being here with these magical people?

LIZBETT: I like being with these people and the fairies a lot. I heard about the fairies where we used to live, but now I can see them. They are very friendly. They like us. They come up to us and they are playful. They have jobs. They help the flowers and trees. They help the earth. They help everybody live their best life, whether it is a plant or a flower or a bumble bee or a person. They know how to vibrate with the right colors and the right sounds. They work best with the sun and the elements. They help everything work right together.

CLAIRE: It sounds like you know a lot about the fairies.

LIZBETT: Yes. Nana has told me about them and how they help the herbs that go into making tea and salves. The fairies somehow get the herbs to do what they are supposed to do so people can get well. She calls them devas and angels.

CLAIRE: Do these people work with the angels?

LIZBETT: I think they do. I don't see the angels yet. The angels are bigger. I can see the fairies and the elves when I am in this special place like I did in certain places near the big mountain where we used to live. I think I will get to see the angels soon. Nana says there are fairies and elves in the new place we are going.

CLAIRE: Do you think you will share what you have discovered about the fairies with your daddy?

LIZBETT: Yes.

CLAIRE: Do you think he knows about these little people?

LIZBETT: Yes. I think he plays with them, too.

I think too many of the older people are worried right now. It's kind of like a fog...umm...

CLAIRE: ...over their minds?

LIZBETT: Yes, over their minds. Sometimes I feel that worry, too. I'm glad the Roman soldiers haven't bothered us. There were two or three times when they stopped us. Uncle Joseph talked to them in their language and showed them some papers with special writing on them. Then they let us go. They are still a worry though. And now that winter is coming, there might be storms that will keep us from going in the boats. We have to hurry to get everything ready.

{*Lizbett's story continues in Avalon, Britain – see PART 3, Chapter 19*}

— Chapter 12 —
LAZARUS OF BETHANY[18]
Mount Bugarach, 36 AD

{*Lazarus, the brother of Mary of Bethany and also one of the disciples who participated in the Christ Drama, steps forward in his current environment at Mount Bugarach. He shares information about his familial relationships and work with the Magdalenes.*}

CATHERINE ANN (*Henceforth: CA*): Please share with me what you notice.

LAZARUS: It's dark. I am standing inside the doorframe of a small room looking out. As I look outside I can see that I am on a hillside where there are silhouettes of trees against the night sky. Some of them seem to be oaks and conifers. There is a haze that obscures the stars.

CA: Is there anyone else around?

---

[18] Lazarus is Anna's grandson, the adopted son of Joseph of Arimathea, who is also Lazarus' uncle. He is Mary of Bethany and Martha's adopted brother. He was the orphaned son of Joseph of Arimathea's wife, Mary of Magdala's sister. Bethany was his primary home where he assisted his mother and sisters to provide shelter and healing for the homeless and infirm. He spent short periods at Mt. Carmel and longer periods at the Essene community of Qumran. He joined John the Baptist for a three year retreat on Mt. Sinai before Yeshua began his formal ministry. Lazarus then became one of Yeshua's devoted disciples. He is best known as Mary and Martha's brother who died and was brought back to life so that others might believe in the healing power Yeshua demonstrated. He was a living example of the true nature of the Soul that survives death. This healing set the stage for Yeshua's own resurrection. Lazarus continued to serve as a protector of the Magdalene women and children in France and Britain. He spent his last years with his sisters in southern France and died near an area presently called St. Baume. One of several Biblical references: John 11: 1 – 45.

LAZARUS: There are several men who are asleep not far from me. I don't know about the others.

CA: Can you see your body or is it too dark?

LAZARUS: My body is in shadow. Perhaps it will assist if I go out the door into the star light. There is a bench outside.

CA: OK. Move to the bench outside.

LAZARUS: There is a gentle breeze rustling the leaves and dry grasses. I don't know why I am not able to sleep in the moment.

CA: What are you wearing?

LAZARUS: I am wearing a robe of rather course weave. It is made of linen, the kind that is worn under outer robes. I am wearing it to cover my nakedness at night.

CA: Are you a man or a woman?

LAZARUS: I am a man.

CA: What are you called?

LAZARUS: Most call me Lazarus, but not everyone.

CA: What do you prefer to be called?

LAZARUS: For this purpose you can call me Lazarus. That identifies me with my father's family.

CA: What is on your mind tonight?

LAZARUS: I have been reviewing my life to this point. There has been so much to do and not enough time for quiet contemplation. It feels good to arise and be in this quiet space now. I can hear the gentle sounds of the others sleeping and the crickets nearby. There is a balmy breeze from the distant sea mixed with the heat of the earth. These last few days have been very warm.

CA: And what sea is that?

LAZARUS: The Great Sea.

CA: Tell me about this place. Do you live here or are you visiting as a traveler?

LAZARUS: It is my new home. We have been here over three years. My understanding is that we will be here for some time, but at some point many of us will move to Britain. I don't know yet what my choices will be for the future. Even though there is a great deal of uncertainty, I am glad to be here. I am glad we now have an opportunity to rest.

CA: Who are the others that are sleeping?

LAZARUS: They are the brothers of this community who do not have mates. Those who have mates sleep in another area and the women without mates are in yet another dormitory space.

CA: Is this your home?

LAZARUS: This is our community near the mountain you call Bugarach. It is a monastery patterned after Mount Carmel.

CA: How old are you?

LAZARUS: I am approaching my 35th year.

CA: What are you doing at this time and place? What is your life like?

LAZARUS: During the day I have been assisting the brothers with harvesting the fields of grain. I have also mended the fences that were in need of repair. We are going to erect the new storehouse in a few days and I will be assisting with that. The late summer season is a busy time and today we will have many things to do. Even though I am very busy, I am glad to be here where I can rest from what used to trouble me.

CA: What troubled you?

LAZARUS: Our last years in Palestine were often very challenging. Even though it has been six years since Yeshua's resurrection (*April, 30 AD*), the impact of the experiences I had when I walked with Yeshua still rest heavily upon me, at times. We worked very hard to support our dear cousin, Yeshua, and also our beloved cousin, John.[19] Our trials were many. It was very difficult for me to hear of John's wretched death. I could not have imagined such a heinous thing could happen to someone so pure and powerful. He had been my beloved teacher for years. I still have mixed feelings about our keeping his skull when I know others of John's disciples believe it is theirs to safeguard.

---

[19] John, called The Baptist, is Anna's nephew who lived in the Judean desert and more particularly in the Essene community of Qumran on the western shores of the Dead Sea. He was the victim of a vengeful plot instigated by King Herod's wife, Herodias, who had John beheaded. All four New Testament Gospels speak of John the Baptist.

If this were not hard enough to bear, there was the day of Yeshua's brutal trial and crucifixion. I was present for the Passover Feast and I was with the others in the garden of Gethsemane. But when Yeshua was put under arrest at dawn, I had to leave and go back to Bethany with some of the women. I could not witness such brutality. I had not been prepared as was my sister, Mary (*of Bethany*), and my aunt, Mary Anna (*Mother Mary*), to be so brave and fully present for what was to follow during the course of that terrible day.

I knew the plan was that Yeshua would consciously still all his vital signs within hours of being on the tree of crucifixion on Golgotha. Then he would allow his body to transmute and be resurrected to a greater level of consciousness within the sepulcher that my father (*Joseph of Arimathea*) prepared for this purpose. I knew he had the power to resurrect his body because he brought my spirit back from the invisible realms after I died in Bethany. I had had a direct experience with dying to this world for four days and then walking once again in physical form! I beheld the Truth that I am much more than my body. Knowing that life is eternal, and that Yeshua could command the elements, gave me courage to endure the harshness of all that happened during those culminating days of the Passion Week. I was able to set aside the fleeting shadows of doubt that arose in my mind. But it wasn't until I saw him for myself that I could begin to fully relax!

You can imagine how overjoyed I was when Mary (*of Bethany*) and Myriam (*of Tyana*) told us that Yeshua was fully alive and shone with the brilliance of the sun. As they spoke of his radiance, I knew he was filled with more Light than ever! But it was not through believing their words alone that I was able to heal from the trauma of the things I witnessed. For indeed, I had seen the savagery of Roman crucifixion displayed on the road that led from Bethany to Jerusalem and other places, as well. But it was with immense solace to my soul that I saw with my own eyes what my sister described!

I was present a number of times when Yeshua showed himself to us in Palestine after the resurrection. I have seen him when he comes to Bugarach. I have felt his loving embrace. I know him to be all that he promises us that we can be, as sons and daughters of a forgiving God. I now know beyond any shadow of doubt that consciousness is eternal and that the Great Work of the Soul is awakening to that fact. Then we can know liberation from our karmas and the suffering that comes through endless cycles of rebirth.

CA: What a powerful experience to have witnessed Yeshua's resurrection. I can understand that all this was traumatic and troubling for you. Go now to the next significant event you wish to share.

LAZARUS: I have not made up my mind yet what I am going to do, whether I will stay here, go to Britain with my grandmother and many of the others who came to Gaul from Palestine, or go on a journey with Philip and some of the other brethren.

CA: Where is your grandmother right now?

LAZARUS: She is in the dormitory with the women.

CA: Is Yeshua here?

LAZARUS: Not at this time. He has been with us and those were very joyful times.

CA: What is Yeshua doing right now?

LAZARUS: As I tune into the ethers, I can see him in a great light. He is smiling and he assures me that all is well. He says he will come amongst us again, but to not expect him at any particular time and not to expect him to come in particular manner of appearance. As always, he invites me to be comforted with the knowing that he is always near, whether I see his body or not.

CA: Did you come with the family on the boat?

LAZARUS: Yes, I came with the family on that harrowing journey (*Chapter 43 of Anna, Grandmother of Jesus*) which almost took our lives. I have seen and experienced miracles before, but this was such a close call for all of us. I continue to be disturbed by its lingering effects when I try to sleep. I still have dreams that hearken back to those very bleak days when I was especially worried for the children.

Now that we are in this safe haven, I awaken every morning filled with gratitude for the grace that moved all the members of my family to come together with an unwavering sense of unity. I would like to share more fully about our extraordinary experience as we crossed the Great Sea in our boat that was stripped of its sail and oars.

The elders among us counseled us how to be at peace. Thankfully, as we settled into calmness, everyone recognized the necessity of turning away from fear and selfish concerns. Once there was no more bickering and complaining by the children, who were so hungry and frightened, we began to work with the elements with a unified purpose. We felt each other's hearts and the purity of our souls. Whereas a few moments earlier, some of us were feeling a despairing apathy and were ready to give up, we came into a unity beyond anything I had ever known before – even more so than during the Passion Week when we rallied around Yeshua with all our heart, mind and strength.

I felt a sweet gentleness and a comforting warmth come into my heart, as if a bubble of light were all around and within us. As I looked at the expression on every dear one's face I saw what I can only describe as supreme angelic peace. Then it no longer seemed to matter if we perished or not. We knew we were together as a loving family and we would continue our life as a family on the other side, if that was to be our shared experience. We would walk together into the world of spirit, as one united mind and heart, and no one would be left behind.

An hour or two before dawn, while immersed in reverie and stillness, we beheld a light far out on the water. At first we were concerned that it was a Roman boat with a lantern. The light remained motionless. As the minutes passed we became aware that the quality of the light was not that of fire. It was an iridescent orb of light that began to move toward us. Slowly it grew larger. It moved in an interesting pattern as it approached. Then not far from us it floated silently above the reflective water. In our hearts we began to feel that Yeshua was in our midst and that all would be well. Then the light orb flickered and was gone. Master, as we call him, did not come and presence himself on the boat. A gentle breeze arose similar to the balmy breeze I am now feeling. Somehow the water beneath us felt different. Our listing boat with no sail or oars began to move northwesterly, as if upon an invisible current.

This experience of redeeming grace was a turning point for me. There have been other miracles, but this was the first time I experienced all of us as one unified force, no matter our age or gender. It is very refreshing and affirming for me to know that this kind of Oneness can happen in this world of divisive conflict, war and sorrow.

CA: Thank you for sharing this inspiring story. Is there more you would like to say?

LAZARUS: I am glad for my family members who have made Bugarach their home, but I continue to feel, as many do, that we will not be here for long. Maybe I will go away for awhile and come back from time to time like some of the others do. It depends on the activities of the Romans and whether the women and children are safe. As a consecrated Magdalene, I do feel a responsibility to care for them and to protect them from harm.

There is news that other disciples who walked with Yeshua are imprisoned and there will be more loss of life. There is so much unrest and so many dangers that can come upon us with little or no provocation. We have no more immunity than the others who left Palestine seeking havens all around the Great Sea. There has been a great dispersion – a dispersion of families and disciples, and, most of all, a dispersion of focused energy. We all had a sense of purpose and destiny when Yeshua walked with us. During these past six years it's like being scattered to the winds. There are so many with different ideas about how to go forward. We hear reports of so much conflict and loss of life.

Yeshua has been visiting with my sister, Mary (*of Bethany*), on the inner planes. She says he is going to be coming again for a visit with us before too long. That will be good. Maybe when I hear what he has to say I can make up my mind about what it is that I am to do.

CA: What are some of your other options?

LAZARUS: As I have said, Grandmother Anna plans on going to Britain, which she remembers with great fondness. She would very much like to see her other three sons, my uncles, Andrew, Josephus and Noah. Grandmother Anna wields a strong influence among us. I am leaning most strongly in this direction, also, because my father and sisters are choosing to go there. Our decision is made easier because we are told that the Romans under Julius Caesar were forced to leave Britain. There are few, if any Roman soldiers there now. Britain feels like a safer haven than living amongst the Romans who control southern Gaul.

We don't know exactly when we will go, but Grandmother and Father think it will most likely be next summer.[20] Father is completing making arrangements with his freighting boats. He has already been making arrangements with his brothers and the leaders of the Celts who live on the isles of Avalon. They want to ensure our welcome among the native people and to make sure we will be comfortably accommodated. Father said that I could come and assist him with his trade of tin and other commerce, as well as assist with transporting initiates from place to place. He is feeling like his years of seafaring are drawing to an end and he desires a simpler life in Avalon. He says if I wish to carry on his freighting business he will teach me all he knows. But Father's interests and talents in commerce and diplomacy are not mine. I do not think I can follow in his footsteps with good conscience. I know he understands me and will support any decision I make.

I would like to explain something about my relationship to my father, Joseph of Arimathea and my mother, Mary of Magdala, who are actually my aunt and uncle. I always think of Uncle Joseph as my father and Aunt Mary as my mother; no doubt because they are the only parents I have known. My birth mother, Susannah, who was old in years, died when I was born. My birth mother's sister and Joseph of Arimathea took me in as an infant. Joseph always treats me as his son, perhaps because he has only daughters. I have older siblings on my mother's side and cousins on my adopted mother's side, but I do not know them very well. They live in Galilee. Several

---

[20] The family actually leaves Mount Bugarach in the fall of 38 AD and cross the Channel that same year.

of my mother's relatives joined us in the last years of Yeshua's ministry. My older sister, Mary (*of Bethany*), and my younger sister, Martha, feel like true, devoted sisters. Please excuse my clumsy speaking; I just wanted you to know about my relationship as an adopted son and brother.

CA: Thank you for sharing this information about your family. There are so many of you, sometimes it is difficult to remember who everyone is and how you are related. Are there additional options for the direction of your life you would like talk about?

LAZARUS: Another option is that I could find my other cousins who still live in Galilee or find those who migrated to places around the eastern shores of the Great Sea, Turkey and India. I know that I don't wish to go back to Jerusalem where James (*Yeshua's brother*) and Peter (*the disciple*) still live. We have heard that our sanctuary for the poor continues in a modest way, but I do not feel there is more I can do to support its outreach from Bethany. I suppose it is best to wait until after I have had an opportunity to speak with Yeshua. Meanwhile, there is much for me to do here.

It is good to have a sense of being carried forward in my life, even though I do not know my exact direction as yet. It feels good to be still in these quiet hours before the dawn and to contemplate how I am effortlessly supported day by day, just as we were supported on our little boat in the middle of the Great Sea. As I realize I am feeling some anxiety about my future, I recall similar times of anxiety when I walked with Yeshua. I would lose mindfulness about the present moment and of my own God Presence providing for my every need. At those times when Yeshua observed my lack of mindfulness, he would stop me, place his arm around my shoulder, and gently remind me, saying, "Peace be unto you, Lazarus. Be still. Know I AM God." Or sitting together among the spring wildflowers, he would say to me, "My dear brother, Lazarus, cease to be anxious for the 'morrow. Look upon these lilies of the field, they toil not, neither do they spin, yet their raiment is more splendid than that of kings." As it was then, so is it now, I turn inward and find the Great Peace that passes all understanding.

Though I do not know yet where my footsteps will take me a year from now, I do know it feels good to be here in this peaceful mountain valley enjoying this beautiful night.

CA: What can you share about other experiences you had with Yeshua?

LAZARUS: I would like to say a little about my understanding of Yeshua's teachings. There are things that are difficult for the mind to understand, but the heart knows the full meaning. Master taught me some of the wisdom teachings he learned on his travels to the temples in Egypt and in India. I shared with him what I learned from John when I went with him to Mt. Sinai. Yeshua would smile and confirm what a great soul John was, and still is in the spirit realms, and that living John's teachings is a powerful way to know God. Then he would add to John's teachings. Master opened my eyes to see, my ears to hear, and my heart to open to direct knowledge of the Kingdom of Heaven within me and that it dwells within all beings.

I came to know beyond any doubt that we are pure consciousness. These bodies and all things of this world are temporal. If we cling to our body and to those things that pass away, we suffer with great fear, grief and anger for that which is lost and dies. The only lasting peace is that peace we nurture within our own breast. Gaining a full measure of wisdom and love – opening our heart to love our Father-Mother Creator and to love one another equally – is our only real treasure, where rust does not corrupt and thieves do not break in and steal.

These are the pearls of wisdom which we take with us into the Infinite Light when our bodies return to the earth. We need never be afraid for our lives, for life is all there is. Our physical form might change in a twinkling of an eye. All that is of this world is ceaselessly changing from birth to death. Yet there is also the absolute unborn, undying Stillness, out of which all things have their being and into which all things return – the one indivisible Presence.

CA: Thank you for sharing these beautiful teachings. Could you share how it was for you living with your sisters Mary and Martha?

LAZARUS: Some people find it easier to relate to my sister, Martha, who was very skilled in managing our large household and alms sanctuary, and who, like my father, continues to be a great conversationalist and diplomat. Although she often gets lost in caring for details and sometimes feels put upon, she is also very jovial and meets all manner of people with equal kindness and respect. On the other hand, most find my sister, Mary, who carries the name and mantle of the Magdalene, more aloof in her manner of relating, while also being very attentive and gentle of heart. This gives her an air of mystery. Mary can also be very outspoken when defending the downtrodden and those in need of having their civil rights given fair justice. She knows many things, far beyond my mind's reach. She is much more like Yeshua in that respect. As a couple they exude the same Soul energy, as if they were identical twins in male and female form – to be with one is like being with the other. Their personalities are more complementary because Yeshua is more of the water and air elements and Mary is of fire and earth. Mary is sometimes still a mystery to me. But even so, I am thankful to her for her unflinching strength, honesty and devotion. I love both my sisters dearly.

I also came to love Myriam (*of Tyana*) very much. It was a great blessing and a great learning to witness my sister overcome her jealousy of Myriam. They have become very close; much closer than Mary is with Martha.

CA: Did you ever marry and have children?

LAZARUS: No, I never married. There were times of loneliness when I have had my heart turn to women and I desired their companionship. But, I suppose it was because I spent a good deal of time at Qumran, which was made up almost exclusively of celibates, that I turned increasingly to holding my seed as my path of choice. I was taught within the brotherhood, and also by John (*the Baptist*), how to hold my fire within my loins and not spill my seed, as my path to God. I still find abstinence to be challenging, but I also find there are fewer distractions.

I used to feel conflicted by the part of me that felt a kinship with this pattern of celibacy and the part of me that desired to be a householder and to have children. After Yeshua returned with Myriam of Tyana and their children, and especially after he married my sister, Mary, I sometimes envied his happiness. During the times I was vulnerable to loneliness and feeling self-pity, I wanted to live more in the way he did. As the years have passed, I have resolved this internal conflict. I am happy being of service in the way our monastic life encourages. It is true that there are more married couples in Bugarach than celibates, but I find support for my choice and I am happy. I love being an uncle to Sar'h and Lizbett, and in a sense being their adopted father, as Joseph was mine.

It seems like I have sat in this space of contemplation many times – my head in my hands, my elbows resting on my knees. Just sitting here and wishing somehow that what was mine to do would just be clearer. As I sit here now, I find it rather strange and yet familiar, how I have had so many different opportunities and so many different directions I can take my life.

CA: When Yeshua was with you in the physical, did you feel there was more of a sense of direction?

LAZARUS: Yes, when I walked with him I went about the day's activities and didn't think about the concerns of tomorrow at all. There was plenty to do. Just being with him and serving with the others was enough to think about. There was no time to worry. We were serving so many people day after day. Getting enough rest was a problem, but somehow there was always enough energy to meet each day's need. I learned many practices from Yeshua and my sister that helped me to cultivate life-force energy. It seemed they never needed sleep the way most of us did. That was a time that I hold very precious. I am glad to be living at a slower pace now. But sometimes, I confess, I miss being with Yeshua as it used to be. I miss how sweet and tender he could be. To be held in his embrace, to look into his eyes and to feel of his strength.

I was glad for my sister, Mary – glad that she could be with him completely. Sometimes I felt an energy within me that wanted to merge with him, but we never consummated my fleshly desire. I think I would have liked that. I knew Yeshua sensed my attraction to him in this way. He never was in judgment of me, and neither did he ever encourage me to act out my desire for him. I felt free to work it out within my own mind and heart.

As I reflect on my life, I see it as a whirling wheel of many colors. There are so many choices, so many directions that one can go....Ah, well, I must move along now. I just wanted to share that little piece with you.

There is a gathering light from the east over the great mountain. The roosters are crowing, the doves are cooing, and everyone is stirring. I best get on now with my day. It's been good visiting with you (*Catherine Ann*). I know our sharing is more than a dream. I sense something about you that is very familiar. Perhaps we will have more to share at another time. I know you could look into my future and help me make up my mind, but that is not yours to do. I think I will stay here this season and over the winter months, then I will know what I will do. It is best to bring my mind to the activities and opportunities for service and happiness this day. As Martha reminds me, "This precious day, well lived, is enough!"

CA: I am certain you will make good choices for your life. Thank you for coming and sharing your story.

{*Lazarus did choose to go with the family to Avalon where he lived until 56 AD, at which time, he returned to southern France. He died near St. Boehm in Provence.*}

{*We are introduced next to Joseph of Arimathea, Mary of Bethany's and Lazarus' father, who tells us about his role in bringing the family from Mount Bugarach to Avalon, Britain.*}

— Chapter 13 —
JOSEPH OF ARIMATHEA[21]
Proposed Travel to Avalon
Mount Bugarach, 38 AD

JOSEPH: I am the one you know as Joseph, Anna's oldest son.

CA: Where are you right now?

JOSEPH: I am at the hilltop monastery in the Pyrenees near Mount Bugarach. I have just arrived. This is my sixth extended visit since the family came to live here.

CA: What would you like to share today?

JOSEPH: In the context of time which you call the past — the now which is also the past — I desire to inform you that it is time to leave Mount Bugarach. It is time for us to make our way northward to the shores of northern Gaul and then to set sail to the western coastline called Cornwall in southwest Britain. We will exchange our ocean-going freighting boat for flatboats, as has been my custom for many years, as I have been involved in the tin trade and transport of initiates and supplies. The flatboats will easily carry us through the shallow waters of the Severn estuary to Ynes Witrin, the Isles of Glass, as the Celts speak of what you call Avalon, your present-day Glastonbury.

---

[21] Joseph is Anna's oldest son. Matthias was his father. He played a key role in supporting Yeshua's spiritual training and ministry; as well as providing support to the entire family and Essene community through his financial resources, freighting boats and diplomatic skills. He was a spiritual adept in both the Essene and Druid traditions. He died consciously in Avalon, Britain in 62 AD. See *"Anna, Grandmother of Jesus"* for more details. Joseph is often mentioned for the influential role he plays throughout this sequel. He is spoken of in the New Testament account of Yeshua's crucifixion and burial.

CA: What alerted you at this time?

JOSEPH: There is concern for the safety of the children. There have been some troubling experiences occurring in Rome and other places throughout Gaul among the other followers who call themselves disciples of Yeshua. That is, let us say, many of them are disciples in name only because what they say and what they do are very different. There are many factions. And more factions are arising at an alarming rate. There is increasing zealousness among those who have not been adequately trained to control their emotional and mental states. There is social unrest and injustice. The Emperor Caligula is looking for any excuse to meet out severe persecution. In fact, terrible suffering at his hand has already been reported.

As you know, my sister, Mary Anna, has been expressing a great determination to go to Rome. She wants to see if she can turn divisive hearts back to the simple loving path Yeshua and she have always taught. She will come with us to Britain for a short visit. I have recently promised her that I will assist her passage to Rome and Ephesus, if that is what she is still determined to do.

She greatly desires to do what she can to bring peace and to see her other children whose safety gives her very real concern. I am doing what I can to get messages to Yeshua's brothers in Jerusalem and Galilee so they can meet with their mother in Ephesus, if at all possible. There have been threats on the lives of others of us who chose to remain in Palestine.

Actual persecution has come upon the followers of my nephew, James *(Yeshua's brother)*, Peter, Andrew, my nephews John *(Zebedee)* and James *(Zebedee)* in Jerusalem. We hear that Paul of Tarsus has turned away from persecuting us to evangelizing his understanding of Yeshua's teachings and making them easy for non-Jewish people to embrace. This creates more tension and division. Sadly, most of these brethren seem to be intent on organizing Yeshua's teachings into a doctrine and religion. Even James' *(Yeshua's brother)* more conservative and orthodox leanings are creating division and this greatly grieves his mother *(Mary Anna)*. But these self-appointed apostles, as they call themselves, are like wolves in sheep's clothing. Those who follow them are easily turned by any buffeting wind and they are so laden with fear they cannot observe calm reason.

The brethren in Jerusalem know of our whereabouts. As you know, Nathaniel and some of the brethren of Bugarach were killed earlier this year. I am very concerned for my daughters and grandchildren and all of my extended family.

I am come now, for it is my calling to be a guardian and protector of this family. I can see that it is time to take my loved ones to safety in Britain. I know of no people zealously practicing orthodox Mosaic Law in the regions surrounding Avalon who would deem our way as heretical. There are those of Hebrew descent, such as my brothers, Andrew, Josephus and Noah, but all these are integrating our more mystical practices with Druid spirituality. There are no Roman soldiers in Britain according to my latest reports. Julius Caesar's earlier attempt to conquer Britain was met with failure and he turned tail back to Rome. Our Celtic tribesmen and warriors could not be vanquished. We do not know when next the Romans will attempt another siege and this time take Britain as their prize. And, woe be to us all when they take us by force in order to salve their wounded pride and enrich their coffers.

It is not a matter of "if" the Romans will invade Britain, but "when." Even so, when that time comes, it may take years before they make inroads into Avalon. This is because they will be preoccupied with securing the southeastern region and I know the ferocity of my Celtic brothers when it comes to defending this fair land and her people. But until that dark day comes, we can meet out a measure of peace and well-being in Britain's West Country. There are peace-loving people who call Avalon home. And more importantly, there is a well-established Essene-Druid community already there. As a place of learning and as a mystery school, it has attained some stature over the years since my brothers have been its stewards. My mother agrees that this is the best time to depart even though we are in the midst of the fall season and there may be serious storms threatening our passage over the Channel.

CA: Who goes with you?

JOSEPH OF ARIMATHEA

JOSEPH: Most of those who came with us on the boat to Gaul. My daughter Lois Salome will stay here. Her husband, Daniel, died within a year of our coming to Bugarach. Several years ago she married a good man of noble stature and means in Narbo Martius. Aonghas promises to be someone I can entrust my fleet of boats should I find myself no longer capable of being their captain and a minister of trade. There are several brothers from Mount Bugarach who will come with us. Some will stay in Britain for awhile but then they will return to Mount Bugarach or go to other destinations, as they are guided. There has long been an exchange between Avalon and the Essene communities scattered about the Great Sea.

We make haste. It is rumored that there are ones we cannot trust who know about my boats in the harbor at Narbo Martius, so we will not go there. We will go north on the land route and Aonghas will sail two boats with trade goods and supplies. On earlier occasions when there was risk going by sea, I escorted initiates along this same route. We have our strategic places of refuge and various forms of conveyance made available to us. We have a network that is being very carefully organized, because we know that there will be ongoing unrest within Gaul and we must be prepared to flee whenever necessary. We can take flight in a moments notice. So we have taken everything from the storehouses that will sustain us for several weeks. We are very mobile.

Some of the brethren and sisters along our route are receiving additional training in various kinds of secrecy and reconnaissance protocol. We have had a period of time when there has been relative peace without the need for so much caution. But now it feels like the air crackles with an electrical current that causes our hair to stand on end. We can't allow ourselves to completely rest. We have to be awake, vigilant and at the ready.

CA: This training in various kinds of secrecy and reconnaissance protocol - were the secret codes verbal, visual or a method of touch?

JOSEPH: All of those.

CA: What happens next?

151

JOSEPH: We do not require much commentary on the trek north, other than to say we will go west toward the Atlantic Ocean and then proceed to the northwest coast of Gaul (*Brittany*). There are several locations where I have access, by agreement with those who are fishermen and freighters, to use boats to cross the Great Channel. We will cross an expanse of water; stopping briefly at the Channel Island you call Guernsey, then around the coastline of Britain's Land's End and the Cornwall coastline. We proceed finally to the Severn estuary and Avalon, as I described earlier.

I think you will be very glad to meet my brothers and others who live in Avalon whose voices will be heard. There are more mysteries to be revealed. It will be a very edifying journey for those of us witnessing from this side of the physical veil. Our stories will also be edifying for you, where you find yourselves today. I welcome those who come on this journey of words. I welcome those who know how to travel the pathways of light. Then we can progress together into our unfolding story in much the same way as the family and I journeyed to Avalon long ago.

I am glad to have an opportunity to bring words that carry something of my essence and my point of view, as one representing the male gender and the masculine perspective.

CA: Thank you very much for coming forth and sharing your wisdom and your voice. Is there anything else you wish to share?

JOSEPH: Thank you for so graciously receiving me. No, there is nothing more at this time. Fare thee well until we meet again.

{*We proceed to PART 2, in which Mary Anna (Mother Mary) travels to Rome, Ephesus and India with Myriam of Tyana. Other people who were integral to her travels during this time also share their stories.*}

PART II

The Suppression of the Feminine Voice

ROME (Italy)

EPHESUS & TYANA (Turkey)

39 – 45 AD

— Chapter 14 —
MOTHER MARY (MARY ANNA)
Rome, Italy, autumn, 39 AD

MOTHER MARY (*Mary Anna*): I am walking down a city street – a cobblestone street.
CATHERINE ANN (*Henceforth: CA*): What city are you in?
MOTHER MARY: I am in the large city you call Rome.
CA: And what is your purpose for being in Rome?
MOTHER MARY: I am hoping to talk with the brethren. My heart feels heavy with concern. I am very desirous that the brethren find a place in their hearts for what I might say. The discord that is occurring among Yeshua's followers troubles me. There is so much noise. There are so many people......
CA: And who is accompanying you?
MOTHER MARY: My son, John Mark (*15 years old*), and my daughter, Ruth (*34 years old*). There are others among my family: my brother, Joseph of Arimathea; Myriam of Tyana; Philip and his wife, Sara, who is my niece. There are several other brothers and sisters I have known in the past from our days in Palestine. It is not necessary to name them. There are some of the brothers from Mount Bugarach.
CA: Where are you headed at the moment?
MOTHER MARY: To find the company of brothers and sisters we knew in Judea and Galilee. They are abiding in this city for a time. They come and go throughout the lands bordering the Great Sea.
CA: Do you know where to find them?
MOTHER MARY: I do not know myself, but we have Joseph and Philip who know how to contact them by sending messages through trusted runners. They know certain passwords

MOTHER MARY

and other ways of secretly signaling our presence. I am confident that we will find one another.

CA: What is weighing most heavily on your heart?

MOTHER MARY: I have continued to hear that some of our beloved brothers and sisters have lost their lives. There continues to be arguing amongst my son's (*Yeshua's*) followers, even more than when I was with them in Jerusalem. There are so many who are arguing needlessly. It grieves me to have my family so at odds with one another and with my son's simple message of loving-kindness. When he was openly traveling with us, many felt a truth within his words. We could feel a deep peace within our hearts. His message was intended to be a simple and direct passage to greater love and peace for all people.

But now that he is no longer as accessible as he used to be, there are ones among us who are having difficulty interpreting and living his words. They are wondering how to share his message and the story of his life. Who should lead? What should be taught? What seems to be emerging with the passing of time is the opposite of what we intended. This is bitter for me.

I don't know if they will listen, but I feel compelled to do something. I have come a great distance and now I am in a very strange place which is contrary to my way of being. I desire to be in non-judgment, but it goes against my grain to be here. The dreadful noise and constant movement impacts my nerves and my constitution. I must practice abiding in calmness and compassion with great concentration, while breathing very consciously to keep my heart open to all that I am experiencing. I know in the Oneness there is no difference between what is within me and what I perceive to be outside. As I rest calmly in a sense of spaciousness in my mind, I experience the all-pervading Peace.

CA: Is this your first time in Rome?

MOTHER MARY: Yes. I am desirous of giving my messages and departing as soon as possible. There are others of the brethren who are scattered, doing what they feel they must do. I feel a desire to embrace them, to touch them with my love and to see if they will change the direction they seem to be taking.

ANNA, THE VOICE OF THE MAGDALENES

My nerves are very much on edge. I don't fear for my life. I have faced that fear in my training since I was a young girl. I know the greater Truth that removes death's sting. I simply desire to accomplish what is mine to do with my mother's love. I desire to bring peace to my children. As I look ahead into my children's future, I am troubled; not just in regard to the family of my loins, but in regard to the greater family of this Earth. I don't know if I can make any difference, but I must try. The Father/Mother of Life walks with me and gives me strength. For this I am thankful. There are some who have advised me against this journey. . They say it is futile and dangerous, but I must follow my heart and do whatever I can.

There is a brother and sister approaching us now. They embrace and kiss me in the way that lets me know they are also Essenes. The brother places his hand in the crook of my right arm and the sister takes my other arm. I can feel their great loving strength. I am thankful for the renewed vitality I feel coming into my body as we are led down many narrow streets. There is the press of large milling crowds as we move along. The air is filled with smoke from burning fires; the kinds of fire that are used for burning refuse and torches and cooking food. My senses are bombarded. The noise gets louder the more we penetrate into the inner city. The deafening sounds seem to be coming from everywhere.

We are now going through a heavy gate. It is much quieter on the other side and I am thankful. There are trees, small gardens and plantings of flowers. We climb many steps. As I go up, I have a view of the buildings the proud city-dwelling Romans have built. These monuments are quite extraordinary. The architects' and engineers' handicraft is remarkable. Looking from a distance, where it is more peaceful, I can see that this city is truly amazing. I can see the great palaces where the Emperor Caligula and his many attendants live. There are temples arrayed on the hilltops. There is a kind of beauty in it all – but, as you know, I prefer the simple and unpretentious grandeur of Nature.

My guides encourage me to not linger and I am nudged to continue up the steps. There are lovely trees filled with songbirds. I am feeling better. As we go through a much smaller gate, I feel a gentle hush. It feels like the other more familiar sanctuaries and monasteries I have known. I am glad that quiet places like this can be found in the tumult of great cities; even so, in the midst of great chaos, peace is always to be found within the sanctuary of a calm mind.

We go through a low door. Even, I, who am quite short, have to bend down just a little. There are some steps descending into the darkness. There are several torches which give us light. It's smoky. I cover my face with my shawl. I can hear a little water dripping. I smell dankness, mold and sewage. There are places where there are no steps in this network of tunnels. But then there are more steps to climb or descend, as we continue our way up and down, right and left, as if passing through a labyrinth. I trust that we are being led aright and we will safely find our way out of the city when it is time to leave.

CA: How are you feeling about this in this moment?

MOTHER MARY: A little nervous, but again, I am able to align my fears with my breath and with my inner vision. I can see what is before me clearly enough to place one foot in front of the other with some confidence. I can feel the people who are awaiting me. Some feel welcoming and others feel resistant to my coming. I sense a kind of shame and agitation within them. We go through yet another gate made of iron. The hinges are rusty. I don't like how it sounds when it opens and closes. It reminds me of some of the underground passageways in Jerusalem and Egypt. We are now in a long tunnel that is going slightly down. There are rivulets of water underfoot.

CA: Is it still difficult to breathe?

MOTHER MARY: Not so much; there is more fresh air. The passageway is quite narrow now and we must walk single file. We proceed up a few steps and I can see a light ahead coming from under a door. After one of the brothers knocks, using a secret code, the door opens from the inside. I am inside a large vestibule that leads to a much larger room. There are no windows that I can see at this point. My eyes are growing accustomed to the difference in light. There are candles and oil lamps illuminating the space around us.

CA: Is this where the people are who have been awaiting you?

MOTHER MARY: Yes. But as I look about, I do not see any familiar faces; the ones I thought I would be seeing are not here. Perhaps we will be meeting later.

CA: How many people, other than your party, are assembled here?

MOTHER MARY: I would say there are less than two dozen. Some are in the shadows. It is difficult to be certain right now exactly how many there are.

CA: Are they all men?

MOTHER MARY: No, there are men, women and several children. I feel a little chill now – perhaps it is just my nerves.

CA: What happens next?

MOTHER MARY: I am given a seat and some fresh water to drink. Bread, cheeses, figs and other fruit are served. Several of the sisters beckon me to eat, relax and rest a bit. The brothers and sisters with me are likewise given sup. No one seems to be surprised by our arrival. They have been waiting – perhaps a long time.

CA: Can you tell me how many years this is after Yeshua's resurrection?

MOTHER MARY: I would say about nine years. I have been told that the old Emperor Tiberius has been replaced by a very cruel man called Caligula. I do not want to speak of the great suffering this man has caused. He is one of the main reasons we must be so careful. *(Sigh)*

CA: Now you are eating....

MOTHER MARY: It feels good to be seated and to have a little refreshment. I am especially appreciating the quiet stillness. I can feel love coming toward me from those who are gathered. The opposition I felt earlier must be held by other people who are not in this room. These brothers and sisters seem very reserved. This surprises me since I feel so much energy coming from their hearts. After I eat and have more strength in my legs, I stand up. We all choose to be in silence as I go now to each dear soul.

I place my hands on the shoulders of each one in front of me. I look deeply into their eyes and into their souls where I can feel of their hearts. I hear their thoughts. I can sense many are in awe of me, or they are experiencing a kind of innocent disbelief. I suppose it is like a child who desires something for a long time and has almost given up having it, and then all of a sudden there it is. My sense is that it's like that for these precious ones as they behold me. I think they might have thought they would never be with the mother of Yeshua their beloved Teacher of Righteousness, for whom they have come to have so much reverence.

I realize they have been heavily influenced by the stories that are circulating, in which my son is portrayed as a deified being. Because they view Yeshua in this way, it feels like they are giving me more energy than I deserve to receive. I wish them to know we are all equal in God's eyes. I desire to assist them to know the simple truths so that they can give themselves and each other the same love they are giving me. Can we simply love each other as our loving Father-Mother Creator loves us; no one above another?

It concerns me that this misplaced devotion comes to my son and me to the extent that it does. I can see this is one reason why there are increasing disputes and differences of interpretation of Yeshua's teachings. As I look more deeply, the concerns are justified that I have about some of the brethren's motivations. I can see that over time there will be those who would take advantage of the simple hearts who want to believe that Yeshua is a god with the power to save them from themselves – to somehow miraculously remove the effects of their karmas. Those who seek power, in the years to come, will preach sayings that give me cause to grieve *(Tears)*. I have heard these stories and now I see for myself that it is so.

It is unfortunate that there is so much ignorance and misunderstanding about the great mystery teachings, such as those of Osiris, Isis and Horus; which form the basis of our work as Magdalenes. Often that which was intended to remain as parable and metaphor is taken literally. Yes, we literally enacted the ancient story of "The Dying and Risen King," but it was for the purpose of demonstrating that there is only Life permeating all physical forms. Death and birth are but transitory passages through which the Absolute emanates its unborn/undying Being.

This is why Yeshua emphasized that anyone who loved God and their neighbor with all their mind, might and strength, in Oneness, could directly know the Resurrection and the Life, as he did. But those looking for a savior "King," do not see Yeshua as a reflection of their own Infinite Divinity...instead they deify him as the "King of Kings" – God in flesh. And sadly, they see themselves as unworthy outcasts. There is deity worship all around me in this great city. There is little wonder that, like seeds cast before a mighty wind, all manner of false teachings are spreading.

Breathing deeply, I let go of these concerns and I turn to the love I am feeling for the children. I place my hands on their heads and shoulders. There is so much lightness in their being compared to the adults who carry life's many burdens. I gather them to me and they wrap their arms around me, pressing their heads innocently into my belly and my bosom. I kneel before them and take them into my arms and hold them on my lap. I softly sing a psalm into each one's ear.

It feels so good to have us all feeling relaxed – just being simple and free together. Thank God for the children! Would that we could all have the lightness of being these children do. *(Tears)* My son often said to those in positions of authority, who thought themselves wise and powerful, "You say that you are servants of the Most High. You say you represent Creator's Power and that you can take yourself and others into the Kingdom of God. But I say unto you, unless you become as a child, and are born anew, you cannot enter in." They had such a hard time hearing this teaching.

I can see that, like the Pharisees, some of those who profess to be disciples, have turned their hearts inside out. Their minds have become clouded. They shut out the light that used to shine so brightly. Thankfully, they are not as hardened as I experienced the priests of Jerusalem. But it grieves me that some of the brethren are different from the way they were when we walked together years ago.

I am told that we will be abiding here for several more days awaiting Simon Peter's arrival. I have heard that Paul *(of Tarsus)*, who once persecuted us, may also be coming.[22] We will have places to rest and be comfortable upstairs in this large home that serves as a haven for ones such as us. There is access to the passages that go deep into the earth. We will depart in the same way we came.

CA: Did you counsel with Yeshua about coming here?

MOTHER MARY: Yes, we discussed it on our earlier journeys near Mount Bugarach. He showed me what I might expect. He, too, is concerned about the increasing discord. However, I experienced him as rather detached, not indifferent, but not as attached as I presently seem to be in my emotional body. Perhaps it is a mother's nature to be concerned about the dangers we are all passing through. Yeshua cares, but he knows what is required of us now is that we continue to do our work, as best we can. It is always unwise to be zealously in opposition – indeed, to resist is to feed the flames.

He encourages us to go about our lives and to assist others to know inner peace – where there is an allowance. He says it is important to continue our energetic work with the consciousness grids of the planet; to plant, as it were, seeds to ripen. To look ahead and trust and know that there will come a day when more hearts are ready to awaken. To look deeply into the rich storehouse of our minds and lives and transform any seeds of discord we might find there. To be as a child who is willing to be innocent, simple and free.

He encourages us to let go of our fearful dramas and to put our attention on being engaged in the simplicity of loving and serving one another; and to remember our beloved Mother Earth who grieves for her children even while she quietly and patiently serves them. She judges us not, even when we abuse her. She does not withhold her love and her bounty that sustains her children's souls and bodies. She is our Great Teacher who, like a clear mirror,

---

[22] Although there was the hope of Peter and Paul's coming to Rome, this did not happen because they were detained in Jerusalem.

reflects our folly, and allows us to reap the seeds we sow, until wisdom and self-mastery are attained.

CA: You desire to help in some way?

MOTHER MARY: Yes. Against the counsel of many of my family at Mount Bugarach, I stood determined to bring my mother's heart to these dear ones. So it was that I came. And now, seeing what I see, I am determined to go to those places where the evangelists have been teaching. I feel that I can bring some kind of balance, some kind of light – not to contradict their teachings, but perhaps through my presence, I can assist those who did not walk with Yeshua to understand my son more fully. I hope to also speak with my son, James, whose zealous stubbornness troubles me and Simon Peter and the sons of Zebedee (*James and John*), if possible.

There are others teaching in Asia Minor and I will find them also, if the way is prepared to do so. I confess that sometimes my mind is confused and I pray earnestly for clarity. Perhaps it is my attachment as a mother, who has great concern for her children, which causes a certain amount of confusion in my mind. I will look deeply into this. I will go only if I can be of real assistance. Myriam of Tyana has said she will go with me to Ephesus and beyond, perhaps to her ancestral homeland. Perhaps we will even go on to India. How wonderful it would be to see my beloved son, Joseph (*the Younger*), who was but a young lad when last I was with him! We will proceed only as we are guided. We shall see what is best.[23]

---

[23] Mary Anna did travel with Myriam to Tyana, Turkey and they went on to Varanasi (Benares), India, where she was reunited with her son, Joseph. She had the opportunity to finally embrace grandchildren she had never before seen. She also made pilgrimages to various sacred sites and spent time with masters and saints. Particularly meaningful to her were the months during which she was embraced by the presence of Yeshua's Guru and Friend, Babaji. He took her to the place where her beloved husband, Joseph ben Jacob, had taken his ascension, which still retained its vibration. She returned to Mount Bugarach and Avalon in 48 AD with Myriam. She lived in Avalon and Wales until 56 AD until it was decided that the concern for safety required a dispersion of the family. Mary Anna moved permanently to Ephesus, where she lived the remainder of her life until her conscious death ten years later.

CA: There is much speculation and myth that have grown up around the origins of the Magdalene lore. Can you tell us about the origin of the Black Madonna?

MOTHER MARY: I would like to speak about this mystery. The origins are very ancient. She was a representation of Isis brought forward by the Roman Catholic Church. The Great Mother, Isis, had her origin in Egypt and Atlantis and other civilizations before that. For it is that the Great Mother has always been amongst us, though she is called by many names. She is black because she represents that which lies hidden beyond the veils of unawakened mortal mind. She is black also because she has worn the skin of darkness in Africa, Mesopotamia and India, whose origins go into the far distant past. She, with her brother/soul mate, Osiris, and their son, Horus, had their beginning in Atlantis. They migrated to Egypt and began a powerful civilization. They amassed great spiritual powers and political influence. They initiated many souls into the great mysteries of awakened mind and eternal life. Their teachings flourished into my day. Many of my family still practice these mysteries. Those of us who wear the mantle of the Magdalene also wear the mantle of Isis, for in truth, they are one and the same.

Long ago there was one who wore the mantle of Isis, who was called Sheba. She was most wise and extraordinarily beautiful. She was powerful in the ways of magic; in the ways of healing; and in the ways of inter-dimensional travel. She amassed great wealth and was a queen among her peoples, who lived near the headwaters of the Nile River, in what is called the land of Ethiopia. She was part of an ancient matriarchal lineage. She was very powerful and many obeyed her word as their command.

Solomon the Wise knew of her and desired that she come to his kingdom. He invited Queen Sheba to live with him, for a time, in his beautiful temple and palace which he had erected. He entertained her and created a liaison with her. He lay with her, and conceived with her, a child. When it was time for Sheba to return to her motherland, he sent her away with many riches. These riches included many of the magical talismans he had kept secret within the interior of the temple crypt, which were of the ancients. She took these treasures and her child; and with a great retinue, traveled back to her lands and people. She did not leave her lover empty-handed, however. She left with Solomon one of the greatest treasures of mystical literature, "*The Song of Songs*."

From these two a lineage was born and a genealogy was kept. It was of this seed of Solomon that, in time, through David, and thence, through my loins, came a mingling. My mother has shared about the two Marys who wed my son, Yeshua. Both of these women carry the blood of Sheba. She called herself, Isis, as is common among those initiated into her rites. These Marys both bore daughters. One of these daughters bears the name of our great matriarch, Sarah, Father Abraham's wife, who was initiated in the temples of Isis. In Egypt, she is called Sar'h. (*Consequently, the daughter of Yeshua and Mary of Bethany is called Sar'h*). The other daughter is called Miriam (*daughter of Yeshua and Myriam of Tyana*), named after Moses' mystical sister. Both Sarah and Miriam, in olden time, wore the mantle of Isis.

You have heard of the mysterious representation of the Black Madonna, who is said to be Sar'h, the Egyptian, who is honored in your day, in a crypt of the church at Saintes-Maries-de-la-Mer. It was nearby that our crippled boat landed years ago. It was here that the legend of the Marys was passed on daughter to daughter.

We will now create space for the Marys and others to weave their stories. In this way "The Black Madonna" shall come into the light of awareness.

May love prevail and peace reign in every heart.

I bid you adieu until we embrace again.

CA: And now move forward to the next significant event that happens.

{*Mary Anna's story continues in Part 3, Chapter 27*}

SARA OF MOUNT BUGARACH CONTINUED

— Chapter 15 —

SARA OF MOUNT BUGARACH

Mount Bugarach, 41 AD

(This chapter is a continuation of Chapter 10. Sara is Anna's granddaughter and the daughter of Isaac and Tabitha. She has returned to Mount Bugarach with her husband, Phillip, from Rome, Ephesus and Tyana.)

CATHERINE ANN *(Henceforth: CA)*: Let's move forward now to the next significant or important event in your life.

SARA: *(Sigh.)* Everything is speeding by very quickly, like leaves fluttering in the wind.

CA: We will stop at the appropriate time and place where you can share some event that is important to you.

SARA: *(sighing)* My eyes have seen so many things. I feel much older, wiser and very travel-worn.

CA: Where are you now?

SARA: I am in the part of the countryside where you can behold the Great Sea. It is not far from where our poor boat landed years ago *(Saintes-Maries-de-la-Mer)* when my Grandma Anna and other relatives first came with me to Mount Bugarach from Palestine. I am with my beloved, who is known in your book of scriptures, as Philip. We met not far from the town called Capernaum on the Sea of Galilee. I will say more about our meeting later. We are on our way back to Bugarach from a journey that has lasted almost two years. Perhaps we can go to our home in Bugarach and then continue my story.

CA: Yes, let us return now to your home in Bugarach. Tell me more about your beloved Phillip.

SARA: Yes. Let me fill in more of the story so that you can understand my weariness and who my beloved Phillip is.

165

It was in the autumn of 28 AD that Uncle Joseph (*of Arimathea*) came to Mount Bugarach for one of his visits. He told us Yeshua had returned from India and that he now was prepared as a Teacher of Righteousness to minister unto the people of Galilee and Judea. When he spoke of these things I felt a deep calling within my breast to go and be with my dear cousin (*Yeshua*). My parents and Uncle Joseph told me more about my Light Conception and that the time had come to fulfill the purpose of my birth. I took their sayings to heart and contemplated them during a three day retreat in one of Bugarach's caves. It was made clear to me during these days of silence that I was to go to Galilee.

So it was that a number of the brethren from Mount Bugarach and I went to Jerusalem and Bethany with Uncle Joseph on his return voyage. After enjoying a short rest and the wonderfully nourishing meals prepared by my younger cousin, Martha, we made our way to Mount Carmel in Galilee. I was overjoyed to meet Grandma Anna and Aunt Mary Anna (*Mother Mary*), and many of my relatives I had only heard stories about before. After a time of celebration we went on to the villages along the Great Sea. It was at the seashore, near Capernaum, where I first met Yeshua and his growing inner circle of disciples. Already he was drawing large crowds of people who sat enthralled with his sayings and charismatic presence. I was taken immediately into the inner circle of Magdalene women; in whose company I felt deeply at home.

There are no words that can adequately describe how I felt when I first beheld Yeshua. Without hesitation, I knew him to be the Beloved incarnate. Right away I began calling him, Master, as did the others. When I first beheld Phillip, one of Yeshua's disciples, I knew him to be the beloved for whom my heart had yearned all these long years. With great rejoicing we were betrothed and married, soon after our meeting.

The year and a half I walked with Yeshua and the Magdalenes were filled to overflowing with divine grace. Each day was also encompassed by an aura of terrible majesty – a time of ominous awe. I was intoxicated with Divine Love. I often felt deeply humbled – laid low in humility and compassion for the souls of humankind, whose suffering I have come to know as my own. Although less naïve, I still believe in, as I did in my youth, all that I shared with you earlier. I value all that I told you about myself. This has not changed, but I have also been added upon by much wisdom; and by experiences I earlier could not have known to be possible when I was a child. Where I was once blind, I now see.

There is no need to add to my grandmother's story about our final days with Yeshua and our joys and hardships after his resurrection.[24] You know about our safe delivery upon the shores of southern Gaul and my glad return to my parents and our beautiful Mount Bugarach in the fall of 32 AD.

CA: Thank you for sharing about your part in the Christ drama.

SARA: After some months of much needed rest, I felt a stirring within my heart. I felt a soul desiring to enter my womb. Within the first year of our homecoming, Phillip and I conceived a handsome son, whom we call Justus. Then we conceived our beautiful daughter, Ceres, almost two years later.

We continued to live very happily, at peace with our quiet existence with family within the vale of Mount Bugarach. Grandma Anna and many of the family left Mount Bugarach in the fall of 38 AD and moved to Avalon, Britain. The following year, Aunt Mary Anna (*Mother Mary*), Yeshua's mother, felt compelled to go to Rome to speak with the brethren, and to travel, as well, to the isles of the Aegean Sea. Uncle Joseph brought her and Myriam (*of Tyana*) to Mount Bugarach where Mary Anna reminded us of her intention to go to Rome.[25] She also told us that she desired to return to her birthplace of Ephesus. Her hope was that her older children, who live in Palestine, and perhaps her son, Joseph (*the Younger*), who lives

---

[24] Sara is referring to the sayings of Anna in the book, "Anna, Grandmother of Jesus."

[25] Mary Anna had attempted a journey to Rome in the late spring of 38 AD, but returned to Mount Bugarach because of her concern for Mariam's well-being, after the community received the news that Nathaniel had been killed that winter in Carthage, Africa.

in India, might all come to Ephesus where they could be in reunion with her for a time.

Philip gladly offered to go with Uncle Joseph and Mary Anna to the Imperial City. He also wished to speak with the brethren about the many concerns that were on his mind. I, of course, could not be persuaded to remain in Mount Bugarach, and made arrangements for Justus and Ceres to stay with my aging parents and my sisters.

We have thankfully returned safely to our children and our families.

CA: How old are you now?

SARA: I am approaching my forty-fourth year.

Our bodies are somewhat broken down with all the many months of travel and our spirits are rather heavy with our labors amongst the peoples whose ways are so very different from those of us who live a contemplative life. We were touched by many people, who without ever seeing or hearing Yeshua, believe in him and the teachings which are given to them. The teachings, whether transmitted accurately or embroidered with fantasy and cultural bias, are received by growing multitudes of people – men and women, old and young, rich and poor. We were amazed to find the Gentiles responding in the same way, perhaps with even greater receptivity, than the humble Jews of Palestine.

What especially brightened my days in those foreign lands were the children. It seems that wherever we went there were crowds of children milling all around us. Many of them were orphans with little hope for the future. Yet their innocent, smiling faces spoke of their gladness for a little bread; and our warm arms holding them close. It was a blessing that we had the means to bring a small measure of comfort to so many children, adults and the elderly. This ministry to the outreaches of the northern coastline of the Great Sea and the high plateaus of Cappadocia reminded me of the blessed years of service we gave as Magdalenes with our beloved Master, Yeshua.

A number of us have suffered greatly. We must turn within to find comfort and peace. Finding peace within us, we offer the Great Peace to others, as best we can.

SARA OF MOUNT BUGARACH CONTINUED

CA: What has caused you so much suffering?

SARA: It has been over eleven years since I first left Bugarach to join with Master Yeshua. During this time there have been innocent souls among us whose bodies were stricken by the hands of tyranny. Some have died and some are maimed. (*Sigh*) Those of us who have returned home count each rising of the sun to be a blessing. We continually express gratitude for the simple things of life, for the beauty of Nature and for our precious bodies. Our physical vehicles, which carry us so faithfully on our many journeys, are a gift. They are never to be abused or cursed, as some do. Our bodies deserve to be respected and given great care. In the same way that we care for our bodies, so likewise, do we give our care to our Mother, the Earth; the giver of all blessings.

I am reminded of my youth when I placed beautiful adornments upon my body. I no longer do this to the extent that was once my custom. I still wear the serpent upon my arm and some gold upon my ears. But my ways are much simpler now. My robes are the same as those my brothers and sisters wear. I still dance, especially when I feel particularly heavy with the burdens I carry along my life's journey. At those times, I know I am not alone in my suffering. When we are especially heavy with concern, I invite our community to join with me in glad rejoicing. We exchange our sorrows for lightness of being. Together, we celebrate the fact that Master still lives and walks among us – although, I confess, he is not with us as often as I would prefer. All in all, there is so much for which to give thanks. And so it is that we awaken each morning singing psalms and praises to the Birther of all things.

CA: Is there anything else you wish to share about the wisdom you gained in this life?

SARA: Each soul who resonates with our stories will find what is needed to awaken. Each precious soul will remember what is required for healing. Everyone is seeded with the same Light that awakened us in our time. It is that same Light that has returned us once again to the Earthplane to carry on the Great Work, which shall remain until all suffering ceases.

It is enough for now. I am very thankful for our sisterhood and for this time of awakening which has finally come. What has been sealed up may now come forth. All that I have revealed has been given freely for the blessing of all.

CA: Thank you for your willingness to share.

SARA: I bid all my family to remember that we are collectively held in the arms of the Great Mother. Whether you carry our literal genetic codes or you are the whole of mankind carrying the energetic codes of light – the light codes Master Yeshua and the Magdalenes impressed into the atoms of the earth; you are the Christ child – the luminous, awakened child the Divine Mother is birthing.

It is the Mother Divine who takes you up in her arms and holds you to her nurturing bosom. The stars swirl around her head and she stands upon the mighty serpent of Wisdom. She parts the veil of separation and takes us into Divine Union. She commands whither the Life-force energy goeth and cometh. All Creation is in her care. It is good. I am at peace.

I bid you peace and fond farewell.

— Chapter 16 —
PHILLIP OF BETHSAIDA[26]
Ephesus, Turkey, 40 AD

{*See Sara's words in Chapter 15 for the context in which to better understand what Phillip is sharing.*}

PHILLIP: You may ask me questions.
CATHERINE ANN (*Henceforth: CA*): What is your name?
PHILLIP: I am called Phillip. (*Sara's husband*)
CA: Where are you now, Phillip?
PHILLIP: As I look down, I see great stone steps.
CA: Are you going up or down?
PHILLIP: Up the steps.
CA: And what is your destination?
PHILLIP: I must make haste. I have a message to deliver.
CA: Who are you delivering it to?
PHILLIP: To the brothers and the sisters who abide in Ephesus. I want to make sure that everything is prepared.

I understand there is a messenger waiting for me who can relay my words on to the people who are preparing for our arrival. My wife, Sara, is walking with our Master's mother, Mary Anna; his brothers, Thomas (*also called Thaddeus*), Simon and John Mark; his

---

[26] Phillip is from Bethsaida, a fishing village located on the northern shore of the Sea of Galilee. He spent a number of his early years in training at Mount Carmel where he met and befriended Nathaniel Bartholomew. He was a member of Yeshua's inner circle called "The Twelve." Sara, the daughter of Isaac and Tabitha the Egyptian, is his wife. Phillip accompanied Anna and the family on "the boat without sail or oars" to southern France, where he, with rare exceptions when he traveled, continued to live the remainder of his life. Biblical references: Matt. 10: 3, Mark 3:18, Luke 6: 14, John 1: 43 – 46.

sister, Ruth; and his uncle, Joseph of Arimathea. They are behind me walking with the others who made the journey to Ephesus.

CA: Where have you come from?

PHILLIP: Joseph of Arimathea brought Mary Anna (*Mother Mary*) and Myriam of Tyana from Britain to Mount Bugarach, which is close to the great mountains of southern Gaul. Mary Anna's children, Ruth and John Mark, also came. She left her two younger children, Esther Salome and Matteas in Grandmother Anna's care in Avalon. We have come from Bugarach on a long journey that has taken many months. Fortunately we have had the use of Joseph's freighting boat which has made our travels much easier. We have gone to many different cities within the Roman occupation, including the Imperial City of Rome. We have visited some of the brethren and sisters who walked with us in Palestine. They now abide within the cities and villages that are located upon the many isles of the Great Sea including Ephesus, Antioch and Tarsus. It was in these areas that Simon Peter, Andrew, and John and James ben Zebedee spent a brief time teaching and making contact with some of the congregations. They have since returned to Jerusalem where they choose to spend most of their time.

We have heard stories about how Peter has aligned with Paul of Tarsus who once persecuted us, but is now drawing a large following; especially among the Gentiles. Yeshua's brother, James, remains in Jerusalem fulfilling his many duties which he feels are his responsibility. We hear there are many arguments between Paul and James over fulfilling the Mosaic Law of circumcision. We are looking into the many factions, contentions and disputes that seem to be sprouting like seeds in the springtime.

We have all come together to lend our support to Mary Anna's (*Mother Mary's*) mission to bring peace to the hearts of those who must walk now without Yeshua's close presence. There is much conflict among the brethren because few remain with the ability to hear Master Yeshua's direct oral guidance from those of us to whom he still speaks. There is disbelief that he still lives. Others cling to the rumor that he does live; but hope without direct knowledge, breeds fear and confusion. There is jealousy and distrust of those of us who carefully guard and keep the mysteries of spiritual transmutation from the people who are uninitiated. Unfortunately, there is jealousy and distrust among Yeshua's closest disciples who knew him intimately and witnessed his resurrected body.

Sad to say, there is increasing dispute regarding Yeshua's oral teachings; how to transmit them and how to organize the teachers who are choosing to lead the growing congregations. We have come to bring unity rather than division. We have come to console those who have suffered persecution and the death of loved ones. My beloved friend, Nathaniel, was recently killed and I still grieve his loss. We bear great burdens.

Mary Anna's *(Mother Mary's)* sons, Thomas of Nazareth *(Thaddeus)* and Simon of Cana joined us in Corinth almost four months ago. We have been in Ephesus for several weeks. We have sent word to James of Jerusalem and Jude of Nazareth to join us in Tarsus in a month's time. We hope this can happen before we press on to Tyana. Mary Anna has much concern over James and wishes to embrace and console him with her mother's love.

(Pause)

It is necessary to move to another household in the outskirts of Ephesus.

There is a sense of urgency. We are not sure what the outcome is going to be.

My legs are…..

CA: Is something happening to your legs?

PHILLIP: My legs are cramping. They feel like dead weights because I have been running a long way. I have been climbing many stairs.

We must get to our destination before dark. The house where we can find refuge for the next several nights is located beyond the main city of Ephesus. It is inland, southeast of the city. Now, after climbing to the top of the hill, I can glimpse part of the Great Sea shining in the distance. The large home where we will stay serves a purpose that is kept quite secret. It is the same purpose for which many homes in the communities we have visited serve; to harbor ones such as ourselves.

(*Hushed*) It feels like I am being followed...

CA: Go to the next significant event.

PHILLIP: We are eager to get away from this place. We need assistance to go further east to the lands of Cappadocia and the source of the Indus. Mary Anna and Myriam of Tyana will go to Myriam's birthplace in Cappadocia and then they will go on to the great mountains of northern India where other family members live. Mary Anna desires to see her son Joseph (*also called Joses or Joseph the Younger*). Myriam of Tyana will go on with our Master's mother, so that she can be reunited with her son, Johannes, whom she has not seen since he was a small child. Mary Anna reminds us there are grandchildren she has never seen. They both remind us they have not been with family members who live in these distant places for many years. Sara and I, together with Ruth, will accompany Mary Anna and Myriam to her ancestral village near Tyana, but no further. We will return to Ephesus where we will rendezvous with Joseph of Arimathea, who will take us in his boat back to Mount Bugarach.

CA: How long has it been since we last spoke when you were in Ephesus planning your travel to Tyana?

PHILLIP: It has been almost a month. We have moved to several different households near Ephesus and we are now in Tarsus. Master's brothers, James and Jude recently arrived in Tarsus. Jude's wife, Galeah, and two of his four children, were able to come with him, much to Mary Anna's delight. Mary Anna has spent much time with James in solitude. Sometimes I see that she has been crying and James seems more sober than usual. I pray for them and all of us who feel rather lost without our beloved Captain's steady physical presence to steer our course.

When it is time to travel on to Tyana, James will return to Jerusalem and Jude will go back to Nazareth. Myriam desires us to meet her family in Tyana. We will also go and spend the winter there as the season of cold is coming upon us. She, Mary Anna and their escorts, including our Master's brothers, Thomas, Simon and John Mark will go on to India; but Sara, Ruth and I will return to Ephesus for vernal equinox and the Passover. Our prearranged plan is to meet Joseph of Arimathea there. He will take us back to Mount Bugarach.

I am concerned for Mary Anna's and the others' welfare. We want to make sure all the supplies are gathered and the appropriate guardians are....

CA: Guardians?

PHILLIP: There are men who are wise in the ways of travel to and from the Orient. They know how to outfit our group so that we can travel with greater safety and comfort. They know the roads that pass through here from Egypt and Rome to the exotic lands of upper and lower Asia. (*What are termed the Silk and Spice roads.*)

CA: Do you need guardians because of the threat you are under?

PHILLIP: Yes. With the increasing threats the Roman emperor, Caligula, is making toward us, as well as the persistent animosity we feel from the orthodox Jews, it feels like the high mountains of India will be the safest place where Mary Anna (*Mother Mary*) and Myriam (*of Tyana*) can go now, instead of returning to Britain. Even so, there is still great concern for their safety, and our own, as well. I traveled those long, arduous roads with Yeshua and our small company of disciples before our public ministry in Judea and Galilee. Fortunately, we only suffered minor skirmishes then. I have heard many stories about cruel robbers lying in wait to prey on innocent travelers; not only robbing them, but also taking lives.

As I have said, Ruth, Sara and I will not be going all the way to the great mountains. We will go as far as Tyana and then return to Ephesus. Ruth will remain in Ephesus with relatives while awaiting her mother's return. Sara and I plan to set sail with Joseph to Narbo Martius where we will be supplied with horses and make our way back to Mount Bugarach.

It's been such a long time away from our beloved children, Justus and Ceres.

CA: How long have you been on the journey?

PHILLIP: It feels like we have been uprooted far too long. Great weariness is settling into our minds and bodies. We have been gone more than a year. It is difficult to say with certainty when we will return. We continually surrender our small wills. It may not be as we have planned at all. Often it feels like we are walking blindfolded along a great precipice. At times it seems like we must gather sufficient faith to leap over the edge into thin air. When we least expect it, a major change of direction, happens; and suddenly there we are - taking a leap of faith.

CA: Why does it feel like you have to surrender [aufgeben] your own will?

PHILLIP: It has often been challenging to let go of expectations we have held as we have identified ourselves as being Yeshua's disciples. We never know where our journey with him will lead us – that is, on the physical plane.

Since his resurrection, our lives have been very different than we thought they would be. Sometimes, in the moments when there is much suffering, we experience momentary despair. Thankfully we have each others' support. Together, we remember a greater truth; which is, we are servants of an unchanging, everlasting Truth that lives in us – an unwavering Truth that is all-knowing and all-merciful. Our bodies are nothing, but our soul's Awareness lives on forever. Our small wills and bodies are the servants of Love and Wisdom. These eternal truths are our treasure, which we lay up during our lives. It is love and wisdom which continue beyond the physical veils. When our bodies and minds surrender to our Infinite potential beyond our thoughts, feelings, sensations and perceptions, which are of our bodies and this physical world, we often experience miracles unfolding before our very eyes. Knowing this Truth makes surrendering our wills much easier.

CA: Yes, thank you Phillip for sharing your wisdom. Now, go forward to the next significant event in your life.

PHILLIP: We are preparing to leave. I am told we will meet some important people in several more days.

CA: Are you still in Ephesus or are you on your way east?

PHILLIP: We are on our way east from Tarsus. We are on our way to Tyana and other villages where relatives live in Cappadocia. The warm season is coming to an end. We feel an urgency to move on so that we can be back in Ephesus before spring. We have received word that Joseph of Arimathea will be awaiting us in Ephesus during the time of vernal equinox and the Passover celebration. With each passing week our hearts turn increasingly to our children and our family at Mount Bugarach.

CA: If there is anything more you wish to share about your journey to the east?

PHILLIP: No.

CA: Move on to the next significant or important event in your life.

Mount Bugarach, spring, 49 AD

PHILLIP: Yeshua is here. It's always a joy when he is with us.

CA: Is this a surprise visit?

PHILLIP: He's been with us for several days. In this now moment, the fact that he is here is not a surprise. But yes, usually it is a surprise when he first comes, because he usually does not announce his coming in advance.

CA: Where are you now?

PHILLIP: I am in Mount Bugarach. Yeshua has come. He invites us to go with him to a nearby cave where we will fast and pray together. We are accustomed to doing this when he comes among us.

CA: Who does he take with him?

PHILLIP: His beloved mother, Mary Anna, and his wife, Myriam of Tyana, who have recently returned from India. Myriam has her youngest son, Johannes, with her. Johannes recently came to Mount Bugarach after a brief time of visiting relatives and several temples in Egypt. He and his wives will be returning to Egypt in a few weeks and Joseph of Arimathea is readying his boats to take Mary Anna, John Mark and Myriam back to Britain as soon as possible. It has been ten long years that they have been away from their other children. They will be embracing many changes, I am certain of that!

CA: Is the family based mostly in Bugarach or in Britain at this time?

PHILLIP: More in Britain.

CA: Is there more you wish to share about Yeshua's visit?
PHILLIP: No, not at this time.
CA: Please move forward to the next important event you wish to share.

Mount Bugarach, early spring, 55 AD

{*We have progressed much further in the story. Phillip's following account may be read as a kind of preview of what is coming or you may wish to proceed to the next chapter and then return to Phillip after reading "The Great Gathering" in Part 4, Chapter 26.*}

PHILLIP: Yeshua is visiting us again. But this time his visit is very brief.
CA: What is significant about this particular visit?
PHILLIP: He is telling us there is to be a conclave of the Great Ones in less than three month's time and we are invited to come. People will be coming from many places and it would be wise for us to begin to prepare the way now for our long journey.
CA: Where is the conclave going to take place?
PHILLIP: It will be held in a land that is located in the north of Britain.[27] I have not been there. I am looking forward to going; it will be a blessing and honor to be in the presence of Great Ones.
CA: Who will be attending the conclave in northern Britain?
PHILLIP: There will be ones who are living masters coming from many different places. They were not with Yeshua during the time of the great ministry when I was with him. On a number of occasions; however, I have met such ones who have won mastery of the physical plane. Many of these masters live in the high mountains of India. Perhaps some of these Great Ones will be coming.
During our time in India (25 – 27 AD), before the years of Master's outward ministry (28 – 30 AD), my beloved Sara and I had opportunities to visit the sanctuaries and retreats of the masters.

---

[27] Phillip is speaking about 'The Great Gathering' held in Fortingall, Scotland in the summer of 55 AD. See Part 4 for more information.

There are ones of us who have been issued a call to attend "The Great Gathering," as we all have come to call it. I feel honored. It is a great privilege to be one who still has so much human focus to enter into such a conclave as this one promises to be. I am not given the names, nor can I see with my inner vision, those who will come. But I can feel the energies that will be present for this great gathering of higher consciousness. It will be very powerful. We must put everything in order within our own selves and also issue invitations to other initiates we know, whom we feel guided to bring with us.

CA: Is there more you wish to share?

PHILLIP: My way is to not speak much. My way is more of keeping records of my contemplations and memories.

CA: Is that your primary focus?

PHILLIP: No, it is not my primary focus. As with all the men who are Magdalenes, my primary responsibility is first of all to awaken my soul to the Infinite Light beyond birth and death; and secondly, to protect and support the Magdalene women and our children within our Essene communities.

(Claire's legs are involuntarily jerking and her speech becomes hoarse and slow.)

You may wonder why my speech is so slow and my legs are twitching now. I have a desire to explain if you wish me to speak about this.

CA: Yes, I was wondering. Please explain.

PHILLIP: This body was damaged in an experience I had on one of my travels to the great mountain valleys of eastern Gaul.[28]

(Pause)

I will share briefly what happened as I was on my way back home to Bugarach.

(Pause)

---

[28] An Essene monastic outpost had been established decades earlier near the present-day border of France and Switzerland. Among others, Mary Anna's daughter, Ruth, moved there in 41 AD after being in Ephesus while her mother was away in India.

There were four other brothers on this journey. Thankfully, none of the women were with us. We were overtaken by some Roman civilians and native Celts. We were fortunate to have our lives spared, though we did suffer. Hot iron fagots were applied to my body, particularly to my legs. They were going to cut out my eyes, but thank God, I still have vision, although my face is scarred.

CA: Know that you are safe, here in this conversation, no longer feeling the pain, but just observing this scene. Why were they doing this to you?

PHILLIP: They tried to force us to tell them where they could find Yeshua.

CA: What were their intentions toward Yeshua if they found him?

PHILLIP: To do to him what they were doing to us – only worse. They wanted to see if the stories about Yeshua, being a god, were true. They had heard that he had died and now he lived. They wanted to see if he had the power to stop them or if they crucified him, would he save himself and continue to live. If he could not do these things, then they could prove he was human after all; and all the stories about him were false. They were divided among themselves – some wanted to believe Yeshua was a god preparing everyone for the "end times" and others wanted to prove he was a false prophet.

CA: What were the stories about the end times?

PHILLIP: The stories said there would be massive destruction and upheavals of the earth; and that the wicked would be slain and left to die and rot. They would suffer endless torment. But if you believed Yeshua was God then you would be saved in a heaven world.

CA: Were the stories of "the end times" new to this time period or have there always been tales of end times?

PHILLIP: Yes, there have been prophecies of "the end days" spoken of for many generations. Such sayings are a way of controlling people. At best, seers who can see the future, give us warnings that can help us make different choices about our lives. But, at this time, there seems to be a great apocalyptic fervor because the effects of the Roman occupations are becoming so difficult for so many people. This is especially true for those people who do not conform to the Roman laws and the arbitrary whims of local magistrates and tax collectors. Even those who are completely innocent are taken into their circuses and prisons. They are tortured and thrown to the lions. Crucifixion is still used as a deterrent.

Thankfully, this did not happen to us. I am not certain why the ones who attacked us did not continue their abuses or throw us in prison or sell us as slaves. They simply stopped and ran away. Many of us believe Yeshua somehow intervened; but I cannot say for certain. There are others, such as my dear companion, Nathaniel, and his son, Benjamin,[29] whose lives were not spared. This is a mystery best left unsolved by the analytical mind. There is more to karma than our minds can understand. As Yeshua advised us, "Judge not, lest ye be judged." "Forgive those who falsely accuse and persecute you, for they know not what they do."

CA: Thank you for explaining. Is there anything more you would like to say at this time?

PHILLIP: No, there is nothing more for now.

CA: Thank you for coming, Phillip.

PHILLIP: Thank you for listening and being so patient.

---

[29] Benjamin was Nathaniel and Mariam's son, who, at only sixteen years of age in 31 AD, was stoned to death (*together with others*) by a mob led by Saul of Tarsus (*Paul*).

— Chapter 17 —
JOHANNES

(Youngest Son of Yeshua & Myriam of Tyana, Age 22)
Cappadocia, Turkey, 48 AD

CATHERINE ANN (*Henceforth: CA*): Who is speaking now?

JOHANNES: I am one of the sons of Myriam, one of the Magdalenes, as you know her. I am called Johannes. You didn't think to call my name because you did not know me – or only very peripherally.

CA: No, I did not think to call your name.

JOHANNES: That is all right. My coming is just a little surprise.

CA: You are the son of Yeshua and Myriam of Tyana, the son who stayed in India?

JOHANNES: Yes, I lived in India until now. I am presently 22 years of age. I remained in the household (*in Varanasi*) of my father's brother, Joseph (*the Younger or Joses*), until my mother and Grandmother Mary Anna came. They stayed in India for almost seven years. I could say many things about our travels and adventures together; how we met with the Great Ones who live in the Indus Valley and the high mountains; how my father came and the rejoicing we all experienced. But I am told that telling is not for me to share.

Now we are traveling westward toward the Great Sea and beyond. We joined a caravan to make our trek across the great wastelands. It is a long journey with many stops along the way. We are visiting my mother's family in Tyana for an extended time. They have never met me and there is much celebration.

CA: Who is traveling with you?

JOHANNES: My father's mother – my grandmother, Mary Anna (*Mother Mary*), and my mother, Myriam, and my father's brothers Thomas, Simon and John Mark, and my two consorts, whom I now call Ruth and Salome, instead of their Sanskrit names. My wives are sisters and they are quite lovely. We were married less than a year ago and we have not borne children yet. It was an arranged marriage, which is often practiced within the Brahman caste. Although we do not condone such control and divisiveness among people, it was decided by Uncle Joseph (*Yeshua's brother*) and his father-in-law, that such a marriage, among royal bloodlines, would be best for us and coming generations.

CA: Your parents are thought of as being of a royal lineage?
JOHANNES: Yes.
CA: Tell me more about your journey.
JOHANNES: I have met many very interesting people all along our route. Here in Cappadocia, I am meeting some very wise teachers and sages who used to live in the high Himalayas. There is a wonderful exchange that goes back and forth between these two regions. I like them a great deal. It is good to be reunited with several teachers I once knew when I was a lad. Not far from here, there is a large cave which is used as a library. It is filled with ancient records and artifacts of all kinds, shapes, and sizes. Grandmother Mary Anna (*Mother Mary*) and my mother have told me about my great-grandmother, Anna, and how much she would have enjoyed seeing these treasures. I am very much looking forward to meeting her, and learning from her, as my father did.

There was quite an extraordinary teacher who joined us on our journey through the country you presently call Afghanistan. We had stopped to rest and there was time to share our common interests and acquaintances. Making certain that we were of equal spiritual understanding, he told us that he had been in deep retreat with several beloved masters. It turned out that one of these was my father! He said he had also had a very empowering experience with the one we call Mahavatar Babaji. He did not openly say this; for to do so would not be honoring or wise, but he said enough for those of us who know Babaji and my father, to recognize who it is to whom he gives so much reverence. Without saying more, we joined our new friend in a ritual of paying homage to these beloved masters.

Grandmother Mary Anna and my mother had an opportunity to be with Babaji for almost six months. I went with them but I was not sufficiently prepared to meet the Master face to face. I did have visitations with Babaji on the inner planes. I also had the good fortune to visit the site where my father's father, Joseph ben Jacob, took his ascension. The stones within the cave rang with his vibration. And most dear to me, I must confess, were the weeks, here and there, that my father spent alone with me during the almost 23 years I lived in India.

Those times with my father, especially after his resurrection, were a turning point for me in my spiritual life. Over the years, I had increasingly become preoccupied with my medical studies and personal affairs. But in saying this, please let me reassure you I was not completely overtaken with the mundane world. I did immerse myself for long periods with the great teachings of many masters (*both Hindi and Buddhist*) and I participated in extended meditation retreats in complete solitude.

This prepared me for my more recent experiences with my father. Remembering his clear Light still assists me to know the True Self, whom I seek to reveal and express day by day. After having those glimpses of the Absolute, I experience my often absent father, more as a Great Soul and less as a father. Now I am able to see my path with greater clarity. There are times I miss my father's physical presence; but I also I know he is always with me in spirit.

CA: You said an extraordinary teacher joined you. Can you say more about him?

JOHANNES: As we shared our family connections, it turned out that this extraordinary teacher is a relative of my mother. They are cousins, which makes him my cousin, also. He is called Apollonius of Tyana. He was born several years after my father was born.

CA: Did he ever encounter your father?

JOHANNES: Yes. They had encounters in India and in the high Himalayas.

CA: Did they spend time together?

JOHANNES: Yes, as I said, they spent time with beloved Master Babaji.

CA: They were in training together?

JOHANNES: Yes. Let's pause for a moment, so we can feel the energy of their combined Presence.......... (*Pause*)

CA: Thank you. It is good to pause and actually have an experience of what you are telling me. Did Mary of Bethany and your mother have this same training?

JOHANNES: My mother (*Myriam of Tyana*), indeed, had training with the masters of India and the Himalayas, whereas Mary of Bethany had only relatively brief encounters with them when she came to India with my father before the great ministry. Most of Mary of Bethany's training was with the Essenes at Mount Carmel. She also passed through initiations with the Pythagorean and Osirian Alchemists and the Essene-Therapeutae of Egypt. My mother spent a relatively short time with the Essenes when she was young – before she and Father met. I desire to go to Mount Carmel and Egypt. I don't know if that will occur on this journey or not.

CA: You mentioned you had some experiences and exposure to the spiritual masters and teachings in the land of the Indus Valley. Please tell me more.

JOHANNES: For reasons I do not fully understand, my father, mother and siblings went back to Galilee to begin the great ministry and I was given into the care of my uncle, Joseph (*the Younger*). I was only one and a half years old at the time. Perhaps they thought I was too young for the arduous journey and the unsettled circumstances they knew were ahead. As the years passed, I became reconciled and resisted moving away from the only home I knew.

Like many of my family, I have been through many initiations over the years of my short life. When I was a youth I was trained in the ways of my father and my mother. I think I was motivated to be diligent in the practices, in part, so I could spend more time with them...that somehow by immersing myself as a good student, they would come back to India. I hoped they, and my older siblings, would stay with me instead of being so far away. We received a message that told us they had gone far to the mountains of the West.

Quite often, over the years, I was consoled with lucid dreams in which my mother came and comforted me. And, as I have said, Father appeared out of the ethers and walked and sat for hours with me. During these past years that my mother has been with me, he has also been with me much more than he used to be. This has been a great joy and healing.

But, I must confess, there is still some residue of feeling anxious about being abandoned; toward which I continue to bring compassion to myself and others who are afflicted by this strong emotion.

As I look back on how I have held the thought, "It was I who chose to stay with family members in India," it was no doubt to remove the sting of feeling abandoned. In truth, of course, since I was only a child when they left, it was my parents and Uncle Joseph who really made that choice for me. However, I am certain Father and Mother left me with great reluctance. When it was time for them to leave India and return to Galilee, they lovingly communicated with me in such a way that I did not feel abandoned. I was too young to really understand. But somehow, I knew they would return for me when the time was right.

As it turned out, it was for the best that I stayed in India. I can see that my parents understood both my independent nature and also my need for stability. I believe they also could see that India and the master teachers which abound everywhere would give me the best possible training. At a very young age, I began to study Ayurvedic medicine. The healing arts were to be my calling in life. I knew Uncle Joseph (*the Younger*) also had this knowing as a boy. He became my trusted and beloved mentor. I had the very best schooling a young, ambitious young man can receive in both my spiritual life and in my career. Thankfully, I have the wisdom to practice integrating both endeavors, as one and the same.

Besides my medical studies, I spent a full year in pilgrimage to sacred temples and shrines. I received the blessings of beloved teachers who follow both Krishna and Gautama Buddha. I spent much time in hermitage. I walked far up into the mountains and I also wandered in the hot, humid valleys of the Ganges. I gladly put away my clothing and exchanged my comfortable life for a beggar's bowl and a loin cloth; leaving my hair uncut and my heart filled full. Even though I had a natural affinity for such utter simplicity; I also knew my path included holding a position of influence so that I could be of service to others who walk many different paths.

CA: Were you alone or did you meet with others?

JOHANNES: I was with others on occasion, but I was alone for longer periods. There was a time, shortly before I came back to my studies, in which I was sealed up in a cave in the same way that my father and mothers have been. I have many more initiations yet to experience. That is why I desire to go on this journey with my grandmother (*Mary Anna*), to visit those places she and my parents know so well. Perhaps I will go to Egypt and Britain. I desire to walk in my father's footsteps as best I can. I also desire to be with my siblings, Joses Simeon, Jude (*half-brother*) and Miriam, who live in Britain. They are much older than me. I do not remember them. It will be a blessing to have our family all together.

CA: Can you share more about your Uncle Joseph (*the Younger*), your father's brother, as your mentor?

JOHANNES: He is a very skilled doctor. He prepared me for advanced courses in which all manner of medicine are studied. I was shown how the body, the mind and the soul are inseparable from one another – how expanded brain states; light, sound and color; sacred geometric patterns; earth and cosmic energies; nutrition, conscious breathing, life-force cultivation, exercise, energy cycles and harmonious thoughts all contribute to well-being. I will miss Uncle Joseph and his large family very much.

My grandmother was so overjoyed to be reunited with Joseph. It had been many, many years since Mary Anna (*Mother Mary*) let him go away with my father and his other brother, called James. She had seen Joseph on the inner planes, but this was the first time to share a physical embrace in many years. She confided that although she missed him terribly, and was concerned for his welfare during his long absence, she was glad he was removed from the drama in which my father and mother and so many others of the family were involved. She was so happy to see her large flock of grandchildren. She was so filled with joy to embrace me and to celebrate my recent marriage to Ruth and Salome. I think of her as a true saint; an embodiment of the Divine Mother.

CA: Do you also think of your mother (*Myriam of Tyana*) as being a saint, an embodiment of the Divine Mother in the same way you do your grandmother, Mary Anna?

JOHHANES: I feel that my mother possesses a greatness of spirit and a sweetness of presence. I am thankful for these past years in which we have come to know each other better. (*Pause*) I must confess in this moment, as I contemplate your question, I feel a shadow of grief and anger coming over my mind. I see that the feelings I have denied about being abandoned by my mother, as I have perceived it, are causing me to not see her clearly. Thank you for assisting me to bring light to my unacknowledged darkness. I shall take this revelation to heart and bring more healing to my heart and mind. Because I know all time exists in the present moment, and that I can change future outcomes by bringing conscious awareness to any choice, I shall now investigate what I have been shown.

How fortunate that I can now bring a greater love, compassion and honoring to my beloved mother. For it is she, who gave me life in this realm of existence in which there are so many favorable conditions for me to awaken my full potential in this body. Thank you, my sister, for your insight and willingness to bring healing to my soul.

CA: You are welcome, Johannes. Thank you for coming and sharing your story. Please move forward to the next significant event in your life.

{Johannes continues his story in Part 3, Chapter 24}

PART III

THE VOICES OF AVALON

The Druid-Magdalene Voice Emerges

THE ISLES OF AVALON

YNES WITRIN (Glastonbury, England)
&
YNES MON – MONA
(Anglesey, Wales)
38 – 54 AD

— Chapter 18 —
MARTHA OF BETHANY[30]
Avalon, 38 AD

{*The family arrived in Ynes Witrin (The Isles of Glass – Avalon) from Mount Bugarach in the late fall of 38 AD. Martha is with family members celebrating Winter Solstice on the Tor of Avalon.*[31]}

MARTHA: It feels cold! (*Claire is holding her arms, shaking and shivering.*)
CATHERINE ANN (*Henceforth: CA*): Where are you?
MARTHA: I am at the top of the hill that you call the Tor. There is a cold, biting wind whirling small flakes of snow. We are huddled around a fire my father (*Joseph of Arimathea*) has made. We are waiting for the sun to come forth.
CA: Is there a particular reason you are up at the Tor before dawn on this cold morning?
MARTHA: It is Winter Solstice.
CA: Who am I speaking with?
MARTHA: You have asked to speak with Martha, and I am she. It is so cold! The freezing air goes right into my bones. I want to warm up so I can talk clearly. Maybe you can assist me.

---

[30] Martha, born at Bethany in 3 AD, is Anna's granddaughter. She is the daughter of Anna's oldest son, Joseph of Arimathea, and the younger sister of Mary of Bethany and Lazarus. She lived in the large family home Joseph of Arimathea built for his second wife and Martha's mother, Mary of Magdala, located in Bethany near Jerusalem and the Mount of Olives. She lived in Bethany before going to France and Britain. She returned to southern France in 56 AD, where she lived the remainder of her life. Biblical references: Luke 10:38-42 and John 11: 1-45, John12: 1-11.

[31] The Tor of Avalon is a prominent landmark located in present-day Glastonbury, Somerset, England.

CA: Is there a need to stay here at this moment or can we move forward to a time when you are inside and warm?

MARTHA: Oh, I would like to go in where it's warm. I don't always enjoy these kinds of rituals. I go because I want to show my support. And sometimes I find there are things to learn.

CA: Whatever it is that you experienced during this ritual you will retain and remember, if it is appropriate to share later. Now move forward in time to a place where you are inside and warm. When you are able to talk comfortably tell me where you are.

MARTHA: I am in my Grandmother Anna's hermitage. Some would call it a hut. Compared to our spacious home in Bethany, I would call it a very humble abode. It's nice and warm here close to the fire, which is burning in the center of a large round room. The fire and oil lamps light up the space; otherwise it would be very dark. There are long flickering shadows dancing on the walls and thatched roof. When I look up to follow the patterns of light and shadow, I see them disappear into the darkness at the top of the pointed ceiling, high overhead. I would never have imagined living in such a place. It is very different from my other home in Bethany. But it is typical of such homes, to be like this, that are made by the people who are native to this land.

CA: And what is the home made out of?

MARTHA: The floor is made of a mixture of flat stones and hard packed earth. Grandmother has covered most of the floor with thick woven rugs made from wool and reeds. The outer wall is a ring of stones supporting a thatched roof. There are large, smooth, erect timbers sunk into the ground encircling the central hearth. These massive oak posts support smaller timbers that radiate out from a central point at the top to the outer ring of stones at the bottom. All this holds the thick reed thatching, which looks like a coned hat.

CA: Is the inside one large room or are there other rooms?

MARTHA: It is one large room with an entry vestibule attached. The great round room serves a number of different purposes. Part of it is used for sleeping; part of it is for the taking and preparing of meals; and part of it is for socializing, study and meditation. My grandmother has a little table the boys made for her in the vestibule. Boys – that's what Grandmother calls my uncles Andrew, Josephus and Noah, even though they seem like old men to me. This is where she does her writing. There are many stacks of parchment and papyrus on shelves and other tables. There are a few of her treasured scrolls she brought with her from the old country. And there are other texts my father, the one you call Joseph of Arimathea, brought here during the many years he has journeyed to Avalon from Carmel; and to and from other monasteries bordering the Great Sea.

Along the stone walls are niches and shelves which hold many kinds of storage items, such as dried foods and herbs, olive oil, blankets, oil for the lamps, medicinals, a few plates and bowls and other things. I'm not sure what they are. There are woven baskets and pottery that carry water, household and personal items, and a change of clothing. The hearth is in the center and there is an iron grate over part of it for cooking and the warming of water. But most of the cooking is done elsewhere.

Further up the hillside valley, which lies between the Tor and Chalice Hill[32], is a larger compound where some of the other single women and young girls live. That is where the large communal kitchen and dining room are located. This hearth is just a place where my grandmother can warm up a little soup or an herbal tea for herself and her guests. In this way, the fire also serves the infirm

---

[32] In present-day Glastonbury, Somerset, England, the Tor is the highest natural prominence and Chalice Hill is the next. The Tor has inner chambers, mostly caved in and not opened to the public. This is where Yeshua, as a youth, experienced a profound initiation. The exterior Tor and the "White Spring," at its juncture with Chalice Hill, are still used for ceremonial purposes. The adjacent Chalice Hill received its name from the legend that Joseph of Arimathea brought the chalice used at Yeshua's Last Supper here. Some say it is buried near the "Red Spring" which flows from a deep well on the hillside below the location of Anna's abode. Today, the Chalice Well Gardens National Trust stewards this very sacred place where the Divine Feminine is revered.

or dying who may be in her special care, from time to time. The primary purpose for the fire is mostly to give light and warmth.

At especially cold times, like today, some chilly air comes in through the cracks. If there isn't time to replace the mud wattle, we stuff the little openings with moss or pieces of cloth that are no longer wearable – you call them rags. I am noticing that Grandmother has recently done this to keep the icy winds at bay. Otherwise, the large room has several simple wooden benches and chairs for the seating of ones that come to visit, such as myself today. At the back of the room there is a narrow bed behind a hanging rug, which is used as a partition. Grandmother usually sleeps in her special place in the communal dormitory with the rest of us. But she is sleeping here more and more. I'm not certain why she is doing that. I will ask her if something is troubling her. Often she spends time alone in deep contemplation when there are heavy things weighing on her heart. She takes her position as the Wise Great Mother very seriously. She wants no harm to come to us.

I like the vestibule room the best because it has windows covered with tightly woven cloth and some kind of stretched, very thin leather which is oiled so that light can come through. Now it is dark because the shutters are closed. We do that so the cold can't come in. The walls of the vestibule are made mostly of mud and wattle with an extension of the main thatched roof covering the interior space. It has a heavy, oak plank door. My father has promised to bring some glass ingots that will be crafted into windowpanes to replace the old ones. Then Grandmother will have much more daylight in this special room. And my uncles, Andrew and Josephus have promised to expand the vestibule this spring when there is less rain, so that Grandmother has more room and light for her writing. She is very happy about that.

Just outside her door, under some very old apple trees are several benches, where I love best of all to sit in the sunshine with Grandmother. There is a wonderful view of the hillside vale, the flowing spring grottos, the Tor and Chalice Hill. The vast watery flatlands and marshy lakes extend to the west as far as the eye can see. They reflect the sky and sun like glass. I think that is why the local Celts call this place, Ynes Witrin – the Isles of Glass. My uncles and Grandmother prefer to call these isles, which grow many apples, Avalon. When the sun shines, which has been very infrequent since we arrived, I am reminded of Bethany. I do miss my old home where we had so much more sun and comforts.

I've just come down from the ceremony. It's later in the day. I am still feeling a little cold. I haven't completely thawed out.

CA: Know that as you share with us, you'll feel warmer and warmer.

MARTHA: That is good to know. I will be glad when it is the spring season.

CA: Is this your first winter here?

MARTHA: Yes, it is. I am not accustomed to so much cold.

CA: Yes. Is there anything about the Winter Solstice ritual that you wish to share?

MARTHA: Not really. To be honest, it doesn't pique my interest like it does many of the others of the community. For me it means that the days are lengthening and there will be more light and warmth; and good things to eat out of the garden. The days are so short now and it has been raining almost continually. It's gotten colder and everything seems to never dry out.

I don't mean to complain, but I do find this dark, wet climate depressing. I am thinking when the ones who are from Bugarach return to the sunny land of Gaul, near the Great Sea, I may go with them. I will wait and see if this is wise. Even though I miss my home in Bethany and my more recent simple life in Bugarach, I am glad that I can be here now with so many of my family. I feel safe. The Romans are not here. I feel that I can help with the children; that I can help my grandmother; and that I can help many people in the community, like I've always done. I am learning many new things and I have my place in the household. That is enough.

I don't understand completely what it is about the Mysteries that attract so many of my family. I have been surrounded by people, all my life, who know about the invisible realms and who can do things most people cannot do or even think about. My mother taught me about the Goddess from my infancy. For many years, she served as a Magdalene high priestess at the village of Magdala, on the Sea of Galilee. I experience the Great Mother's ways as being very exciting and beautiful.

I know those who have soul Awareness beyond their mind's concepts, and who are present with their breath, are much happier and calmer than the ordinary people I meet. But many of the alchemical practices of the Magdalene seem too difficult to understand; and they take so much time and energy. How the others, like my sister, Mary (*of Bethany*), and my brother, Lazarus, do these things so effortlessly escapes me. I prefer having good conversations with my family and spending my time with what I can tend to with my hands, such as making clothing and preparing healthy foods.

I am good at creating very soft and durable garments. I can weave all kinds of fibers and piece fabrics together. I know many things about how to keep our bodies healthy and functioning well. There are some of the communal meals which I like to create, especially when we are observing a special feast. I have learned how to help with certain foods that are good for individuals so that their bodies are ready for fasting retreats. I also enjoy being available to provide rejuvenating meals when they are finishing their time of cleansing. If anyone is ill or injured, I can administer healing tonics, which soothe them and speed recovery.

I am thankful for our Essene practices of cleanliness and eating only vegetables, fruits, nuts and grains. I try to continue eating only raw food but that is not always easy in this cold, dark climate. Before long, as the light increases, it will be time to fast and cleanse. There will be ample fresh produce from the gardens and orchards. I am glad that the coming days will help us all feel lighter in our bodies and minds.

I love children. And perhaps, because I never had any of my own, I like to spend a lot of my time tending the babies and teaching the children. I especially enjoy teaching the different languages that I have learned over the years to anyone who is eager to converse in them, no matter their age. I am somewhat facile with a number of spoken languages, but not so good at writing them. I confess that I find this ability helps me to feel some measure of intelligence, especially at those times when I don't understand more esoteric subjects.

CA: Tell me more about your ability with languages, Martha. Are you able to read or speak more languages than the others?

MARTHA: I know how to speak, read and write Hebrew, Aramaic and Greek. I can read Latin and speak some of the Latin vernacular that the Romans use in Palestine and Gaul. I also understand a little Egyptian and some of the language of the Samaritans. I very much enjoy learning a few new phrases that Yeshua, Myriam of Tyana and my sister teach me when they talk about their travels to India. While we were in Bugarach, I learned how to speak some of the native dialects.

Now I am learning the Celtic tongue that is spoken by the native peoples here in Avalon. I am able to discern several different dialects because there are numerous Celtic tribes who speak according to their origins. My ears are able to hear nuances of sound. With a little practice and a kind heart, I can often engage conversations with almost anyone. People come here from different places, just like they did in Bethany and Bugarach. I am very interested in their stories and what brings them here – and how I may be of help in some small way.

From the time I was a small child, Father (*Joseph of Arimathea*) hosted many guests from many places, who came to our homes. He often invited me to sit with them and I quickly learned that I could carry on a conversation with little effort. I learned how to interpret and translate so that we could all understand each other. This gave my father and me much pleasure. And because Father was away so much, I must confess that I, like my siblings, enjoyed his attention in all the forms it came to us.

CA: It is really wonderful that you are able to communicate with so many different people.

MARTHA: I like that very much, as well. Sometimes I write, but more often what I do is communicate through speaking. These past years, in which I have had much more time to be with Grandmother Anna, she has begun helping me to learn how to memorize some of the oral spiritual teachings in Aramaic. One of my favorite recitations, treasured among the Magdalenes, is the "Song of Songs," which Queen Sheba gave to our great patriarch, Solomon the Wise.

There has always been an oral tradition among us who practice the mystical path of the Essenes and the Great Mother. Some of it, I learned from my mother (*Mary of Magdala*) who was also skilled in oral rendition. Because I chose to stay in Bethany, where I was the mistress of our large household, I did not learn much of the ways of arcane wisdom, as did my siblings and cousins, who went away to the places of initiation at Carmel and Egypt. I tried to learn at the synagogue and I visited Qumran a few times, but I found their formal teachings too dry and boring; so I gave it up.

After Yeshua returned, I found his way of teaching much more to my liking. His words communicate directly to my heart and not just my mind. This is true of my sister and brother, as well, when they share their great wisdom. It is a wonderful treat to sit in my adventurous family's company and receive the many teaching stories they have gathered over many years of study; and their travels near and far.

Grandmother (*Anna*) also has a way of making her teaching stories very interesting and meaningful. My family's example motivates me to memorize and recite more than I would otherwise. It is for this reason that I feel somewhat hesitant to go back to southern Gaul. Avalon is a great place of learning and I have a wonderful opportunity for enriching my later years by being here. I have also been told there is a much bigger center of Druid culture, what you would call a university, far to the west of us where the land of Britain extends out into the great Atlantic. Just beyond this far shore, there is an entire island which is given to sacred practices. It is called Ynes Mon or Mona[33]. We also call it an Isle of Avalon. I hope to go there someday.

---

[33] Ynes Mon or the Isle of Mona (Anglesey) is located off the northwest shore of present-day Wales.

There is a very sophisticated oral tradition among the Celtic people that has been carried on since ancient times. I learned a little about this while in Bugarach, but here in Avalon it is given great emphasis. Those who keep and transmit oral wisdom are called Druids and Bards. My father and uncles, Andrew, Josephus and Noah, have been taught how to transmit these oral traditions. They are highly respected, especially Noah who is already considered a great Druid and Bard. I was very surprised to learn that my beloved father has been trained in the Druid wisdom; and that he is looked up to by many of the Celtic kings and chieftains who come to visit him. Many years ago Yeshua shared some of the experiences he had with my father and uncles when he came to Avalon as a boy of thirteen. Now that I am here, his stories come more alive.

My grandmother wishes I liked to write better than I do. She's a little disappointed in me, but she is glad that I can pick up languages so quickly. It pleases her greatly that I am developing skills as a keeper of oral wisdom and history. It gives her comfort to know that so many of her family can carry on her work of sharing the practices through the written and spoken word. She loves the teachings which help make life in this world more peaceful and prepare us for going on into the Great Light after death.

CA: What you are learning sounds very useful. Go forward now to a future time in Avalon. Do you see many people?

MARTHA: We have been here for a full year. (*It is now late winter of 39 AD.*) I have seen that our community in Avalon welcomes strangers for the most part. Sometimes we are guarded and we hesitate to welcome some of the people who come. We perceive that they do not understand the purpose of our community and we are concerned that they might create a distraction for those who wish to be quiet and contemplative. We are friendly and helpful toward all, but we only encourage continual fellowship with those who can most benefit from our way of living and our view of Life's greater purpose.

CA: I would like to ask you about your relationship with Yeshua. How do you feel about his involvement with the Mysteries? What is your relationship with him?

MARTHA: I think of him like a beloved brother, and I am his beloved sister, more so than just being cousins. I feel very, very close to him. My sister and brother pick up on the deeper meaning of his sayings right away, but for me they often go over my head. That troubles me some. It feels like I can't be as close to him as I would like to be. But there is a part of me, in my heart – yes, in my deepest heart – where I know he knows me and I know him. I can feel his beautiful energy melting away all my tension when I am in his arms. Sometimes like right now (*Claire's body is shaking*) I can attune to him and he helps me relax. I can breathe and let go of my worries and my cares.

I don't see energy patterns like my sister, Mary (*of Bethany*), does; but I can feel subtle energy as a movement of warmth in my body. I can feel a vibration like when the sunlight comes through a window and the little particles of dust dance in the light. Sometimes the little hairs on my body stand on end. The top of my head, my skin and my muscles vibrate. Sometimes I vibrate very gently – the vibration is hardly noticeable at all – other times my body quakes all over. The energy feels like the warmth of the sun. I feel more warmth throughout my body and my muscles become softer. In my stomach, where I often feel the tension, it begins to loosen up and go away. My mind gets very still and I can feel a soft glowing energy between Yeshua and me. All sense of being in separate bodies dissolves. I can tell that Yeshua likes it when I become soft.

Lots of energy flows through his hands when he strokes me. I feel like a kitten that's being stroked. I am really a simple woman in that way. My sister is so complex. She knows so many things that go over my head. But I can understand how a kitten or a mother cat relaxes when I stroke her. When Yeshua strokes me, and holds me close to him, I relax. I can feel his heart and my heart growing together. It is as if delicate jasmine tendrils grow out of my heart into his heart and from his heart into mine. It's as if our entire bodies become one giant pulsing heart, which is like the sun giving its light and warmth forever to the sweet earth. It is very lovely. I have not felt this kind of energy with the other men I have known.

CA: Have you known many men?

MARTHA: When I was younger I liked to be with men. This troubled my mother very much. She was reluctant to tell my father. I liked how I felt when we lay together. Often I felt ashamed for the feelings that I had because I knew that women who had many lovers were despised. If they were caught in adultery, by their husbands, they were usually stoned to death. I witnessed that such women, especially the ones who received money, had troubled hearts and troubled lives. I did not want a hard life, nor did I want to be thought of as a harlot.

My mother, who was a priestess of the Great Mothers Isis and Ishtar, tried very hard to teach me a different way to use my sex. She taught me about the Goddess and her powers. Some of the rituals I liked a lot. We worked with the elemental energies of fire, water, earth and air. We sometimes took various herbs that opened our minds and bodies to more energy. We learned how to breathe consciously and recite words of power. We used certain oils to anoint our bodies so that we had more stamina and flexibility. We moved and stretched, taking postures that were very ancient. We danced until we attained ecstatic states of trance.

I love to dance – to sway with the music and make myself hot in my loins. All this makes me feel powerful as a woman. It took many years and some difficult experiences to learn how to tame this powerful energy. As I became less selfish, I slowly learned how to use my life-force as a way to benefit others instead of just myself and the men who gave me their brief conditional attention.

Our homes in Jerusalem and Bethany were very well-appointed because my father was wealthy. He hosted many dignitaries who traveled great distances. When my Aunt Martha, whom I was named after, was the mistress of the household in Jerusalem, she had maids who helped her. After Father married my mother, Mary of Magdala, and Aunt Martha was no longer strong enough to carry on her previous duties, my mother gladly accepted help with our new home in Bethany, where she preferred to live. My mother had a great love of people who were of all stations in life. She especially wanted to serve those who were in great need. Father added on extra rooms so that we could give temporary shelter to the homeless: unwed mothers, orphans, battered women and the infirm.

Before Mother died I learned much of what I know at her hand. Lazarus and I carried on her healing work when she became ill. When my sister (*Mary of Bethany*) was home recuperating from her grave illness, which came upon her in Egypt, she joined us in our efforts. Then Father added even more rooms and acquired other properties for our humanitarian outreach. Our sanctuary was well known and we sadly had to turn people away. Much to the Pharisees' dismay we took in several lepers which astonished many people. One of these was called Simon, the leper. He is mentioned in your Holy Bible with reference to our home in Bethany, during one of the times when my sister, Mary, anointed Yeshua with spikenard oil.[34]

But I am getting ahead of my story. Let's return to the maids and my youth when I was discovering my sexuality. Some of the maids, who worked in our home, lived a secret life. My keen ears overheard them whispering among themselves. What they said intrigued me. They accepted me into their circle of confidence. After I was opened to these mysteries, they taught me how to mix and drink certain herbs if I lost my monthly bleeding. I knew at those times that a child might be coming and I assisted it to move out with my blood. Afterwards I felt very badly. But I continued in this way for more years than I would like to admit. Part of the sadness was keeping so much hidden from those who loved me. But the greatest sadness came when I wanted children. Then, like my sister Mary, I found myself barren. Her barrenness was caused by the extreme Kundalini energy that coursed through her body during an initiation in Egypt. Mine was caused by unbridled lust. (*Softly crying*)

I had one lover I liked very much. In fact, I believe I really loved him almost as much as Yeshua. If he had been willing, I would gladly have married him. His name was Judas. In later years he became a devoted disciple of Yeshua. You know him in your

---

[34] One of several Biblical references about Simon the leper: Luke 7: 37 – 50.

Holy Bible as Judas Iscariot. In the last year of Yeshua's ministry I was Judas' Magdalene consort.³⁵ In the days of our ardor, he came to be with me from the nearby desert monastery of the Essenes called Qumran. Sometimes I went there, but I did not like it very much. It is a harsh place. Their rules and demeanor are far too stern for me. Later I joined with Judas and my brother, Lazarus, in following John the Baptizer for a short time. That was after Judas and Lazarus had gone with John to Mount Sinai. They were in retreat with him for three years. This was before Yeshua came back to Galilee from his second journey to India.

(*Claire's face and body start showing signs of agitation.*)

I am shaking. I don't know why I am shaking so much. I suppose we are calling up some experiences that have been difficult for me to bear.

CA: Know that you are safe, Martha. And if you need to shake that is perfectly okay. Breathe with the shaking, sink into it without attaching words or a story to it. Let the energy do what it wants to do. As we gently embrace it, the uncomfortable energy will be free to move through your body.

MARTHA: Yes. That is what Yeshua, my sister and Aunt Mary Anna tell me to do.

(*Calmly*) I would like to tell you more about Judas.

He was also my sister Mary's dear friend, but he was never her lover. Judas had a special way with me that was very tender. His eyes were dark and deep and so knowing. He was extremely sensitive. I felt sorry for him because his father was harsh and demanded so much of him. He tried very hard to please his father – so much so, that he would ache with despair in his heart when he thought he had failed in some way. Each time Yeshua came back from his journeys

---

[35] Within Yeshua's inner circle of twelve men there were also twelve women – the "outer/seen twelve" and the "inner/hidden twelve". "The Twelve" acted as an alchemical chalice/circle that surrounded and supported Yeshua and the Magdalenes who stood in the center – "The Thirteenth." These twelve couples served as an energetic unit throughout Yeshua's and the Magdalenes' formal ministry, especially during the times of their ceremonial ministry that included healing and teaching large audiences.

with greater wisdom and abilities, Judas became increasingly awestruck. He was the kind of person who was deeply devotional. He believed strongly in the scripture's promise of the Messiah. He recognized Yeshua as a fulfillment of those scriptures, as he understood them.

I was present when John the Baptizer announced Yeshua to be the Master Teacher – the Teacher of Righteousness – the Messiah, which the scriptures prophesied. John said that his purpose, as the one who had come to prepare the way, had been fulfilled. When Yeshua was ready to begin his public ministry, John asked his disciples to follow Yeshua instead of him. Many did, but some remained faithful to John, even after he was brutally murdered. There remains a division among those who still follow John's teachings and those who follow Yeshua. This is difficult for us, for we truly desire unity among us all. We still venerate John and we keep his skull as one of our most precious secret treasures. I think this fact is perceived as a great loss and travesty among those who think John is greater than Yeshua. Some even think Yeshua betrayed John and they call him a false teacher. It is a sore thing when we hear these rumors.

Judas was so taken with Yeshua he began to see him as the Hebrew god, Jehovah, walking in the way of flesh. His adoration was similar to that of the Romans who bring offerings to their gods and their goddesses. The emperors even call themselves gods and require their subjects to worship them. The priests, who serve at David's temple altars in Jerusalem, bring forth sacrificial offerings to appease Jehovah. Blood runs deep. Although blood sacrifice was an abomination to Judas, and remains so for all Essenes, he was willing to offer his whole heart and his very life, as a sacrifice, if that were asked of him. Judas felt Yeshua really was an incarnation of the one true God, as monotheists believe. He did not fully understand the Oneness Yeshua taught and he expected great things of Yeshua. When Yeshua did not live up to Judas' expectations, he felt not only very disappointed, but betrayed. This created much internal conflict for Judas.

He, like his father and other Zealots who lived at Qumran, wanted Yeshua to rise up as their earthly king. They passionately yearned to have Yeshua rid them of the Romans, whom they saw as the embodiment of evil – the Sons of Darkness. It was in this way that my friend, Judas, and some of my other lovers, spoke of the coming Messiah. However, in my household, we believed differently.

When I was with Yeshua I knew in my heart that he never intended to rule the people as a political king. For those of us who could truly hear him, we knew he spoke of the Kingdom of God within us; and that it is not of this world. I weighed Yeshua's and Judas' sayings in my heart. Sometimes I felt confused. I wanted to keep this confusion out of my mind. I wanted to keep my life simple. So I withdrew from such conversations and turned to the things that I could do within our household and hospital. I preferred to serve the downtrodden people who came to us for healing; and left talking about politics to others.

Then our lives became more exciting and more challenging at the same time. Yeshua said it was time to fulfill the purpose for which we had come to earth. Everything we had done to prepare ourselves was now to be lived in such a way as to be examples to others of how to not only serve God, but BE God. He taught us that God, the infinite Father/Mother Creator, is not an angry, jealous god. He said when we feel separate from God we try to make a god in our image. But in truth God is an unnamable, unborn-undying Presence, whose essence is both emptiness and bare intrinsic awareness, expressing as pure BEING and Love. This Great Presence manifests in all forms and walks in earthly bodies, as one family of humanity. He says it is time to establish Heaven right here on earth – right here in the gentle beating of our hearts – in the loving expression of our lives, moment by moment.

As I spent time with Yeshua, especially during the last year of our outer ministry, I allowed my view of him to change from being my older cousin to that of being a Teacher of Righteousness. I came to know with all my heart that he had attained Oneness with the Father/Mother of Life. From then on I called him Master.

Even though we looked to him as our most beloved teacher, he always remained humble and very approachable. He asked me to join with the company of women who walked with him. I was thrilled to be part of his support team who made his path much easier. I agreed to not allow distractions to interfere, except to briefly oversee my duties in Bethany, from time to time.

During those intense months he took me aside and opened me in ways I had never known before. Besides learning how to circulate and transmute my life-force energy for the benefit of Yeshua's ministry, I attained the great stillness beyond the constant chatter of my mind. In the Great Silence, I came to directly know Yeshua as one of the Great Ones who had realized his True Nature, beyond time and form. I came to know him to be a Son of God and a Son of Man. And even though it took longer, perhaps because I had always thought of my sister, Mary (*of Bethany*), as just my older sister, I came to know her as an incarnation of the Great Mother. During those extraordinary days with Yeshua, Mary, and Myriam of Tyana, I came to know what it means to be in the presence of awakened Christ-Magdalenes.

There is one last thing I wish to say about Judas. I think he understood his most difficult role, as best anyone can. I barely understand myself what was asked of him in those last days. My heart still breaks when I look back on that very anxious and terrible time. I do know this though; Judas was greatly loved by Yeshua. Yeshua, Myriam and my sister, Mary, spent a great deal of time with him so that he would be prepared to do what was his to do, as a Christ-Magdalene initiate.

As the Osirian mystery goes, in the enactment of the raising of Osiris by his beloved Isis from spiritual death (*the ignorance that is separation/duality consciousness*) into life (*spiritual awakening/Oneness*), someone must play the role of the "villain," Set. (*Set is Osiris' jealous brother who betrays and kills him. Isis, the Divine Feminine – Wisdom and Love, raises – awakens Osiris' awareness of who he truly is.*) Set personifies separation consciousness: selfishness, greed, avarice, resentment, jealousy, lust, betrayal, and so forth. Set is the inner "enemy" – the betrayer of life and the inner Christ. Set is the part of us, as unrealized sentient beings, that obscures our true nature – the Christ Light.

Judas stepped up to play that very misunderstood "dark" role – the role of portraying Set, the antichrist – Set, the opposite of love and light. Set, the brother who attempts to betray and kill his brother – his own true Self – the Christ. But, in fact, sets in motion the very process of the inner Christ being raised into full awareness. This is the great paradox within the Osirian-Isis mystery – the mysteries of the Christ-Magdalene. Yeshua demonstrates the raising of Osiris – the victory of pure love transmuting fear in every moment – in every breath. As a Magdalene, I have come to know Yeshua IS the resurrected Christ. Yeshua IS the Love, the Life and the Light. And in truth, Judas and all beings can know we are already the Christ – we just don't know it yet.

My heart continues to ache for Judas' soul. In spite of everything he, and everyone, did after Yeshua's crucifixion and resurrection, he continued to sink into a deep depression. I think his internal conflicts since childhood were compounded by the hysteria of the angry mobs. And then added to this was the unbearable weight of his own self-doubt, compounded by the scape-goating among those of us who misunderstood him and his role. There were some among us who had not been fully initiated within the Magdalene mysteries. They did not understand the role Judas innocently played. And so it was that his mind was besieged and battered, until he could no longer bear the pain.

CA: That must have been very difficult for you. What other significant events with Yeshua do you recall?

MARTHA: There was the time that my brother Lazarus became very sick. He died and Yeshua raised his body back into life.[37]

CA: Lazarus?

---

[36] For an expanded teaching on the roles Yeshua and Judas played in the Osirian-Isis/Christ-Magdalene mystery, see "Anna, Grandmother of Jesus," chapters 38 – 41.

[37] The Biblical account of the raising of Lazarus: John 11: 1 – 45.

MARTHA: Yes. Yeshua had gone away with some of the brothers who had not experienced the initiation temples of Egypt and the Far East, such as Simon Peter and his brother Andrew. He wanted to give them teachings that would help them be able to face the hardships Yeshua knew lay ahead. My father was also away on one of his travels. Thank God, my sister, Mary, and Myriam were with me. My beloved brother, who chose to remain in Bethany, became very ill. He died and we placed his body in a nearby sepulcher. Yeshua knew of Lazarus' death in his heart before a messenger came to tell him. It was four painful days later that Yeshua arrived. (*Tears*) He went to the tomb, had the stone rolled back and spoke Lazarus' name loudly. Lazarus came forth and did not smell of death, whatsoever. I will not say more at this time. Let your Bible accounts suffice for now....

CA: (*Claire's body is shivering again even though the room is warm and the season is summer.*) Are you still cold? Would you like a blanket?

MARTHA: Maybe that would help. My feet are cold aren't they? I think it is all the hard things I have witnessed and have held in my body all these years.

CA: Now it is safe to share and be at peace, just as if you are in Yeshua's arms.

MARTHA: I so wish he were here. He is telling me now to go on with my story of my life in Britain. There is no need to revisit those last difficult years in Palestine.

CA: Did you ever marry?

MARTHA: There was a betrothal that my parents arranged because they were concerned about my affairs. They did not want me to bring shame and perhaps even death upon my self. The man was someone my father knew, he seemed to be kind enough, but we didn't have affection for one another. After the betrothal, when he found out that I was not a virgin, he was quite angry and he wanted his dowry back. He was good enough to not have me put away. I think Father secretly came to my rescue. I was very relieved to be brought back to my parent's house. He was an older man, a widower and I was only sixteen. I am so glad the marriage fell through. Once a woman is divorced, it is very difficult to ever marry again or to find support for her physical well-being. It is not that way for men. Men have a very unfair advantage and many women suffer as a result.

CA: And in your culture were people only married to one partner at a time or ….

MARTHA: Mostly. But there were some men who had more than one woman.

CA: Did Yeshua marry?

MARTHA: Yes.

CA: Did he have children and did he marry more than once?

MARTHA: Yes, he had children, and yes, he married two women. His first marriage was with Myriam of Tyana, whom he met shortly before his first journey to India. Before he returned to India with Myriam the second time, he became betrothed to my sister, Mary. They never formally married.

CA: Did he have children with Myriam of Tyana and Mary of Bethany?

MARTHA: Yes. With Myriam, he has three children; Joses Simeon, Miriam and Johannes. Jude, who is Yeshua's consort Radha's orphaned child, was adopted by Myriam and my sister. My sister, Mary, was barren when she and Yeshua were betrothed. Years later a miracle of healing occurred on the night you call Yeshua's "Last Supper." Mary conceived Sar'h then. In our first year at Mount Bugarach she conceived another daughter; we call her Lizbett. They are here in Avalon and they have their stories to tell. I will let them tell what they wish to share.

CA: Thank you for sharing this information that has been hidden so long. Is there any last thing you wish to say?

MARTHA: Only that I am so glad that we have had this opportunity to share our voices. These things that have been hidden are at the surface of so many hearts and minds. My story, like many women's stories, speaks of the burdens we have carried – so much shame, guilt, abuse and sorrow. It is time for us, as women and men, to put aside the wounds of our hearts and our minds. It is time to forgive and allow healing – as individuals, families and society. I know when we do that we will take far better care of our mother, the Earth. My vision is that we will be one family without jealousy and distrust of one another.

We women will put aside our insecurities and not vie for husbands or ceaselessly try to get our fathers' and men's attention. We will not compete and betray and libel one another. Ours will be a true sisterhood where we can rejoice in one another's intrinsic beauty and support each others' different talents. We will be present for each other with our nurturing abilities from the moment of conception. Through our unfailing love, we will make sure no one is left alone to suffer during life's inevitable passages – birth, sickness, aging and death. We will see our suffering with greater patience and compassion so that all beings may know happiness.

In my vision, I see men no longer competing with or using women or the Earth Mother for their aggrandizement, their gluttony and their lust. Our men will not go to war to prove themselves, nor take offense in order to gain power. With a greater sense of communal Oneness, there can be less defensiveness toward possessions and borders. They will no longer be so busy filling time with constant distractions, unaware of the joyful, present moment. Then there will be fewer regrets of the past and worries for the future. They can bring their full presence to their lives, as spiritual beings first. Then they can be good sons, brothers, husbands and fathers. As a true brotherhood, they will inspire and support both men and women to be all we can be for the benefit of all beings.

When I speak of men, let it also be understood that the masculine energy expressing through women will also be brought forth in the ways I have spoken. And so is it also true, that the feminine energies expressing through men will be cultivated and honored for the benefit of all.

In all these ways we will honor each gender's divine complementary gifts and bring union, balance and wholeness to all our relationships. With a sense of equality that embraces our diversity, we will co-create the Earth to be a home of harmony, healing and holiness. That will be a truly glorious New Day, as Grandmother Anna calls it. (*Emotionally*)

Grandmother is so dedicated to the New Day. She also sees a time when we can all be one family, at peace with one another – a time of loving without regret, shame, guilt or sorrow. My hope is that my story can assist my sisters and my brothers to lay down our burdens. Your "Holy Bible" tells us, "Repent and sin no more." This means to simply turn away from those thoughts, feelings, and actions that bring harm to self and others. Instead, we can think, feel and act in ways that increase life's abundance.

When we are aware that we are far more than our separate bodies and minds, our Divine Soul is given space to live and act. The compassionate heart of the Soul guides the human mind to listen and obey its quiet, inner voice. Then there is a greater ability for peace. It is said that in the New Day, the lamb and the lion shall peacefully lie together, and the Earth Mother shall thrive as a fertile garden. There will be no more animosity amongst the species of earth, neither wars within the heaven worlds, nor discontent and suffering anywhere within the worlds of time and form.

CA: That is a beautiful vision to hold during these troubling times.

MARTHA: I feel a deep peace knowing my sharing may somehow bring more love to your heart and to the way you live your life. May your ability to love increase as you relate to your brothers and your sisters; to your mothers, your fathers, your children and all beings. Thank you for hearing my story and my voice. That is all I have to say for now.

CA: Thank you, Martha, for coming and sharing your vision and words. They help us have greater understanding and wisdom.

{*Martha continued to live in Avalon until 55 AD when she returned to southern France with her brother, Lazarus, after "The Great Gathering." Before this turning point, Martha fulfilled her dream of living several years on Mona at the great Druid sanctuary. Martha and Lazarus were instrumental in assisting Sar'h and Andrew with their humanitarian efforts of expanding a network of hospitals, orphanages and hospices throughout southern France. Martha died at the age of 84 in 80 AD near Mount Bugarach.*}

— Chapter 19 —

LIZBETT

(The Daughter of Yeshua and Mary of Bethany)
Avalon, 41 AD. Age 7

{*This chapter is a continuation of Lizbett speaking in Chapter 11. Claire is facilitating Catherine Ann.*}

CLAIRE (*facilitating Catherine Ann*): I ask you now to go ahead in your journey and tell me where you are.

LIZBETT: I'm on a green hillside twirling around. It's sunny and the grass feels warm beneath my feet. Things are peaceful now; at least today... the Romans aren't here. Sometimes we see a few who do business with Uncle Joseph (*of Arimathea*). But we don't see the soldiers anymore. It's mostly peaceful. I've heard stories about the nearby tribes fighting amongst themselves; but now it is peaceful.

CLAIRE: Tell me about this place and hillside.

LIZBETT: I can see far away when I stand on the top of this hill that is called the Tor. It is close to where we live. Today I am by myself. I am just twirling and feeling the sun on my face. I twirl and twirl until I get dizzy, and then I fall down. And then, when I fall down, I roll over and over down the hill. Then I just lie there until the world stops spinning. And then I run up the hill and do it again.

CLAIRE: Is this a place where you have come to live for a long time?

LIZBETT: Yes. We will have been here three years when the days are very short and it is cold. I just turned 7 years old a week ago.

CLAIRE: Tell me about your home and who lives there.

LIZBETT: There is a kind of fence made of big thick branches that are roped and woven together so there's no space between them. The fence surrounds our entire village. It is a kind of protection and it keeps the animals from wandering away. We also have another kind of protection. The people who live here know how to make a mist come up when they want our village to be invisible. Inside the gates, we have our houses.

CLAIRE: Tell me about your house. Who lives with you in your house?

LIZBETT: I don't live in just one house. The houses are round with pointed tops made of stiff straw and reeds. Some are big and some are small. They are mostly clustered close together. Nana's (*Grandmother Anna*) is a ways off all by itself. Sometimes I stay with the other children in one of the big houses, but sometimes my sister, Sar'h, and I stay in Nana's little house. We have a place to sleep where we don't bother her.

CLAIRE: Do the children live with their parents or do they live by themselves?

LIZBETT: It's different here than it was at Mount Bugarach, mostly because it's so much colder and wetter. We still share everything – all our food and work and clothing. Some of the families that have always lived here, all live together – the grandparents, the parents and the children all share the same space. Those of us who came here from the Old Country live more in dormitories. The older children live together with a few grown-ups who take turns looking after us. The men and women who are not married live together, but in their separate dormitories. The couples who are married have their little huts. There is a large roundhouse where we come together to eat and share prayers, singing and stories. Guests who travel a distance sometimes sleep there. It's in the middle of the circle of roundhouses where we live. There are several large gardens and springs nearby. The sheep and cattle roam over the hills and there are fields that grow our food. There's a special place where the animals; their food and the wagons and tools, are kept.

CLAIRE: Is there a school and things to learn?

LIZBETT: We always learn. We go to different houses to learn different things.

CLAIRE: Do the girls get to learn with the boys?

LIZBETT: Yes. Sometimes the girls learn different subjects. Sometimes we go and sit at different teachers' feet. Some of the teachers are old and some are not much older than me. Each one has something special to teach us; like how to watch the movement of the stars and how to predict the weather, how to care for the animals, how to count and measure and build things and how to keep from getting sick. Some show us how to grow food and how to prepare it for meals. There are drum and harp players, also singers who teach us songs and special dances. Some know how to make things that are useful and they know how to decorate them with pretty designs. Others are master storytellers. They train our minds to memorize many things and how to recite them and how to think clearly. We also learn how to speak different languages and how to write and read some of them.

CLAIRE: Do you like being taught how to think?

LIZBETT: Yes and how to focus my mind and concentrate until everything feels very still and full of light. We learn about our breath and how it's connected to our thoughts and feelings. We work with our imagination and with our dreams. They make it all into games. Sometimes there is laughter; but most of the time we work and practice with lots of determination and focus. I think the older children do the same things, but what they learn is more difficult. Right now, we mostly just practice.

CLAIRE: Does your mother (*Mary of Bethany*) sometimes teach you things?

LIZBETT: Sometimes she teaches me and the other children. When we are alone together she sits down in front of me and she puts her forehead to my forehead. Then she holds my hands and touches her feet to my feet and her hands to my hands, palm to palm. She smiles and breathes with me. We practice and practice gathering the energy. It feels nice and warm when she sends the energy through my body. Then she has me send the energy through her body. It goes around and around. I can feel it. I like doing this with my mother very much.

CLAIRE: She seems to know a lot about energy.

LIZBETT: She does. She's not here all the time. She, Nana and my daddy (*Yeshua*) come and go. I don't think they go too far away. Myriam (*of Tyana*) and Mary Anna (*Mother Mary*) have been away for a long time. They went with Uncle Joseph (*of Arimathea*) to the big city where the Roman emperor lives. I have heard they are now visiting a far away place in the Orient where Daddy and Myriam (*of Tyana*) used to live. Some of their children[38] are here with me. I know their mothers will come back someday. Mariam is here. She doesn't travel so much. She still doesn't talk. I'm used to her being quiet. We understand each other very well even though we don't talk in the usual way.

CLAIRE: Do you think you will grow up to be like your mother?

LIZBETT: I don't know – maybe.

CLAIRE: Maybe you will get to travel with them sometime. How does that feel?

LIZBETT: I would like that. Even though we have horses and provisions when we travel, my parents, sometimes, can also travel differently than other people – it's like they can come and go and just kind of reappear.

CLAIRE: That sounds like a lot of fun.

LIZBETT: Yes, it's not so cumbersome, like when we have to travel. I don't understand why they don't do it that way all the time. Maybe it's because we don't all know how to disappear and reappear like they do. I will think about this and talk to Nana about how to learn to travel with them.

CLAIRE: Are there other children who have talents and interests like yours in these mysterious things?

LIZBETT: Some of the boys have some special training.

CLAIRE: Where do they go for the training? Who trains them?

---

[38] Mary Anna's children: Esther Salome and Matteas; Myriam's children: Joses Simeon, Jude (adopted) & Miriam.

LIZBETT CONTINUED

LIZBETT: The great uncles: Uncle Joseph (*of Arimathea*), Josephus, Andrew and Noah take them to train with the Druids in the lands to the west (*Devon, Cornwall and Wales*).

CLAIRE: Do the Druids come and visit the village here sometimes?

LIZBETT: Yes, they are close friends with the people of our village.

CLAIRE: Tell me about Anna – your Nana. Does she live alone or does she have a companion?

LIZBETT: Sometimes there are people that come and visit with her. She is always very happy to see them. Her heart is very joyous. I'm not sure who they are. Some I have seen before. She gets very excited when they come to visit. There is one man friend she sees a lot. His name is John. I think she loves him because she looks at him and touches him in a way that says he is very special. Sometimes she blushes when I ask about him. I'm not used to seeing Nana this way. I'm glad. She's not so serious.

CLAIRE: I ask you now to go forward to a time when you are with the maidens whose blood time has come. Your breasts are developing and there is a flow of blood which you have learned about from your teachers. You are not afraid of it. Your body is able to have babies and you have talked about this with your mother and Nana. As you look down at your body, please tell me what you see.

Avalon, 47 AD, summer, Age 13

LIZBETT: We are having a ceremony – a "coming of age" ritual. I am dressed in a very fine bluish, flowing material. It's almost see-through. I have an embroidered dark blue ribbon on my head which covers my third eye. Then the ribbon comes back behind my ears where it ties. There is a small crystal sewn to the ribbon where it covers my third eye. My dress also has a ribbon with the same embroidery and it comes across my chest in a cress-cross pattern. I have long, medium brown hair. It's parted down the middle and it goes below my waist. I have very fair skin. It's pale like my Grandma Mary Anna's (*Mother Mary*). There are very few of us with such pale skin. Almost all of my relatives who came from the Old Country have olive-colored skin. There are many more light-skinned people who live here in Avalon. I am standing with my hands slightly away from my sides, with my palms forward. We are having an initiation.

CLAIRE: Initiation. That's a grown-up word. What does it mean to you?

LIZBETT: This is a special initiation day when we get to actually experience, for the first time, what we've been taught. This initiation means we get to take the light and move it in a special way through our bodies. We take our light from the earth, moon and sun. And not just the sun we see with our eyes, but the sun beyond the sun. We take all the light into our head and move it down into our energy centers. We focus it down into our organs where babies are made. It is a powerful golden light that comes down and connects into that energy center and into those organs. It sets up an energy field that carries a particular frequency. It connects with the moon's blood that comes upon reaching the threshold of womanhood. It connects with all the blood that flows through our whole body and all the energy that flows through all our being.

In this way, our blood carries the vibration of spirit. It is an anchoring of spirit into our consciousness so that when the time of shedding our moon blood comes, we can use our thoughts and our words to benefit life and give birth to good things. It is a time of responsibility in which we bring nurturing care for others; and it's a fine-tuning of self. It is a time to be more like the Great Mother – to be her daughters in true sisterhood.

CLAIRE: You are growing up, aren't you?

LIZBETT: Yes. But I am still in-between a bit. I am being shown I don't yet have the full responsibility and the full knowledge of an adult.

CLAIRE: Who is leading this initiation?

LIZBETT: Grandmother Anna, my mother (*Mary of Bethany*) and Noah's wife, Dancing Wind.

CLAIRE: How are they dressed for this occasion?

LIZBETT: They are wearing long, midnight-blue, hooded tunics. They are each holding a long wooden staff. It anchors and directs the flow of light and energy. They use it to calibrate the energy for our group of eight girls who are in the inner circle and for each of us individually. They have a band across their forehead that holds a crescent moon over the third eye point. They breathe deeply while they tone sounds and sing chants. They form a triangle at the center of our circle of eight new initiates. There is a larger circle of women and older girls surrounding us. Some of the women are the girls' mothers.

At first, we girls are standing at the threshold outside of the triangle getting ready to enter, one by one. Even though we have had this energy come down as a group, each one of us goes and stands in the center of the triangle. There are stones arranged on the smooth ground at the center of the sacred grove. There are two large inter-twined circles in which we all stand. Five other priestesses come forward and make a pentagram, the symbol of the sacred feminine. Within the shape that is formed, where the circles overlap, it is the shape of our eyes, our mouths and the shape of our sacred female gate. Grandmother Anna, Mama and Wind Dancer make a trinity to amplify the energy at the innermost center.

We walk one at a time into the space they create. They move and dance around us, lifting their staffs toward the full moon. She is bathing us with her silver light. They chant and beat their hoop drums and bring the energy in. They bring it in and bring it in until we are trembling and almost swooning – the energy is so strong.

CLAIRE: The way you describe the triangle that is formed is similar to the toy you loved when you were a little girl.

LIZBETT: Yes. I think it was kind of an imprinting. Now it's an entry point to many other worlds and dimensions. Each point and each surface allows a different kind of access. And in this initiation, we are being granted the permission to move into another level of teaching. We are having the energy that follows sacred geometry to be imprinted within our being to allow this unfolding. It is very exciting. It's something we have been taught from childhood. We are working very much with our planet, our beloved Mother Gaia. We are learning more about the Divine Mother, how to hold her great energy and how to be a conduit, or a sacred container, through which other energies can pass and come into harmony. That is part of what we do.

CLAIRE: Do the boys get a teaching like this?

LIZBETT: Yes, they have their own initiation. The uncles; Joseph, Andrew, Josephus and Noah, the boy's fathers and brothers lead the rituals of becoming a man.

CLAIRE: Are the rituals always done outdoors?

LIZBETT: No. Sometimes when there is a bad storm we gather in the large round house or in a cave. But mostly we meet in sacred groves, by holy springs, or in standing stone circles. Sometimes we gather on the Tor and sometimes by one of the lakes.

CLAIRE: How old are you, Lizbett?

LIZBETT: I am thirteen. I will be fourteen in two more months. Some of the girls are twelve. The oldest is sixteen. Some of the girls in our village have children at our age, but we are on a different path. It is not that we are not allowed to have children at some point later in life; it is just that we are choosing a different training or path of teaching. We young girls, who are coming into our womanhood, are being taught how to carry the information and the codes to a different fruition. We are taught how important it is to be able to utilize our wombs for a higher energetic exchange and a higher alignment with our mates. Whether we do this for our enlightenment or for allowing a greater divinity to come forth when we have our children; it is done with much more loving awareness.

CLAIRE: Did your mother and daddy bring you into the world in this way?

LIZBETT: Oh yes. It was a very sacred exchange, a blessed moment, sanctioned by all the Councils of Light.

CLAIRE: Why do you suppose your mother is called Magdalene?

LIZBETT: She is of that family and that spiritual lineage.

CLAIRE: Does that make you a Magdalene now?

LIZBETT: Yes. Not a fully initiated Magdalene; but a Magdalene at the first level of training.

CLAIRE: Please tell me what your understanding is about being a Magdalene.

LIZBETT: I carry the genetics and the potential for being a Magdalene, which are carried from generation to generation. But just having the Magdalene genetic codes does not make me a Magdalene. There has to be a willingness and readiness of mind, body and soul. Much study, contemplation, and cleansing of thoughts and emotions are required. There are activations or transmissions of spiritual energy that must come down and awaken the codes that are held in the earth elements of the body. Then there can be an ignition of a spiritual fire within. When this happens it ignites internal pathways of knowledge to be expressed in external paths of service. Then you can be addressed as a Magdalene.

Some Magdalenes have to look back many generations to find their genetic connection. To be a Magdalene is not by birthright alone. It is through a deep desire and a willingness to be trained and taught. It is accomplished in collaboration within a lineage of those who have gone ahead of you. It is an honoring of those who walk with you; and it is an honoring of your own physical and emotional self. When all the required elements are present, there is the uniting of the memory and the ancient wisdom that is carried through lifetimes into the present incarnated self. Then one holds the mantle and the staff of the Magdalene. It is a great honor to never be taken for granted. A Magdalene vows to never bring harm or to feel superior or prideful.

CLAIRE: Are there men who are Magdalenes, or is it only women?

LIZBETT: There are men aligned in a similar order. They are the protectors or knights of the Magdalene. They receive their own similar experience of teaching and fusing higher dimensions of divinity into awakening the codes held within physicality. The frequencies are a little different for the men whose path of service brings together the union of spirit and flesh; but they go about it with a slightly different focus than the women.

It is important to understand that the codes may be carried in a female body in one lifetime and then in a male body in the next. The soul has the opportunity to experience a full spectrum of how the Great Mother, through her Magdalene sons and daughters, helps all living beings return to her full embrace. Some of the Druids carry this ancient wisdom and they work in harmony with those of us who are called Essene-Magdalenes. On certain occasions of teaching and ritual, the men and women come together.

Because there is a slightly different complementary frequency and function, the initiated men and women can come together like a lock and key. There can be a powerful fusion. This is needed for conceiving more awake children in the Light, for conscious dying and rebirth, for the Rites of the Sepulcher, and other things that we do not share with those who would not understand.

CLAIRE: Do you need a partner to have these fusion experiences?

LIZBETT: No. You can do it all by yourself. But it is very helpful to learn in increments with a partner. The partners may change with time, as either one may develop faster than the other, or one may be better suited for a particular ritual and not the other. My parents (*Yeshua and Mary of Bethany*) and sister (*Sar'h*) and other relatives were my first partners, like when my mother and I circulated energy with each other. There may be a series of partners, both men and women, until we are ready to be with our partner who perfectly meets our highest destiny.

Then there is a perfect fusion and a perfect fit on all levels. Then we can create an incredible energetic field. There is an energetic interpenetration like a pulse that goes out and then it returns, amplifying and magnifying the joined partners as they join with the Light of the Beloved on High (*as Grandmother Nana calls the unnamable God*). It is like the sacred triangle. The two people are the base of the triangle and the Beloved is the point at the top, where they both join. They are equally joined at every point of the triangle. Then the triangle becomes a powerful generator of energy like the Great Pyramid in Egypt where my parents took some of their Magdalene initiations. Information and wisdom is gathered and experienced. There is a spiraling out and in of greater and greater magnitudes and more and more dimensions.

CLAIRE: Do the boys and the men come to the priestesses and maidens to learn from them?

LIZBETT: Yes. That has not happened to me yet, but I know that in a year or two, after I have the training, then those experiences will commence.

CLAIRE: Would you like to go forward now to that time?

LIZBETT: I'm not quite sure I am ready at this moment to view that experience. I have much to integrate.

CLAIRE: Is there something more we need to learn before we leave this experience of being with the older women who have so much wisdom to give you?

LIZBETT: Yes. I am seeing a different part or aspect of them. It's like they are not my Nana or my mother. It is like they are the face of the Goddess. It is like something beyond what I have known and how I have known them, and yet it's very familiar.

CLAIRE: Will your relationship with your Nana and your mother change now?

LIZBETT: Only in the sense that I cannot get away with being a little girl now. I don't know yet if it will change, or how it will change.

CLAIRE: Will you get to live in a different kind of situation?

LIZBETT: Actually, yes. There is another place where the initiated maidens live together. I also know I can go and be with my Nana and my mother when I need to do that.

Avalon, 48 AD, Age 14

CLAIRE: Go forward now to a time when you are living with the maidens. How does this feel?

LIZBETT: It feels kind of exciting because we get to share and talk about things that girls our age get to know – things we didn't know or care about when we were younger. There is much practice that we do, but we also have fun. I get to live with my sister, Sar'h, now. We also have our house mother, who lives in our home with us.

CLAIRE: Is this one of your relatives?

LIZBETT: No. She's usually one of the women in the community who doesn't have children. It is thought that it would be better to not have anyone's relative so as not to have any favorites. Occasionally, a relative comes when there is a need. Usually our house mother takes turns with other women.

CLAIRE: Please bring your awareness to your uncles: Uncle Joseph, Andrew, Josephus and Noah. Tell me about them and anyone else, if you would like.

LIZBETT: Andrew and Josephus were more involved here in the community in the early days. They have not been around so much in these later years. I only saw them once not long after we arrived. I am told they live in the southern part of Wales and on the isle of Mona. They are getting very old and their bodies are stiff and don't move very well. They don't travel very much. They work with the Druids. I don't know if I will get to see them again. (*Both Andrew and Josephus pass away within weeks of each other later this year.*) Uncle Noah and his wives live here. They travel to the West Country a lot. I get to see them and my cousins in Avalon most of the year.

Uncle Joseph (*of Arimathea*) was gone with Mary Anna (*Mother Mary*) and Myriam (*of Tyana*) for several years (39 – 41 AD). He came back to Avalon when they went on to visit relatives in Tyana and India (41 AD). He left this summer to bring them back home. He has a great sense of responsibility for our community and for overseeing its welfare. I miss him. He's very old, too; but he doesn't look as old as Uncles Andrew and Josephus. In fact he is quite spry. He has a wife named Nueme whom he married soon after his return to Avalon in 41 AD. In 43 AD Nueme gave him two boy children who are twins. He is very proud of them and I know he must miss them very much. I think when he gets back this time it might be his last long voyage.

And of course, I miss Grandma Mary Anna and Myriam (*of Tyana*). I can barely remember them – their kind and beautiful faces linger in my childhood memories, as does Uncle John Mark. (*Lizbett was not yet six years old when they left.*) They will come back to many changes. Myriam's children, Joses Simeon, Jude (*Lizbett's half-brothers*) and Miriam (*Lizbett's half-sister*) are all grown, as are Grandmother Mary Anna's children, Aunt Esther Salome and Uncle Matteas. They are all married and most of them have children. Myriam and

LIZBETT CONTINUED

Grandmother Mary Anna are supposed to be back in Avalon sometime later this fall.[39] I can hardly wait! Maybe my other half-brother, Johannes (*Myriam of Tyana's son*), will come to Avalon. I can barely contain the happiness that comes with the thought of having all my brothers and sisters and mothers together for the first time ever! I know Daddy will come and we will have a wonderful celebration!

CLAIRE: That will be wonderful! The Romans – are they nearby?

LIZBETT: Five years ago our peace came to an end. The Romans invaded far to the east and many lives were lost. Now there are thousands of soldiers, just like in Gaul; except there is more fighting in the fair land of Britannia, as the Romans call it, because this is Rome's new frontier. The Celts of Gaul have long been suppressed under the rule of Rome. The Britons are very brave and fierce warriors. But they are not able to keep the Romans from pouring onto our sacred land. The legions keep coming and it is easy to see they are here to stay. The Emperor Claudius even came for a few weeks.

Not far from here, legions of soldiers passed by earlier this year. They were on their way to create more forts near the tin mines of Devon and Cornwall. They are improving the primitive road and calling it the Fosse Way. The local tribal leaders did not put up much resistance. But there are other tribes in Wales that are fighting to the death. The Romans are in pursuit of the great tribal chieftain King Caradoc, whom they call Caratacus, who fled the Eastland to take refuge with the Silures and Ordivices of Wales. The bards are already singing his praises and telling troubling stories about the loss of life everywhere. They tell of many atrocities: women and girls being raped, houses and fields being burned and many men, women and children being taken away as slaves. The Celtic tribes did such

---

[39] As it turned out, they did not return to Avalon until the spring of 49 AD, ten full years since they left in 39 AD to travel to Rome, Turkey and India.

things to one another for many generations; but not like this. The old worries have returned.

Right now we are being ignored, which is a good thing. We continue on with our ways and our life. But we pretty much need to keep to ourselves. We blend in as much as we can with the common folk. It is best that way.

CLAIRE: What is the place called where you live?

LIZBETT: Avalon.

CLAIRE: Have you heard of some of the other places in Britain called Avalon?

LIZBETT: Yes, there are other places sometimes referred to as Avalon. It's like Avalon is a consciousness, not so much the name of a physical place. As a consciousness, it is the combined wisdom of the Magdalene-Essenes and the Druids; it is an ethereal realm of peace, beauty and magic that lies beyond the mists of the ignorant mind.

CLAIRE: Does your father (*Yeshua*) come visit this place?

LIZBETT: He comes, but he comes less and less now. I have not seen him in quite a while, although I know he is here on the inner planes close to my heart. It seems that he spends more time in the mountains you call the Himalayas. I think that is partly the reason his mother and Myriam went there. I see some things in my inner sight. He shows me things. Mama, Sar'h and I sit together often and ask for Daddy's presence. We can feel a part of him come and be here with us. Sometimes he actually shows up for an hour or two. I think Mama sees more of him; but she doesn't talk about it much with me. She knows how to travel to the great mountains in her light body. I am still learning.

CLAIRE: Very good, Lizbett, I would like you to go forward to the next significant event in your life.

{Lizbett continues sharing her story in Part 4, Chapter 27}

— Chapter 20 —
ANNA and JOHN
Avalon, 39 AD

ANNA: The sweet aroma of evergreens and wet leaves permeate the air. I glimpse patches of a dark grey sky through the thick forest canopy overhead. A gentle mist envelopes me as I walk. I am wearing a thick woolen, hooded cloak and my feet are bound with leather and lacings. Each step is cushioned with layers of soft lamb's wool and moss, which also keep my feet warm and dry.

CATHERINE ANN (*Henceforth: CA*): Is it cold out now?

ANNA: Yes, it's rather cold. An early winter chill goes deep into my bones. Thankfully, the wind is not blowing, nor is it snowing.

CA: What are you wearing under your cloak?

ANNA: I am wearing several layers of heavy homespun tied with a sash girdle which wraps around my waist. There is a small bundle held within the sash so that I don't have to carry it. My hands are free to hold my walking staff and a larger bundle, which is also supported by a sling that goes over my left shoulder.

CA: What are you carrying in your bundles?

ANNA: There is an assortment of ground herbs I will use to make tinctures and poultices. I also packed a little food, primarily brown bread laden with nuts and dried fruits, together with some root vegetables and several withered apples. A clean robe, other personal items and an assortment of small gifts are also included.

CA: And who is speaking?

ANNA: This is Anna.

CA: I figured it was you, Anna. How long have you been in Britain?

ANNA: Almost a year.

CA: What is significant about this moment?

ANNA: I am on my way to visit a friend who is ill. I am going to see what I can do to assist him to feel better. I will probably be away for two or three weeks. Two of the brethren from Avalon escorted me to our agreed rendezvous point. I can see from this vantage point that one of my friend's family members has already arrived and is finding some shelter on a covered wooden bench. Such benches are often provided for pilgrims going to and from the Isles of Apples – our beloved Avalon[40]. He will lead me in the rest of the way.

CA: Where is it that your friend lives?

ANNA: Near the Mendip Hills just to the north of Avalon. He has family there; but he doesn't always live with them.

CA: Can you tell us your friend's name?

ANNA: Yes. John is one of the brethren from Avalon who returned to his village a month or so ago to help a number of his family and village people who are quite sick. Some have died. He is giving support to his grown children and close relations who are grieving the loss of family members and friends. Now he is also quite ill. I am concerned for his welfare and that of his family and village.

I first met John shortly after I arrived in Britain. In the following months after our meeting, he was often away taking our trade goods to other villages and bringing back needed supplies. On the brief occasions we saw each other there was a sense of deep recognition and a mutual desire for further communion. Once we claimed this great boon to be our good fortune, it did not take long to begin a deep mutual exploration of our souls. We found our times together quite refreshing. We were just getting to know each other in this way when he was called to his mother's ancestral village.

CA: Have you known John in other incarnations as Anna?

---

[40] Anna and the family refer to the place where they live as the Isles of Apples and Avalon; the Britons refer to it as the Isles of Glass – Ynes Witrin.

ANNA: When I look into the records I can say that this is so. We both sense we go back a long, long way and that we are of the same soul energy.

I sense a flickering of Joachim's presence. It feels that if we were to choose to spend time together we might be able to access more of the soul consciousness that incarnated as Joachim.

I realize I am feeling a pang of sadness as I say this. Unfinished grieving beckons. I can see that John is touching a place in my being I have not allowed myself to feel in many, many years. As I look more deeply, I sense a part of me wishing John to fill up this empty, aching place in my heart. I have avoided visiting this too "sacred" chamber, which I had given completely to my beloved Joachim. For more years than I wish to count, I have been so absorbed in the Beloved on High and so preoccupied with healing the universal grief of others, I have not realized the extent to which my own heart is actually closed. I see that in avoiding this deeply personal grief, I have not been fully present to my human experience or as fully present for those who are in my care.

The power of intimate relationship to awaken insight into what I had denied within my consciousness startles me. It is good that I have these moments of reflection before seeing John; else I project my unhealed wound upon him and not see him clearly for the being he is. If we were to bring our lives together, I would commit to open my heart in ways that I have not previously in the dance of personal relationship. I am seeing that I am crossing an unexplored threshold late in this long life. The portal feels familiar, while what is rising up to meet me is a veiled mystery I have yet to fathom fully in this incarnation.

As I draw closer, I feel a cellular vibration and a soul kinship with John that quickens me. He seems to be an essential part or aspect of me. I can't help but feel an attraction. A wild kind of curiosity about this man and our unfolding process ripples through my consciousness. There is something here to be experienced that is more than I knew with Joachim. When I allow my mind to open to exploring a greater shared purpose, I sense our present life circumstances being lifted into a lightness of being that promises an unprecedented level of fulfillment and joy.

To allow myself to think these thoughts feels like a kind of heresy. It feels like a betrayal of the oaths I made with Joachim. Yet, as I approach John's door there is the same irrefutable knowing I felt when the breathless runner arrived with the invitation to come to John's side. I knew then, as I know now, I must come and ease his condition. I know that in being near him, regardless how many hours or days or years we may be given, it is important to remember our soul connection and our greater Soul Purpose. Just as I felt exceedingly shy before running into Joachim's arms, so am I now feeling a peculiar shyness mixed with a secure confidence that calms me.

Now that I see John's pale, drawn face, I feel a profound concern for his well-being. I realize that a priceless gift has been given. I do not want to lose its physical offering before we have opened ourselves completely to the potential we both sense is possible.

CA: Allow yourself to move forward to the next significant or important event that occurs.

ANNA: Several weeks have passed. I smell smoke rising up from a crackling fire. John is lying on a sheepskin pallet by the wall of the round house. The weather has cleared somewhat and I am grateful I can open the door and allow more fresh air and light into the small, cramped space. Today I may even take John outside for a little walk. He's coming along nicely. His fever has broken. He's taking more substance and digesting it well. He is gaining strength. I am grateful.

CA: Can you share what John looks like?

ANNA: In some respects his appearance is similar to Joachim's, in that he is quite tall and slender. His cropped black hair is graying at the temples and his beard is almost completely white. His kind eyes are a very dark brown and his skin is olive-toned. He has told me he comes primarily from Celtic stock; but that his grandfather came to Britain from Rome as a soldier during Julius Caesar's campaign (55 and 54 BC). As often happens, the soldier returned to his homeland leaving his lover pregnant. John's grandmother gave birth to a boy who later became John's father. He was born into a family that operated a freighting business based in Exmoor (*to the west of Avalon*) which takes supplies to the tin mines in Devon and Cornwall. Their wagons also haul lead from the mines in the Mendip Hills where John's father met his mother. John helped his father in the freighting business until John's wife died and his children were grown.

Many years ago my son, Joseph (*of Arimathea*), contracted this freighting service to carry tin and lead to his boats, which were then, and still are, moored on the coast of Cornwall and Devon.[41] Over the years Joseph and John developed a fondness for each other. John loved to spend time at our growing Celtic-Essene community in Avalon. He eventually left the freighting business to his children; most of whom wished to remain close to their grandmother's family in the Mendips. He was glad when the time came that he could move permanently to our beloved Isles of Apples. He rejoiced in finding a peaceful communal life that removed itself from many of the cares and distractions he had known in the poverty-stricken mining villages. The miners and their families suffer unbearable hardships. He continues to maintain several freight wagons; but they are serving a different purpose now as they support our community of Essene-Druid initiates.

CA: Is John an initiate of the mystery school in Avalon?

ANNA: His formal journey as a probationary initiate only began a few years ago. He is keenly interested in the basic teachings I have begun to share with him. I observe John having a natural endowment for the mystical. I would say he has an affinity for the realms of spirit combined with a love of beauty and a generosity of heart. He has an innate ability to still his mind and calm his emotions. He has been practicing the powerful connection between

---

[41] It is also to be understood that Joseph kept a small number of boats moored at Narbo Martius on the west coast of the Great Sea in southern France. These are overseen at this time by his son-in-law, Aonghas, Lois Salome's husband's sons.

conscious breathing and mindfulness of the present moment. He is looking deeply into his mind; his stream of thoughts and feelings and how there is no difference between his mind and how he experiences his outer world – how it is all a dream and he is the dreamer of the dream. He is consciously entering his sleeping dreams and his daytime dream as a more awake and compassionate witness; a conscious human being capable of changing his dream of life to be more joyful, thus assisting the collective dream to be more harmonious and happy.

Though somewhat challenging, he is already developing a keen awareness that everything that appears to be solid is actually without substance and cannot be independently separate from the web of Oneness. Everything is energy vibrating – coalescing and dissolving according to how he is focusing and aligning his consciousness – either expressing its infinite potential as harmony, wholeness and balance or as myriad kinds of suffering. He knows to ask himself, "Am I resting my awareness in the essential emptiness out of which the All rises, while retaining an awareness of pure, fresh Beingness – an abiding sense of peace and freedom – or am I yielding to my old, conditioned mind's grasping to make my transitory experiences real and permanent? Either way is all right, but the choice of loving-kindness and calm abiding in the present moment feel better. One choice brings harm and isolation, the other nurtures the heart of life rather than creating an arid wasteland. In these ways, I am assisting him to take what he already knows intuitively to deeper levels of awareness.

In the days we have been together he is becoming more aware of his energy bodies, which has grandly assisted his healing process. It won't be long before he'll actually be able to travel beyond the confines of his physical body.

CA: Does he have the same awareness you do of your soul connection?

ANNA: Yes, he does. He also feels an affinity for me, as if we are magnets pulling each other into a remembrance of an eternal embrace. It feels enlivening for us to be in this unfolding relationship. His family is quite glad we are finding a measure of happiness late in life. I am told there is more sparkle in my eyes. I am feeling lightness in my steps. We are both experiencing an increased energy rising in our loins and a delightful expansion of our hearts. It has been many years since we have felt this vibrant energy, I assure you! It is all quite extraordinary and mysterious. I am happy to say that I have come to feel that John is a gift from Joachim.

CA: Now move forward again to the next significant event. What is happening?

Anna and John on Chalice Hill, 45 AD

ANNA: John is living with me in my home on the hill above the red spring.

CA: How does it feel to be living with John?

ANNA: I am finding our life together very nurturing, very comforting. John is happy to have found that he has a talent for reading and writing. Now that he has more time, he is expanding his love of carving all manner of hardwoods into beautiful household items, such as bowls, as well as doors and furniture. He has learned the craft of making harps. He is beginning to learn how to play simple melodies and to recite stories and psalms. He is such a dear and gentle soul.

CA: Is he learning more of your ways with the mysteries of cellular regeneration?

ANNA: Yes, on a basic level we are exploring some regenerative practices – those that are a routine part of the Essene way of life. Our sexual lovemaking, though somewhat infrequent, seems to be the most effective gateway for him to ignite his erectile life-force energy. This motivates him to be disciplined in channeling this heightened energy in meditation and energy practices. Consistent practice of the basics is required, not only for enlightenment of consciousness, but to facilitate the rejuvenation of the body.

John has had some remarkable glimpses into the still heart of the Beloved on High. Over the few years I have known him he has gained many accomplishments. The benchmarks which indicate an initiate's authentic spiritual progress are evident. Even more important, however, I am relieved to observe his innately abundant patience, compassion and humility increasing rather than diminishing. I have counseled him to never speak of his experiences to others or to not "show-off" his emerging spiritual powers as a way to influence others for his own selfish gain. I am happy to say he is quick to receive this counsel and immediately applies it inwardly and outwardly. He is truly without guile and quickly rejoices in the progress his fellow initiates make. He seems to intuitively know that his transitory experiences – epiphanies of insight and bliss that have not yet been stabilized – do not mean that he is fully enlightened. I see many looking up to him, not just because of his association with me, but because he deserves such respect. However he knows that the level to which he has arrived does not qualify him to be a teacher and guide in whom other initiates can fully rely. He walks gently and speaks with wise, patient restraint.

I am watching years of hard work, sorrow and loneliness lift from his previously stooped posture. There is a lively spring to his step, a constant smile, a merry twinkle in his eyes and a robust luster to his skin. Every time he enters into and transmutes his core separation patterns and feels his afflictive emotions deeply, I experience him to be more and more present for his life; and gratefully, more present for our moments of mystical union. His vitality level is equivalent to a much younger man, which I admit I very much enjoy. This gives me an incentive to likewise preserve and increase my life-force.

I must say though, I am increasingly becoming aware that I am experiencing less and less motivation to continue the arduous Rite of the Sepulcher practices I used to participate in without hesitation. Before coming to Britain, I, in greater or lesser measure every decade, went into extended times of deep retreat in order to fulfill my purposes as a physical immortal. I am glad to pass this wisdom on to my son, Noah and his wives, Rhia and Dancing Wind, and several other initiates. Noah and his wives are very motivated to practice the disciplines involved. I am pleased that this and other ancient wisdom practices may continue through their lineage. My oldest son, Joseph (*of Arimathea*), has long participated in the basic Rite of the Sepulcher practices. It is for this reason that he is still so physically active and capable of rendering so much continuous service as an adept to our family and community.

I am sensing more and more that I am to hang up my physical robe, so to speak, and allow the natural declination of this physical form. I don't know how long this aging process will take because of all the energy cultivation practices I have done to prolong my life. I will continue our Essene way of diet, cleanliness, strenuous walking and physical labors, yogic postures and meditation. This harmonious way of being has long been my way and life. It is my offering to the Beloved on High. His unfailing Breath flows unhindered through me and is the source of my abiding joy. I dedicate my life-force and calm presence of mind to the upliftment and happiness of all beings with every breath. I am nothing; my body is nothing; for it is the Beloved on High who IS and uses this body to bring Love and Light into this world in Oneness.

Keeping occupied in this way assists me to feel that I am a useful instrument in service to our beloved community. Continuing to teach the young maidens, to facilitate the rituals of the Magdalene, and to offer wisdom within our council meetings all provide an opportunity for me to feel that my life in this body continues to have purpose and meaning. Now that John is here, my very rich life is even richer.

{Anna continues her story along with Mariam in Part 4, Chapter 27}

— Chapter 21 —

DANCING WIND

(Anna's Daughter-in-Law and Noah's wife)
Avalon, 49 AD

DANCING WIND: I smell roses. I love the smell of roses. (*The essential oil of roses had been applied to Catherine Ann's and Claire's throat and heart chakras.*)

CATHERINE ANN (*Henceforth: CA*): Please tell me who is speaking.

DANCING WIND: I have many names. For this record you can call me Dancing Wind. I am one of Noah's wives. If you wish to know, I am the younger one.

CA: Do you mean Noah, Anna's youngest son?

DANCING WIND: Yes, Noah is the youngest son of Anna the Wise. I have given Noah three children. He was married many years ago to another woman I never met. Noah called her Ariadne. She was the daughter of a now deceased tribal king of the Silure tribe, named Arviragus (*not to be confused with King Caradoc*). This great king, who is my great-grandfather, invited my husband, who was only a boy then, and his older brothers, Joseph of Arimathea, Andrew and Josephus to live here upon the Isles of Apples, called Ynes-Witrin or the Isles of Glass, as they are called by the Celts. Ariadne bore Noah five healthy children and then she died the year before I was born. Their last child, Vivian, was Light-conceived in the same way as others of Anna the Wise's grandchildren.

During the last years of Ariadne's life, when she was very ill, Noah married Rhia, who is my aunt. Noah and Rhia cared for Ariadne with a deep love that helped her pass peacefully into the purelands. Rhia is very wise and beautiful. She spent most of her early life in training within the Druid sanctuary of Mona. Now that Anna is here with her wisdom about cellular regeneration, Noah,

Rhia and I, with a few others, have been taken under her careful tutelage. This is a very challenging and sometimes dangerous path, but we are committed to carrying on this great work of the ancients. We are just beginning to see results in terms of our increased energy levels and more youthful appearance.

CA: Does Noah know you by the name Dancing Wind or something else?

DANCING WIND: I don't like to be limited by one name because I am so much more than a name can describe. I am glad Noah calls me by many names. But the one I like best is Dancing Wind. I like to be free as the wind that comes and goes. I like to take many forms and I like to be invisible to the physical eyes. Most of all, I like to feel boundary-less, at one with the enormity of all space and all beings. I immensely enjoy losing all sense of being in a separate body, while at the same time also experiencing being just me, like a little drop of rain in the sea or a snowflake in a field of winter snow. I enjoy teaching these ways of feeling free; and I also enjoy learning many new things, as I progress from level to level as an initiate.

Now that Anna the Wise is here, I am able to learn much more than I had known was possible before. She sets a wonderful example for me. She inspires me to also be wise and loving. When I think of her as my beloved teacher, I think of her as a great Druid. When, as a young woman, I confide in her, I experience her as my beloved grandmother. When I sit beside my husband and Rhia, we honor her equally as the Great Mother. Sometimes when I feel insecure in her eyes, as Noah's mate, I think of her as my mother-in-law. But in truth, I refrain from labeling her at all because I know she, like me and all beings, is much more than a name or many names.

CA: How old are you and what would you like to share with us today?

DANCING WIND: I am now in my 34th year. I would like to share the ways of the sisterhood, the ways of the Magdalene-Christ, the ways of the Grail Mother and their codes of light. I would like to share the ways of purification of the soul, the body and the mind.

These practices are important because this is how we protect our purity of intent, so that we might be a blessing instead of a curse upon life. I wish to share how it is that we bring beings of light to come from the other side of the mists into this Earthplane to help us. We call them forth because we know we human beings cannot be happy living solitary lives inside a self-imposed fortress of mental constraints; and the fields cannot be fertile if we are at war.

We see evidence of what human arrogance brings, as does blight bring hunger and suffering to all when innocent plants are dying and greed levels the forests. All beings flourish when we nourish one another and respect our interdependence. In truth, we who walk with two legs are small and weak. No matter what our mind attempts to create in order to impress others of its feigned power, our mind, in truth, controls nothing. It is best to be humble servants of the Great Mother and make beneficial alliances among all beings, both seen and unseen.

Among those we seek for help are the angels, as Anna the Wise calls these energy beings who show us how to walk our earth path lightly. These dear ones help us to be in human form. They remind us that our bodies are a precious momentary gift that allows us certain experiences and opportunities that can only be found here on earth. As we walk, as the angels walk, we bless all life born of the Earth Mother's body. When we are awake and aware, as the blessed angels are, we bless all her creatures in all their forms. As we see with the eyes of the Great Mother and her angels, we behold all creation's dancing energy fields. I love to see the beautiful color patterns radiating from our intermingling bodies of light. The beauty is beyond words. When we refine our senses to be more like those of the angels', we have the ability to bring a greater knowing of those places of pure light from whence we have come, but have forgotten.

We can know the ways in which the plant kingdom maintains their angelic essences, their voices, and their properties for healing. We can communicate with many forms of creation and know our relationship with different species. Even though all things pass in the twinkling of an eye, in the few moments we have, we can experience peaceful harmony, fertile beauty and healthy bodies. When we are fully present for each moment the Great Mother gives us, we can know joy and be a source of abundant love.

This is true even at those times when our losses and physical pain are great. With awareness and disciplined practice, we can extend our earthly sojourn until we are very ripe in wisdom. Then our lingering presence is a true blessing to many beings. All these practices have been passed down from before time by the Shining Ones who came first from the stars and then migrated to this ancient land from the islands you call Atlantis.

(*Thoughtful pause*)
There are some things that I wish to share with you which may seem strange. I am rather hesitant to voice them because you may misunderstand.

CA: It's OK if you feel a little uncomfortable at first. What you say may seem strange, but I'm sure as you are sharing, we will come to know it all as wisdom. What you have to share may be of great assistance to us in a future time so that we can remember and make shifts in our beings. Thank you for coming so that we can bring forth a greater consciousness.

DANCING WIND: I must look into my heart. We safeguard these sayings and teachings very carefully. There are ones in your time who remember a portion of what we have hidden from the profane. These souls are remnants of the lineage that we safeguard. This is the primary reason I am here with you today. We are able to communicate because we feel a mutual resonance. We understand each other because we share in the same purpose and design which is imprinted into our genetic pool.

(*Pause*)
I am continuing to look, and as I look, I feel our familiar resonance. While I have words to share, I am seeing I am here, in this moment, simply to welcome you back into our circle of sisters.

CA: We thank you for that.

DANCING WIND: There are a number of us who have a desire to utter our stories with the hope that you can feel and remember our vibration. We see that what you bring to our circle is a greater clarity of ourselves cast forward into your time, into your season of being. We see that some of you are our future selves. We bring wisdom and clarity to each other from both directions across the passage that is called time.

CA: What do you call your circle?

DANCING WIND: You would not understand the Celtic words. But in your understanding of the ways of the Great Mother, you know us as a circle of Magdalenes.

(*Smiling and laughing*) It makes me very happy to hear these words spoken.

CA: It makes me happy, too.

DANCING WIND: Some of us are wives of the brothers of this community in Avalon. Some of us are choosing to be celibate for a time so that we can go through rituals which prepare us to pass across dimensional thresholds. We are at various levels of training and expertise. Some of us, who wish more advanced learning, also spend time on the great Isle of Avalon (*Mona or Ynes Mon on the coast of northwestern Wales*) far to the west by the shining sea. Many of these brothers and sisters who are trained at the great school of wisdom in Mona return to be teachers of great wisdom here. Some of the initiates preparing to go to Mona for their first time are my husband, Noah's relatives. They came to Avalon with my mother-in-law, Anna the Wise.

Do not be distressed that we might bring only a small portion of all that could be said forward at this time. It seems to us, as we survey those who shall partake of this co-creation, there will be a timely unfolding until everyone receives their promised portion. There's no reason to be anxious. It's like slowly unwrapping a quilt of many different patterns and a spectrum of colors all pieced together. We unfold here and we unfold there, but eventually all will be revealed. All that is to be made known will be given, whether through my grandmother's story or through the stories others of this lineage bring. It will all be told in due time, you can be assured of that. All that has been hidden, I am glad to say, will be revealed.

Now we are in a time of building bridges and opening doors which have been long locked shut. It is as if those who have guarded the way have grown into pillars of salt and the hinges of the old heavy door are rusted. The locks and keys have melded together. It takes time for all that has been silenced in the cold darkness to awaken. The door must be opened from the inside out. But the opening cannot occur until the time of awakening is here. We know that time has come because you stand at the door and knock. We hear you. Now we shall do our part to open the door from our side so that we can cross the threshold. Then more and more of us shall meet and embrace each other on both sides of time.

We are somewhat reluctant to speak of things that we would not have dared bring forth to the uninitiated ear in our day. Our training asks us to be very, very cautious and careful. We follow the counsel of the adepts, "Know, be, do and keep silence." Rest assured we are making certain that what we share will serve a good purpose and it will not bring harm. We marvel that so many more ears can hear us now. We are amazed that so much can now pass our lips. We are thankful that it is so.

CA: We are thankful that the time has come for sharing your wisdom. May I ask if the symbol and scent of roses has anything to do with the Magdalenes?

DANCING WIND: Oh, yes, especially red and white roses. The red rose represents our womb and monthly blood and the white rose represents our brothers' seed.

CA: There have been times when each of us has smelled roses, without any particular source of the scent being apparent. Does that indicate the presence of a Magdalene?

DANCING WIND: Yes, or it could be the scent of the Mother herself. One of the functions of the Magdalenes, besides facilitating spiritual awakening and mystical union, is to introduce you to the Mother of All Things. The scent of roses attunes you to her Presence and great love. You are lifted up into her Heart when you attune to the high frequency of roses. The angels of the mystical rose convey you on their wings so that you may take your ascent into the heart of the Great All. The rose helps you bridge the gulf that seems to separate the domain of the human and the domain of spirit.

ANNA, THE VOICE OF THE MAGDALENES

(*Thoughtful pause*)

We apologize somewhat, but not altogether, for the sobriety with which we come forth so often. It is not always like this. We do have times and seasons of celebration in which we come out of our cloaks to dance in the moonlight. We dance more often in her light because the moon moves through her cycles more frequently than does the sun. The springs and meadows, hilltops and mounds, stone circles and groves welcome our singing and dancing; whether at night or in the light of day. We sing and dance with and without musical instruments; with and without clothes. The beings of the elemental and fairy realms have energetic intercourse with us. There are times when beings come in large spheres of light from other worlds and dimensions.

I have come to know the one called Yeshua, my husband's nephew, who has joined our circles from time to time during these past years. He has taken us on spirit journeys and he has given us many wisdom teachings. Sometimes he takes the form of some of the gods and goddesses and introduces us to other great beings he has met on his many travels. He displays these beings before us by "impersonating" or merging with them. Then he tells their epic stories. We, who have been trained in the art of shape-shifting and the oral traditions of storytelling and theatre, especially enjoy listening to him for hours on end. I am very happy when he invites us to enact a role or dance the dances of the gods and goddesses. His mother and Myriam (*of Tyana*) are with us again after their long absence in India. Even though they come and go more than I would like, we are greatly blessed by their extraordinary wisdom and gifts of spirit. So, you see, it's not always so serious and sober.

Sometimes the uninitiated misunderstand the occasions when we bridge the worlds and make the earth fertile in her seasons and cycles of time. To such ones the celebrations, and the things that we do, may seem very strange. Often the curious and naïve, even though they mean well, misunderstand. When they attempt to do what they do not understand, they often have disappointing and sometimes even painful experiences. This is because they do not have sufficient insight or preparation of their minds and bodies to benefit from what they superficially observe or imagine us doing.

Even greater mischief and harm has been done by those with ambitious designs to aggrandize themselves or maliciously hurt others. They attempt to do this by learning how to use the energies of the earth, sun, moon and stars to control beings for their selfish purposes.

Most of these are ignorant of their inner shadows, which obscure and distort the wisdom and love that remain hidden in their minds and hearts. Some innocently join us, while others feign sincerity. We read their energy fields and minds before admitting anyone into the most basic training. Some are turned away immediately. Those who are admitted are placed on a probationary status. They are closely observed and given initiatory tests which determine their readiness to proceed to another level. But some, before they have healed their minds and souls sufficiently, leave their training and the wise teachers who can help them heal. Among these, there are those who refuse to use their acquired skills responsibly. These unfortunate souls are slowly but surely beginning to know the painful consequences which inevitably come when powerful energies are abused.

Let me say more even if I repeat myself; so that you may clearly understand the importance we give to our vows of harmlessness. Everyone who enters our community must pass through cleansing processes before more is given. This preparation is a responsibility we do not take lightly. The ones with selfish motives, who are overcome by the poisons of their minds, often find these increasingly challenging initiatory passages too difficult to bear. They either depart on their own, often with much resentment, or they are firmly asked to leave, much to their chagrin and shame. Some of these try to gain some measure of esteem and mastery by using the little knowledge they have gained in some form of lesser psychic and astral mediumship. But often this meets with frustration.

For those whose intention is malevolent from the beginning, lower forms of alchemy and magick are learned elsewhere. Such ones use the sorcerer's craft because this is all their fearful hearts care to do. This brings much harm to their souls and injury to the souls of others. They have not opened their hearts to the importance of loving-kindness and a higher form of alchemy that benefits everyone. I have witnessed this and it brings much pain to my heart. I have great concern for their souls. I join with the other elders to prevent the damaging impact such ones can have on our community. It is like a rotten apple damaging the whole basket of apples. It is best to escort such ones away before they ever enter our door.

Now you can begin to understand why it is that we are reluctant to let go of our concerns and conditioned control which takes various forms of secrecy. As we look at the many awakening souls during the season in which you live, we see a greater good coming forth by sharing more with you. So it is that we are beginning to let go. We are realizing that to hold onto control, even though we mean well, can also bring harm. This is a delicate undertaking. To reveal enough to bring forth wisdom, but not so much that there is harm.

CA: You said you are married to Noah and that you are his younger wife. Please tell us more about your relationship with him and the custom of having more than one wife. How do you feel about that?

DANCING WIND: Among the people I know; the Silures and other nearby Celtic tribes, I have come to know it is customary to have multiple partners. However, a couple who wishes to be monogamous is equally supported. When such a couple is well-suited to each other, we encourage being mated for life. We are also pragmatic and know life's circumstances bring unexpected changes. A couple, or another configuration of people, is given a "hand-fasting" ceremony that bonds them for a certain amount of time. Then when that time comes to an end, they can reconsider and dissolve the bond if they choose or have another bonding ceremony for an agreed time. There are ones, like Noah, Rhea and me, who have committed to be faithful to each other for life. I am also aware that some family clans abuse their responsibilities as mates and parents. I would like to see the ideal being lived; however, I'm aware we sometimes fail and many suffer as a consequence.

By suggesting that we participate in multiple partner relationships, does not mean I am encouraging promiscuity or that I am advocating polygamy or polyandry – I am aware that much suffering arises from these practices when love and deeper understanding are not present. Because we practice as we do, as has been our custom for many generations, does not mean it is beneficial for everyone or for all societies; in my time or in yours. Within our community we take the responsibilities of being devoted couples and being dutiful, loving parents very seriously.

In this same light, we do not condemn a responsible choice to have more than one partner. It is possible for a man to have more than one woman, and for a woman to have more than one man, for the length of time that is mutually agreed. This also extends to those of the same sex. I prefer to not describe the various methods that are used to discourage the abuse of vows. I simply want to emphasize that we, in Avalon, take our responsibility to be harmless in our relationships quite seriously.

CA: Is this a common practice?

DANCING WIND: Generally speaking, we find openly honoring each other in this way serves our society better than to have liaisons in secret. Our families are cross-generational and often cousins marry each other. Family bloodlines are carefully monitored so that the children are as healthy as possible. Sometimes marriages are arranged for various reasons, such as Noah and Ariadne's. We try our best to be sensitive to a couples' appeal for marriage when it is genuinely based in love, even when an earlier arrangement by the parents to marry someone else has been made. Children are always welcomed with love and they are given great care, especially here within our community of Avalon.

I readily admit there are many exceptions to this ideal, as I have described it, among the Britons generally and among the Celtic-Essenes of Avalon specifically. We are far from perfect. Sometimes there are quarrels and jealousies among us. Within some tribes there are wars and many atrocities waged against one another over the breaking of oaths and alliances. In these situations there are all kinds of political intrigue and long-lasting feuds. But for the most part, we, in Avalon, are a community of spiritual initiates who bridle our human appetites and weaknesses. We are very motivated to do this for the good of all within our community. Knowing our interconnectedness, we extend our good to the greater circle of humanity and all beings.

CA: Is this practice of multiple partners congruent with the Magdalene circle or is it only a Celtic custom?

DANCING WIND: I have learned many things from my husband's family about the great wisdom mysteries, especially from Anna the Wise to whom I am devoted as a student. The work of the Magdalenes to awaken consciousness and restore Awareness of Oneness has been upon the Earthplane throughout time. The names may be different but the source of the lineages is the same. We have a long oral history that tells us we come from a very ancient origin. We try to preserve the practices that have helped us to be a happy and basically kind people. Anna has told me this manner of honoring relationships is a very ancient practice that can be found not only among the Celts, but among the Magdalenes in many other cultures. Some of our ancient practices are kept secret and are given only to qualified initiates. These are energy practices that have more to do with enlightening consciousness and developing self-mastery than they do with sex; that is, as most experience their sexuality.

We see our ancient energy practices becoming misunderstood, distorted and abused. Much suffering has come as a result. Monogamy is the better choice until there is a greater sense of reverence for the sacredness of life; and even then, monogamy is best for most couples who are consciously choosing relationship as their path of spiritual awakening.

Many have strayed from the truths of Oneness and love. There are many territorial battles and much ignorance, disease and poverty. Many conquerors from other lands, being ignorant and coarse in their being, have abused women and children for as long as anyone can remember. The men feel entitled and have many wives; the despots have harems; human flesh is trafficked in the slave markets.

Great suffering has come from this base ignorance. We, in Avalon, struggle to preserve a more mindful way of life that lessens suffering and brings peace instead of war and famine. Sometimes we are successful and sometimes we are not. Now that the Romans have returned to our sacred lands we are very concerned for our welfare and our ability to maintain an unbroken lineage of truth bearers.

We have noticed an uncomfortable influence that has come into our circle from those who have migrated here from the lands where my husband was born; as well as people who come from other lands that border the Great Sea. Unfortunately, this seems to be especially true of those who have heard Yeshua's teachings and are confused about their true meaning. They try to understand according to the old ways in which they have been taught. Many of the ones who have recently come to Avalon try to separate spirit and matter, mind and heart, male and female, good and evil. It seems to me that when there is a split like this in their minds, there is a disharmony and an imbalance in the way they relate to other people; the Earth Mother and her seasons and cycles of life. It is as if they separate themselves from themselves. It is a sad thing. We see more mistreatment and abuse. This is a dark time upon the earth.

But we, as Magdalenes, do what we can to keep the Earth Mother's body, including our bodies (*as her gift to us*), and the ways of our sexual expression and creativity wholly unified and sacred. Whether it is the conception and forming of babies in our wombs and caring for their rearing, the creation of patterns with cloth and stones, or other forms of creation; we honor the sacredness of life. We also express this in the way we weave our stories and dance our dances or merge in sexual love. We praise and find great joy in our physical senses as we embrace all forms as expressions of one divinity. It makes no difference that the Great Mother takes the form of deer, ants, clouds, stones, trees, or running and still water. We are all one family. I have my being in all of these. They are all my brothers and sisters, expressing as the Mother's many forms. We give them many names but still they have their being in me and I have my being in them.

You must look deeper than my words to understand. The heart knows all in wholeness. The mind and its words separate what is inseparable – the naked suchness beyond names and concepts.

There are traditions among the Celts that have always troubled me, such as various kinds of blood sacrifice or the ways of war or the ways of cursing others. Whether they are expressed by men or women, I experience them as being the outer manifestations of deeply troubled hearts and minds clinging to the idea of being a separate, solid and self-existing identity. I have noticed more men than women aligned with these dark practices. I feel this is because men generally perceive blood and reverence for life differently than women.

I have also seen exceptions. I find the female warriors short-sighted and calloused when they come to our community to rally support for going to war, as if war justifies the shedding of life's blood. I have witnessed village women angrily trying to correct an abuse. They seem to hold more resentment and anger than eunuchs who feel cut off from their power. I have seen male warriors in their full power, more caring than fearful women feeling powerless to change their lot. Since the Emperor Claudius marched his troops upon this sacred land, I am seeing an increase of anxiety and unrest among both men and women. Suppressed survival instincts are rising to the surface more frequently. We invite harmony and peace, but our words seem to fall increasingly on deaf ears.

My sister-in-law, Mary Anna (*Mother Mary*), since her recent return from Rome and the Far East, has told us that this warring spirit seems to be expressing more and more. Yeshua's wives, Myriam of Tyana and Mary of Bethany also tell us how most of the men on their travels do not know the ways of the Great Mother; the nurturing ways of the feminine heart, the ways of knowing through feeling. Sadly, more and more women are forgetting the Goddess' mysteries in which there is an honoring of their blood; their cycles and seasons. I thank the Goddess that Noah and Rhia are not like these unfortunate souls who have created a self-made wasteland. I am glad Yeshua and others in our community honor and keep these powerful energies sacred in the way they relate to all women, children and the whole of life.

CA: Thank you for sharing your wisdom. Is there more you wish to share?

DANCING WIND: I hope you like being here in this circle that honors you and all life expressing in your day.

CA: Yes, thank you for including us in this beautiful circle that feels so familiar. Is there anything more you would like to share?

Dancing Wind's Guided Meditation

DANCING WIND: Yes, I would like to invite you to come with me on an imagined journey.

I wish you to imagine a most beautiful night sky. We are laying together arm in arm on the soft grasses covering the great Tor of Avalon. At our heads is a large standing stone, which is part of a stone circle. The circle embraces the inner sanctum, the place where the dragon lines[42] marry and dive deeply into the womb of our Earth Mother. Our feet point toward the center of the wheel where there is a small sacred fire. We look up and we behold the heavens. The stars are pulsing with light.

Spiraling energies are coming down to make love with us. We breathe in the energy of the Earth Mother below us. Her body is pulsing. She invites us to join with her in a seamless way that unites our mutual yearning for Father Spirit to mate with us. Our bodies are as the trees and the standing stones which deeply amplify and focus the descending and ascending energies. As we lie here upon this ancient mound we can feel the Oneness of all things. This has been our way since the dawn of time when we all spoke the same language. We remember we are the Ancient Ones returned to create

---

[42] Dancing Wind is referring to electro-magnetic energy lines or ley lines that run through various levels of the Earth's surface; just above, on and below. These lines are psychically discerned through dowsing rods or through precise instruments. On the Tor these lines weave a pattern which the Druids ceremoniously follow as a kind of labyrinth. The electric and magnetic lines converge ("marry") at the apex of the Tor and create a very powerful energy vortex. They are called dragon lines because of their undulating properties. Druids who are trained in geomancy are often called Dragons.

a holy temple in which heaven and earth can touch, embrace and merge. The Earth Mother wears her most resplendent wedding robes. All beings are at peace.

We can feel the great chambers below us emitting their light. We can feel the light of Earth's inner sun and the great crystal beings who remember the history of this sphere. Patterns of light, sound and color weave intricate designs all around us. We hear fine music, the tinkling of bells, delicate cymbals and stringed instruments, horns, and celestial voices. Tall beings of gossamer light are descending; angels, Pan and the faeries gather around us. They are all dancing and leaping, weaving intricate patterns of scintillating rainbow light. As we attune with them we feel a lightening and a lifting up. Our physical bodies rest in calm repose while our etheric doubles rise up to join in the dancing and merriment.

Returning from the space beyond time, our ethereal bodies quicken the cells of our physical bodies. We feel the heat of the sacred fire at the center of the stone circle. Our hearts and bellies are aflame with ecstasy. We rise up and dance around the fire that touches the stars. Effortlessly and joyfully, we leap through the flames. Round and round we dance. We are ignited and intoxicated with Great Love exploding and flowing through us.

We are the dancing flames, the flowing air, the fecund earth, the ambrosial water and the Great Emptiness – the Beloved holding us to his lips – breathing us into the Holy Grail of Love. We surrender completely into the Breath, breathing our exalting dance. We weave ourselves into all manner of creation within the chalice cup! We melt into emptiness beyond our mind's understanding; aware only of bliss and the sacredness of all things – letting go – just Being as we are!

I invite you to be a part of this dance, forever and ever, weaving your body anew as a receptacle of light. You are a keeper of the sacred grail, the holy blood, the keys and codes of remembrance of the worlds from whence we have come and the Great Home beyond all worlds of form. As you remember me and our Grail family, may you remember the sacredness of your life and the sacredness of this magic-making.

I have come to be with you so that we can all create a greater happiness to be known in every beating heart. Whether it is a heart flowing blood or sap, may we weave our magic beyond time and beyond words within the Great Silence.

You can think of me as the dancing wind carrying you to the Home we never left. The place we call Avalon beyond the farthest shore.

— Chapter 22 —

NOAH

(Son of Anna & Husband of Dancing Wind)
Mona – Isle of Anglesey, Wales, spring, 47 AD

NOAH: I see beloved ancient trees. I see evergreens of pine, cedar, fir, yew, and holly. Among these great beings are deciduous trees, shrubs and thickets. They bear leaves, blossoms and fruit of every color and variety. The verdant rolling landscape, which supports these groves and orchards, is covered with grasses and wildflowers.

CATHERINE ANN (*Henceforth: CA*): Is this an area in Britain?

NOAH: Yes.

CA: What are you doing there now?

NOAH: We are a company walking on a well-worn path. Several of us are leading horses with packs on their backs. I am wearing a long, heavy, woolen, hooded cloak that is dyed a very dark blue – almost black. My feet, which are the feet of a man, are covered with leather. They show the mud, grime and wear from much walking. We have walked a long distance.

CA: Are you a young or older man?

NOAH: I am what you would call in my middle years, although I consider my years different than you reckon the aging of the body in your social consciousness at this time. My years are many, but my body does not reflect the passages of the sun.

CA: Is that because of the training you have had?

NOAH: Yes.

CA: Who are you?

NOAH: My mother and father call me Noah. I go by other names in Avalon.

CA: Who else is traveling with you?

NOAH: There are twenty-four men and women including my wives Rhia and Dancing Wind; my mother, Anna; my half-brother, Joseph (*of Arimathea*) and his wife, Nueme; my niece Mary of Bethany and her daughter, Sar'h. Myriam of Tyana's children: Joses, Jude and Miriam. Some of our older children are with us, as well as other adults from our community in Avalon.

CA: Do you have children by both of your wives?

NOAH: Yes. My first wife, Ariadne, who passed into the purelands many years, ago gave me five children. Rhia has given me two healthy children and Dancing Wind, three. Two of my older children are with us. My wives are wise in the ways of healing herbs, the seasons and the cycles of time. They know how to bend time, as it were. They can become invisible and change the shape of their form. Their souls are ancient like mine. We have walked upon this earth in many forms.

Raven-haired Rhia is noble in bearing, tall and strong of limb. Fiery-haired Dancing Wind is quite small, agile as a deer and just as gentle. Unlike some men who choose younger wives, that is not my purpose for choosing these beautiful women. It is that their season for coming forth onto the Earthplane came in my later years and it was only at this time that we could meet. We deeply recognized each others' souls. It is not because of their youthful appearance, stamina or abilities to please me as a man that I chose them. Although I admit I do appreciate these gifts the Great Mother has given me. There is so much misunderstanding amongst many men and women about these concerns which are not our concerns.

Joseph (*of Arimathea*), my half-brother, who is well-advanced in wisdom and years; but who appears much younger, has his mate, Nueme, with him. They were married in 41 AD soon after Joseph returned home from his voyage and travels with my sister, Mary Anna (*Mother Mary*), and Myriam of Tyana to the lands to the east. Nueme is of the tribe of the Celtic peoples (*the Silures*) who live upon the land through which we are passing. In your tongue you call these beautiful mountains and peaceful valleys, Wales and this region, Glamorgan.

My mother, Anna, also has a companion with her, named John, with whom she has ceremonial intercourse, a Tantric energy practice which is familiar to a number of us. There are a few men and women with us who have not participated in these rituals. Most, I believe, will enter into this way when it is in a ripeness to do so.

CA: Would you be willing to share more about ceremonial intercourse?

NOAH: We may do that at another time. Not now.

CA: Is there a purpose to the journey that you wish to share?

NOAH: Yes. We have been invited by one of the Ordovician tribal kings who lives in the north and by leaders of other tribes to come and make ceremony with them. They want to fortify the energy around and within several places where they abide in the West Country. We have already visited three large villages in the region you call Glamorgan, where my elderly brothers Andrew and Josephus live. Sadly, they are not faring well; Andrew is quite crippled and Josephus is ailing. I see them passing into the purelands within the year. (*Andrew and Josephus do pass away within weeks of each other at the end of the year.*) There are five more villages to visit before we arrive at the one that is of grand significance to us. It is far more than a village center. An entire island is given to the high Druid arts and sciences. You know this sacred hidden isle of Avalon or Ynes Mon, as Mona (*present-day Anglesey*), the heart of Druid culture and education.

In the four short years since they penetrated the southeast coast of Britain, the Romans have begun building many roads and forts. They already stretch in all directions from their primary occupations along the river Thames. An almost straight road is almost completed which extends far to the northeast. It crosses the flat levels very close to our community of Avalon and then onward into the depths of Cornwall to the southwest. They call the road the Fosse Way. Already there are tributaries extending their reach into Wales. Forts are being constructed. Skirmishes and heavy battles are continually being waged. My Druid brothers and sisters are deeply concerned. Our alliances and family ties are inextricably connected. Therefore, we share our destiny with that of our brothers and sisters of the Celtic tribes who call this land home.

Alarming reports are brought to our council meetings by those who have traveled and seen the increasing numbers of Romans forcing their customs upon our Celtic brothers and sisters to the east of us. The Romans have taken command of ancient gold, silver, lead, iron and tin mines; which are operated by slaves and indentured servants. We are intensifying our efforts to preserve our peaceful way of life in Avalon. It reminds us too much of the stories my Essene family tells me about the Roman occupation of Galilee, Judea and Gaul.

We have heard King Caradoc (*the Romans call him Caratacus*), who has led the resistance against the Roman occupation in the East, is already on his way to Mona. We know him well, having taken sup and counsel together many times over the years. It will be good to be with our loyal friend once again. It is understood that the Silures are looking to Caradoc to lead them to victory.

Many of us with inner sight repeatedly see a most tragic vision of the Romans storming the Menai Strait (*the narrow water-way separating the mainland of Wales and the isle of Mona*) and laying siege to our most sacred Druid sanctuary and mystery school. We do not know when, or if, this will occur, but we must do what we can to prevent it. We are not openly resisting, but we are making necessary preparations to ward off potential desecration and abuse. Although the Romans claim they are here to maintain peace, over the short years since Claudius' arrival in 43 AD, we have seen our valiant neighboring peoples subjugated and some taken into slavery.

The simpler, rural folk are forced to join their armies, work in the tin and lead mines and stone quarries; and build lavish Roman villas, baths and fortified cities. The Romans are an ambitious, extremely industrious, urbane people. Their materialistic influence grows at an alarming rate. If the Romans were not enough to give us concern, there are also the conquered peoples from other lands brought here to serve as indentured soldiers and laborers. Even though the Romans bring improved sanitation, roads and water systems, the fact is, the rapid change which is imposed upon us creates much unrest among the freedom-loving Celts. This is especially true of the tribes in the east that are heavily impacted by the growing number of Roman cities, such as Londinium (*present-day London*). We are concerned that this subjugation will, all too soon, be our lot, as well.

Our indigenous people can be fierce when provoked. After all, Julius Caesar turned tail twice, in 55 and 54 BC, when he met our opposition long ago. But these are different times. With improved ships, the Romans breach our coastlines by the thousands. They are becoming more entrenched by the day and the peace they try to maintain is fragile.

For these reasons we have answered the invitation to join our brothers and sisters who protect Mona and our other centers of Druid learning in the West Country. It is important to stabilize our alliances and to assist our allies as best we can. We have already visited a number of our satellite communities and made ceremony with the elders who live along the course of our journey. Some of these leaders have joined us. Others have gone on ahead to set up camp. We hope to be in Mona within three weeks to prepare for a very large gathering.

It is now the spring Beltane season. We will abide in Mona until we complete the autumnal Samhain festival. A number of initiates who have come with us will be receiving preliminary training during the months we are here. If they are accepted, they will remain in Mona until they are finished with their advanced courses. It is understood they will return to Avalon sooner if their safety is threatened. There are several initiates who have already lived on Mona for several years. They have accomplished their initiatory work and other purposes for being at the sanctuary of Ynes Mon. We will take them back to Avalon with us this fall. There is safety in numbers.

CA: How long have you been in Britain at this point?

NOAH: I have been here many decades. I first arrived in 22 BC when I was only a lad of twelve. It is now 47 AD.

CA: Why haven't you taken Joseph's (*of Arimathea*) boats to Mona?

NOAH: As I have said, there are village leaders throughout Wales we wish to see; to voice our concerns for them and to invite them to the gathering on Mona. Walking through the inland vales has been our preferred way of travel. However, if time is of the essence, then we do take our boats. Although the journey by boat would have been faster and easier for the women, we chose this time to go on foot, for the reasons I have told you. There is much unrest, but we feel confident that we have our allies' protection.

Our community still has four of Joseph's boats moored in one of the safe harbors on the coast of what you call Cornwall. Two more are safely harbored on Devon's shore. We use the boats to transport family members and initiates to France and other destinations near the Great Sea. Joseph very seldom chooses to set sail anymore, having turned most of his boats and freighting business over to his aging daughter, Lois Salome's husband Aonghas' sons who live near Narbo Martius in Gaul. Joseph prefers to travel only when the family is in need of his boats and diplomatic expertise, such as his more recent trips with Mary Anna and Myriam (*of Tyana*) to Rome and Ephesus.

He is enjoying a simpler life with his beloved Nueme and staying close to his children and extended family. As a Druid, he also spends many hours providing wise counsel for the wide spectrum of people who seek him from near and far. He is planning on a voyage in the summer or fall of next year to Bugarach and Ephesus in order to bring Mary Anna and Myriam back to Avalon, as they earlier agreed. He tells us this may well be his last long journey by sea.

We are enjoying our visits with the tribal chieftains and communities along the way to Mona. The distance between villages is not great. There has been ample opportunity for rest and renewal of familial connections. Even though some of the women are advanced in age, they are in extremely good physical health. The hardships are minimal.

CA: Move forward now to the next significant event that happens.

NOAH: We arrived in Mona several weeks ago. The early Beltane ceremonies have been celebrated. We have had days of feasting, music, dancing, storytelling and matchmaking. Now I am sitting in a large wooden chair made for ones who hold positions of leadership. I am in a great hall constructed primarily of tall wooden timbers, stone, mud and wattle, and thatching. There are a few windows. The space is dimly lit with most of the light coming from fires laid on great stone hearths. There are also torches that extend from the walls. There are several hundred people gathered; men, women and older children. The young children and infants are being cared for in what you call nurseries in the domiciles, which are set apart for them.

This is an important council meeting. We are gathered to hear the general populous' concerns, as well as to listen to respected tribal leaders, such as our dear King Caradoc; all of whom have prepared long dissertations on a variety of topics. I am awaiting my turn. Of course the primary concern on everyone's lips is the encroachment of the Romans. Both women and men give forth equally, perhaps more men than women, but the women's voices are honored, including Caradoc's good wife.

CA: Are the people who are attending this gathering from Mona or from all over?

NOAH: They are from a number of different tribes, as I described earlier. I understand that it is difficult to remember all that we say and how it all interrelates. I have great patience, so proceed with your questions without concern of offending me.

CA: Thank you. Yes, at times all the unfamiliar names and topics are confusing and difficult to keep straight in my mind.

NOAH: Back to your question: yes, this gathering is being attended by different tribal leaders and representatives from all the regions of the West Country.

The council meetings last several days, followed by a time of feasting and merriment. It is at the end of this time that a very old custom of blood sacrifice is enacted, if there is a reason to do so. This year the council has found what they consider to be a good reason. Joseph (*of Arimathea*) and I will reluctantly attend, as there does not seem to be a way out that would create less harm than

NOAH

adding our witness. My mother and the other women did find a graceful way to excuse themselves.

We Essenes abhor this and other rituals which use blood sacrifice. The more traditional Celts, in the hope that a greater good may be accomplished for the land and people, have pressed their case for a sacrificial scapegoat this year. None of the reasons they have offered, in our opinion, justify the loss of life. It is our truth that these ritual dramas have a deeper meaning, better conveyed as archetypal drama and alchemical metaphor. They were never intended to be enacted literally. Thankfully, on Mona, these rituals are rare and only done after careful consideration. As I speak, I am aware that my young nephew, Yeshua, did literally enact the role of "scapegoat;" but it was for the purpose of ending blood sacrifice, not perpetuating it.

At this time there are seven men being held whose boat came on shore during a storm. It was not until it was too late that they realized where they were. It did not take long to recognize that this island was the legendary Ynes Mon – a Druid sanctuary. They remembered the agreement among the Celts that Druids, living in sanctuary, are considered beyond the arm and acts of war. They were recognized as a scouting party of a marauding tribe from the far North Country. Ordinarily, such ones would be firmly sent on their way after surrendering their weapons and making a solemn oath to never return.

But with the rising anxiety mounting over the Roman invasion, these men were not reprimanded and released, but rather captured, chained and put into a large man-shaped wicker basket. (*Heavy sigh*) It was decided at the tribal council meeting that these pitiable men would be offered as a sacrifice to ward off an even greater travesty, the capture and annihilation of Mona by the Roman armies. Those of us from the inland isles of Avalon petitioned for these men's lives. But our efforts were to no avail.

Tonight and tomorrow many of the adults will become intoxicated. They will also use various methods to enter into deep trance states. Before the sun goes down we will gather to the large open field where the captive men are being held. Many curses and incantations have been placed upon them for many days. More will be placed when the bonfires are lit. We will remove most, if not all, of our clothing to reveal our tattooed bodies, which have been painted with a dye made of blue woad. I have tattoos myself, indicating that I have been adopted into the Silures tribe and that I am recognized as a Druid priest. As the first stars come out and the crescent moon is on the horizon, the men in the wicker basket will be set on fire and offered as scapegoats. Any physical remains will be sealed up in a bog, together with their weapons, armor, gold and silver ornaments, and coins.

These extreme and cruel traditions are very difficult for us to witness. Earlier in the day, we separated ourselves from the others in order to prepare our minds and hearts, as best we could. My mother and John; Joseph and our wives; my nephews and nieces; and the others from Avalon joined together with me in a quiet, removed place apart from the others' increasingly cacophonous sounds. While the native Celts were participating in their preparatory rituals for many long hours, we examined our minds to find any marauding fears and shadows lurking there. We courageously and mercifully brought the Light of merciful awareness to our internal enemies: anger, greed, jealousy, pride, despair and all manner of non-virtuous thoughts, words and actions with which we have harmed ourselves and others during the course of our lives.

We breathed in such a way as to stoke the alchemical fires of transmutation within our bellies. Not in judgment, anger or fear, did we breathe, but in compassionate knowing that all fearful thoughts and emotions that arose from within our minds into our unblinking awareness was the cause of endless suffering and rebirths for all beings who sleep in ignorance. We saw that the content of our minds, which still clung to a separate self, was no different than that of these brothers and sisters who ignorantly chose to cling to and enact their familiar traditions. With compassion for ourselves and them we affirmed that they, as we, only wish to flourish and be happy; that they, as we, do not wish to experience harm.

So it was that we turned to our chosen and familiar path which is to open our hearts with compassion so that our own internal adversaries may be embraced and transmuted through the power of love and wisdom. For it is that we have come to understand that all enemies are really not outside attacking us (*though we may indeed be attacked*), but they dwell consciously or unconsciously within our conditioned minds. We see that our enemies, which are actually illusory displays of infinite mind's potential, show us how we wall ourselves off from our true nature. And so it was that in this sad situation; and in this same manner, that we turned to compassion, mindfulness, insight and forgiveness. We humbly bowed and surrendered our minds, bodies, and emotional armor - those stubborn aspects of ourselves, which when triggered continue to cling to a separate identity. We placed these afflictive shadows into the Grail Fire which was ablaze within our bellies.

By doing so we could bring forth the needed change from within ourselves first. Once this was accomplished, we could face the collective mind's projected fearful and destructive forces with calm equanimity and clarity. In this way more harmonious options often presented themselves. And if death was to be our lot, we would go forth with calmness into the Light and serve with compassion from the other side of the veil.

And so it was that we breathed all suffering and causes of suffering into our bellies and hearts, as if they were the most magnificent fuel. We placed our entire sense of separateness and unquenchable greed for "having and being more" – "for protecting perceived 'me and mine' and bringing harm to 'other'" – into the flames of an undying, unifying Love. We opened ourselves and made ourselves naked to the vast Infinite Light that is our true being. We prostrated ourselves upon the sweet Earth Mother and poured forth our tears and sweat into the ground as we breathed in and felt the suffering of all beings. Our Love's labor was freely given, for in liberating "other" we found freedom and great joy abounding in our expansive hearts. With unified minds and hearts, we did this for ourselves and all beings, through all the times and all the realms.

In this way we remained until we could feel and see the wastelands of ignorance within us blooming and giving forth compassion's sweet fruits of forgiveness and brother/sisterhood.

When we felt sufficiently clear and stable, we united as a circle and energetically connected with the souls of the captives. In this way, while the others were preparing themselves to act out what they feared within themselves, we prepared ourselves to be of service to the Mother's Great Mystery. It was our hope to lessen the inevitable karmic suffering all beings experience.

We did this until we heard the voices and drums move to the killing field, which for them was perceived as a sacrificial altar. My mother, Anna; my wives, Rhia and Dancing Wind; my sister-in-law, Nueme; my nieces, Mary of Bethany, Sar'h and Miriam; and the other women, continued to work with the energies from a distance. We brothers walked slowly to the killing field where the terrified men were about to be sacrificed. We stood together a ways off from the others as the bonfire was lit. The "wicker-man" was held within the pyre. As the flames engulfed the "sacrifice," we attuned with the men's traumatized souls. We internally recited our soul-liberating mantras and assisted their souls to pass quickly into the Light, as we psychically accompanied them. Our unified intention was that they might not linger as tormented ghosts; that they would meet their guides and karmic choices with clear minds and hearts.

(*Reflective pause*)

I feel burdened by a deep weariness when I witness such displays of ignorance. I feel deep weariness as I share this dreamlike scene with you. (*Deep sighing*)

CA: Give this sense of being burdened permission to lessen and allow yourself to move on to an occasion when you feel more comfortable.

NOAH: We have returned to our beloved Avalon. Ominous dreams and visions still come, showing us terrible things that may play out in the not too distant future. It is a dark and dreary time for all beings walking the earth. It is difficult to maintain a lightness of heart these days. But at the darkest of times, I pick up my harp and sing; I love my wives and play with my children and grandchildren;

and I remember the sayings of my nephew, Yeshua and his beautiful Magdalenes.

I have had the privilege of witnessing a great Light come upon this plane. I endeavor to follow it and embody it until all darkness flees. We, who bring a ray of the Infinite Light into this dark dream, continue our practices of loving-kindness as best we can. Places such as Mona serve their divine purpose. But I can see her days, as a sanctuary and haven of wisdom, are numbered. Meanwhile, we gather together upon our blessed isles veiled in the gathering mists. We count each new day's dawning a great blessing.

Even though it seems "the troubles" follow us everywhere, I remind myself and my family that we do have many days of gentle peace. Making good use of the time we are given, we prosper in the ways of spirit. As long as the Great Mother showers us with her blessings, we will continue to create a place of wisdom where we may serve all beings with compassion. We invite others to come and experience the light that shines within them. Looking ahead, we pass on our oral and written spiritual teachings as a blessing to the coming generations. There have been many seasons of deep peace. For this, I give thanks.

CA: Is there more you would like to share?

NOAH: What I have told supports my mother's desire to assist souls in your day to make new choices with their lives. Sacrifice through blood, in all its forms, must come to an end. War, the disregard of life, the trampling of the Earth Mother and the raping of her sons, daughters, animals, plants and elements must cease. The taking of life into slavery of all kinds, whether it is self-inflicted abuse, addiction or the subjugation of household members or those who are perceived as different, must cease. All causes of separation must be brought to the heart of compassion and healed back into wholeness.

I emphasize once again, suffering must cease within all beings. So it is decreed. So it is that we assist all beings to be released from their chains of bondage. We come forth with our familiar vibration through the seasons of time. So it is that I, Noah, have taken a vow to remain close to this Earthplane where I join with you and many others to bring forth a new way of life.

I have been with my nephew, our beloved Yeshua and the Magdalenes. We have fasted and sought visions within the sacred groves and within the caves. We have looked into your day and into your children's generations to come. We see a different Earth – a garden resplendent with the beauty of peaceful harmony. We know this Earth already exists; it is but to chose it and awaken within a new dream. For this purpose, we live our lives with a sense of destiny. We do what we can. Sometimes we stumble upon the rocks of our own ignorance. We are saddened when the ears that hear our sayings remain deaf. This, our present generation, gropes blindly, even while the sun shines clearly. Though the darkness gathers, much has been seeded into the genetics of our lineage.

These seeds of light have come forth into your day. It is you who carry our stories and codes within your genetic memory. We are here to strike the bell of remembrance.

I have been blessed with many experiences in the Light. For this I give thanks. I give thanks to you for coming and listening to my voice beyond the mists. I shall come forth again, in yet a future time and future life where you may know me by a different name. You may recognize my vibration as a Merlin (*the Merlin Taliesin*) who weaves the tapestry of time. Now I bid you fond farewell, for this time and into eternity.

Noah = Merlin

— Chapter 23 —
SAR'H

(Daughter of Yeshua & Mary of Bethany)
Avalon, 49 AD, Age 18

SAR'H: You can ask me questions.
CATHERINE ANN (*Henceforth: CA*): Look down at your feet and tell me what is on your feet.

SAR'H: I am wearing small lightweight sandals, the kind we wear at home. They are not used for walking long distances. My feet are small and my ankles are quite trim. When I lift my skirt, my legs are slender, as are my arms. You would say I am quite thin, or even scrawny, as you say in your language. I am wearing a simple, one-piece, woolen robe that is of fairly thick weave. It is dyed a deep, maroon red. The cloth feels supple and soft against my skin. I like it a lot. There is a cotton scarf tied around my waist and I have several rings on my fingers. They are small, narrow bands of gold. My hands are delicate with long, slender fingers.

CA: Is there anything on your head?

SAR'H: Just a narrow woven band which I use to pull back my long, thick hair. It falls in tight curls and is a rich brown color, somewhat auburn; like my father's. When I look at my face in the bronze mirror, I see that I have rather large, almond shaped eyes with long eyelashes. My eyebrows are rather heavy, but nicely shaped. I have fairly high cheekbones and my nose is small and narrow.

CA: Is your skin fair or dark?

SAR'H: It is a light olive complexion. It tans easily in the summer months when I can be outdoors for hours at a time. I enjoy being outdoors more than being indoors. Sometimes, I confess, I envy the freedom the boys and the men have to be outdoors as much as they like. I feel very fortunate to be a young woman in this community compared to the constraints most girls and women experience in the outlying region.

CA: How old are you?

SAR'H: I turned eighteen years at the coming of the last winter solstice sun.

CA: What are you called?

SAR'H: I am called Sar'h.

CA: Do you live with your parents?

SAR'H: I live with a lovely, large family. My mother is usually here, but sometimes she goes away with my father. I don't get to see him very often. I have asked to be schooled in a way in which I can feel good about not having my parents close to me. I know many children who do not have any parents or family. Some of my adopted siblings are orphans. My father and mother give them parentage, protection and a good life.

CA: What are your parents' names and how many siblings do you have?

SAR'H: My father is called Yeshua and my mother is called Mary (*of Bethany*). I have a younger sister birthed by my mother. She was conceived on my birthday in 33 AD. My father calls my little sister, Lizbett; so that's the name we all call her. She is also known as Elizabeth Hannah. I have three older half-brothers: Joses Simeon, Jude and Johannes, and one half-sister: Miriam. Their mother is Myriam of Tyana, who, just a month ago, returned to Avalon with Grand Ma'ma Mary Anna and Uncle John Mark. It is such a joy to have us all together again. It had been so many years (*ten*) and I only had my childhood memories of them to hold close to my heart. Now they are more beautiful and wise than I remember. I also have seven siblings who are orphans; three are here and the others are at Mount Bugarach.

CA: Do your siblings, those who were birthed by your two mothers, live with you?

SAR'H: Everyone lives here now, except Johannes, Myriam's youngest son, who used to live in India. He is in Egypt now; but when Uncle Joseph's (*of Arimathea*) son-in-law's son, who lives in southern Gaul and commands Joseph's boats, makes his next voyage to Britain, Johannes will come to Avalon to live. It will be wonderful to meet this brother who has been a mystery all my life. Ma'ma Myriam tells me he has two beautiful wives.

There is a fair amount of travel; coming and going like the wind. Sometimes we are concerned for our welfare and we leave for a time. Sometimes it's so that we can meet and spend time with certain people. We share stories with them and assist with their healing when they are sick. We do this in a way that does not draw large crowds. We go where we can best serve.

I live in Britain now; in a place we call Avalon.

CA: Have you been participating with the Magdalenes who train the young maidens in Avalon?

SAR'H: I have been introduced to some of their ways. We have received trainings from wise ones who have been a part of this community from their very first breath as well as from other teachers who arrived here later in life. Many of the women and children are curious about me. They like to listen to the things I have to share about my journeys. With some of the people, I feel quite guarded. I have a certain knowing that I can share some things with certain ones; and some things I must hold very close to my heart.

I was born in Egypt; and lived there almost two years. Then we moved to the mountains of southern Gaul and an Essene monastery near Mount Bugarach. We lived there for over five years. Even though I was very young, I feel more of an affinity with the places we visited near the Great Sea than I do with this cold, dark land. My heart sings more easily in places where the sun shines a lot. I desire to return someday to those places where I remember being warm; filled with light and beautiful flowers. But I will go wherever I am called to serve. That is a certainty.

There are difficulties here with the Romans, just like we experienced in Gaul. The soldiers were not here when we first

---

[43] Johannes and his wives, Ruth and Salome, do come to Avalon in 51 AD.

arrived, but they invaded Britain four years ago. I, myself, have seen them. I try to put them and the troubling stories I hear out of my mind. Being in deep meditation and serving in all the ways I can in our community help me to be calm and at peace. I treasure the extended moments of serenity I have in nature.

Mother Earth calls me to go into her caves and drink from her streams. She beckons me to climb the hilltops and sit among the groves of trees. The Ancient Ones speak to me through the mists. I visit the places where the Druids meet and feel of their presence after they are gone. There are patterns of energy imprinted into the stones, oaks, and holy wells, which I read as easily as the inscribed words Great-Grand Ma'ma Anna writes. Fewer and fewer of the local Druids are openly gathering these days. It is known that the Romans are aware of the Druid's power. They are most concerned about the Druid's persuasive ability to encourage resistance against the emperor, Claudius, who would take away our freedom.

CA: What is it like when you are with your parents and younger sister?

SAR'H: Mostly I am with my extended family within the monastery of our Essene-Druid community. But sometimes I get to be alone with my mother and sister. Lizbett has passed through her "coming of age" ceremony and we get to live in the same dormitory set apart for the young and unmarried maidens. In the times we get to be alone together, my mother, sister and I comfort each other with singing and holding each other close. Sometimes we light an oil lamp and gather around it. We join hands and we sing and we attune to a greater Light. It's what you would call God.

We often allow a sense of connection with my father. My mother knows how to draw him close. Sometimes he actually appears for a short time and that is always wonderful. She has taught me how to do this also. Father tells me I can attune to him anytime. So even though I do not always get to embrace him, I can feel his loving presence. Father is a mystery in many ways to me. Our relationship feels like a paradox. I feel extremely close to him and yet distant at the same time. I desire to heal my internal conflict and feel my father's presence all the time.

I feel closer to my mother because I see much more of her. But even with her, there are times when she feels far away, even when her arm is around me. This used to bother me. My other mother, Myriam of Tyana, and my grandmother, Mary Anna, could feel my pain and confusion when I was quite young. They taught me how to "go" with my mother into the spirit planes, instead of feeling badly that she was not fully present with me in the physical world. Great Grand Ma'ma Anna also taught me how to do this. Now when Ma'Ma and I are sitting close, we fly together in our bodies of light. I can feel her love and her spirit. She helps me to know more about who I truly am.

CA: What is it like being with your father?

SAR'H: Whenever he is here, he always takes me into his arms and makes sure that I know he loves me. We sit very, very still together. It is like when we gather around the lamp and look into the flame with a soft gaze. There is a stillness that deeply comforts me. I love it when he sings and plays one of the stringed instruments my mother brought with us from Bethany; or he plays Uncle Noah's harp. Sometimes he surprises me with a visit when I am alone, walking slowly on one of the many paths, or while I am sitting in solitude at one of my favorite nature spots. Unless I really need him, he usually does not come with his physical body, especially when I am being insistent and selfish. He does not intervene, if, in wisdom, it is better for me to work out a personal difficulty by myself. He is like this with Lizbett, too. The only difference seems to be that he is more playful with her. It is her nature to be playful; mine is to be more contemplative.

CA: Tell me more about Lizbett.

SAR'H: When she was little, I remember her as being something of a little imp. Great Grand Ma'ma Anna also tells stories about Father also being rather mischievous as a boy as well. Lizbett loved being outdoors, singing little songs to herself and playing with her invisible friends. Then she grew into a lovely young lady. Now we share our love of nature, meditation practices and learning about healing energies. As we get older, we find more about each other that we truly love. We comfort each other, as we sometimes feel like orphan children who do not get to be with their parents. We help each other to open our hearts and to not be selfish and disgruntled. Although Ma'ma Myriam's children, my half-brothers and sister: Joses Simeon, Jude and Miriam are older than us (*they were in their 20's when Myriam went to India*); we know they miss their mother very much. They often spend time with us and our mother (*Mary of Bethany*). We always rejoice when Father comes. He always takes each of us aside so that we can share our heart with him in private. He is so loving and kind. He inspires us to be like him; though he remains a mystery to us in many ways. As we enter into our spiritual practices more deeply, we understand and appreciate our parents ever so much more.

There are many orphans in our community's care. Their very real sorrows are so much greater than ours. Often they surprise and humble us with their ability to forgive, smile and laugh, and give so much love – they are wonderful teachers. I hope to do more for the orphans and homeless and ailing beings when I am older; just as my mother, Aunt Martha and Uncle Lazarus continue to do every chance they get.

CA: Does it bother you or seem strange to you that you have two mothers?

SAR'H: No, it's all I have ever known. It doesn't seem strange. It is a comfort to have two loving mothers. Ten years passed during my childhood without Ma'ma Myriam, so it has been more like what most children experience with one mother. But Ma'ma shares her parenting of me with others, as is the case of most of the children in our community – so I feel like I have many mothers. I have many close relatives who love me. There are Great Grand Ma'ma Anna, Grand Ma'ma Mary Anna, Mariam (*my father's cousin*), my half-brothers and half-sister, and lots of aunts and uncles, for example.

I really missed Grand Ma'ma Mary Anna when she was away in India. I am so glad she came safely back to us. She is so very beautiful, tender and sweet. She can be very firm with me, too. She often says, "There's a lot expected of you, Sar'h." I do not feel controlled or manipulated by such a statement, because she always holds me close and gazes softly into my eyes when she says these words. She helps me see my infinite potential. She reflects back to me my true nature and helps me to see through my human veil as we come into Oneness. In the Oneness, I know what she means by; "Where much is given, much is required." Or as my father says, "The lord is also the servant to those given into his stewardship."

Of my two mothers, I would say that I feel a greater affinity with my own mother than with Myriam (*of Tyana*), although, in some ways, as I grow older, I am finding my other mother is much more accessible to me, as my personal confidante. Now that I am a young woman, Myriam and I have much more to talk about that are the mutual concerns of being a woman. Although it has only been a few weeks since her return to Avalon, it seems like hardly any time has passed. We know each other so well on a deep soul level. She tells me I can call her Myriam. She feels like a wonderful older sister.

CA: How does it feel to have a father who is so different from other fathers and ordinary men?

SAR'H: I do not think about it very much. Many of the men, who are my relatives, are not like the men I see in the nearby villages. I am glad for the example of all the men and women who live in Avalon. Everyone is devoted to a spiritual way of life. When I see the poverty and hardships of the people who do not live as we live, I can see that they create their circumstances according to how they view themselves. They talk among themselves in a way that is belittling and coarse. Their lives hold so much suffering and there is little opportunity or incentive to change. They could choose to come to our community where teachings are available; but most resist our invitation to learn unfamiliar skills that might ease their burdens.

We go among the people stricken with poverty and help where we can. But changing old traditions takes a long time, so I am told by the elders. As I mature in wisdom, I see that change is possible, but it is a delicate process which requires much patience and generosity of spirit. It's best not to judge and demand that a person change into someone like yourself. Unconditional acceptance and encouragement borne of a happy and kind example, is the better choice.

CA: Do you feel that you are very different than most people you meet?

SAR'H: I think that they think that I am, especially the older people in the villages. I do not think the younger children experience that I am so different. They seem to be attracted to me. When they see me coming with my baskets, they run up and gather close to me. They follow me around, asking me all kinds of questions; pulling on my sleeve to come see something. I have heard stories how the children would do that with my mothers and father in the Old Country. You have your story of the pied piper. I think my father is a pied piper because I see the children running to him right after they first hear he is with us. They gather around and follow him like bees attracted to the nectar of flowers.

CA: How do you think most people view Yeshua?

SAR'H: With the local people who do not know Father, we keep who he really is — a resurrected Teacher of Righteousness, a secret. For those who have some awareness or have heard rumors, we try to evade their questions that come from idle curiosity. Only the initiates know who he is and how it came to be that he is still alive. They come to know the truth according to their ability to attune their Soul awareness to be in resonance with how they feel in his presence.

The stories that circulate are more fantasy than fact. There seems to be an allure about Father dying, then coming back to life for a short time, and being taken up into the heaven worlds as a god and savior. As you can imagine, such ideas attract attention. There are many variations on that theme, so there are many factions and much confusion. In a way this is good because it creates a kind of veil that protects the truth within his sayings and our spiritual practices; only those with ears to hear, know how to discern the mysteries. But this veil does not protect the many people who try to follow their own limited understanding according to their varying beliefs about Father and his words. Many of these dear souls are being persecuted and martyred for their belief. It does not protect us, as Magdalene-Essenes, from the fearful projections others place on us. Some of us who have the direct knowledge have also been martyred for our supposed heresy. We are mostly looked upon, at best, as a peculiar people and we are left alone in our hermitage retreats.

I think, by and large, most people, who hear about Father, think of him as a kind of revolutionary who promotes change – and change is usually resisted because most people fear the unknown and what is different from their conditioning. I feel somehow that I am to carry on the kind of revolutionary change my parents' example instills in me. It is not clear to me yet how I am to do that. I am only a young woman just coming into my own as an adult member of our community. I am certain, though, that I am not to carry on Father's work in a way that intentionally stirs up trouble; although "trouble" always seems to accompany change and it always seems to follow us wherever we go. My family members, in spite of the challenges, all seem to share a singular vision of peace and harmony. Because we live in this way, we are calm and unassuming most of the time.

I like to study people and human nature. I think my father is like that, too. He can size someone up very quickly. He determines where they are on their soul journey and how well they are accomplishing their soul lessons. He can see where they are fooling themselves by denying and resisting their inner darkness. They might not be wearing metal armor over their bodies, but it feels to me, as I think it does for my father, that such ones wear their inner darkness as heavy armor over their hearts and minds. I feel sadness for people's suffering.

My mothers tell me I have a sensitive heart, and that this is good. They say it is important to keep my heart open, because there will always be opportunities to give a smile, say a word of kindness or gently touch a hand in a way that deeply comforts. It might be that someone has an ailment or their heart is crushed with grief. Love is needed everywhere.

So my family, extended and personal, often comes together to support each other in our way of loving-kindness and in staying strong in our minds and bodies.

CA: Thank you for sharing your wisdom and love. Please go forward now to the next important event in your life.

{Sar'h continues her story in Part 4, Chapter 26}

— Chapter 24 —

JOHANNES

(Son of Yeshua & Myriam of Tyana, Age 28)
Stonehenge, Salisbury Plain, England, 53 AD

{Chapter 24 is a continuation of Johannes' sharing in Chapter 17}

CATHERINE ANN (*Henceforth: CA*): Go now to the next appropriate event in your life. As it is coming clearly into view, please share what you are experiencing.

JOHANNES: I wish to say that I did go to Egypt with my wives *(called Ruth and Salome)* and several of the brothers from Mount Carmel. I met Great Uncle Joseph of Arimathea in Ephesus. He took all of those who had gone to India on one of his freighting boats to Caesarea near Mount Carmel and then we went on to Alexandria. Those of us who were to linger in Egypt made our way to Heliopolis; the others returned to Mount Bugarach and Britain. Approximately five cycles of the sun have passed since I was in Tyana. I have lived in Avalon the past two.

Now we are gathered in our white robes to initiate a spring equinox ritual. The mark of a spiral is drawn upon our foreheads. We are walking slowly and mindfully on the path that takes us through a certain pattern laid out on the Earth's surface. This pattern aligns us with the stars above and the electro-magnetic lines that weave through the Earth Mother's body. Twilight is approaching. The stars are just beginning to come forth as we approach the heel stone. We pause and further attune our body/mind with great awareness. We slowly proceed on our walk. We approach the great blue stones which you call the Henge that rests in massive majesty upon the Salisbury plane.

CA: Is this Stonehenge?

JOHANNES: Yes. We are progressing through a long processional. Many from near and far are gathered into this space.

CA: Is it a Druid ritual? Are both men and women present?

JOHANNES: Yes. And yes, both genders are present, because there is a belief in balance. Both polarities, in equality, are required.

We know we are being observed at a distance by a small company of Roman soldiers. Our large number arouses attention.

CA: How many are you?

JOHANNES: Seventy-two. There is plenty of room for us. We are still in the waning energies of vernal equinox and the waxing of the passage called Beltane (*May Day or May 1st*). We have been observing and conducting the energies for several weeks.

CA: When you say a number of weeks are those weeks spent at the stones in Stonehenge or are there different locations?

JOHANNES: There are different locations in this general area. It is an opening portal for interdimensional energies and it will also be a place of closure. We will return to the Henge to close the portal when the moon is made new after celebrating Beltane at the Great Processional Henge of Avebury.

CA: Is there more you would like to share about the nature of the ritual or your training?

JOHANNES: You have asked about the congress of men and women, the training of the initiates to incarnate the heaven worlds and to make both males and females receptive and fertile. By this, I mean fertile in the way of calling in souls to be born, the harvest of crops to flow in abundance and our well-being to be felt harmoniously. It is the time in which to lie with one another, to burn the ritual fires, to join one with another while bridging heaven and earth.

It is a time to commune with the stars and the wisdom therein. It is a time to bring much light into the cells of our bodies and into the womb of the Great Mother. These stones assist us to do this. They are like a light-craft made of stone. As we join together in mantras and mudras, we begin to spin our energy fields. A great mandala of light is created. The Henge begins to spin. The stones become very ethereal – a very powerful vortex is created and we all become exponentially expanded through the night.

There is a large light-craft above us. I am told the consciousness within it is from the Pleiades. Some of us have been learning and practicing the ways of Light-conception, as taught by my great-grandmother, Anna, and my paternal grandmother, Mary Anna. Both of my mothers (*Myriam of Tyana and Mary of Bethany*) understand and have practiced these ways of conceiving children; both with and without the seed of a man.

These mysteries are very ancient and they have been corrupted through time. We are doing our best to preserve them in a way that honors both men and women. Our desire is to bring unity and balance. Our way is to provide an immaculate space for the most evolved consciousnesses to have physical bodies. I have listened carefully to Great-Grandmother Anna's, my grandmother's and my mothers' wisdom. I have also listened to my father (*Yeshua*) and my great uncles – Joseph of Arimathea and Noah, who are powerful Essene-Druids. They call this the work of the Magdalene.

They tell of a time when these ways were only practiced by women without the seed of man. Then there came a time when men sought to personify and embody the "gods," with whom the women mated on the astral planes. This is true today. Sadly, there has been much corruption, abuse, conflict and suffering. We seek to find a way to bring men and women together in a way that heals separation consciousness and opens the portals beyond duality. We seek a way that goes beyond the agendas of gender identities, which express as dominance and submission and all manner of war, pestilence and famine.

My female forebears have experienced virginal conception and also conception with physical seeding by their conscious, male partners. With every conception, there was a triangulation of man and woman with the Beloved on High; who directed the flow of energy in every aspect. Each soul to come into physical incarnation was conducted to the Earthplane from the spirit planes by the angels and Great Ones. Each soul's journey into the Earthplane was physically supported by the grounding energies of initiates, whether close or at a distance.

Some of my relatives, as I have said, conceived children with ethereal "Light-seed," but not with the physical seed of their fathers; such as the Light-conception of my grandmother, Mary Anna (*Mother Mary*) and her Light-conception of Yeshua, my father. Most of our family members are Light-conceived with the physical seed of our fathers. This is true of my siblings and me; except for my half-sister, Lizbett, whose conception (*after Yeshua's resurrection*) was facilitated with my father's ethereal seed. My mother (*Myriam of Tyana*) has confided in me that she is preparing for a Light-conception with my father in the same way that Mary of Bethany conceived Lizbett. She is overjoyed with the prospect of such a union and the coming forth of another child even though her monthly bleeding is no longer regular.

CA: Please share more about how the Light craft and Stonehenge assist Light-conceptions.

JOHANNES: I could say many things about this topic. It is one of my favorites – one that I have been studying these past years with great interest. I will do my best to refrain from getting too carried away.

What I will share with you is that there is a rather complex interdimensional matrix of energy aligned with interdimensional purposes which are accomplished by the interaction of Light-craft and stone circles, as in this case. This is also true with other Light-conceptions which occur within mountain caves, such as the conception of Lizbett, within the mountain cave in Mount Bugarach. I have also been told there was a great confluence of Light-craft and intergalactic consciousness, which facilitated the Light-conceptions of my father and some of my aunts and uncles, who are of my father's generation.[44]

---

[44] Johannes is referring to the Light-conception which took place in the desert oasis of Kadesh-Barnea, in present-day Saudi Arabia. See *"Anna, Grandmother of Jesus"* for more information about Light-conception in general and about Yeshua's and Mary of Bethany's conceptions specifically.

JOHANNES CONTINUED

It is that on occasions such as this one at Stonehenge, we are now over-lighted by a Pleiadian Light-craft. That is to say, it is of the Light – beings of light, in complete unified Oneness, have co-created what is called a "Chariot of Fire or a Chariot of the Sun" – some call this living Light-craft a group Mer Ka Ba energy field. This Light-craft is not physical. Although it utilizes the energies of the Earth, it is not bound by gravity or by physical plane frequencies. It is more aligned with cosmic frequencies of Light, Sound and Color. It is intergalactic in origin; although the beings present on this particular Light-craft are attuned with the higher ascended consciousness vibration of the Pleiades.

Of the kinds of cosmic technology present, sound technology is particularly important for the regenerative work we are currently facilitating. Sound technology especially enhances the harmonic interaction of the Light-craft, the blue stones, and our unified consciousness – the Magdalene-Druids who are very carefully attuned and calibrated with one another. When you understand that all manifest creation is comprised of frequencies; and that frequencies are sound; and that the conscious awareness of sound facilitates manifestation; then you understand on another level why Stonehenge was created.

And so it is that we consciously use our voices which are amplified by the power of each stone. Then we work through the collective harmonic arrangement of the stones, together with the Earth's electro-magnetic frequencies in alignment with the Earth's core and elements. And last, but not least, cosmic harmonics are sounded through the Light beings/Light-craft in Oneness; unifying and amplifying all that we are anchoring on Earth through our bodies. All together, in unified harmony and balance, WE SING THE STONES!

Depending on our purpose, whether it is bringing fertility to the Earth and to the well-being of our minds and bodies, the Light-conception of children, or affirming peace and harmony among all beings, Sound, Light and Color are the technologies we use as Druid-Essene Magdalenes. In concert with the Earth Mother, sun, moon and stars – we are in harmonious attunement with the creative energies of the Music of the Spheres and the All That Is.

I became aware of these technologies in my medical studies in India. My father and mothers freely shared their understanding with me. I also entered sound-healing temples; which are dedicated to the Greek physician Asclepius, when I was in Cappadocia and Ephesus. When I went to Egypt, I entered into the Temples of Hathor[45] and became aware of my profound intergalactic life-stream which carries the consciousness of the ascended Hathors into the Earthplane. In ways that you would not now understand, I bring forth these technologies for the benefit of all beings in my time and in your day. I do this for the awakening of Light-seeds encoded within the Earth Mother; including all her stones, such as these of Stonehenge. There is also the awakening through the Voice of the Divine Mother (*the Magdalenes*) of the Light which is seeded within the crystals and limestone of mountains, and within the elements wherewith your bones and blood are composed.

I leave these words for your contemplation and further exploration. As I have said, I find this topic not only of great interest, but of great importance for Earth and humanity in your day of planetary crisis.

CA: Thank you for sharing so much about the importance of sound for the facilitation of Light-conception. Will Light-conception happen here on this occasion?

JOHANNES: No, I do not believe it will occur here. I will add further that not all who are present have come with the intention of conceiving children. It is more for the purpose of impregnating the land with Light so that there may be peace and prosperity among the people; especially in regards to manifesting a

---

[45] Johannes is referring to the intergalactic beings called the Hathors, called forth by our planetary logos, Sanat Kumara, to assist with the preservation and enlightenment of humanity and the Earth. See *"Anna, Grandmother of Jesus"* and *"The Hathor Material, Messages from an Ascended Civilization"* by Tom Kenyon and Virginia Essene for more in-depth information about the Hathors and their important role as mentors of ascending consciousness.

JOHANNES CONTINUED

greater generosity of spirit within the consciousness of the Romans, who give us increasing concern.

CA: Is there any more right now that you wish to share about these rituals?

JOHANNES: What I can say is that there are other rituals, as well, that bring forth the Divine Mother's infinite love, compassion and wisdom. We attune to her regenerative powers to heal and bear fruit upon what has become a sterile and arid physical plane of consciousness. I am not speaking so much of the Earth Mother, although in her wisdom she reflects the arid consciousness of a male-dominant society. Both men and women have lost their connection to the feminine heart of compassion and the interconnectedness of all beings – the Law of Oneness. We all suffer as a result. We must be mindful and alert as a community to protect the ways and the body of the Great Mother. We men, who are trained as Magdalenes, do this with our women, children and the stewarding of this verdant land. We grandly respect and honor the Goddess and her powers.

My great-grandmother (*Anna*), my grandmother (*Mary Anna*), and all the beloved women, as I look about me, right now, are nodding their heads and smiling. They are all raising their hands and collectively sending a great deal of energy into the opening of the seals that have bound the voice of the Divine Feminine – the Great Mother, as the Magdalene – and her resurrecting powers of unconditional love.

I have made peace in my heart concerning my childhood wounding when I perceived that my mother abandoned me. I have come to see that we all need to heal this collective wound of abandonment; actually self-abandonment, that comes from perceiving as a separate self. Feeling like a castaway, we experience afflictive emotions which relentlessly cycle through us, causing us to feel unloving, unlovable and unloved. Our grief and anger push the Great Mother's ever-present love away. Blind to the love and the mercy and the goodness that are always present within us, we bring harm to ourselves and others. We need to feel the Divine Mother's love so that we can love all beings, including our human self.

Then we will all flourish. Our Mother, the Earth, will don her glorious garments of light and fertility. This is my vision and aspiration. I dedicate my life to this purpose. With these great stones and the radiant stars over my head as my witness, this night and forever, I consecrate the life-force flowing through me to the benefit of beings, through all the times and realms.

It is all good. This is a time of great healing and goodness. Even in the midst of the greatest darkness and chaos, this is the grandest of opportunities for love to come forth and heal the minds and hearts of all beings. We have but to relax, let go and let the love that we are just simply BE. Through non-judgment and non-efforting, we will bring forth our intrinsic wisdom and take compassionate action.

I am called Johannes and I am available to assist you from the other side as a healer who understands the mending of broken hearts; whether you require physical, emotional and/or spiritual healing, I am at your service.

Peace be with you.

CA: Thank you for coming, Johannes.

PART IV

"THE GREAT GATHERING"
Fortingall, Scotland
&
The Dispersion of the Seeds of Light

(England, Wales, Scotland, France, Spain, Eastern Europe, Turkey and India)

*The Magdalene Voice
Withdraws into Silence*

55 – 186 AD

— Chapter 25 —

LIZBETT

(The daughter of Yeshua & Mary of Bethany, Age 21)
Glamorgan, Wales, early spring, 55 AD

{Chapter 25 is a continuation of Chapter 19 with Claire facilitating Catherine Ann}

LIZBETT: I am being sent out into the world, away from my beloved home in Avalon. I feel some trepidation, yet I know I am to carry the flame of divinity and the codes of the Magdalene to other people, especially other women.
CLAIRE: How old are you?
LIZBETT: I am twenty-one.
CLAIRE: Are you alone?
LIZBETT: I am alone for the moment, yes.
CLAIRE: Where are you?
LIZBETT: I have gone to the land and villages of the Silures in southern Wales where my uncles Andrew and Josephus used to live. They began a monastery here when I was very young and still living in Bugarach. They are no longer living, but there are some relatives and people I used to know in Avalon who call Glamorgan home. My other mother's (*Myriam of Tyana's*) children: Joses Simeon, Jude and Miriam; and Grandmother Mary Anna's children: Uncle Matteas and Aunt Esther Salome live here much of the time; as do I. We come and go between here (*Glamorgan*), Avalon and Mona. They (*the children just mentioned*) are all married now and they all have children. I would say more about them except that I know trying to remember all their names and where they live would be difficult for you to keep straight.

It is difficult being here because the Roman soldiers have encampments and forts everywhere. Most of the local people do not

LIZBETT CONTINUED

trust us. We refuse to fight, and because of this, they think we are siding with the Romans. They do not hide their anger toward us and their hatred of the Romans. Many of their villages and people were destroyed when the Romans were trying to capture King Caradoc. He fled to the north of Britain to find refuge with the queen of the Brigantes tribe. But she betrayed him to the Romans. He and his family were taken in chains to Rome. There's been some peace, but I fear the unrest and occasional surprise raids by the Silures and Ordovices warriors on the soldiers when they are in small scouting parties will be met with terrible retribution.

Right now I am crossing many fields and rolling hills on my way to a village where I have been invited to share my knowledge of healing herbs and midwifery. I have a large hunting dog (*predecessor of the Irish wolfhound*) with me for protection. He is a good stalwart friend. We are walking very briskly; as fast as we can along the muddy track, and we should arrive at our new home well before the sun reaches its zenith. I usually don't travel alone. But I am confident I will be safe. My inner sight is well-developed and I know how to be invisible. This is an opportunity to use what I have practiced. This is my first journey alone. In the past I could lean on others. This is my first journey being really responsible for my self and listening to my own inner counsel/council. Although I know I will find brothers and sisters among the Druids and my relatives, and there will be teachings and camaraderie, I am truly my own timber, so to speak, at the moment.

CLAIRE: Do you have a mate?

LIZBETT: Not at this point.

CLAIRE: Is your mother (*Mary of Bethany*) still on the Earthplane?

LIZBETT: Yes, she is also living in Wales (*near Mona*), but, like my father (*Yeshua*), she comes and goes. Sar'h is here. She is receiving training at the Druid sanctuary on Mona. I may go there for my advanced training. It has not been revealed to me if this is mine to do or not.

CLAIRE: Does Anna sometimes travel or does she stay in the place where you spent your youth?

LIZBETT: She mostly stays where I spent my growing up years. Occasionally she comes to this land and spends time on Mona. She's always very thrilled every time a member of the family comes to visit her in Avalon. We are rather scattered now. It's getting more difficult for her and the others from Avalon to travel because there are so many Roman soldiers and forts separating them from the West Country. We have to be very careful. There's a lot of talk about how we can protect ourselves and make our travels safer.

CLAIRE: Tell me about your life with the common people.

LIZBETT: Because I have been more isolated, living all my life with contemplative brethren who have set themselves somewhat apart from others, I am being guided now to live among the common folk in order to serve them and blend in with them. It is important for my own safety to not "stick out" like a sore thumb, as it were. The people who work the land have an arduous life. They have suffered much at the hand of the Romans. It is good to learn their ways and to gain their trust. My half-brothers (*Joses Simeon and Jude*) and my half-sister (*Miriam*) and also Aunt Esther Salome and Uncle Matteas are married to good men and women who mostly carry the blood of the Britons. This fact does not go unnoticed by the local people; nor by the Romans. We walk a delicate balance.

I am now approaching the little village. Someone is coming to meet me.

(*Long pause*) {*Catherine Ann's consciousness returns.*}

CATHERINE ANN: I am feeling very tired. I think it is time to rest.

{*Anna reveals more about Lizbett's later life in Chapter 33.*}

— Chapter 26 —
SAR'H SPEAKS
"THE GREAT GATHERING"
(Daughter of Yeshua & Mary of Bethany, Age 24)
Fortingall, Scotia (Scotland)
Summer Solstice, 55 AD

{*Chapter 26 is a continuation of Sar'h's sharing in PART 3, Chapter 23.*}

CATHERINE ANN (*Henceforth: CA*): So move forward now to the next significant event in your life.

SAR'H: ….The land is very different here. There is a cold wind that bites into your skin and into your cheeks. My lips are dry and cracked. I have to wear a heavy shawl around my head and shoulders. My little thin body has a difficult time with it being so cold. But as I look upon the land, it is truly glorious! The great towering hillsides are windswept. The light that illuminates everything is so crystalline. This is the land of Scotia and this valley is called Fortingall.

CA: What is your purpose for being in Fortingall?

SAR'H: As you know from the stories others have told, we are attending what we call "The Great Gathering." We are expecting many people from many places, because Father, my Pa'Pa (*Yeshua*) has sent an invitation for us to come and gather. We have arrived somewhat early, as is Uncle Joseph's (*of Arimathea*) pattern. In just over three weeks it will be Summer Solstice and the return of the full moon. We came on one of Joseph's boats and landed on the west coast of Scotia, where there are many islands. Years earlier, I visited some of these islands with my mothers and siblings after

Ma'Ma Myriam returned from India. It felt good to feel of the islands' sacredness again and to be reunited with the brethren who live in these remote places.

Some of the brethren we had met earlier escorted us to a special place on the coastline where we were met by guides with ponies and carts. Many of us walked or rode ponies. Those who are aged or infirm were carried in various conveyances. We traveled over hill and dale for several days until we came to the beautiful valleys located in what is called "the heart of Scotia." (*Perthshire in present-day Scotland*)

We are expecting Father to come at the time of Summer Solstice and the full moon.

CA: Now move forward again to the next important thing that happens.

SAR'H: Before we arrived, a great evergreen arbor was created for protection from the cold wind. Part of it incorporates the far-reaching arms of a very ancient yew tree.[46]

My mother (*Mary of Bethany*) is here. There is a glow about her. She is looking especially pretty and robust — well-rested and full of life. There is a glow in her cheeks. Her smile is tender and her teeth look healthy. This is good to see. My sister, Lizbett, has also come with us. Ma'Ma Myriam (*of Tyana*) is also here. She is beautiful, as usual; but I note she is more serious than I have ever experienced her before. She is busying herself with taking care of various responsibilities and tending to details. Great Grand Ma'Ma Anna and Grand Ma'Ma Mary Anna are here as well. We are blessed to have their steady, warm presence.

There are many members of my family who have come from near and far. I am glad to see some who have come from Bugarach whom I have not seen since I was a young girl. My cousin, Sara, and her husband, Phillip, are here with their son (*Justus*) and daughter (*Ceres*). All of my other siblings, Myriam's children, are here, including my half-brother, Johannes and his two wives, who came to

---

[46] This ancient yew tree still is living today near the chapel located in the small community of Fortingall, Scotland.

SAR'H SPEAKS - THE GREAT GATHERING

Avalon from Egypt in 51 AD. Finally meeting Johannes was even more wonderful than I had imagined it would be. He is truly a bright light.

There is a large magical mountain not too far away that I have had the blessing of exploring. I can feel the Ancient Ones gathering in the ethers. The hills are covered with forests; the moors are rich with blooming broom, gorse and heather; and abundant wildflowers grace the meadows stretching out around us. There is a gurgling stream running through the green valley and ancient standing stone circles are scattered here and there. Many tents have been erected to create a temporary village. There are hundreds of fires for cooking and warmth. I am glad we are so far to the north in this season of very long days. Besides having the comfort of the sun's heat and light, the lingering summer solstice sun gives us ample opportunities for visiting and celebrating late into the night. This is a wonderful gathering for unmarried people like me to meet other kindred souls. It makes finding a suitable husband or wife much easier. There is much laughter and merrymaking. Those who are skilled at matchmaking are very busy!

CA: Did you meet someone special at this gathering? If so, please move forward in time and tell us about your meeting.

SAR'H: Yes, I did meet someone very special to me – an old friend I used to know!

His name is Andrew. He came with my relatives from Bugarach. I first knew him when we were children living at our Essene monastery. It was so wonderful recognizing each other as cherished friends from the past. Andrew is very kind, gentle and generous of heart. He is stalwart in the way of the Essenes, the wisdom of the goddess, and in Druid wisdom, too.

We have a great affinity toward one another. We are a good match. My mothers approve of him and they are very happy for us. I am certain Pa'Pa will be happy, too. Toward the end of The Great Gathering there will be a time for couples to announce their intentions for betrothal. We are, of course, making plans to step forward and receive a Celtic hand-fasting ceremony.[47] Andrew will accompany my mother and me back to Avalon and Mona, where we and several other couples will have two more ceremonies with family members and friends who could not be here in Fortingall.

CA: What is it like being at this gathering?

SAR'H: It is like the way you would want a family to be. There is no complaining; just a lightness of being pervading everyone, everywhere. There are some of the Celtic men, native to Scotia, who are a bit coarse and gruff, but we all get along well together. There is camaraderie and enthusiastic laughter all around. There are times when we are very quiet. Our meditations take us deeply inside where we rest for many hours in the Great Silence. There are other times when we gather for storytelling, singing, dancing and praying. It is very, very harmonious, even blissful being here together.

(*Reflective pause*) There are no Roman soldiers here. Perhaps that's one reason we feel so free to just be ourselves.

There are many people from different places. I have not ever experienced anything like this before, where there are so many different kinds of people. It's like being one happy family. This feeling of harmony is very, very nice. It helps me to think that maybe, someday, our human family can be like this; no wars, poverty, or suffering of any kind. We all care for each other. We all enjoy an equal measure of abundance. Don't you think that would be lovely?

CA: Yes, that would be lovely, indeed. You said you were expecting your father. What was it like when he came? Move forward to that event during the gathering and tell us about your experience.

---

[47] Celtic hand-fasting is a betrothal ceremony is which a couple is "bound" to one another for "a year and a day." If, at that time, the couple desire to be married for life, another "hand-fasting for life" ceremony is held. Or the couple after "a year and a day" can dissolve their marital contract and seek another mate. Ribbons, scarves, tartans, cords, etc. are used to bind the couple at the wrists and hands.

SAR'H: He came for three days toward the end of "The Great Gathering." It was quite extraordinary! I had never experienced my parents (*Yeshua and Mary of Bethany*), Ma'Ma Myriam, Great Grand Ma'Ma Anna, Grand Ma'Ma Mary Anna and Aunt Mariam (*actually Sar'h's cousin; but referred to as an aunt because she was Yeshua's adopted sister*) in the way I came to know them during those last days. The day of the gathering in which Father arrived, actually began during the early morning hours of darkness. I was surprised to awaken at dawn's first light with the sound of small bells pealing for an extended time. We had been holding silence for three days prior and we had also been fasting from food.

When I arrived at the great arbor I was stunned by a radiant light that was almost blinding. As my physical eyes adjusted, and my inner eyes attuned with the frequencies, I beheld an extraordinary sight! Father was seated on an elevated platform in equipoise; in the full-lotus posture. Flanked on his right and left were the Grand Ma'Ma's, Anna and Mary Anna, and my two mothers. Mariam also sat with my two mothers. Then to their right and left, and behind them, was a dazzling array of beings emitting a rainbow profusion of light!

All of us, who were invited to come into the arbor, entered in a single file. One by one, we came forward and prostrated ourselves before my father and all the Great Ones who were seated with him. Each of us received a blessing and was escorted to the place which was designated for us to sit. Later, during that amazing first day, after we had all become completely unified in mind, body and soul; we were blessed with the ethereal appearance of Father's beloved spiritual brother and Guru, Mahavatar Babaji and the future Christ-Buddha, Maitreya.

Words cannot adequately describe all that occurred within our sacred circle on that day and the remainder of our visit within the heart of Scotia's hallowed vales. I simply invite you to ask for entry and an attunement, so that you, too, might receive these awakening energies, as I received them that extraordinary day.

I did not see my mothers or Mariam during the three days prior, the three days during which my father officiated, or the three days that followed. And it was only after I returned to Avalon that I learned that all three "Marys" had been impregnated during this auspicious gathering with Yeshua's Light-conceived children! Their story is not mine to tell. I can only say now that my mother (*Mary of Bethany*) gave birth to my brother, Michel, and Myriam (*of Tyana*) gave birth to my half-sister, Zariah. Mariam conceived a child; but she did not bring her baby to full-term. I have seen her child on the inner-planes and I know Mariam (*Yeshua's cousin*) shall surely bring this child of the Light forth in a future incarnation, a time now not known.

As for me, I was reunited with my beloved Andrew. Together, we joyfully look to the fruition of our days with a glad heart. And surely, being a witness of my father and mothers, radiating forth their true essence within the Infinite Light those three days of "The Great Gathering," shall burn forever in the depths of my being!

CA: Thank you, Sar'h, for so beautifully sharing this sacred occasion. It feels to be a culmination of all that your father and mothers brought to the Earth.

SAR'H: Yes. And as I look into my beloved parents' last years on the Earthplane, I feel that even more was accomplished for the benefit of all beings – more than we can ever comprehend with our limited minds. We are so very blessed that such ones have come to serve us through all time.

CA: Is there anything more you wish to share about "The Great Gathering?"

SAR'H: No, not at this time.

CA: Please move forward to the next important event in your life.

{Sar'h continues her story in PART 4, Chapter 32}

— Chapter 27 —

MARIAM & ANNA
Avalon, 57 AD

{*Chapter 25 is a continuation of "Mariam," PART 1, Chapter 9 and "Anna and John," PART 3, Chapter 20. Both Mariam and Anna blend their voices in this chapter which describes pivotal events leading up to "The Great Gathering" and the cause of the dispersion of the family from Avalon as the Seeds of Light after 55 AD.*}

CATHERINE ANN (*Henceforth: CA*): Who is here?
MARIAM: I am called Mariam (*Yeshua's cousin and adopted sister*). Many years have passed since we last shared. I am now living in Avalon. My grandmother had such a blow. I can feel the injury she sustained within the holographic matrix of this body (*Claire's whip-lashed neck*)[48], [49]

---

[48] See the *"Laying of the Foundation"* section in which Myriam of Tyana gives an invocation of *"The Opening of the Mouth"* initiation for the purpose of lifting and healing the suppressed collective feminine voice during this patriarchal era.

[49] Note from Claire: It is not to be inferred from this statement that I am a future and fully embodied incarnation of Anna. I do believe that I am one of Anna's literal descendants and that I was a witness of many of the recorded events in Anna's account. Because of this, my DNA holds cellular memory of this incident. I also believe that on a soul level I have agreed to have access to the holographic record of this injury (the Akashic Record or Book of Life) and the other events communicated through this sequel. It is interesting that a coincidental physical out-picturing occurred when my neck was whiplashed by an intense rising of Kundalini energy several weeks earlier during an *"Opening of the Mouth"* initiation. The literal pain I was experiencing made these references to Anna's neck injury feel quite real.

ANNA, THE VOICE OF THE MAGDALENES

Perhaps it is best that Grandmother Anna tell you about her experience in her own words. Then I shall return to share more of my experiences in Avalon.

Anna Speaks:
The Ambush on the Way to Mona, autumn, 55AD

(*After "The Great Gathering" in Fortingall, Scotland*)

CA: You just spoke of an attack that severely injured your neck. Is this the same one that Mariam mentioned? Could you share more about it and the impact it had on you and those who lived in Avalon?

ANNA: Yes. I will speak of this incident because it was pivotal to the decisions we made soon thereafter that have so grandly impacted my family.

We were taken unawares.

CA: Who was with you?

ANNA: My sons, Joseph of Arimathea and his wife, Nueme; and Noah with his two wives (*Rhia and Dancing Wind*); Myriam's children: Joses Simeon, Jude, Miriam and their spouses; and four of the brothers from Avalon including my beloved friend, John. Thanks be to the Mother of Mercy that Mary Anna and her children; Myriam (*of Tyana*) and her son, Johannes; Mary of Bethany and her children; and Mariam were not with us. Mary Anna (*Mother Mary*) and Mariam chose to remain in Avalon where they cared for Nueme's two young sons and fulfilled their other various duties.

CA: Where were you headed?

ANNA: We were on our way to Glamorgan in southern Wales where my sons, Andrew and Josephus, started an Essene-Druid monastery several years before I arrived in Avalon in 38 AD. They were well on in years at that time. They passed beyond the veil within weeks of each other in 47 AD, never seeing the fruits of their labors in Glamorgan. But Mary Anna and her children, Esther Salome and Matteas; and Myriam and her children: Joses Simeon, Jude, Miriam and Johannes; as well as others from Avalon and Mona, including Lizbett, have faithfully carried on their work. They are in the process of expanding the function of the Glamorgan monastery to include serving as a hospital, orphanage and hospice.

These family members have not all stayed in Glamorgan, but rather they have chosen to come and go over the years; giving what they can to our various communities in Avalon, Cornwall, Devon and other Essene-Druid outreaches throughout the West Country, you call Wales; including the scattered islands off Scotia's west coastline. We are also exchanging initiates with our brothers and sisters of Eire (*Ireland*), far to the west.

Our plan was to visit family members living in various communities in the south and west (*of Wales*) and then press on northwest to the great Druid sanctuary on the isle of Mona where Myriam and Johannes; and Mary of Bethany and Sar'h were awaiting us. They had gone to Mona straightway from Scotland, almost a month earlier in the late summer, after we had all returned from "The Great Gathering" in Fortingall. As you know, it was in the heart of Scotia where we attended this most memorable gathering led by Yeshua and other masters.

Besides reuniting Myriam (*of Tyana*) with her children, we were eager to pass on the teachings and energies we had received during "The Great Gathering." There were many who lived on Mona and the scattered communities who had not been able to attend. Joseph (*of Arimathea*) and Noah had papers in their possession which had been recently stamped with the seal of the Roman governor Didius Gallus. Months earlier these documents had served us well on our journey to and from Fortingall, which was then beyond the reach of the Romans. Though much of our travel to Scotia was accomplished by using Joseph's freighting boats, there were times that we were required to pass by Roman sentinels, who, when seeing our credentials, allowed us unhindered passage.

CA: Did you make it to Mona?

ANNA: No; that is, most of us did not. We had already left our flat boats which we used to cross the Severn estuary, and we were beginning to make our way westward on the new Roman road which was being built to Carmarthen and other sites leading to Mona. We had successfully passed by a hill fort that was previously used by the Silurian warriors, but which, during the Roman campaigns in Wales between 48 AD and 50 AD, had been taken and restructured in the manner to which the Roman military was accustomed. It was during these earlier tumultuous years that the great hero of the Britons, King Caradoc; Caratacus, as the Romans call him, successfully fought against the Roman legions using guerilla warfare in league with his rebellious Welsh tribal allies. He retreated from the mountains of Wales and was finally betrayed and turned over to the governor, Ostorius Scapula in 51 AD by the Brigantes' queen, Cartimandua.

As I was saying, we were walking through a heavily wooded stretch, when, without any hint of warning, we were overtaken from the rear and sides by an angry Silurian mob of loudly screeching men and women. John and I were among the last in line, followed only by Maldwyn, one of the brave Celtic brothers from Avalon, who was large in stature and trained in his youth to be a warrior. If it had not been for the quick response of my companions; my beloved John, Maldwyn, and my sons, Joseph and Noah, it is likely that our entire company would have been killed. At the first encroachment, Maldwyn turned and faced off the attackers with his staff. John instantly took me in his arms and stood between me and the onslaught. But it was too late.

John took the full blow of an ax. Then the ax's dull end glanced off the back of my head, neck and shoulder. Before losing consciousness, I reached out to John, lying next to me, and felt his traumatized soul leaving his lifeless body. My ears pounded with blood. Before everything became dark and silent, I heard my brave sons shouting Druid words of power over the deafening cacophony, commanding the mob to stop.

Recognizing the Druid command, the attackers halted in mid-air, as if frozen in time. Then the woad-painted (*indigo dye*) ruffians ran away into the forest. John was the only one of us to die. Two escaped with no physical injuries; others suffered serious wounds and some received only bruises. I lay unconscious for several days. It was only upon our return on the flatboats, as we weaved through Avalon's misty marshes, that I came back to any awareness of my body and what had befallen us. Even then, I drifted in and out of my body, my soul seemingly unsure of remaining incarnated or taking my leave and fully joining John on his journey into the light.

Returned to my hermitage by the three brothers from Avalon, it was Mary Anna (*Mother Mary*) and Mariam (*and later Lizbett who left Glamorgan for a time*) who nursed me back to health. Joseph and Noah took Myriam's children, together with their spouses, on to Mona after resting at the new monastery at Glamorgan. It was a tragic wake-up call; one that changed our lives forever.

CA: Why were you attacked?

ANNA: As I said, the Romans were obsessed with stamping out any resistance to their conquering and occupying Britain. They saw the resistant Celtic tribes, and especially the Druids, as a major threat to their intent of taking control of Britain's peoples and her resources. Most of the tribes in the east, who had resisted them and survived, moved westward to Devon, Cornwall and Wales. Mona was, and had long been, the seat of Druid power; which sustained the spirit of the Britons. The Romans were determined to achieve peace on their terms and break the Celtic spirit. The tribal Britons; especially those located in the frontiers, were determined to defy them.

As King Caradoc so boldly stated, as he rallied support for his resistance movement, "They defile our fair land; and when they have made the world a desolation, they call it peace." The continued desecration and loss of life up to this point was a grave and constantly irritating sore for the Celtic tribes whose love of the virginal land and nature was so different from the urbanized Romans. Unfortunately, no end to the turbulence was in sight.

Although we had had an alliance with the Silures since Joseph (*of Arimathea*) had first begun to come to Britain many years ago; and he and my son, Noah, had married Silurian wives, it was clear that some among the native people no longer recognized us as allies and family. Rather, we were seen as traitors because they saw our passive resistance as unsupportive of their cause. In our refusal to fight, we

---

[50] See bibliography in the Appendix.

ANNA, THE VOICE OF THE MAGDALENES

were seen as nothing more than pawns of their sworn enemy. But those who attacked us did not realize we were initiated Druids. But when they heard my sons speak the ancient Druid words of power – they indeed knew, and that realization saved us.

CA: Thank you for sharing your tragic story, Anna.

{*Note from Claire: At the outset of this session, as Anna's consciousness first presented itself, I was aware of looking down on the coastline of southwestern Britain. As I continued to look, the specific area surrounding the Bristol Channel came into view. As you recall, several weeks before this session I experienced my neck being severely whip-lashed as a result of Kundalini energy rising suddenly during an "Opening of the Mouth" initiation. Now, as I was "out-of-body" looking down on the scene below me, I noticed that I was completely free of pain. When Anna's consciousness entered more fully into my body I became aware of the ambush scene and a searing pain in my neck. It was difficult to stay conscious. It was then that Anna revealed the details of the attack that injured her neck.*}

ANNA: Let us return now to Mariam who wishes to share her wisdom.

Mariam Speaks, Avalon, winter, 57 AD

MARIAM: As I was saying - the powerful energies released during Claire's experience of "The Opening of the Mouth" initiation are held within the holographic universe. I am finding the interdimensional holographic universe a very magical place. I am learning how to travel within it beyond the ways I had been taught in my youth. We had all been prepared to take flight from our bodies, but somehow the training I have received since I have been in Britain feels different. It seems to be part of my healing that brings me to a new level of mastery in which I can better match Yeshua's ascending frequencies when he comes to visit us. This was especially true during the time I was recently with him in Fortingall. Contemplating these experiences of ever deepening union brings me great joy. (*Emotion*)

Since arriving in Avalon in the fall of 38 AD, I have experienced deep healing. I am glad that I still walk upon this beloved earth, although I spend more and more time on the other side – beyond the mists that shroud these isles in mystery. As I walk between the worlds, I know I'm not completely finished with this physical realm. There is something more that I am here to do with my sisters and brothers – on this side and the other side – both in form and beyond form. There is more healing and awakening of my consciousness. There is more to experience with Yeshua. I am thankful beyond measure for the leisure that is gifted to me in which to study, meditate and heal my mind of any thoughts that cause me to imagine I am separate from my Creator Source and my Divine Mother's manifestations; and my beloved Yeshua.

Mariam Offers a Wisdom Teaching on Consciousness

In these past seventeen years I have returned to my spiritual roots. I am studying and practicing more of the ancient texts Grandmother and Uncle Joseph (*of Arimathea*) brought to Avalon from Mount Carmel and other Essene monasteries scattered throughout the coastline of the Great Sea. Myriam (*of Tyana*) and Johannes also recently brought texts from India and Egypt. By reading and contemplating the great teachings, I am sustaining my deep spiritual practices more than ever.

More and more I am witnessing a permeating light and eternal perfection in all things and in all experiences. Like a dream from which I am awakening, I am discerning what is real and what is illusory. In this awakening the solid world is seen as pure light, space and subtle frequency.

But the concepts of emptiness, and the forms that emanate within space, merely point to an even greater subtlety – the essential nature beyond all mental concepts. Increasingly, I am experiencing this infinite, empty luminosity and the bliss of awareness as my true nature – the essential nature of all things – all that is, is of an inseparable Oneness. It is difficult to talk about such truths because my discursive mind cannot describe what is unnamable. In order to know all that I have feebly named, it must be experienced directly with naked, present awareness. That is the nature of Gnosis and the awakening path of enlightenment. But it is more than just glimpses.

Regardless of how frequent or how wonderful the moments of clear insight seem, or how much bliss is experienced, the emptiness and awareness must be stabilized and brought into inseparable union. This takes consistent and diligent practice and a great "letting-go" into the Mystery. I am certainly not enlightened; but I am making progress on my path; knowing any progress I make is only due to the grace of the Beloved on High and the Great Ones in my behalf. And so it is that I dedicate any greater capacity to know the Oneness as benefiting all beings, who, in Oneness, are my own self.

My temperament is much calmer and more even than it used to be before the traumas of my son, Benjamin's, and my husband, Nathaniel's, deaths. My thoughts and emotions – both pleasant and unpleasant, float within a gentler and more merciful spaciousness; which helps me to feel more compassion toward myself and others. More often than not, no matter what is happening internally or externally, I find my sense of self settling easily into a pervasive peace, joy and gratitude. Sometimes my body feels heavy and dense because I have a lingering preference for "just being" – actually, I realize "just being," while having a physical body, is a form of escape – escaping into the realms of light and bliss, fleeing the limitations of physicality. When this happens, I realize I have split myself in two, identifying with "this" opposed to being "that." Conflicted, I have obscured the Peace and Lightness that is my true nature – including my body's essential nature, as light manifest.

I am gaining mastery, day by day, in how to let go of defining myself in ways that take sides. In fact, I am letting go of being any particular identity needing definition or reflection. When I return to being mindful in Oneness, it's easy to embrace the wholeness and the sameness of everything while appreciating its distinctions and diversity. I can be at peace while embracing all that arises in my inner and reflective worlds – the wonder of it all passing by while pure awareness remains calm and still is such divine grace. The infinite potential of Infinite Mind to express every possible imagining is truly amazing.

I am finding it easier to be in physicality and not be disturbed by its beauty or its ugliness. These judgments are just my conditioned mind wanting to make real what is actually empty – light particles dancing like elusive rainbows. While I still prefer the subtle realms of spirit, I am realizing a growing joy in being present for my physical relationships and mundane tasks. Simultaneously, I am also aware of the Infinite Light that IS everything, including the "relative darkness" that defines "relative light." No "good or bad"; no "right or wrong"; no effortful striving to be or to get somewhere or to have something better. All that I Am is the Great Perfection – and That is enough!

I am finding an increasing stability and constancy beyond anything I knew before. Being awake in fresh, present mindfulness – doing and being whatever I am – aware in my body, aware in my breath, aware in my sensations – is being "spiritual." Being awake is nothing to shout about! It's just being who you really are – a sentient being with a heart filled with compassion and a mind filled with wisdom. What is true of me is true of you and is true of all beings.

Instead of avoiding looking into deeper levels of suffering, within and all around me, as I used to do, I am bringing merciful and clear inquiry into how my mind clings to the idea of being a separate self – from breath to breath. I see how my, and everyone's, thoughts and feelings create all manner of afflictions – dramas in which we seek to hold onto fleeting pleasures and push away reoccurring pain. When something intense happens and I become identified with the drama, like the ambush that threatened Grandmother, I can see how it is that I am clinging to illusory shadows.

Instead of being unconsciously pulled in and becoming automatically reactive, I find myself stopping, pausing and responding with greater mastery and true compassion. Feeling spacious and less anxious, it is easier to align with the Light that illuminates and dissolves my mind's projections. I can just be in equipoise wherever I am, whatever I am doing; allowing the parade of my thoughts, feelings, sensations and perceptions to simply pass by. Instead of challenging events becoming obscured with self-concern, I am calmly bringing clearer awareness and more authentic support to everyone's experience of separation, suffering, and fleeting pleasures. Instead of "my" pain and joy, it is "our" pain and joy.

As the years pass, I am more appreciative of the full spectrum of human feelings — my feelings and other people's feelings merged in Oneness — be they sensory, emotional or a quickened awareness of the most subtle energy. I honor our ability to be aware through feeling, because feelings enliven us and provide a bridge between the physical and spiritual worlds. Awareness and wise discernment of our "gut" feelings is the foundation of our intuitive guidance. A keen feeling awareness, free of obscurations, such as fear and anger, provides clear choice and a greater sense of freedom and well-being.

I am also becoming aware; once again, that in the midst of constant movement and change there is a great stillness and peace. This is the essence of the Magdalene teachings. Even though impermanence — all things which have a beginning have an ending — can create suffering when there is attachment to things, people and ideas, impermanence is also a gateway to freedom. Resting in the space between inflowing and outflowing breaths, I know the great unborn, undying Silence — the Beloved on High. In stillness, I experience my thoughts as if they are ephemeral clouds passing by and my feelings as elusive rainbows dissolving into a clear blue sky.

As I enter more fully into the way of the Beloved — the very fountainhead of love, I feel Yeshua taking me as a bride to stand together before our Creator. Turning to face our greatest suffering — the intense pain that comes from thinking we are separate, abandoned and unlovable, we behold a light within the darkness. The Infinite Light which has the power to burn away all fear, anger and grief. Entering Love's temple we come into the presence of a transmuting Cosmic Fire which is aflame upon the altar of our hearts. Being love, lover and beloved, "I" gives itself to perceived "other."

Letting go, we enter into the Beloved's fiery embrace and die only to emerge spiritually reborn in Love's consuming flames. Knowing love at last, we relax into the Peace that abides beyond form — the Truth that removes death's sting. Resting in the great stillness, we feel the Beloved breathing. Being the Beloved's breath, we join as one breath and breathe into the worlds of form. Being Peace, we bring glad tidings to all who feel bereft of Love's eternal presence. Remembering — awakening — we choose love.

At the Beloved's altar, I offer up my commitment to bring blessings and harmlessness to all sentient life. I reaffirm my vow to do my part in releasing all beings from our collective karmas and endless despair. Into the Beloved's heart of compassion, I bring the pain of all who feel lost and bewildered. Merged in mystical union with my beloved, Yeshua, as the Beloved on High, All That Is becomes a vast ocean of shimmering light.

Another breath arises and I become aware of a "self" coalescing like a pulsing, crystalline dewdrop bejeweling an apple blossom. And I gratefully return into my body consciousness, as Mariam, a simple woman sitting on a bench in my grandmother's garden.

(*Pause*)

CA: Thank you, as always, for sharing your love and wisdom. You give us much to contemplate. Refocusing now back into your awareness as Mariam, please tell us where you are in Avalon. Is anyone with you?

MARIAM: I am aware I am stepping into Grandmother Anna's cottage, as I prefer to call her thatched roundhouse. She is sitting right here, smiling. Her face is becoming withered these days and she moves more slowly. She looks very different from the youthful woman I used to know. Soon after the accident she lost most of her hair. When her hair started growing again it was white. Now it is completely silver. She no longer holds her head in an erect manner. It is somewhat tilted to the side — her right shoulder is drawn up closer to her ear. She still loves to have me comb her hair which is growing surprisingly long in such a short time. Sometimes when I sweep her comb through strands of silver, instead of the dark chestnut tresses I used to know, a tear or two spills from my eyes. I fondly remember her thick, long hair, which I used to plait into a braid and wrap upon her head like a crown. Somehow the harshness of the accident and the many stressors that she still faces since the Roman invasion[51], have caused her to age, as if overnight.

CA: Does Anna still practice cellular regeneration?

MARIAM: As I speak, I am recalling Grandmother taking me aside shortly after our coming to Avalon. She confided with me that she would no longer be participating in the rituals of cellular rejuvenation which used to be so much a part of her long life. I was surprised at first, but then she explained she had become aware that her purpose for being embodied was coming to a close. I knew it was important for me to align with her wisdom and to let go of any attachment that would create any suffering for her, our community, or for me, as her faithful granddaughter.

Her last time of retreat was within a cave at Mount Bugarach in which I took part as one of her attendants, just as I have done a number of times before. Somehow I thought attending Grandmother in this extraordinary way would continue through the remainder of my life. But I am slowly accepting and serving her in an even more profound way during this time of transition. I know not whether I shall pass before or after her. It matters not. What is important is to continue to receive Grandmother's vast wisdom and to love her while we can still embrace and walk together upon these green hills. And more important still, is for me to cultivate the same capacity to love all beings as effortlessly and as purely as does this amazing woman – this grandmother whom I have known and served all my days.

---

[51] The Romans first invaded Britain under Julius Caesar in 55 BC. Any attempt at occupation was met with heavy resistance from the Britons and without the necessary legions the campaign was soon aborted. Except for ongoing trade, Britain remained free of Imperial Rome until Emperor Claudius successfully invaded Britain in 43 AD. The Roman occupation continued until 425 AD. Much of Scotland was never occupied and Ireland was never invaded by the Romans. The Anglo-Saxons invaded Britain in 450 AD.

I am slowly realizing Grandmother is choosing to bring great compassion and love through her choice to face her own physical impermanence. Like Yeshua and his mother; she, and all we Magdalenes, walk the same path all beings must walk. In a very conscious way, just as she chose to extend her life in order to be of greater service to more people over a large expanse of time, she will continue as she always has, whether in, or out of body, to bring love and wisdom to every being who suffers. By allowing her body to age, she will embody and transcend the suffering through which humanity and all forms must eventually pass – the passage we call dying to physicality and birthing ourselves back into spirit.

Although Yeshua's path demonstrates the continuation of life within physicality, albeit a very subtle physicality; he, too, will eventually release all identity within form when he passes from this world. He will ultimately dissolve his most subtle bodies of light in order to BE the Beloved. Then he will be Love manifest, taking form within the cycles of time. He will continue to come as one of the living masters (*avatars*), completely awake within the great Emptiness, while knowing all things across all time and space.

He lives to exemplify that everything is possible for those who would know the Truth that sets them free. He shows all beings how to find their way Home through the awakened and purified heart. Heaven – the Great Love – is to be found where it has been all along – within every heart – no exceptions. He has spoken of these things with me. He is showing a number of us a more expanded view. We are receiving great comfort as we try to live it – simply by being the love we already are. This is the way of true enlightenment and liberation.

CA: Are you practicing cellular regeneration in the same way Anna did?

MARIAM: There are some of the simpler practices that I feel are in alignment with my soul's purpose in this incarnation. They do seem to give me more energy and clarity of view when I practice them. I am in my 60th year. I look and feel much younger, as do my other Essene-Druid relatives who have carefully practiced disciplined care of our bodies. Grandmother taught me many of the essential aspects of cellular regeneration all through my life. The primary purpose of this teaching was to become a skilled and trusted attendant so that I could provide her and a few others at Mount Carmel with the support they needed. My interest in this strict discipline is to be in service to the courageous souls who actually participate in the Rite of the Sepulcher, as did our beloved Yeshua when he went into the sepulcher after his crucifixion. It is to understand, of course, that this was not the first time he had stilled his vital signs and passed through the Rites of the Sepulcher. As for me, I have never felt that my actual participation in it was mine to do. I am thankful for the wisdom and profound experiences I have had as an attendant.

Mariam Offers a Teaching on Physical Immortality

I have observed that there is much misunderstanding about physical and spiritual immortality. It is important to demystify it – to remove overly romantic or fearful ideas many may have. Advanced spiritual adepts who choose to practice cellular rejuvenation and physical immortality are motivated by compassion for all sentient life. They deeply desire to release beings from suffering in all the realms of consciousness. They have a compelling desire to attain mastery of the physical plane in order to be of benefit to as many beings as possible for an extended time.

It is possible for anyone with sufficient discipline to attain considerable skill and spiritual powers through any deep practice – physical and spiritual immortality being one of a number of the fruits or signs of such activity. It is important to understand that these powers do not indicate full enlightenment. They may, in fact, be an obstacle and a distraction in a soul's awakening process. Spiritual powers are gifts that come with amplified karmic consequences, for they may be used for beneficial or harmful purposes. This is why anyone on a genuine spiritual path of opening to their True Nature must take a vow of harmlessness and always be motivated to bring benefit to all sentient life.

Some naïve souls approach cellular rejuvenation from a very superficial and self-gratifying level. They may be motivated to avoid aging or they are in denial of death and wish to put it off. Few, if any of these, progress beyond the most basic disciplines. Their improved well-being is a benefit and this may facilitate an awareness of compassionate caring. There are more sophisticated, though wounded practitioners, who wish to satisfy their lust or take revenge or bring harm to others through the use of occult powers in order to manipulate. These, too, usually do not stay with the practices for long. The harm they bring comes back to them many-fold. It is true that there are also highly skilled, but extremely misguided souls, who are motivated by a strong wish to be impervious to the effects of their karmas and their inevitable death; but, these, too, invariably realize the consequences of their self-delusions.

When such extremely selfish souls acquire the spiritual powers that accompany cellular rejuvenation, they can extend their physical incarnation long enough to accomplish their self-centered goals, and then they consciously die. They know the life-force they cultivated and channeled into their earthbound astral body will go on for a long time before it eventually dies (*a lesser form of spiritual immortality*). Then they can do many things they could not do in a physical body for the purpose of gaining power over others. You call such ones, when they are embodied, sorcerers and lesser alchemists,[52] and malevolent, "hungry" ghosts after death.

---

[52] Alchemy involves the transmutation of one or more substances from a form of lesser value (impermanent forms) into another of greater value (immortality – extending form through time and/or realizing the Absolute – beyond form). Purely physically based alchemy is the art and science of transmuting base metals into gold. There are two forms of spiritual or energetic (Tantric) alchemy: lower and higher alchemy. The result depends on the motivation of the alchemist. The more physically based and self-aggrandizing the intention is, the "lesser" the alchemy. "High" alchemy involves the transmutation of the physical body and human consciousness until full enlightenment and liberation are achieved for the benefit of all life. This requires heightened brain states which activate the endocrine system and neurotransmitters to secrete high frequency "elixirs." Some form of mind

The Egyptians call this subtle body which lives on after physical death the KA body. It is neither intrinsically good, nor is it bad. It is simply the second of seven interpenetrating bodies – the gross physical body being the first, on to the seventh which is a very subtle light body – then there is the unborn and undying formless Body out of which the All has its being. Grandmother, as a spiritual adept, is deeply aware of her KA and other light bodies. As practitioners of high alchemy, spiritual initiates and adepts carefully cultivate life-force energy and direct it into these bodies; but instead of doing this out of fear, they are motivated by Great Love. They know how precious their human birth is and how powerful it can be when they are in service to the Light.

They are not limited by the physical dimension. Death is not feared, but welcomed, as a portal into Homecoming. Knowing various degrees of Oneness, each is in the process of stabilizing their awakened consciousness, until they are a realized Christ or Buddha, according to their spiritual lineage. Realization of their true nature is an organic process of transmuting obscurations. Self-realization is experienced in the now moment without effort or pretense.

Only a pure desire to be harmless and of loving service can motivate the practitioner of cellular regeneration to invest the degree of discipline that is required to undertake this very arduous, alchemical process. It is important for the uninitiated to be aware of the effects of having most of your consciousness removed from the body for an extended time. While the body is comatose and passing

---

expanding Awareness meditation is used. In this way extrasensory perception, omniscient awareness, and unified consciousness are realized. The base human consciousness involves dualistic thoughts and emotions. These are called poisons of the mind or the "base elements" used in spiritual alchemy: anger, lust, greed, jealousy, fear, habituated ignorance, etc., which are embraced and transmuted into love, compassion, wisdom, equanimity and joy. The "high" alchemist is not above others but rather practices alchemy for the purpose of attaining enlightenment or the Light Anointing: i.e. realizing the consciousness of a Christ or a Buddha who has attained the Immortal Rainbow Body or The Golden Raiment in order to bring benefit to self and others in this lifetime and all lifetimes.

through profound transmutation, the consciousness or Soul Awareness is awake and highly alert. Depending on the intention and length of time involved, the physical body often goes through profound biological changes; such as a minimal to total loss of skin, teeth and hair. All the body's organs and its entire nervous and circulatory system are affected. Then there is the critical time of new cellular growth. This can take many months and then there is a lengthy time of recuperation and rehabilitation.

As Grandmother's attendant, a keen clarity of perception is required in order to be able to follow her consciousness into the multidimensional realms, while simultaneously holding an immaculate space/frequency container around her body. When it is time to "rise from the sepulcher," it requires an especially precise, continuously focused attention, to assist her to bring her harmoniously back into body awareness.

Full cellular regeneration, or physical immortality, is a calling that very few initiates begin and even fewer repeat during the course of their extended lives. It is a great responsibility for initiates and even adepts, such as Grandmother, to undertake. For me, as Grandmother's witness and attendant, I have felt my participation to be a profound honor. But sometimes it also feels like a heavy burden because of the exacting measures that must be taken in order to prevent injury to the body and to safeguard against mental illness or loss of life. To be honest, I must confide that I am actually relieved that I will be serving in this capacity with much less frequency within our community.

As I said earlier, fully embodying these practices and becoming a physical immortal is not mine to do in this incarnation. Being fully conscious at my death and during my soul's journey into its next conscious birth seems more than enough to master during this lifetime. Of course my Great Desire is full enlightenment and liberation. If not in this lifetime, then I am working out my karma to bring about favorable conditions in the next.

CA: Please tell me more about where you learned these skills.

MARIAM: Besides learning from our grandmother, Mary of Bethany and I also learned how to refine these skills during our initiations in Egypt. We did not know at that time how important these abilities would be until they were enlisted by our beloved Yeshua when he fulfilled his commitment to "rise from the sepulcher," after demonstrating the crucifixion initiation.

CA: Are others in Avalon practicing cellular regeneration?

MARIAM: Two of my uncles: Joseph of Arimathea and Noah. Uncle Joseph has benefited from the basic Rites of the Sepulcher which have extended his life and given him many spiritual powers. Noah recently began more advanced practices. I am aware of several initiates living at Mona who began the basic exercises, but I do not think they intend to master it to the extent Grandmother and my uncles have.

Noah is especially interested in this science. He and his two wives, Rhia and Dancing Wind (*also known as Blodwedd or Wild Spirit*) are meeting quite often with Grandmother so they can practice the advanced skills with her wise guidance. Sometimes I am asked to assist. Uncle Joseph made the decision to cease practicing the Rites at about the same time Grandmother did, soon after we arrived in Avalon. I have observed him also aging rather quickly since the ambush. He was injured, but not as severely as Grandmother. The other Magdalenes, like me, have varying degrees of awareness about what is involved; but we do not practice the full Rites.

CA: What are the experiences like when you and Yeshua meet?

MARIAM: When we are together it is like we enter into a different frequency reality. This physical plane feels very dense. The frequency of the energy that manifests into physical form is very slow compared to the frequencies of the subtle realms. In the simultaneous dimension where we meet, I would say the frequency is very fast. There is also a sense of fluidity. There is a recognizable vibratory signature. I would say that I experience a greater constancy of consciousness that has a far vaster view of many interpenetrating realities – a clearer View of the Oneness, Nowness and Emptiness of all things. I experience everything as being more like liquid light. There is much more a sense of harmony and unity. Love prevails. My heart and mind are open like a window that allows a gentle breeze to blow through. My perception is clear and everything is transparent, fluid and unified.

When Yeshua comes amongst us, he sits and we gather around him. Just being with him brings us into a unified attunement. There's no effort. No need to do anything special or try to be a certain way. As we gaze into his eyes, we know we are clearly seen and loved just as we are. He becomes an energy portal or a matrix, like an expanding orb of light. We can feel our energy wheels[53] spinning faster, matching and joining with his, like spokes coming together at the hub of a large wheel. He is the center – the hub and also the embracing circle that enfolds us – like your symbol for the sun. Together we come into a singular accord.

Once we have arrived at complete Oneness, he shows us the most amazing things. Our consciousness travels to places where other beings live, both on and within this planet and on other worlds. Those in need of healing are often healed. He tells us, "I am the open door. I am the way and the truth and the life. Come, follow me. Do what I do, be you as I am. Hold on to no thing, including saving your life, if it be for your sake only, or for the seeking of riches, which become tarnished and lost. Grasping desire and aversive aggression cause endless suffering – know that all things must pass away. Who you think you are, is a no thing. Yet, you are everything. Bring the above and the below together – know the Oneness of the within and the without – make male, female and make female, male. Be all that is – Love manifest."

Then we laugh. There is so much joy! Yeshua often leads us into a kind of game the children especially enjoy.

As I share these memories, I recall the times when I would go to the special roundhouse where we have our community gatherings

---

[53] Hindu yogis refer to these spinning energy vortexes as chakras. Acting as portals, they are located at significant points of the body where they bring life-force from the subtle realms into the physical body. The primary chakras are associated with the endocrine glands which bridge the physical and subtle realms. The secondary chakras are located in the palms of the hands, soles of the feet and at the knees. In adepts, such as Yeshua, the entire body is an awakened energy portal – every pore of the skin an "eye."

and where the children are schooled or to the places in nature where they love to come together and play. It is especially joyful to be with these little innocent ones when they take turns being Yeshua! (*Wonderful laughter*)

CA: What would they do?

MARIAM: There are groves of apple trees scattered upon the hillsides and meadowlands. Of all the trees, there is an ancient apple tree the children love the best. They love to climb into her limbs, have picnics in her verdant shade and play their games, bowing to her revered presence. One of their beloved games is to take turns imagining being Yeshua or one of their other favorite teachers. Near the great apple tree is a large round stone. The one whose turn it is to be the "Master Teacher for the Day" climbs atop the stone and assumes his or her role. The other children gather around. With rapt attention, leaning into the day's teaching, they respond with affirming nods and extended silences, punctuated with laughter.

They are so sweet and innocent sitting there, hands folded quietly in their laps or assuming various mudras![54] All the while, "The Master for the Day" sits in calm equipoise, smiling just as Yeshua does. She or he leads the students in prayers, psalms and mantra[55] recitations followed by the day's teaching story and energy practice. (*Delightful laughter*)

The energy practices often take the form of games such as "hide and seek," lifting and moving objects with their minds, cultivating energy in their hands and watching the rainbow colors streaming from hand to hand, astral journeys, levitating their bodies, and observing auras fluctuating in color and brightness according to what the volunteer is thinking or feeling. Sometimes a playmate or

---

[54] Mudras are body postures and hand/finger positions assumed by the Hindu and Buddhist yogis and yoginis which facilitate specific flows of life-force energy through the body/mind to enhance concentration in meditation and to expand consciousness.

[55] Mantras are carefully prepared and repeated sequences of seed syllables (the primordial sounds of creation), such as OM AH HUM, used by yogis and yoginis to greatly enhance their energy practices. They are spoken or chanted vocally or internally within the mind.

grown-up in the community is sick. The children send healing energy from a distance. They are so happy to find their friend or elder feeling better.

Besides Yeshua, they have other favorite teachers they enjoy "being." There's Grandmother Anna – the one they call the Great, Great, Great Grand Ma who lives in the little hut down the hill! (*Laughter*) They also love memorizing and reciting the teachings that Mary Anna, Mary of Bethany and Myriam of Tyana have given them. Their other favorites are Joseph of Arimathea and Noah – they never tire of impersonating these very impressive Bards and Druids.

CA: Are you still maintaining your vow of silence?

MARIAM: It is interesting that you ask me this. I did so for many years as I worked very hard to restore my body to its full strength. I am glad to say that it is perhaps more vigorous than ever. Even though I have aged, I feel more vitality and suppleness. And there is almost always a song in my heart. I suppose it's because I feel my beloved Yeshua is so close and is at one with me.

But to answer your question – Yes, a day came when I absolutely knew it was time to allow my voice to be heard. It was right after the ambush that almost took Grandmother's life. Sadly, it did take her beloved companion, John's life. I did not go on this occasion. I had responsibilities to tend to in our community while the others were away in Mona.

I was utterly surprised and grief-stricken the day John's lifeless body was returned to Avalon. Grandmother and several others who had been wounded were also brought to the infirmary on litters. Almost everyone in the entire party had received some kind of injury – some with only abrasions and bruises, others with more serious wounds.

Thank the Great Mother that Joseph and Noah knew how to stop the attack at its very outset. They both speak the Silurian tongue and rose up as mighty Druids. The guerilla band had come unexpectedly out of the forest and, though they were intent on killing, they recognized the high Druid command to desist. They immediately stopped their attack and ran into the forest. The attackers were very angry because they thought we, Druid-Essenes, were supporting the Roman occupation because we refuse to go to war.

This was an opportunity for us to make peace and take stock of how we would handle our future interactions with the Welsh tribes. It caused us to particularly reconsider our involvement with the Druid sanctuary at Mona and to begin dispersing family members to places of safety.

But in the moment of seeing Grandmother so close to death, I did not think of the future.

Without thinking, I could not suppress my voice! Grandmother had accepted my vow of silence and we had developed an effective way to communicate; but in this moment, I knew deep within my soul she needed to actually hear my voice calling her soul to come back into her body from the other side. And so it was that my deep heart's voice reached out to my beloved Grandmother. I sat with her day and night – softly and audibly calling her in…calling her in. I have been speaking in a rather reserved tone ever since. Our community still expresses their gratitude that I helped Grandmother Anna's return to us in one piece. I think they are glad, as well, that it is easier to communicate with me. They say I don't seem so distant. I feel so very blessed to be able to serve through my voice once again.

I also thank you, my beloved Magdalene sisters, for assisting me from your time to revoke my vow of silence. I can feel the healing continuing across time, even as I speak.

CA: Have you ever had the same kind of intimate relationship with Yeshua that Myriam of Tyana and Mary of Bethany have had?

MARIAM: No, not in the physical sense in which they had physical intercourse with him or in the same way I had physical intimacy with Nathaniel. Since Nathaniel's death my relationship with Yeshua did change, however. There is a greater intimacy, but it has been without physical penetration. As his body becomes more and more ethereal, so does our intimacy. That is also true for Myriam and Mary. I confess I dearly desired Yeshua to be my husband and lover in my youth. I was very disappointed and even hurt that he chose to marry Myriam (*of Tyana*) when Mary (*of Bethany*) and I were away in Egypt. Mary's already bruised heart, which was recovering from her near-death experience during her Egyptian Rite of the Sepulcher initiation, was stunned with grief when she learned of their marriage.

It took most of the years Yeshua was in India for us both to heal our wounded hearts. But I can say this, in the ripeness of our unfolding lives and in the maturation of my soul, I have come to prefer the bonfire of every cell being ignited in Mystical Union with Yeshua, than to be a small candle flame lit in an act of unconscious carnal intercourse!

CA: You have said you feel like you are being prepared to be with Yeshua in a more expanded way. What do you mean by that?

MARIAM: First of all I would like to say that I entered into a deeply committed and conscious relationship with Yeshua, Myriam of Tyana and Mary of Bethany. A simple betrothal ceremony honored us about a year after we arrived in Avalon. The relationship that the four of us had known for years immediately changed and deepened. We have always been a close trinity of feminine energy - Myriam, Mary and I – even though we earlier had to work through our difficult emotions of jealousy and distrust. Over time we became a bonded and true sisterhood in support of Yeshua's ministry.

One example that stands out is the time when Mary of Bethany conceived Sar'h. This was on the evening before we all went into the Garden of Gethsemane to prepare for Yeshua's coming travails and resurrection. Myriam and I were very united in supporting the opening of Mary's womb so that she could receive a most powerful Light Conception with Yeshua. We were also very present and supportive of Mary's conception of Lizbett with Yeshua in what we called "The Light-conception Cave" within Mount Bugarach.

All these experiences prepared me for the initiations that occurred at "The Great Gathering" three summers ago in Fortingall (*Summer Solstice of 55AD*). Earlier, Yeshua announced that a great gathering was being prepared in the ethers. It would involve bringing many of the Masters, adepts and initiates together in one place. The location that had been chosen was to be far to the north in the land of Scotia (*Scotland*). Within a sacred valley there is a place you call Fortingall. It is removed from the influence of the Romans. It and some of the islands on the west coast of Scotia are places where some of our sacred texts and initiates are being taken where they can be kept safe. Myriam's children, Johannes and Miriam, are establishing a new Celtic-Essene community in Fortingall. It will be an expansion upon a much earlier initiatory center created by our earlier Celtic/Hebraic ancestors.

Our collective intention for the gathering in Fortingall was to accomplish many important purposes. Myriam (*of Tyana*), Mary of Bethany and I (*now known as "The Three Marys"*), felt a calling to be with Yeshua in a special way that would seed something of benefit for many generations to come. We all shared a mutual commitment to do whatever was necessary to support the safe passage of those who were called to come to this unprecedented gathering. Joseph (*of Arimathea*) readied his boats and gathered support wherever he could find it. Whether it was to provide safe passage for those of us living in Britain, Gaul or the eastern shores of the Great Sea, Joseph did what he has always done best – the gathering of resources to accomplish a higher good. Everything was quickly and efficiently put in order, as time was of the essence. We only had a few months to prepare.

I choose not to disclose all my experiences with Yeshua in Fortingall. My heart still feels too tender. I continue to know I would be dissipating a sacred energy if I were to say more. Trusting that you understand, I choose to hold the energy close to my heart in Silence. What I can say is that we served Yeshua in all the ways we used to do during the public ministry in Palestine long ago. We also participated in the energies of Light Conception. As I contemplate this event, I know it was for me, personally, the purpose for which my soul has taken birth – it may, in fact be the culmination and fulfillment of this lifetime. That is all I can say for now. Perhaps others will speak what they have to share. I pray that you understand my reluctance to say more.

I will share that Yeshua has strongly encouraged me to make the long, arduous journey to join with him, Myriam (*of Tyana*) and

Mary (*of Bethany*) in the high mountains of northern India. He says his days upon the Earthplane are waning and he desires his "Three Marys" to be close to him. Of course, I cannot refuse my beloved's beckoning. Perhaps this is the Calling for which I have truly taken incarnation. Myriam awaits Mary of Bethany and me in southern France. Joseph is making preparations for our sailing when the winter storms have abated.

Since "The Great Gathering" and Grandmother's accident, we continue to be surrounded near and far by prevailing unrest. There are ongoing massacres and pillage throughout Wales. The great tribal chieftain, Caradoc (*the son of King Cunobelinus, who inspired Shakespeare's "Cymbeline"*) was betrayed by the queen of the Brigantes and taken to Rome. There are threats of retribution on every side, whether by the tribal Britons or by the Roman legions whose intent it is to bring the peoples of this fair land to our knees. We only seek peace. But ever darker clouds cover these isles and portend unspeakable violence. It is not difficult to see the gathering storm that is threatening our every effort to maintain good-will among our Celtic neighbors.

Because of the potential danger to the children, as I have said, we are executing a careful dispersion of the family. Last winter there was a most serious council meeting where we took up the heart-wrenching decisions of which of Mary Anna's grandchildren and Myriam's children and grandchildren would remain in Britain and France. Sar'h and Andrew have chosen to return to Mount Bugarach. Lizbett will stay here. Mary and I await our departure from these fair, green lands. I confess it saddens me to think of leaving my beloved Nana (*Anna*), whom I treasure with all my heart. A new life and a Great Love beckon upon the winds that sweep these misty isles. When next we meet with Yeshua, we shall see where the winds have taken us.

CA: I thank you for all that you have shared with us. Is there anything else you wish to share? If so, please move ahead to the next significant event in your life.

{*Anna continues her story in PART 4, Chapter 28 and Mariam continues her story in PART 4, Chapter 29*}

— Chapter 28 —

ANNA

THE DISPERSION OF THE SEEDS OF LIGHT

ANNA: The ambush that occurred in the fall of 55 AD, on our way to Mona, was a pivotal turning point from which our lives radically shifted as many of us chose to turn away from our beloved Isles of Avalon. Regretfully, we knew it was time to begin withdrawing from Mona, and even to begin removing ourselves from Avalon (*Glastonbury*) and from the lands to the west (*Devon, Cornwall, and Wales*), as necessary.

More and more of us were, and still are, experiencing visions of devastation which haunt us with increasing frequency. The signs of increasing turbulence are all around us. It was decided as soon as I was healed sufficiently from my neck injury, and was able to participate in the Council meetings which occurred over the winter months; we would begin the process of relocating family members. Slowly, so as not to arouse too much attention and concern, Joseph (*of Arimathea*), and the other good seamen among us, began taking volunteers, as they were guided, to their variously chosen destinations.

We know that even if the Romans are in greater numbers, such as in Gaul and Turkey, their long-standing presence in those places also means there could be greater opportunities for safety and a long-life. Finding reasonable safety during this time of great uncertainty seemed especially important for all the descendants of the generations that had been Light-conceived – my living children, grandchildren, and particularly Yeshua's children.

ANNA: THE DISPERSION OF THE SEEDS OF LIGHT

The Dispersion of Anna's Family from Avalon
56–59 AD

{See the Anna's, Joseph of Arimathea's and Yeshua's Descendants charts and "The Seeding of Light" chart in the Appendix}

And so it was that a dispersion of the family began almost immediately, as soon as the winter storms had abated in the spring of 56 AD. Of my remaining children, Joseph (*of Arimathea*) and Noah are choosing to stay with me in Avalon. Mary Anna (*Mother Mary*) and her children, John Mark, Esther Salome, Matteas and most of their children returned to Ephesus in 56 AD. They will use Ephesus as a home base from which to relocate to other places in Eastern Europe, Greece and Turkey. Joseph (*of Arimathea*) took Myriam (*of Tyana*) and her children, Joses Simeon and Jude (*and most of their children*), and her infant daughter, Zariah, to Mount Bugarach on the same voyage in which he took Mary Anna on to Ephesus. Of Joses and Jude's children, three went with Johannes and Miriam (*and their families*) to Fortingall this spring. One of John Mark's and one of Esther Salome's older children also went to Fortingall. One of Esther Salome's and one of Matteas' older children are with me in Avalon. Two of Joses' and Jude's older children are with me and the younger ones went with their mother to France. It was decided at that time which of the children would stay with Martha, Lazarus and Sar'h in France and who would go on to India.

In the spring of 57 AD, Joseph took his daughter, Mary of Bethany and her children, Sar'h and her infant son, Michel, to Mount Bugarach where his other children, Martha and Lazarus, are living. (*Martha and Lazarus returned to Bugarach after "The Great Gathering" in 55 AD*). Mariam also went with Mary of Bethany to Mount Bugarach where they will join Myriam and her children. They will then begin an extended time of traveling through southern France until they are guided to go to Ephesus and prepare for their relocation to India.

Lizbett and her new husband remain with me. I am happy to say that she renewed her friendship with a wonderful man in

Glamorgan shortly after "The Great Gathering." I first enjoyed his acquaintance during his early Essene-Druid training here and in Mona. They moved to Avalon soon after the ambush and it was here that we joyfully celebrated theirs and Sar'h's marriage to Andrew.

We will no longer travel to Wales for the foreseeable future. We have also abandoned the monastery at Glamorgan for the time being. It will remain basically closed as a monastery and hospital until we can be assured that it will be safe to relocate initiates there.

I realize that my words may feel rather terse and emotionally detached. I only speak as I do to emphasize the urgency in which we made these most difficult decisions.

Anna Speaks
Years of Destruction, 56 – 61 AD

As the grim Roman historical records of Cassius Dio and Tacitus reveal, our decision to follow the guidance of our inner sight to disperse and relocate the family, was not acted upon any too soon. After the Emperor Nero began his heinous reign of terror in the year 54 AD, he appointed his legionary general, Suetonious Paullinus, to bring the unruly Druids and Celts of Britain, including us, to our knees. They attempted to do this by destroying the very heart that enlivened our way of life; our beloved sanctuary of Avalon, we call Ynes Mon or Mona. In the years following the attack that befell us on our way to Mona in 55 AD until 61 AD there began to be a siege of unthinkable atrocities, of which I prefer to say little.

If you wish to know more of the massacre of innocents throughout Wales, including our beloved Glamorgan, Mona and other sacred sites, you may find enough in the Roman annals to open the vaults of cellular memory. Lest sides be taken, let it be

---

[56] See "The Seeding of Light" chart in the Appendix for details concerning Mary Anna's and Yeshua's children relocation.

[57] See bibliography in the Appendix.

known that it is likewise recorded that both the Romans and Celts took turns playing the roles of tyrants and victims.

Though it may be easier to assign the Romans the role of tyrants, while justifying and romanticizing the role the Celts played; it cannot be denied that the Britons, while waging revenge against the Romans, became tyrants themselves. Under the impassioned command of the queen of the Iceni, known still as Queen Boudicca's revolt, thousands of Roman men, women and children were raped, tortured and massacred in turn; and three Roman cities were pillaged and burned.

As in all tragedies, all who play their parts as tyrants and victims play in ignorance – knowing not what they do. Tyrants deserve the greatest of merciful compassion, for the suffering of their karmas, through all the times and realms, is great.

Sadly, the subjugation of Britain by Rome did not end in 61 AD but continued until Hadrian built his wall in 120 AD, separating occupied Britannia (*England*) from the frontiers of Caledonia (*Scotland*). Their occupation enforced years of relative peace called the Pax Romana (*Roman Peace*), which lasted for three more centuries. Gladly, Eire (*Ireland*) was never invaded and much of Scotia (*Scotland*) remained relatively free of Rome's heavy suppression. But nothing remains in status quo; and so it was that much of what became England became romanized, only to be invaded by the Anglo-Saxons and thence the Normans, and so on, and on. It was Wales, southwest England and Scotland that were to retain the voice and mystical ways of the Britons and Hebraic Culdees, which I, for so many years, embraced. As with all that passes away, inevitable change marches down the corridors of time. What comprised the past merges with, and takes on, the face of the new. History is written by the victorious. The Church of Rome, which curiously adopted the name "Christian," eventually created an empire that far exceeded the imperial gluttony of all the Caesars. And, to a large measure, the voices of the Christ-Magdalenes were silenced and shrouded for 2,000 years.

Even so, as I look to your day, the Infinite Light we seeded remains within the genetic codes of your current generations.

319

ANNA, THE VOICE OF THE MAGDALENES

Gladdened songs of awakening sing from the ancient stones lying deep within the isles of Avalon – the codes of Light vibrate within your blood and bones. The Christ-Magdalenes are awakening and ushering forth a new voice – a song of unity and peace!

— Chapter 29 —
MARIAM

Mariam Heals Martyr Consciousness
Northern India, autumn, 62 AD

{*We pick up Mariam's story, which continues from PART 4, Chapter 27. She is now relocated in the mountains of northern India.*}

MARIAM: I am seeing how Yeshua's brother, James' was martyred in Jerusalem. (*Weeping and a long pause*) (*James is stoned to death in 61 AD.*) I am seeing his offering as a true sacrifice. It was not because he wanted to die a martyr, but that he offered himself and all that he was upon the altar of true service to life. Even though his tendency was to be more zealous and conservative, compared to the rest of his siblings, his steadfast devotion also set an example for us all to follow. I know he deeply desired to demonstrate peaceful coexistence. He was willing to exchange anything within himself which was unlike love, for a greater capacity to love. That is true sacrifice and renunciation – a true offering. Nothing more is required. It is time to dissolve the fetters of our minds, which cling to the false belief that there is a need to suffer a greater suffering, as a way to atone for the fact that suffering exists.

CATHERINE ANN (*Henceforth: CA*): Just as we dissolved the oath of silence, let us now release any remaining false beliefs held across all time and space about the need for blood atonement and blood sacrifice. Whether those beliefs are held in the collective consciousness, as myths or religious doctrine, let us now release them as pure energy and life-force that is available for the benefit of all. Wherever guilt, shame and fear are held in any structure or tissue, chakras, and DNA, which attract old patterns of sacrifice, know that these emotional and mental formations are now dissolved. They hold no power, whatsoever. Likewise, all traumas resulting from torture and dying a martyr's death are dissolved. The released energy is now available for nurturing and opening your mind and heart to well-being and joyful living on all levels through all time and space. May this be so for all beings! *(Pause............)*

MARIAM: *(Smiling)* I give you great thanks and honor, my Magdalene sisters, for the sweet and gentle manner of this co-creation in this day when a new consciousness is dawning. We are rewriting the stories of our lives with clarity, compassion and mercy – we are rewriting past and future history!

I see now that the experiences of suffering that I may have misinterpreted during the season of my life, long ago, were not in vain. I am seeing them with clearer vision now. It was very difficult for me to see clearly in those days which were so fraught with trauma. I forgive my obscured vision as I behold an immense light around my life as Mariam. Even now, in this conjunction of time, I am able to create my remaining days in this body with greater freedom and insight. I am glad to have my voice reclaimed for this day and through all time.

CA: Yes, we are so thankful that you have come forth and have shared your voice.

MARIAM: I do not wish to distress hearts, but I also know that hearts will be relieved of their burdens when what has been so suppressed has an opportunity to arise into the light of conscious awareness. Then there can be greater self-forgiveness and compassion for all beings. Then all that we gave will have deep meaning and purpose. Then all beings can be at peace. This gives me great solace.

My life is full to overflowing with all that is unfolding with Yeshua, Myriam *(of Tyana)* and Mary *(of Bethany)* as we take one initiation after another within the sacred mountains called the Himalayas. I ask that you attune with our sacred experiences and know an even greater Truth than we are or can reveal through the words within this sequel.

I thank you, my sister, for co-creating this brilliant sphere of remembrance, illumination and fulfillment. I thank all of you with all my heart, my beloved family of Light, who are reading my words. I bid you a fond farewell.

Ω

The Magdalene Voice
Withdraws into Silence

61 – 82 AD

— Chapter 30 —
MOTHER MARY (MARY ANNA)
Age 80
Ephesus, Turkey, 61AD

{*Chapter 30 is a continuation of PART 2, Chapter 14. Mary Anna (Mother Mary) did travel with Myriam of Tyana to Tyana, Turkey and went on to Varanasi (Benares), India, where she was reunited with her son, Joseph the Younger, in 41 AD. She had the opportunity to finally embrace her grandchildren and their families. She also made pilgrimages to various sacred sites and spent time with masters and saints. Particularly meaningful to her were the months during which she was embraced by the presence of Yeshua's Guru and Friend, Babaji. He took her to the place where her beloved husband, Joseph ben Jacob, had taken his ascension, which still retained his vibration. Mary Anna returned to Avalon, Britain with Myriam; but after the ambush that threatened Anna's life in the fall of 55 AD, she came back to Ephesus in 56 AD, where she remained until her conscious death ten years later in 66 AD.*

In this chapter Mary Anna, identified as Mother Mary, speaks of the martyrdom of her son, James and the growing dishonoring and silencing of the Divine Mother/Feminine among the brethren and the misogyny emerging in the doctrines being taught.}

MOTHER MARY: It is difficult to speak. My heart is filled with grief.
CATHERINE ANN (*Henceforth: CA*): You can verbalize it. Perhaps in sharing your grief, it will be healed.
MOTHER MARY: I am in a small community not far from the great Roman city of Ephesus, on the western coastline of what you call Turkey. It is a very ancient city. It is the place where my beloved mother gave me birth. I have heard that my son, James, has

325

been tortured to death in Jerusalem. (*James was stoned to death by a Jewish faction.*) (*Restrained grief*)

My bones ache with sorrow. John Mark, Esther Salome and Matteas; and most of their children, are with me. They are a great comfort. I am relieved that they have chosen to live nearby. My daughter, Ruth and her husband are here from the great mountains of eastern Gaul (*the French Alps*), where John Mark also lives, as needed from time to time to fulfill his duties. My son, Jude and his wife, Galeah, are here from Nazareth for a season. I am told that Thomas and Simon will be coming with their wives and some of my grandchildren for a short time.

We mourn great losses – so many more than I wish to count. It is such a troubled time. There is a mixture of despondency and an increasing zealousness among Yeshua's followers because of the exploding degree of suffering which is afflicting so many. It is like an insidious poison. Those who have a voice of authority won't listen to what I have to say. They seem to have some measure of respect for me because I am Yeshua's mother, but otherwise it seems that they have no patience for me or my words. (*Great sighs*)

CA: Did you meet with Simon Peter and Paul of Tarsus?

MOTHER MARY: Yes, I finally met with them in Antioch. I have seen my nephew, John ben Zebedee, on a number of occasions. He has great concern for me. His brother, James, was killed in Jerusalem during the time I was India. (*James ben Zebedee was beheaded in 44 AD by order of Herod Agrippa in order to please zealous Jews.*) It is difficult to bear the sadness at times. There's not a lot to say, my dears. (*Tears*) What can I say? I lament the suffering of the women and children. As one who knows the Goddess and serves her, I lament the rampant trampling of her ways into the dust. Peter and those who follow him speak of Yeshua's love of his consorts, Myriam (*of Tyana*) and Mary (*of Bethany*), with continued resentment and bitterness. He and others, like Paul, speak of the Great Mother and the Magdalenes with disdain. (*Tears*)

I confess I feel a greater kinship with the men and women who go to the grottos of the Goddess than I do with many of these brethren, who call themselves the followers of the Word, or the

MOTHER MARY CONTINUED

Logos, as they call it. It has so little heart, my sons and daughters. In their zeal, they are trying to find a way to proselytize Yeshua's subtle Gnostic teachings among people who are steeped in the worship of Apollo and Zeus; spiritually ignorant people who take their words literally. They are making Yeshua into a god; just as the emperor makes himself into a god to gain power.

The role of women and the Goddess is often demonized, and at best, women are made inferior and subservient to men. My counsel is heard out of respect for me, but it is dismissed as soon as I am escorted away. I am searching for a way to assist, but it seems there are few who can really hear me. I do not wish to bring further division, so I am increasingly withdrawing into the Great Silence.

Yeshua comes on occasion, which is always a great blessing.

Myriam (*of Tyana*), Mary of Bethany and Mariam spent this winter season (60 – 61 AD) with me before they pressed on to Tyana and India. They plan to remain with Yeshua in the great mountain retreats of India. Myriam's children Joses Simeon, Jude and her young Light-conceived daughter, Zariah, went with her.[58] Johannes remains in Britain (*Fortingall, to be exact*).

This brings me to the very difficult time my family had as we gathered in council meetings in Avalon during the winter of 55 and 56 AD. With very careful consideration, which involved the children themselves in the final decisions, we decided that it would best serve the children's safety and spiritual growth if Yeshua's and my older grandchildren be dispersed to various locations in Britain, Gaul, Asia Minor and India.

Although being parted from our children is always a heart-wrenching experience for us, it has long been our practice to dedicate our children to their highest spiritual growth and to provide them with as many opportunities as possible to accomplish this. We make aspirations and ritually consecrate ourselves and our children,

---

[58] During "The Great Gathering" of 55 AD, in Fortingall, Scotland, the Three Marys experienced nonphysical Light-conceptions with Yeshua. Myriam birthed a daughter, Zariah, and Mary birthed a son, Michel. Mariam's pregnancy did not come to full-term.

throughout our lives, so that we might realize our greatest potential for the benefit of our families, communities and all life.

Because of our strong inter-generational family ties and community commitment to care for each other in every way, it is somewhat easier to let go; as I did Yeshua to Britain at the age of 13. Yeshua's journey to India also meant again saying farewell when he was 17. But more challenging for my mother's heart was also letting go of his brother, James, who was 16, and his brother, Joses (*Joseph the Younger*) when he was only 12 to accompany Yeshua on his long and dangerous pilgrimage. In this same way, my beloved mother (*Anna*) and father (*Joachim*) set an example by dedicating me to the inner sanctuary of Mount Carmel when I was only three years of age.

And so it is that my compassionate heart goes out to all families who are required to experience the loss of any child; and to every child who feels abandoned and unloved.

CA: Yes, this must be very difficult in many ways for all of you. How about Mary of Bethany's children; where are they?

MOTHER MARY: Mary of Bethany's daughters, Sar'h and Lizbett, chose to stay in the lands they have come to love – the lands far to the west where the family genetic lineage can continue to seed the Light of Christ consciousness. Sar'h lives in southern Gaul and Lizbett lives in Avalon, England and Glamorgan, Wales. Mary (*of Bethany*) also conceived a boy-child named, Michel, at the same time Myriam (*of Tyana*) conceived Zariah in Fortingall (*Scotland*).⁶⁰ Michel and Zariah are with their parents in India.

The Three Marys' (*Myriam's, Mary's and Mariam's*) initiatory Light conceptions occurred at "The Great Gathering" in Fortingall in the land of Scotia in the summer of 55 AD. Mariam conceived a

---

⁵⁹ See the "Seeding of Light" chart for details about which and how many children went to live with their relatives in southwest England, central Scotland and southern France.

⁶⁰ "The Great Gathering" of 55AD in Fortingall, Scotland was overseen by Yeshua and other Great Ones. See Chapters 26 and 29 for more information.

child on the etheric plane but she was unable to stabilize her baby's gestation to full-term. Mariam recovered quickly from her miscarriage and continues to feel the great blessing of being one of Yeshua's spiritual consorts. These beautiful daughters who embody the Magdalene Christ and their Light-conceived children bring me great joy.

CA: Thank you, beloved Mother Mary, for sharing your loving heart and Presence with us. Is there more you wish to share?

MOTHER MARY: There is no more need for words – there is only the need to BE Love. It is my prayer that you may realize true Love in all your relationships, as all that comes to you presents itself to be embraced in every precious moment. Love is the greatest of the Mother's gifts to you and the greatest offering you can give. Love is who you are. BE STILL and know this Truth. Peace be unto you.

I am always with you. I bid you a fond adieu.

— Chapter 31 —

SAR'H SPEAKS

On the Island of Ibiza
Ibiza, Iberia (Spain), 63 AD

{*Chapter 31 is a continuation of PART 4, Chapter 26. Sar'h, as with many others of the family, relocated after "The Great Gathering." She went with her mother, Mary of Bethany and Mariam to Mount Bugarach in 57 AD. She and her husband, Andrew, are now involved in the Essene hospice, hospital and orphanage outreaches in southern France. In this particular chapter the setting for establishing a new hospice/hospital is Ibiza, Spain. Sar'h shares her loving wisdom.*}

CATHERINE ANN (*Henceforth: CA*): Now, move forward to the next important event that happens in your life.

SAR'H: I no longer live in Britain. After "The Great Gathering" and Grandmother Anna's injury in 55 AD, many of my family members moved to various lands with the intention of finding safety for our children. My mother (*Mary of Bethany*), my little brother, Michel, and I left Avalon in the spring 57 AD. Grandfather Joseph (*of Arimathea*) took us and Mariam to Mount Bugarach where we met Myriam (*of Tyana*), Joses Simeon, Jude and Zariah (*Myriam's baby daughter*), who had preceded us in 56 AD. We were happy to see Martha and Lazarus who had gone to Bugarach in 55 AD, immediately after "The Great Gathering." Grandfather (*Joseph of Arimathea*) stayed for a brief visit but soon returned to Avalon. He knew his days on the Earthplane were numbered and he wished to enjoy his remaining years with his young family. We heard recently that he had passed consciously into the Purelands last fall.

SAR'H SPEAKS CONTINUED

Those of us who came to Mount Bugarach traveled together to various places of power in southern Gaul and Eastern Europe (*present-day Macedonia, Bulgaria and Romania*) for almost three years. Pa'Pa (*Yeshua*) was frequently with us during our hermitage retreats. During that time we also visited and participated in the healing work being done at various Essene/Therapeutae hospitals, hospices and monasteries scattered through these regions. We were glad to experience the Romans basically supporting our humanitarian efforts as long as our doors are open to Roman citizens and soldiers requiring our aid. As these beautifully fulfilling three years passed, both Andrew and I began to feel that our calling in life was to give compassionate service in this way. And so we have chosen to remain here in this land which we so much love.

Aunt Lois Salome's (*Joseph of Arimathea's daughter, now deceased*) sons-in-law, who had inherited Grandfather's boats, took them to Ephesus in the fall of 59 AD. They spent the winter months with Grand Ma'Ma Mary Anna. They are now with Pa'Pa in India. Their voices have faded into the Silence; but their loving presence is always felt in my heart.

Now that you know something of how I came to be where I am, I wish to share what is happening in my life now.

I am in a small boat with my beloved Andrew and our two young sons (*ages 4 and 2*). There are two other couples and six more of the brethren with us. Our destination is one of the small islands in the western Great Sea called Ibiza.

We are approaching a little cove where it is safe to land and go ashore. I've heard that it is sometimes dangerous because there are pirates who frequently stop over here. The Romans keep some of their warships moored at a larger harbor which is not too far away. They keep their boats here so they can ensure that these waters are safe for the Roman civilians who come and go to the three islands, including nearby Majorca.

We are now climbing up some steep stone steps that make a path through outcroppings of rocks. There are terraces with lovely cypress and olive trees growing along the way. Small stone cottages are clustered here and there.

331

CA: Where are you going?

SAR'H: We are going to a meeting with the Essene brethren who have been anticipating us for several months. The reason we are here is to create a sanctuary on this island. It will be used for a variety of purposes. It will primarily serve as an outreach of our other hospitals, orphanages and hospices, which are located at several sites on the mainland of southern Gaul and eastern Iberia. These were started many years ago by the Essenes of Mount Carmel and Alexandria, Egypt. There are also a number of these monasteries and hospitals in what is your Eastern Europe; but we have not been there these past years because the distances are great and it is a hardship for our young children. We hope to return to these lovely people when our children are older.

We hope our new sanctuary will be a safe refuge. Islands are not always the safest places to be. We have to trust that we are being guided aright. Our hearts were saddened and the need for vigilance strengthened in us when we heard about the atrocities that have befallen so many in Britain since we left. Our beloved Mona sanctuary has suffered great destruction. I have great concern for Great Grand Ma'Ma Anna; my sister, Lizbett; and Grand Ma'Ma Mary Anna's and Myriam's children who live in Avalon and Fortingall. Our prayers go out to my family and all beings who suffer so much.

We hope our efforts will bring a measure of relief. My grandfather, Joseph (*of Arimathea*), was one of our wealthy patrons; as he was all through his adult life for so many years, beginning with his support of my maternal grandmother's efforts to bring compassionate healing to so many in Bethany (*Mary of Bethany's mother and Joseph's second wife, Mary of Magdala*). Some of our family members, who have grown old, desire to move away from the increasing turbulence in Gaul because of Emperor Nero's cruel policies and the corruption of our regional governors. Some of our elders can come here and have a place of solace – a place to pass from the physical plane in peace. We also desire to bring healing

---

[61] See "The Seeding of Light" chart for details about these children.

SAR'H SPEAKS CONTINUED

comfort to a variety of outcasts, such as lepers. As always, we will also have a place for our Essene brothers and sisters who wish to live a contemplative life.

We are building over ancient Phoenician and Greek ruins. This site commands a beautiful view looking out over the expansive blue waters of the sea. We have gone through the necessary procedures with the Roman governor of Iberia (*Spain*). We feel blessed that he has granted us permission to build and he has promised protection as long as we meet his conditions; which thankfully are few.

I have already mentioned the present turbulence in Gaul, but I wish to repeat how much our lives are being impacted by Nero, the emperor. Unbelievable suffering is being experienced everywhere; so we count ourselves fortunate to be here. We cannot afford to be complacent about our safety. We, as always, are prepared to move away, if necessary. Just as our family visionaries foresaw the carnage on Mona, which caused our families' dispersion, we have heard how our visions actually manifested. Unbelievable atrocities were committed in Wales and the Midlands, by both Romans and Celts, alike. It was Nero who instigated the desecration of our beloved Druid sanctuary on Mona. It has been utterly destroyed and many of our dearest friends, who lived in Wales, have been slaughtered or put in chains! I can hardly bear the thought.

I have heard Lizbett and her husband are in Avalon with Grandmother Anna and that they are faring well. The local people there are generally passive, unlike the mountain tribes of the West lands and those far to the north where "The Great Gathering" took place. It seems that as long as there is nonresistance and they are paying their taxes, the Romans are not bothering our community in Avalon. More and more my family in Britain, like we, are adopting the dress, languages and customs of the local people, including the Romans, so that we can move about freely and not draw undue attention to ourselves. This compliance, however, is only superficial. We, in every other way, still practice our Essene way as much as possible.

Miriam and Johannes and their children are safe in Fortingall, as far as I know. Some of my nephews and nieces (*Joses' and Jude's children*) are living there and in Avalon. Two of my nephews are usually living with Andrew and me. They are presently in Bugarach. We receive few messages these days from Britain. We must trust in Father-Mother Creator for our family's welfare during these times of gathering darkness.

CA: Do you miss your father, your mothers and the other family members who moved far away?

SAR'H: Yes. At times I miss them very much. I know I will likely never see them again on this physical plane. Father comes briefly from time to time; but he is becoming increasingly ethereal. I feel him more as a constant Presence of great love. I suppose, in a way, I have developed a kind of stoic detachment. Yet I wish you to know my heart cares deeply for everyone. I carry on my parents' ways: their humble presence, simplicity, and unfettered ability to reach out and comfort anyone in need, at any time, no matter the cost.

CA: Please move forward to the next significant event or words you would like to share.

Ibiza, 68 AD

SAR'H: Grand Ma'Ma Mary Anna (*Mother Mary*) has passed into the Purelands. (*She consciously died at the age of 85 near Ephesus, Turkey in 66 AD.*) I shall miss her more than I can say. As I contemplate the many souls whom I have loved, who are no longer physically close, I reflect on the meaning of life and my own mortality. I know there is tumult and suffering all around. We could focus on that – how hard everything is – how sad everything is. But, as you know, I have walked the path of mindful, loving-kindness all my life. With much practice over time, I have come to a place of calm, equipoise within the center of my being – rejoicing in the simple, ordinary gifts of each moment – just as they are.

I have great empathy and compassion within the Oneness, as I am aware of the suffering which exists for all beings. I am not

---

[62] See "The Seeding of Light" chart for details about the dispersion of the children.

attached to the phenomenal world. I feel quite free. It is as if my heart is filled with a radiant light; a light-beam shines out of it. When I witness people and events, I do not judge them – good, bad or with indifference. Situations that often trouble and ensnare others, because of emotional attachments, do not affect me in the same way.

I embrace my fellow brothers' and sisters' pain without naming it or judging it. I witness who they really are and I spontaneously take their veils of darkness into the light within my heart. Then I freely give forth my love and send them light so that they might know that same light which is always present within them. I have come to be able to walk my life's path with a steady awareness of this great and beautiful Light. It is the same immense light I witness my father, my mothers and my other family members carrying; it is like they are a lamp that shows the way of peace and harmony for all beings. Like Pa'Pa, I am able to laugh at myself and bring levity to our serious concerns. Laughter and gratitude are the great antidotes to turn suffering around in the very moment it is felt. Instantly there's light to show me where to take my next step.

When I "beam" my heart-light, I experience it is like the stories told about Moses using his staff to part the Red Sea. Miracles of healing occur. All that is needed to support us happens, as if by magic. I do not mean to say that I do not have my personal challenges and heartbreak, because I certainly do. I understand Aunt Mariam's joy and pain because I, too, have conceived and given birth to children, I have "lost" them in death and I have also suffered miscarriages. I am no different from you in my human journey; just perhaps more aware. But I know you can also be just as aware and awake as me. Waking up to one's True Being and knowing abiding calmness and joy in the midst of all the suffering is truly possible – it's an informed choice to be kind and loving moment by moment.

I have learned how to be merciful to myself by embracing my pain as soon as I become aware of any contraction – contraction hurts; it is a signal to breathe and let go. Straightway, any physical, mental and emotional pain lessens. It dissolves into and becomes the immeasurable Light – the pure light of intrinsic emptiness. Sadness and doubt are not my companions for very long. Unlike the hapless fly caught in a spider's web, I see my life as a tapestry of beautiful gossamer threads spun by the Father-Mother Birther of Life. The spider, some call death, is not my devouring enemy, but my Beloved Friend bringing me Home. The web of life is Love's embrace. I don't resist. I let go into love's infinite spaciousness. With each breath I remember I am free to fly. With each mindful and merciful breath, I am already Home.

I am just a little skinny child, doing the best I can to walk with compassionate awareness on the sacred path which is my life – this precious human birth. I desire to be unencumbered and to feel free to love my fellow companions equally, whether they are human, animals and plants, or the waters, the stones, the wind or the sparkling fire's warmth. The sweet Mother, who clothes my spirit, gives me everything. And so it is that I own nothing; but having everything and nothing, I am free to give my ever-replenishing abundance away to all in need.

In these ways, I am at peace and I wish this Peace upon everyone.

Though our voices are receding more and more into the Silence, the Light we carry is seeded into the Earth Mother and into all the elements and into Earth's Akashic Record. Being mindful that this is so, we dedicate our every step and our every prayer to all beings so that we may all awaken and love each other without condition. We, who are blessed to be the children of avatars – my Grand Ma'Ma Mary Anna and my beloved Pa'Pa (*Yeshua*), are leaving a posterity who is seeded with Love's pure Light. You are seeded with this same Light through your physical genetics and through the ethereal cosmos. This Infinite Light, which is your True Nature, is held in our constant Awareness; which is our legacy and gift which we dedicate to your awakening and the awakening of all beings – awakening to the Truth that this is so.

Someday you may go to the little church on the Great Sea (*Saintes-Maries-de-la-Mer near Marseilles*) where there is an effigy made in my honor. But, know it represents much more than a simple girl called Sar'h. As you walk in the places where I have walked – the places within this sweet Earth's garden, which my family loves and tends from one conscious incarnation to the next – be aware of the seeds of Light we have planted everywhere. That same Light is seeded in you because you carry our genetic codes and the frequency of an ascending Earth within the elements of your bones.

Attune and feel us always close – carrying you and all life in our arms. Do not be surprised to find, once you remember fully who you are, that your arms also carry the sleeping ones who also may choose to awaken.

I thank you for your tender caring and masterful way of holding space for my story.

I send forth a kiss from my sanctuary on the Great Sea. I send it forth on the wings of the dove. I send forth an endless prayer so that my kiss of love and peace may find a place within every human heart. (*Emotion*)

May the Light my father lived, and still lives, be seen within all eyes. May we all find that same Light within our self and not look to another as more or less divine.

May we, as one family, join hands in peace and brother-sisterhood.

May we, as Magdalene sisters and brothers, awaken, and find our voices. May we know and live the power of love – the greatest power of all to facilitate needed change. We are the revolutionary embracers and catalysts of change – the kinds of change which foster harmony, freedom and union.

May we reignite our lamps as way-showers and bring them all together to shine a perfect light within the darkness. We, as Magdalenes, shine the Father's Infinite Light and sound the Mother's clarion Voice from the wayshowing Magdalene Tower, as we have always done from before ever there was time.

This is my prayer. I send it aloft with a kiss to every quadrant of this sweet Earth, and into the heaven realms above, and into that which dwells below. Within my heart's embrace, find sweet rest.

Amen and Amen.

— Chapter 32 —
ANNA'S LAST YEARS
Avalon, Winter Solstice, 80 AD

ANNA: I am at my writing table within the entry vestibule of my roundhouse hermitage. Windowpanes of glass were installed in the mud and wattle walls many years ago, just as my son, Joseph (*of Arimathea*), promised. These precious openings, which look out to the southerly meadows below, and eastward toward the Tor, allow the Winter Solstice light to pour gently over the sheets of papyri and parchment spread before me. A crackling fire on the hearth chases away the gathering chill at day's end. Lit candles and a small oil lamp rest next to my ink well and quills. Together with the dimming winter light, the flames cast an illuminating, golden glow upon the words being formed by my hand which no longer writes with the steadiness it once knew.

My days upon this Earthplane, like the few remaining granules of sand in my hour-glass, are drawing to a close. All my children, except Noah, and many of my grandchildren have passed beyond the veil. My remaining grandchildren and their children are spread across many lands. It is time to gather my recent memories and commit them to these pages which hold the recording of all that I have witnessed through this life's long journey. Through many decades of time, I have gathered my family around me, and welcomed those with ears to hear. Together we have partaken of the teachings of the masters – both recorded and spoken. Gladly, I have left messages of love and wisdom, which close the door of fear.

CATHERINE ANN (*Henceforth: CA*): What is happening around you and your community now?

ANNA: It is difficult to describe, exactly. It depends upon your point of view. Some would say that it is a time of bustling activity and growth. But for those of us who remember a simpler life that supported a more direct way of knowing the divinity from within, we see all this activity taking many people further and further away from themselves.

Though I accept inevitable change, there is a part of me, I confess, that misses the simple communal life I used to know. I also wish to share with you, my beloved friend, although there is some nostalgic sadness, I do not in any way regret my life or any experience I have embraced upon my path. My life has been for the seeding of a greater consciousness that may come into fruition at a time I now know not. But as I behold you, I see that what was given in my time is now bearing fruit. Much of the Beloved's Infinite Light, which I have seeded in Oneness, has been in preparation for what is only now, in your time, beginning to stir beneath the dark, fallow earth, before the spring returns.

I have trained others in the way of passing on "Pearls of Wisdom," including transmitting the energies of Gnosis, according to oral tradition. But many of the great teachers have passed away or have departed to more remote regions of Britain and places of sanctuary in other lands. The sites and communities that used to foster the secret training of initiates have been desecrated and deserted; Mona still lies in ashes. Many sacred groves that used to surround Avalon have been burned to the ground. The Druids are scattered and hidden. What remains and continues to grow in number are the Roman cities and legions of soldiers. The Romanized church, which preaches a distorted gospel foreign to me, is looked to as a path of salvation. The voice of the Magdalenes is receding into the Silence.

Our Essene and Celtic way of direct knowing is suppressed. There are fewer and fewer people of influential position who recognize that the awakening of the indwelling Christ is every soul's potential. Much that gave support to true awakening is passing away. But there will always be a spiritual lineage, even if hidden underground, which will support and tend the "seeds of Light" until the great Knowing is realized. For this awareness and my fostering of this lineage of light, even unto your generation, I am most thankful.

339

CA: This seeding, that you are aware of coming into fruition in a future time, how do you see these seeds having been planted?

The Seeding of the Lineage of Light

ANNA: The seeding, for the most part, is a cyclic, self-arising ignition – a radiation, that comes about when infinite, uncreated Mind projects its Light through its creative emanations. These impulses or "seedings of light" express as rounds or seasons of change through which all manner of forms must pass: coming into being, expressing for a sustained time and then dissolving back into the unnamable, formless Mind and Heart of the Beloved – Father-Mother Creator of the Cosmos.

Infinite Mind, so powerful and unlimited in its potential, chooses to create expressions of "limitation" within its vast, boundless "body" of space. One example, with which we, as human sentient beings, are familiar, is the ability to perceive in separation. This divisive process; through which to have experiences of a conceptual mind and contrasting choices, gives rise to the illusion of dualistic distinctions. The consequences within relative being are: a perceived singular self distinct from other, pleasure and pain, clinging and aversion, hope and fear – which ultimately bring forth wisdom and compassion, born of suffering.

Eventually, that (*Infinite Mind*) which is beyond conceptual mind, and the causes and conditions of suffering, is remembered. Meanwhile, a mind that makes distinctions serves a most important function. It is the self-appointed navigator of its own self-reflective, often fearful terrain. Although walking through the increasingly familiar terrain of conditioned habit is like a mine-field filled with hidden explosives, there is a measure of comfort and security in holding onto what is known; avoiding the scarier unknown – denying the existence of the bombs suppressed by a fearful mind. It is this attachment that creates a self-made prison that lasts through endless rounds of suffering – expecting different (*happier*) results, but continuing to do what has always been done in the same way. But change must come – all is impermanent.

ANNA'S LAST YEARS

Eventually the self-induced suffering and abuse becomes too much to bear. Then there is a willingness and readiness to awaken to the Infinite Mind's expansive view and compassionate ways. When Infinite Mind and conceptual mind join in skillful collaboration, the terrain is seen clearly for what it is. An inexhaustible Light leads the way – the explosives are seen for what they are and the lit fuses are extinguished. Instead of running frantically through life, there is a quieting into Stillness. "Peace – BE STILL" – the anchor in the midst of life's storms – the Great Peace beyond understanding comes and cradles the frightened child.

The perceived separate self forgets that it is inherently "seeded" with unlimited, infinite Light potential, which lies hidden behind a "limited self" mask – the mask called "I." But, in truth, "I" is actually the True Self – the Beloved, choosing to have the divine experience of being veiled in forgetfulness, while, unbeknownst to its sleeping self, "I" is really simultaneously awake. What a wondrous, mysterious and imaginative play! Yes! Let us laugh heartily – laughter is the antidote to fear, despair, inflated egos and boredom.

All forms and conditions, no matter how gross or subtle, pleasurable or painful, are impermanent! The mask and the stage crumble and disappear. When all is in ripeness for change, another "Seeding of Light" is initiated, which quickens and resurrects the Beloved's dormant "seeds of light" – the light of intrinsic Awareness. What has always been present – the already enlightened and ascended Self – remembered and realized!

The sun's essential nature is always to emit light, even when obscured by clouds. A gold nugget's nature is to retain its intrinsic value, even when shrouded by encrustations of mud. So, likewise, the True Self remains untouched by relative conditions. Because the goldsmith recognizes the valuable properties of the gold nugget, regardless of the obscuring mud, he gently frees the gold from its dulling accretions. Likewise, an Alchemist of the Soul – a Christ-Magdalene, transmutes the obscurations which have entombed the Beloved's Light, which was previously unknown and hidden. When the season of cyclic change comes, another "seeding" pulsation may spontaneously arise. And, with the "seeding of light," a resurrection of consciousness and the fruition of liberation may be realized – the hidden Christ rises into awareness/Awareness.

But, why wait for the next "Seeding Cycle"? The only time for enlightened Knowing is now – free of conceptual thinking – in this body – in this very ordinary moment! Relax! Let go! Know and BE freedom and unity NOW!

As with the sun and the gold, when beings allow their intrinsic Light to be just as it IS in any now moment; when they simply rest in their essential Nature, it is possible to realize the indwelling Christ-Buddha which is present all along. As gold is treasured, so is our True Nature treasured, even more. With merciful compassion the obscuring veils and dross begin to fall away. An epiphany occurs. A single glimpse of the Beloved's Light catalyzes "Christ-Buddha light seeds" in embryo to awaken and grow. Gradually, with consistent nurturing, what was once unrecognized potential matures and becomes stabilized. The enlightened Mind/Heart – Beloved and beloved are merged in mystical Union!

In the moment of Oneness, the merged mind and heart are liberated from the tomb of selfish ignorance. Wings set free, the Heart of Love emerges and embraces all – knowing the All as its own Self. Hearing the cries of all sentient beings, the awakened Magdalene-Christ becomes aware that the Great Liberation is not attained by and for oneself alone, but can only be fully realized when all beings are free and happy. Such compassionate and wise ones return to the Earthplane to mediate the cyclic "Seeding of Light" for the benefit of all. Consciously taking earthen bodies, they become physical anchors, transducers and transmitters of Cosmic Love. So it is that the Beloved seeds (*transmits or inseminates*) Infinite Light through awakened eyes, hands and feet.

CA: At this time in your life, as your life is drawing to a close, what is it that is letting you know that?

ANNA: Imagine with me that you are sitting by the seashore. You casually note there is a storm far out on the horizon. Taking no concern, you give your attention to the sunlight sparkling upon the watery expanse. Leisurely lifting your gaze, your eyes delight in the soaring flight of birds and your ears rejoice in their uttering forth of fervent song. The surf's slow, rhythmic pulse is calming. Creatures large and small are going about their business. But when you extend your vision and look again out to the horizon, you see that the clouds are deepening in color; they are mushrooming in size. Indeed, the fast, gathering storm is covering the sun.

Feeling somewhat uneasy, you stand and begin to walk briskly along the shore. You notice that the former gentle breeze has become a gusting wind, the surf is rising and its agitated waves are churning upon the sandy beach. Waves crash against nearby rocks, sending sprays of foaming water upon the wind. You begin to notice indicators of a serious storm and that it would be well to take precautions. Familiar with the signs and benchmarks of a gathering storm, you choose to return to the safety and comfort of home.

Just as in the scene I have shared, I am noting there is an unstoppable storm gathering in magnitude all around me. I have done all that I can to take precautions and to preserve what has been given me to place in safekeeping until the storm passes. It is time to let the illumined elements of this body return to the Earth Mother and call forth the angels to guide my soul to my heavenly home where the Beloved on High resides. In another season, I shall come again to the Mother's garden. I shall lovingly attend and nurture the seeds of light I have planted in this life and those planted in my many lives before this.

It has long been my soul's desire that I might come forth during the times of darkness, when hearts turn away from the sweetness of love's pure light. I endeavor unceasingly to bring solace and a greater liberation to those who have forgotten the entombed Christ lying asleep inside. I shall continue the spiraling dance of re-weaving myself back into the Light beyond all forms; and then with the Lord of the Dance, return again and again, dancing seeds of Light into the Earth Mother, re-weaving new bodies in which the Beloved may reside. This has always been my pattern for the sake of all beings from the beginning of time until the All comes Home together. (*Reflective pause*)

ANNA, THE VOICE OF THE MAGDALENES

You could say I'm a bit tired. I feel the aches and pains of my aging body more than ever. I have no more desire to take it through the arduous process of rejuvenation. It is time to bid adieu.

CA: When was the last time that you went through the rejuvenation process?

ANNA: I made a conscious choice to discontinue the full Rites of the Sepulcher within the first several years of coming to Britain. From that time until now there has been a subtle ripening. After the attack that severely injured my neck twenty-five years ago, I began to have the appearance of a young, white-haired crone. Now, somewhat stooped, one shoulder lifted toward my right ear, my head cocked to one side, and my right hand increasingly numb and shaking, I would say I am fully embracing the suffering all beings experience when death comes to their door and beckons, "Come hither and know me as friend, not foe."

I have long prepared myself to take my conscious departure when the time is made known to my heart. Freedom comes with the impermanence of form – birth, sickness, aging and death are portals. Rather than be feared, these rites of passage can be compassionately and serenely viewed as thresholds one crosses on their return to the Beloved's Home.

In the sense of being identified by this body, I have been told that my wizened features seem to be always smiling, revealing the sage wisdom and contentment that shines from within.

CA: Are Lizbett and her husband still living?

ANNA: Yes. They are living, though their peace has been greatly threatened these past years. The monastery, after 58 AD, was for all intents and purposes abandoned on and off until relative peace came after 62 AD. Lizbett and her family have come to Avalon seeking refuge from time to time since then and have returned to Glamorgan when it is safe to do so. Lizbett's family returned to their beloved home in Glamorgan four years ago. Five years ago some very difficult warfare broke out when the Romans, in retaliation against the highly resistant Silures, took full command. Then three years ago a group of Ordovice warriors in the north ambushed and killed a sentry of Roman soldiers. It seems that the hostility on both sides does not stop long enough to heal.

As I said, five years ago, in 75 AD, the Roman general, Frontinus, expanded his Legion in the south of Wales and brought the new generation of rebellious Silures to their knees. The legionary fortress at Caerleon, not far from our monastery in Glamorgan, was reinforced and made even more secure as a Roman bastion. Over the next three years, not being easily persuaded to conform, unrest spread among the Ordovices tribe in the north. Then, in 78 AD, after the skirmish, I mentioned earlier, took place, the mighty Roman governor, Agricola, came and claimed Wales for Rome. Agricola, as a young Senator, had been present when Mona was destroyed in 60 – 61 AD under the command of Emperor Nero and his pawn, Paulinus Seutonious. (*The rugged mountainous country, however, continued to provide sanctuary for the surviving Celts and Druids, enabling them to retain their ancient language and ways for many centuries. There are remnants even today.*) Although Agricola was somewhat more merciful and diplomatically skilled than his predecessor, the resistors who did not comply were killed and imprisoned. And Mona was desecrated again. All was destroyed that the Druids were trying to restore on Mona in order to reestablish our sacred isle as a Druid sanctuary.

Lizbett recently came for a visit; bringing her three children. It was a joy to be with them. They have all grown up in a trust of the Essene way of life. That has been a great comfort to herself and to me and to others of our community who knew Lizbett in our earlier more carefree years. Her children are especially a great comfort since her mother (*Mary of Bethany*), Myriam (*of Tyana*) and Mariam went to India. Her father (*Yeshua*) consciously ascended from the Earthplane nearly a decade ago (*leaving traces of his ethereal body elements as a powerful radiation field*). Sadly, Lizbett has a congestion of the lungs which is settling around her heart, perhaps it is the grief we all bear, as loved ones leave us to walk in our existential aloneness. She knows the Truth of the All-One-ness and in this realization she finds comfort and peace.

Perhaps she and I will be laying ourselves to rest about the same time. (*Anna's voice trails off into a whisper.*) (*Long pause*)

Perhaps this is how it will be, but I am not being shown when her hour or mine will be. I do know this – I will take my last breath quite consciously. I will sit erect in equipoise, as is our custom, and Noah, Rhia and Dancing Wind will witness my journey into the Light. And it will be Noah, my last living son, who will lay this fragile body, which is powerfully seeded with the Infinite Light, back into the dust of this sweet Earth. There is a sepulcher not far from the vault in the Tor where Torhannah rests. This body remnant shall be placed therein and continue to radiate the Great Mother's love to all who come to Avalon – and through the mists to all beyond her furthest shore.

CA: Is there any more about your life at this time that you would like to share?

ANNA: I will pass these records on to Noah, Lizbett and my other Light-conceived descendants who are prepared to receive them. They shall then be passed on to their living seed. My other children and grandchildren have long taken my words (*oral and written records*) to lands beyond the isles of Britain. I fear not should they ever be burned, discarded, distorted in some fashion, or lost. I know that through the seeding born of my loins, souls will come forth (*Several deep sighs...*) with ears capable of hearing my story within the Earth's Akashic mists. Avalon's ethereal mists and stones shall carry the voices of the Magdalenes through the eras of time.

I, and those like me, shall reincarnate again and again with this wisdom and we shall pass it on within the lineage of Light. My posterity will have the ability to recognize me and ones such as myself – they shall see as I see. They shall feel, as I feel, the Infinite Perfection and Awareness that IS awakening all beings. The words spoken by Yeshua and the Magdalenes shall quicken the Seeds of Light. Whether a genetic lineage or one that is purely spiritual, this lineage shall continue as it has from before time's beginning.

During these, my last years, in the midst of very unsettling times, I continue to embroider my life's tapestry and entrust it to the trained ears of those who know how to keep secret oral traditions alive. In the keeping of family and friends, who, as I, are Essene-Druid priests and priestesses, I share Gnostic wisdom and the history of my familial lineage. No ear ever tires of hearing the stories I tell about my grandson and those who wear the mantle of the Christ-Magdalene. And more particularly, do the listeners rejoice when they hear the stories told by those who lived them.

As the years pass, I increasingly seek isolated peace on Avalon's isles. Removed from the world, I am both sought and feared. My mystical ways and powers are little understood by uninitiated ears. So it is that I do what I can to remain obscure, yet available in quite ordinary ways to those in spiritual and physical need.

I welcome pilgrims, such as you, to take sup and rest inside the rounded walls of my simple hut, patterned after the dwellings of the ancient ones who walked the isles of Britain before me. When not roaming the hillsides or tending the communal garden plots, I retreat from the frequent chill under the vaulted thatching that holds the warmth of my hearth's fire. Behind my home, farther up, where the meadow knoll crowns, is a compound of similar structures adjoining others patterned after those of Mount Carmel. These assorted buildings comfortably house my beloved maidens.

Often seated on a bench hewn of oak near the spring that still flows red, I gaze upon Avalon's misty vales, shallow lakes and estuary swamplands that stretch out upon the levels to the sea. Beyond my physical eyes seeing, these waterways extend into the West Country and drain into the vast oceanic waters of the Atlantic. The home I love most dearly, surrounded by pastures and apple orchards fair, host the netherworlds bridging human folk and faerie. I entertain homeless astral wanderers bereft in their ceaseless suffering, as well as those Great Ones whose awakened consciousness weave all the planes, both form and formless.

I thank you, my beloved friend, for hearing my voice and drawing close to my garden gate. I sense my time is soon at hand. Even as I withdraw my voice, so is it cast upon the wind.

CA: Thank you, beloved Anna, for your voice and love which calls us Home to the Mother's Heart.

— Chapter 33 —
BROTHER GEOFFREY
Avalon, 186 AD

{*We have now progressed in years and look back on the family and their purpose for being in Avalon from a different perspective. Brother Geoffrey is an initiate of the Druid-Essenes and a descendant of Anna, who lives in the growing Celtic-Christian monastery in Glastonbury. Just over one hundred years have passed since Anna's conscious death in 82 AD. Brother Geoffrey shares his devotional story which preserves the Voice of the Magdalenes for a time yet to come — and that foreseen time is now.*}

BROTHER GEOFFREY: As I look down, I see that I am wearing a brown woolen monk's habit. My hands and feet are those of a man and my stomach has somewhat of a paunch. My feet are bare except for simple leather sandals. I have a beard and my shoulder length hair is cut in a straight bob.

CATHERINE ANN (*Henceforth: CA*): Are you wearing any ornamentation?

BROTHER GEOFFREY: Just a corded leather belt from which hang some keys. There are big deep pockets in my robe and the hood is large, rather pointed. It falls back over my shoulders.

CA: Where do you live?

BROTHER GEOFFREY: Near the Celtic village of Ynes Witrin or the Isle of Glass. You call this place Glastonbury. Some in your day know, as we know, these are some of the mythic isles known as Avalon.

CA: About what year is this?

BROTHER GEOFFREY: It is 186 AD according to the Gregorian calendar.

CA: Do you live in a monastery there?

BROTHER GEOFFREY: Yes. There is the beginning of a larger structure which will eventually, as I look into future time, be known as Glastonbury Abbey. We are building a small, but substantial stone structure which will be used for the men's dormitory and refectory.

CA: What are you called?

BROTHER GEOFFREY: Some in the small village call me Father Geoffrey. But I am usually called Brother Geoffrey by my monastic brothers and sisters.

CA: Is there anything in particular that you would like to share?

BROTHER GEOFFREY: It's not really clear why I am here right now.

CA: Are there others with you?

BROTHER GEOFFREY: Yes.

CA: What is your particular work that you do in this monastery?

BROTHER GEOFFREY: I prepare the daily missals and vespers. My primary work is in the library where we make copies of the fragments that have been passed to us by the church fathers from Rome and Antioch.

CA: What is contained in these fragments?

BROTHER GEOFFREY: There are several of Paul's letters and some of the other brethren of the early church.

CA: What are your feelings toward the information in these fragments?

BROTHER GEOFFREY: To tell you the truth, I have mixed feelings about these things. (*Hesitantly*) I am reluctant to say anything because much of what I do, I do in secret. (*Hushed voice*) Not what I just told you, that's open to everyone, but there are other things that I do, of which only a very few are aware.

CA: The things you do in secret – is that something that has been asked of you to do? Or is it something that you have taken upon yourself?

BROTHER GEOFFREY: It is mine to do because I see that it is to be done. It rings a truth for me.

CA: Know that you are safe in sharing. Whatever is shared will not be for the time that you are in; it is for a different time.

BROTHER GEOFFREY: We've seen a great deal of turbulence during these many years. The occupation of the Romans continues; but it is not as much a grave concern as it used to be. They have their troubles in Rome and throughout their empire. There have been many sieges and battles. There were times we feared for our lives and for this House of God. For the most part, we feel generally protected; but you never know when another internal conflict will occur or marauders might come and pillage.

CA: This work that is secret — do you feel that you are preserving part of a truth?

BROTHER GEOFFREY: Yes, I believe strongly that this is what I am doing. Thank you for understanding.

CA: Is this information you keep secret possibly about the holy family or something else?

BROTHER GEOFFREY: (*Heavy sigh*) The vows I have taken to keep this information secret are difficult to override.

(*Lengthy pause*)

CA: (*Brother Geoffrey is troubled and breathing very rapidly.*) You are now being contacted from another time far into the future. It is a time when the truths you are protecting are to be revealed. Your vows are serving an important purpose in your time because these truths are being preserved for a greater purpose which can now be fulfilled because of your willingness to share. Our work together is being done on the inner planes and no one need know that you are sharing these secrets. You are safe to share whatever will serve the people who are ready to hear what you have to say. You can lift the vow of silence for our work; if you choose.

BROTHER GEOFFREY: Go ahead and ask questions of me then.

CA: What is it that you are feeling to be precious and that needs your protection?

BROTHER GEOFFREY: I so much desire to keep (*Sigh*)…

BROTHER GEOFFREY

It's like a flame I want to keep lit in the midst of so many forces that work hard to extinguish it. I feel compelled to preserve the precious words of Master Yeshua, his family and those who knew him intimately. I want to protect the documents that contain these teachings and memories, even at the risk of losing my life.

I have been carefully making additional boxes, which are lined with various metals, in which to protect this treasure from the elements, thieves or those who would destroy or corrupt it. Some of the documents are loose sheaves of parchment. A few are rolled scrolls of papyrus. Some are bound sheets of parchment held between covers of heavy leather, wood or metal. A few are thin sheets of wood upon wax has been applied and then words are etched into the wax with a stylus. There are two scrolls made of etched copper. I am currently working on a cover that will lock the loose sheaves of parchment in place. It is made of wood.

More and more, I have to be very cautious during the brief occasions I have these records out of hiding. I consider them to be very precious. Not because of the substance out of which they are made, but because these documents contain the very words written by the hands of those who walked with our beloved Master. I am aware that such records, as these, are indeed rare.

I have received word that there is much intrigue, conspiracy and all manner of conflict arising with those who claim the right to lead the many scattered congregations of believers. There are many schisms and teachers vying for positions of apostolic authority; taking advantage of the exploding numbers of people – mostly slaves, desiring a better way of life – willing to sacrifice their lives, and all they hold dear in order to claim a heavenly inheritance, as children of God. There are many souls willing to join "the dying Christ on the cross" and to rise with him at the time the world is made new. They call themselves, Christians.

I have heard that some of the original oral teachings that were scribed by those who knew Yeshua have been destroyed; others are corrupted in the translation into Greek and Latin – reflecting the Hellenistic philosophical bias and lack of spiritual realization of the translators.

There is an attempt to enforce believing in a conceptualized and idealized savior as the only true way. They say direct personal revelation – Knowing/Gnosis is heresy, and not to be trusted because it is aligned with their belief in evil – calling it Satan or the Devil. Misogyny is rampant; the Divine Mother is trodden underfoot; the Magdalenes who bore Yeshua's children and who supported his ministry are silenced; and women in general are given a lesser stature than men. This is the very opposite of what Master Yeshua taught and lived. I have heard his pure sayings passed on to me with my own ears. These scripts that lay before me testify that what I am saying is so.

And even more relevant for me, is my own testimony concerning these teachings. I have studied and deeply contemplated them whilst in silent retreat. I have borne, through my own experiences, a transformation of consciousness. I have diligently applied these sayings and have found God and Heaven dwelling within me. I have not found "God" to be in a human likeness nor have I found a paradise removed from this world. I have entered those states of being in which I know Oneness with all life. I have known the Great Silence and the Infinite Light wherein the Unnamable abides beyond birth and death, beyond time and form; and yet is present in my breath, in my body, in my food and in the natural world.

(*Lengthy pause*)

I have read copies of epistles, which have been placed in my care, said to be written by Peter, Paul and John, other disciples; and their followers. They give me concern. Within them I find an attempt to convince souls that Yeshua is the one God incarnate. That he is above all beings and that salvation comes through belief in him alone. They claim heretical, the practicing of "the Kingdom of Heaven within us" – being within every one of us. It is a sore thing for my soul to experience that what is being taught in Rome, Ephesus, Antioch and Gaul is also making encroachment into this monastic center. Word has spread to the various Pauline and Johannine centers on the Continent and Asia Minor that we hold to a tradition that they postulate borders on heresy and nonconformity.

BROTHER GEOFFREY

Emissaries have been sent to observe us and to find a way to enforce the gathering sentiment to create a universal church and a canon of beliefs.

We recently received unsettling messengers sent by Irenaeus, a powerful theologian and bishop who lives in Gaul. These men, wearing the garment of humility, tried to convince us of the need to discredit the works of the Essenes, the Therapeutae and the Gnostics. They made compelling arguments that only the gospels of John, Matthew, Mark and Luke contain the full word of God – but they are actually written hearsay, composed many years after Master's ministry. Thanks be to Father-Mother God those who came to investigate our monastic congregation only hold whispered suspicions of the legacy left by those witnesses who actually walked with the Master, Yeshua ben Joseph – the same men and women who lived here and walked these lands of Britain. Hidden from profane eyes, these beloved souls left behind a great treasure – not only a legacy inscribed upon parchment, but a blood lineage that runs within my veins and the veins of those whose names and whereabouts I keep secret.

Persecution abounds; not only from the hands of the Romans, but from those who profess Christ and call themselves Christian. And the Jews, with an even greater vengeance, still persecute those who follow Messianic prophets. I think this is due in part because of their own suffering which was increased traumatically when the Romans destroyed Solomon's and David's Temple – the very center of their faith – in Jerusalem in 70 AD.

Many of those who claim authority to teach and lead congregations have not only taken the first baptism by water, but also claim the baptism of spirit. They say they are reborn but still they are contentious and openly create divisions amongst themselves and use their educated advantage to suppress the ignorant. It is a dark time.

I cannot bear to have this travesty touch these precious remnants which are in my charge; these records, the spoken words and the whereabouts of the descendants of our ancestors who scribed them. I cannot have the various locations of the family, scattered to the winds, divulged. I must be careful and circumspect in every aspect of my life.

CA: Does anyone else know what you doing?

BROTHER GEOFFREY: There are three others in our community who know.

CA: Do they also work with these records?

BROTHER GEOFFREY: Two do. The third is more of an administrative officer within our community. We depend a great deal upon him to secure our way. Our expanded clandestine activity started a number of years ago. We began to create an underground tunnel that will extend in several directions from a chamber below us – beyond the crypt. There is another entrance that leads into this and other tunnels and chambers within the Tor. We meet on occasion in these secret chambers where we have a small collection of bound books, scrolls and chests, like the one I am currently making. Some of the records are kept in a nearby hidden vault in the library wall and some are actually in plain sight within the library and locked scriptorium. This archival and protective activity began long ago during the years Anna of Mount Carmel was the head of our fledgling library.

CA: Did you scribe some of the documents?

BROTHER GEOFFREY: Yes, there are copies that we, and others, have made before us. There are original works as well.

There are numerous extrapolated, excerpted and complete copies of very ancient texts that came from the Orient, Egypt, Greece and the Prophets and mystics of Israel. There are several original texts. Grandmother Anna was a rather zealous librarian and steward who knew the value of these records. She taught her children and her descendants to also value the light held within these many words. And more important, she exemplified how to apply this wisdom within daily life and how to create harmony within relationships.

I would say that most of the records here, the bulk of them, are in the hand of Anna. I feel a great kinship with the wise one, called Anna. I know she carried this lineage forward and I bear her blood lineage myself. I suppose that's one reason why I feel called to preserve and keep this treasure out of harm's way.

We very seldom come into the archives at the same time. We take turns, at carefully determined times, when the least suspicion will arise. We take great delight in reading and re-reading all the letters, diaries, journals and teachings. I have a lot of curiosity about these records which I hold as my stewardship. Some I can't read, as I said, but for the most part, I have the linguistic skills to discern the wisdom they contain. I use them to deepen my spiritual practice as a way to reach into the depth of my heart and soul.

CA: When you go into the tunnels and underground chambers, do you meet with others?

BROTHER GEOFFREY: No. There are only we four brothers right now. There may be more to join with us. I don't know. It's a serious responsibility.

CA: Do the ones who suspect you of heresy know that you do this?

BROTHER GEOFFREY: We pray that they do not. And those who are in leadership positions who are more supportive of our record-keeping are only told what satisfies them — we are protecting the approved missals and epistles sent to us from the churches of Rome, Ephesus and Antioch. I don't especially like keeping secrets, but I see no other way to approach this than to feign ignorance about any rumors that suggest ancient and eye-witness records exist.

For generations, there has been a fellowship of men and women bound by a sacred oath to safeguard these records and the posterity of the holy family. We have hidden the literal records and we have committed much to memory and oral transmission. We have taken aliases and contrived false genealogies. There are legends that offer clues if ears are prepared to hear the encoded truth. Whether these truths are whispered privately or offered publicly, through spoken epic tales or sung in poetic verse, it is possible for anyone who is ripe and ready to receive the Light every authentic teacher points to through their living example and teachings. This includes Master Yeshua and others who are anointed with the Divine Light.

CA: What is the main theme of the legends?

BROTHER GEOFFREY: That the holy family was here. There are the words and records kept by our great matriarch, Anna, the mother of the Blessed Virgin and the grandmother of our Lord. There is a lovely little book of prayers written in the hand of the Virgin Mother. When I say virgin mother, I know she is not a virgin in the way that the letters I spoke of are saying. She lived a deep mystery tradition that is now mostly lost among us. There are other scripts written by Mary of Bethany and Myriam of Tyana, Yeshua's cousin, Mariam, and his daughter Elizabeth Hannah (*Lizbett*). A large volume of history was kept by Anna's son, Andrew and an alchemical treatise was left by her son, Joseph of Arimathea. Her son, Noah, left a great legacy of secreted oral history and wisdom teachings.

If truth be known, I have received some of Noah's vast teachings directly from him through my own eyes and ears. There are others who were his students who received much more. Some of what they received is held within the records I preserve and secret away. Most of these great souls have dispersed to other lands and they have taken their wisdom with them. Several remain; but I cannot disclose their names. It was only eight years ago that Noah laid his body within a sepulcher in the Tor beside his mother and wives. Some privately say he and his wives are not dead; but sleeping. I know they lived to a great age made possible by practicing a very ancient alchemy that comes out of Egypt and the Far East. This is a hidden art and science (*The Rites of the Sepulcher*). I know of no one practicing it today. But then, as I have said, much is kept hidden. Perhaps these eyes will see this great teacher again before my body rests.

CA: You say you are a descendant of Anna. Which of Anna's children was your ancestor?

BROTHER GEOFFREY: Curiously there were actually two of Anna's children who are my direct ancestors. There is Joseph of Arimathea and Noah. From these two brothers, there was intermarriage of cousins who were Anna's grandchildren and great-grandchildren. Of these, there was Elizabeth Hannah whom you know as Lizbett, the daughter of Yeshua and Mary of Bethany, the daughter of Joseph of Arimathea. There were also the descendants of the children of Joses and Johannes, the sons of Yeshua and Myriam of Tyana who are my ancestors. Besides those who are directly descended from Anna's children, there are those of the Celtic tribes who make up my ancestry, such as a son of Anna's beloved companion, John, and those native Britons who married Joseph and Noah.

CA: What motivated you to join the monastery at Glastonbury?

BROTHER GEOFFREY: Well, for many of us it seems to be the most prudent thing to do. It is a way to secure a fairly steady livelihood and it is a place that encourages a contemplative life. We are not bothered for the most part by the concerns and distractions most face in their lives. However, beyond these issues, I believe the primary reason I am here is that my family has resided upon this sacred land for generations; many of them choosing to follow the contemplative path our ancestors have taken for millennia. It also seems to be the ideal place in which to conceal a true testament of our Master.

CA: Are there both men and women in this monastery?

BROTHER GEOFFREY: There is a nunnery a ways off, in the area on Chalice Hill where the women lived in Anna's time. But it is mostly men who live here.

CA: Is there much interaction between the men and the women.

BROTHER GEOFFREY: We come together to celebrate, pray and study. Some of us are married and have children. I was once married and enjoyed having my wife here with me. She, too, was a descendant of Anna through Elizabeth Hannah. We enjoyed parenting four children. Now, I prefer a life of celibacy and devotion in which all my energy is offered up to Father-Mother God. I would say there are more celibates than those who are married at this time. We emulate, as best we can, with our limited understanding, how our Essene forebears lived at Mount Carmel.

CA: How do you deal with the confusion that is arising about the different teachings that are said to be Yeshua's true teachings?

BROTHER GEOFFREY: As I have said, there is so much misunderstanding and it seems to be increasing instead of diminishing. I don't feel it falls upon me to straighten it all out. It is better to allow the karmic wheel to continue to turn as it will. Rather, it is more incumbent upon me to give my attention to being mindful of how I am living each day. At sunrise, I commit my full presence to every moment life offers to me as a gift; be it an opportunity for a kind gesture, or some compassionate action that provides a greater peace and comfort to other souls, or simply to rest in the wonder of each breath. I ask myself daily at sunset, as I take an accounting, "Is it with gratitude, loving-kindness and forgiveness that I have served life during the course of this precious day, as Master Yeshua and the Magdalenes did?"

My heart tells me to hold silence about what is my stewardship and to feel thankful that I may have this treasure close to me. I have the great blessing of actually feeling of its physicality and partaking of its wisdom, its beauty, its grandeur and most of all, its intimate closeness within the display of my life. It brings me very close to my Lord and to those who have gone before me. My other three brothers, likewise, find value in preserving these truths. They, too, are of this family. They carry this blood as well. We are a fellowship, a society unto ourselves. We don't give it any particular name. I'm being told it will have a number of names later on. Right now it is just very pure and simple.

CA: Do any of you have children? Are you concerned about it being passed down through a genetic lineage?

BROTHER GEOFFREY: We are not so much concerned about a genetic lineage carrying on this stewardship. We are more concerned about complete fidelity to the truths within these records, whether the steward of them carries the blood of my family or not. Now it seems that, more often than not, our fellowship is comprised of close family members. But with time the seeding is exponentially spreading. I know Anna and most of her children did not seek to create an elite family dynasty. And most certainly, this was never Yeshua's or the Magdalenes' intent. So I would say it is by resonance and karmic attunement, more than by literal blood lineage, that calls this fellowship together and preserves it from generation to generation.

There is a woman one of the brothers is courting who seems to carry this profound resonance. She has a spiritual readiness to carry on the work. This is a great blessing because her sweet feminine and intuitive nature will be a great boon to our efforts. Perhaps our work can be passed on to their children.

CA: Is there anything more you wish to share?

BROTHER GEOFFREY: Well, I am seeing into the future a bit. (*Pause*)

(*Brother Geoffrey's voice becomes a raspy whisper.*)

I don't know that it is necessary to report all the details I am seeing. It is sufficient to say that I am seeing myself using crutches; my legs having been broken, my tongue is blackened, and my teeth and jaw are broken. But worst of all, I see that some of the records have been lost because they were not taken to another location in time. It is good to have this foreknowledge. I will see to it that the most precious records are taken to our other repositories, especially those in Scotland.

What I see happening with my body is karma, no doubt and an opportunity to bring greater compassion each day to those who suffer. Is it not true that we all suffer to some extent or another until we are returned to the Great Mother's bosom?

(*Great sigh.*)

It will not be long now before my departing. I must make good use of each precious day.

There's no more to say other than to pronounce a blessing upon you in your day: May humanity be quickened with this same Light that I have sought to protect with my very life. May all beings know the Peace that passes all understanding and open their hearts to the same Love that expressed through our beloved Master and the Magdalenes long ago.

CA: May it be so. Thank you for coming and sharing your wisdom and love.

ANNA'S LAST WORDS

Within the haven of Avalon, I chose my body's final resting-place. Here I took my last conscious breath and stepped through the mists into the Light's infinite sea. My embalmed earthy garment remains within a tomb of stone below the place where the sacred mound called Chalice Hill joins with the Druid's Tor.

Today I walk in my body of rainbow light where the fertile red spring of the goddess mates with the seminal god's waters, white. Beside a great yew, that was but a seedling when I planted it almost 2,000 years ago, I often take pause. If perchance you are ever lingering within Chalice Hill's garden, you might remember me and be still. Call my name, dear friend, and you may catch a rose-scented breeze wafting my essence near. Whether or not you walk where once I walked, you may transport yourself from wherever you are by attuning to my pervading essence etched within my words, as you turn these pages.

Through these words, I raise up a new song of ecstatic union and impassioned freedom to go out upon the beckoning winds. Gently I entreat, "Come hither, my beloved friend. Be Anna's guest. Come with me and enter into the fertile vale where, in eternal union, walk the Christ and the Magdalenes. Together, we shall accomplish our work of redeeming love, not by force or untoward manipulation. Rather, we shall gratefully yield up the anguishing fruits of further separation. Yes, as promised before time, we shall herald the glad news with one voice, 'Separation is finished! – I AM the ALL and the ALL is One Life! Amen and Amen."

Know this, my beloved friend, it is not for the purpose of perpetuating stories that I leave these words; but rather it is for the quickening of the "seeds of the Christ Light" within you. And so it is that I transmit the Beloved's voice so that you may be comforted

---

[63] The red spring is located in Chalice Well Garden and the White Spring is located at the foot of the Tor.

and know the Peace beyond all understanding. Now it is you, who continues this Great Work for the benefit of all beings.

My peace I give unto you until we meet again.

And so it is, I bid you fond farewell until another season when we may meet at the Mother's garden gate and tie ribbons of peace upon boughs forever green.

APPENDIX

Transitional Note

{*The following charts are provided to assist you in finding your way through the complex terrain of people and places in the passage of time within the book, "Anna, the Voice of the Magdalenes." The charts may additionally assist you in bridging the material within the first Anna book with its sequel.*

Much of the following information was received telepathically and the remainder from deductive reasoning and written historical records. Please understand that these charts are only "maps" and should not be given misplaced attention. It is the messages and the awakening energies within them which are important; not the names, relationships, and dates, etc., no matter how colorful and interesting they may be. These details serve only to point to much greater and more relevant truths; such as opening to love and to the Reality beyond reality, to which the Magdalenes give voice.

The following detailed information was accessed by Claire through channeled/psychic methods and cannot be substantiated, as such. It may or may not be grounded in fact. It is possible that physical documentation may yet prove or has already proven certain of these data. For those who require some kind of physical evidence, these charts may provide hypothetical "clues" for further research.

The dates and events involving the Roman invasion and occupation of Britain are based on historical resources included in the bibliography.

Please proceed with childlike curiosity while maintaining a healthy skepticism, and most of all enjoy the journey Home; which is this story's ultimate destination. Even though these charts may appear quite complex, the journey is actually quite simple and ordinary. Do not be intimidated or distracted by superficial details. Relax! Rest your mind. Laugh! You already have everything you need. You are the Voice of the Magdalenes and the destination you seek!}

– TIMELINE –

– THE SEEDING OF LIGHT –

– DESCENDENTS CHARTS –

ANNA'S DESCENDENTS CHART
JOSEPH OF ARIMATHEA'S DESCENDENTS CHART
YESHUA'S DESCENDENTS CHART

– BIBLIOGRAPHY –

– ACKNOWLEDGEMENTS –

– ABOUT THE AUTHORS –

APPENDIX

Anna, the Voice of the Magdalenes
Timeline

BC

57 BC
- Anna gives birth to Joseph of Arimathea at Mt Carmel
- 55 BC & 54 BC
- Julius Caesar invades southeast Britain but promptly returns to Rome

47 BC
- Anna gives birth to twins Isaac and Andrew at Mt Carmel

45 BC
- Anna gives birth to Jacob at Mt Carmel

43 BC
- Anna gives birth to Josephus at Mt Carmel

33 BC
- Anna gives birth to Noah at Mt Carmel

25 BC
- Anna's son Jacob moves to Mt Bugarach in the Languedoc of France

22 BC
- Anna's son Isaac (b. 47 BC) moves to Heliopolis and marries Tabitha (b. 27 BC)
- Anna's sons Andrew, Josephus, and Noah move to Avalon

20 BC
- Anna gives birth to Mary Anna (*Mother Mary*) in September in Ephesus

18 BC
- Isaac and Tabitha move to Mt Bugarach

4 BC
- Anna's husband, Joachim, goes through a conscious death process.
- Mary Anna (*Mother Mary*) gives birth to Light-conceived Yeshua
- Yeshua's Light-conceived female cousins Mariam, Mary of Bethany, Sara and Vivian are born. Light-conceived John ben Zebedee is also born.

AD

14 AD
- Mariam and Mary of Bethany journey to Heliopolis, Egypt to take initiations in the Temples of Isis, Osiris and Horus. They become priestesses of Isis within the Magdalene Order
- Myriam of Tyana (Age 19) & Yeshua (Age 17) meet at the well in northern Samaria
- Myriam & Yeshua's betrothal in Mt Carmel, Galilee and wedding in Ginaea, Samaria
- Myriam becomes pregnant with Joses Simeon
- Myriam & Yeshua journey to India via Tyana, Turkey

15 AD
- Myriam of Tyana gives birth to Yeshua's son, Joses Simeon, in Varanasi (*Benares*), India at the home of Yeshua's brother, Joseph (*known as Joseph the Younger and Joses in his youth to distinguish him from his father, Joseph ben Jacob*).
- Dancing Wind is born in Glamorgan, Wales

18 AD
- Myriam gives birth to Yeshua's daughter, Miriam, in India

19 AD
- Yeshua's consort, Radha, dies in childbirth while delivering Yeshua's son, Jude, in India
- Myriam of Tyana adopts Jude as her child

20 AD
- Yeshua's father, Joseph ben Jacob, takes his ascension within a cave in the Himalayas

21 AD
- In late summer, Yeshua (Age 24), Myriam of Tyana (Age 26) return to Palestine from India with their children Joses Simeon (Age 6), Miriam (Age 3) and Jude (Age 2)

22 AD
- Mary Anna (*Mother Mary*) marries her 2nd husband Ahmed
- Yeshua, Myriam, Mary of Bethany and Mariam, together with other disciples, go to Heliopolis, Egypt

24 AD
- Mary Anna (*Mother Mary*) gives birth to John Mark early in the year
- Yeshua & Mary of Bethany are betrothed during the November full moon

APPENDIX

25 AD
- Myriam of Tyana becomes pregnant with Johannes
- Late spring, Yeshua, Myriam and their children, Mary of Bethany, Mariam and Nathaniel go to India with other disciples
- Mary Anna (*Mother Mary*) gives birth to twins, Esther Salome & Matteas

26 AD
- Myriam of Tyana gives birth to Yeshua's son, Johannes, in February in India

27 AD
- In the spring, Johannes (Age 1), is left with Yeshua's brother, Joseph, in India
- Yeshua, Myriam of Tyana and their older children Joses (Age 11), Jude (Age 7), Miriam (Age 8); Mary of Bethany and disciples return to Galilee from India in late autumn

28 AD
- Yeshua is baptized by his cousin, John the Baptist, early autumn
- Sara (*daughter of Isaac & Tabitha*) comes to Galilee from Mount Bugarach in the fall. She meets and marries Phillip of Bethsaida
- Yeshua & Mary of Bethany's wedding is celebrated at Cana in December

30 AD
- Mary of Bethany & Yeshua conceive Sar'h in April during the night of the Last Supper
- Yeshua's crucifixion and resurrection
- Joseph of Arimathea takes Mary of Bethany, together with Myriam and her children, to Alexandria, Egypt
- Mary of Bethany (Age 33) gives birth to Yeshua's daughter, Sar'h, on Winter Solstice at an Essene/Therapeutae monastery near Lake Mareotis south of Alexandria

31 AD
- Benjamin (Age 16) (*Mariam & Nathaniel's son*) is stoned to death in Jerusalem

32 AD The Family Travels to southern France
- Joseph of Arimathea takes family members to Alexandria in the late spring. These include: Anna, Mary Anna (Age 51) and her children: Ruth (Age 28), John Mark (Age 8), Esther Salome and Matteas (Age 6); Joseph's children: Lois Salome (Age 52) and her husband, Daniel; Martha (Age 28) and

- Lazarus (Age 30); Sara (Age 35) and her husband Phillip; and Mariam and Nathaniel, together with several unnamed male disciples
- All the previously named family members, together with Myriam (Age 37), Joses Simeon (Age 16), Miriam (Age 13), and Jude (Age 12); and Mary of Bethany and her daughter, Sar'h (Age 1 ½) miraculously cross the Great Sea on one of Joseph's boats, which had been stripped of its sail and oars
- The family arrives at Sts.-Maries-de-la-Mer mid-summer
- The family journeys to Mt Bugarach in early October
- Yeshua visits Mt Bugarach in early December
- Yeshua & Mary of Bethany Light-conceive Lizbett during the Winter Solstice

33 AD
- October – Anna shares
- Mary of Bethany gives birth to Yeshua's daughter, Lizbett, in early September
- Sara gives birth to Phillip's son, Justus, in November
- Lois Salome's husband, Daniel, dies

35 AD
- Sara gives birth to her daughter, Ceres
- Lois Salome marries Aonghas (*a Celt and Roman citizen*) and moves to Narbo Martius
- Joseph of Arimathea begins transferring part of his small fleet of freighting boats, which are kept in France, to his son-in-law, Aonghas and his sons. The boats are docked at the port of Narbo Martius. The remainder of Joseph's fleet is docked in Cornwall and Devon, England.

36 AD
- Anna's sons, Andrew and Josephus establish an Essene-Druid sanctuary in Glamorgan, Wales

38 AD The family travels to Britain
- Nathaniel (Age 55) (*Mariam's husband*) is killed at Carthage in early winter
- Mary Anna (*Mother Mary*) attempts travel to Rome but returns to Mt Bugarach because of her concern for Mariam. She decides to go with the family to Avalon.
- Anna and the family go with Joseph of Arimathea to Avalon in the late fall
- Martha (Age 35) reports her experience of being in Avalon at the Winter Solstice

39 AD

APPENDIX

- Anna nurses her friend, John, back to health at his ancestral home in the Mendip Hills
- Joseph of Arimathea takes Mary Anna (Age 58), Ruth (Age 35), John Mark (Age 15), and Myriam of Tyana (Age 44) to Rome and Ephesus
- Sara and Phillip's children Justus (Age 5) and Ceres (Age 3) remain with Sara's parents and sisters while Sara and Phillip join Mary Anna on her journey to Rome and Ephesus

40 AD

- Joseph of Arimathea takes Mary Anna (*Mother Mary*), Ruth (Age 36), John Mark (Age 16) and Myriam of Tyana (Age 45) to Ephesus and Antioch. (Myriam of Tyana's children, Joses Simeon (Age 25), Jude (Age 20) and Miriam (Age 21) are in Avalon)
- Mary Anna's sons, Thomas (*Thaddeus, Age 34*) and Simon (Age 34) come to Ephesus and Antioch from Galilee during the summer
- Mary Anna's sons, James and Jude (*with his wife, Galeah*) join their mother and Myriam in Tarsus for a short time and return to Jerusalem and Nazareth
- Mary Anna continues on to Tyana, Turkey in the fall with her sons, Thomas, Simon and John Mark. Sara and Phillip join her.

41 AD

- Mary Anna (*Mother Mary*), Ruth, John Mark, Myriam, Sara and Phillip spend the winter in Tyana and Cappadocia
- Sara, Phillip and Ruth return to Ephesus where they meet Joseph of Arimathea at the vernal equinox. Sara and Phillip return to Mount Bugarach in the spring with Joseph of Arimathea. Joseph stays for a short visit and then journeys with initiates and freight back to Avalon
- Ruth remains in Ephesus
- Mary Anna (*Mother Mary*), Thomas, Simon, John Mark and Myriam of Tyana go on to India.
- Joseph of Arimathea marries Nueme in Glamorgan, Wales

43 AD

- Nueme gives birth to Joseph of Arimathea's fraternal twin sons in Avalon
- The Romans under the command of Emperor Claudius invade southeast Britain

45 AD

- Anna and her friend John live together on Chalice Hill in Avalon

47 AD

ANNA, THE VOICE OF THE MAGDALENES

- Noah goes to Mona with his wives Rhia and Dancing Wind; Anna & her friend John; Joseph of Arimathea and Nueme, Mary of Bethany, Sar'h, Myriam of Tyana's children Joses (Age 32) and his wife, Jude (Age 28) and wife, and Miriam (Age 29) and husband; and twelve others in the spring
- Andrew and Josephus die at the Essene-Druid monastery at Glamorgan later in the year
- The Romans under Legionary General Scapula invade Wales and try to defeat the great Briton chieftain, Caradoc (*Caratacus*), who has taken allies among the Silures and Ordovices

48 AD
- Johannes (Age 22) leaves India with his wives, his mother, Myriam of Tyana, his grandmother, Mary Anna (*Mother Mary*) and his uncles, Thomas, Simon and John Mark in the spring
- They meet Joseph of Arimathea in Ephesus in the summer
- Joseph takes Johannes to Mount Carmel and Egypt in late summer
- Joseph also takes Mary Anna, Ruth, John Mark, and Myriam to Mt Carmel and Egypt and then they go on to Mt Bugarach in late fall
- Thomas and Simon return to their homes in Galilee

49 AD
- Yeshua visits the family at Mt Bugarach
- Joseph of Arimathea, Mary Anna (*Mother Mary*) Ruth, John Mark, Myriam of Tyana spend winter at Mt Bugarach
- Johannes and wives go to Mount Bugarach for a short visit and return to Egypt
- Ruth goes to an Essene outpost in French Alps
- Mary Anna (*Mother Mary*), John Mark and Myriam of Tyana return to Avalon in the early spring with Joseph of Arimathea
- Dancing Wind (Age 34) shares her story and a guided meditation

50 AD
- Caradoc continues to fight with the Silures against the Romans in Wales

51 AD
- Johannes and his wives move permanently to Britain
- Caradoc is betrayed and handed over to Romans

52 AD
- Phillip is injured on his way back to Mount Bugarach from the French Alps

55 AD

APPENDIX

- Yeshua (Age 58) visits Mount Bugarach in the early spring and invites initiates to come to "The Great Gathering" to be held in Fortingall, Scotland during the Summer Solstice
- Martha (Age 51) and Lazarus (Age 53) return to Mount Bugarach with Sara (58), Phillip and other initiates when "The Great Gathering" is finished
- Sar'h (Age 24) marries Andrew in Avalon after "The Great Gathering." They join Mary of Bethany (Age 58) and Myriam (Age 60) and Johannes (Age 29) at Mona
- Anna and her party are ambushed on their way to Mona in fall

56 AD – Dispersion of the Family Begins (*See "The Seeding of Light" chart*)

- Joseph of Arimathea and Noah stay with Anna in Avalon
- Mary Anna (*Mother Mary*) (Age 75) and her children, John Mark (Age 31), Esther Salome (Age 30), Matteas (Age 30) and most of their children return to Ephesus in the spring.
- Joseph of Arimathea takes Myriam of Tyana, her children, Joses Simeon (Age 41), Jude (Age 38) (*and most of their children*), and her infant daughter, Zariah, to Mount Bugarach in the fall.
- Three of Joses and Jude's children go with Johannes and Miriam (*and their families*) to Fortingall in the spring.
- One of John Mark's and one of Esther Salome's older children also go to Fortingall.
- One of Esther Salome's and one of Matteas' older children remain with Anna in Avalon.
- One each of Joses' and Jude's older children stay with Anna in Avalon
- Joses and Jude's younger children go to Gaul (*France*) and later go on to India

57 AD

- Joseph of Arimathea takes Mary of Bethany, two of her children: Sar'h and infant son, Michel, and Mariam to Mount Bugarach
- Lizbett and her husband Simeon stay in Avalon with Anna
- "The 3 Marys", Sar'h and Andrew travel leisurely through southern France, northern Italy and Eastern Europe.

60 AD

- Sar'h and Andrew return to Mt Bugarach
- Myriam of Tyana, Joses, Jude, Zariah, Mary of Bethany, Michel, and Mariam travel on to Ephesus where they pass the winter with Mary Anna (*Mother Mary*).

61 AD
- "The 3 Marys" families travel to Tyana in the early spring where they remain for a year.
- The massacre of Mona by the Romans and Boudicca's revolt (60/61 AD)

62 AD
- Joseph of Arimathea dies consciously in Avalon
- "The Three Marys:" Myriam (Age 67), Mary of Bethany (Age 65), and Mariam (Age 65) travel on to India with their remaining children.

63 AD
- Lizbett and her husband return to Glamorgan and begin to "face-lift" the Essene-Druid sanctuary into a hospital/orphanage

66 AD
- Mary Anna's *(Mother Mary's)* conscious death near Ephesus *(Turkey)*

68 AD
- Emperor Nero dies
- Sar'h (Age 37) relocates from southern France to Ibiza, *(Spain)*

69 AD
- Vespasian becomes Roman emperor

71 – 74 AD
- The Roman governor, Agricola, marches Roman legions north toward Scotland

75 AD
- Conquest of Silures in southern Wales by Frontinus
- Caerleon, Wales, previously a Roman fortress, becomes a Legionary base *(Caerleon is not far from the Essene-Druid sanctuary in the Glamorgan region, which, by now, has become a hospital/orphanage protected by the Romans)*
- Lizbett returns to Avalon for a visit with her three children

76 AD
- Lizbett returns to Glamorgan

78 AD
- The Silures are subdued, the Ordovices of northern Wales still hold out
- Agricola *(known for relative moderation, mercy and justice compared to his predecessor, Suetonious Paulinus, who wantonly destroyed Mona in 60-61 AD)* subdues the Ordovices and takes control of Mona by force

APPENDIX

79 – 80 AD
- Agricola marches into south Scotland
- Titus becomes Roman emperor

81 AD
- Domitian becomes Roman emperor

82 AD
- Anna's conscious death and burial within the Tor
- Agricola makes sea advance along Scotland's east coast and builds the eastern road into Perthshire, the area where Fortingall is located

84 AD
- Agricola's last battle at Mons Graupius. The Romans did not advance beyond this point in Scotland. Agricola returns to Rome.

85 AD
- Britain is controlled by only 3 legions located at Caerleon, then Chester, York and Inchtuthill in south Scotland. The Roman invasion of Britain took 41 years. The Roman occupation of Britain lasts almost 300 more years.

120 AD
- Emperor Hadrian builds the Hadrian Wall separating Scotland from England

142 AD
- The more northern Antonine Wall is built at the Firths of Forth and Clyde

178 AD
- Noah consciously dies at Avalon. His body was placed next to Anna's and his wives within a chamber in the Tor.

186 AD
- Brother Geoffrey speaks about his stewardship of the holy family's writings and the location of Anna's descendants

THE SEEDING OF LIGHT[64]

Through Anna's Child-bearing Children
& Yeshua and the Two Marys

{*The following chart lists the adults and children in* **'bold'** *letters who "seeded" a particular geographical region.*}

THE SEEDING OF SCOTLAND, 56 – 57 AD
MARY ANNA'S (age 75) Children:
➢ ESTHER SALOME'S (age 30) **child (age 12)**

YESHUA'S (age 60) & MYRIAM OF TYANA'S (age 62) Children:
➢ **JOSES SIMEON'S** (age 42) **2 children (ages 18 and 14)**
➢ **JOHANNES (age 31) and his 2 wives and 3 children (ages 5 – 1)**
➢ **MIRIAM (age 39) and her husband and 2 children (ages 12 and 8)**
➢ JUDE'S (age 38) **child (age 11)**

THE SEEDING OF ENGLAND & WALES 56 – 57 AD
JOSEPH OF ARIMATHEA and Nueme: 2 fraternal twins birthed in 43 AD

NOAH and Ariadne, Rhia and Dancing Wind's children: 10 (*plus Noah's and Ariadne's grandchildren through their Light-conceived daughter, Vivian – age 60*)

MARY ANNA'S (age 75) children:
➢ JOHN MARK'S (age 32) **child (age 7) to Avalon**
➢ ESTHER SALOME'S (age 30) **child (age 10) to Avalon**
➢ MATTEAS' (age 30) **child (age 8) to Avalon**

YESHUA'S & MYRIAM OF TYANA'S CHILDREN:
➢ JOSES SIMEON'S (age 42) **child (age 12) to Avalon**
➢ JUDE'S (age 38) **child (age 10) to Avalon**

YESHUA'S & MARY OF BETHANY'S CHILD:

---

[64] The information on this chart is channeled and cannot be documented (as of this writing).

APPENDIX

> **LIZBETT** (age 22) and her husband: 3 children are born later.

THE SEEDING OF FRANCE As of 56 - 57 AD

ISAAC and Tabitha: 8 children (*Light-conceived Sara is the youngest*)

> **SARA** (Isaac's daughter) and Phillip: 3 children

MARY ANNA'S CHILDREN:
> **RUTH** and Nathan: 2 children in the French Alps
> **ESTHER SALOME**: 1 child (age 8) to live with Ruth in the French Alps

YESHUA AND MYRIAM OF TYANA'S CHILDREN:
> **JOSES SIMEON'S** child (age 16) to Mt Bugarach
> **MIRIAM'S** child (age 16) to Mt Bugarach
> **JUDE'S** child (age 8) to Mt Bugarach
> **JOHANNES'S** child (age 8) to Mt Bugarach

YESHUA AND MARY OF BETHANY'S CHILD:
> **SAR'H** and Andrew *after* 57 AD: 4 children in southern France; Ibiza, Spain; and Eastern Europe. After traveling in these three regions, 2 children continue to reside in southern France and 2 reside in Eastern Europe as adults.

THE SEEDING OF THE ALPS & EASTERN EUROPE

MARY ANNA'S CHILDREN:
> **RUTH** and Nathan: 2 children
> **JOHN MARK'S** children: 6 children *after* 61 AD in Avalon

YESHUA AND MARY OF BETHANY'S CHILD:
> **SAR'H** and Andrew *after* 70 AD: 2 children in Eastern Europe and 2 in southern France

THE SEEDING OF EGYPT

MARIAMNE (*Anna's daughter*) and Adolphus' children: 2

THE SEEDING OF THE MIDDLE EAST (Turkey and Israel)

ANNA'S (CHILD-BEARING CHILDREN): NATHAN (14), LUKE (6) and MARY ANNA (10)

MARY ANNA'S CHILDREN:
> **JUDE** and Galeah: number of children unknown

- ➤ **THOMAS** and (?): number of children unknown
- ➤ **SIMON** and (?): number of children unknown
- ➤ **ESTHER SALOME** and (?): 3 children in Ephesus as of 57 AD: 1 child in Avalon, 1 in Fortingall and 1 in Mt Bugarach
- ➤ **MATTEAS** and (?): 1 child in Ephesus and 1 child in Avalon

THE SEEDING OF INDIA AND THE HIMALAYAS

MARY ANNA'S CHILD:
- ➤ **JOSEPH THE YOUNGER** and (?): number of children unknown

YESHUA AND MYRIAM OF TYANA'S & CHILDREN: (*As of 62AD after the dispersion from Avalon.*)
- ➤ **JOSES SIMEON** and wife: 2 children (ages 10 and 7) go to India. (1 in Avalon, 2 in Fortingall and 1 in France)
- ➤ MIRIAM'S **child (age 20)**
- ➤ **JUDE and wife & 1 child** go to India. 1 child in Avalon, 1 in Fortingall and 1 in France
- ➤ **ZARIAH** (infant daughter conceived in Fortingall in 55 AD)

YESHUA AND MARY OF BETHANY'S CHILD:
- ➤ **MICHEL** (infant son conceived in Fortingall in 55 AD)

DISPERSION AS OF 56 AD:

Mary Anna's (Age 75) children and grandchildren

- ➤ John Mark (Age 32) Number of children: 3
  1 child (Age 7) dispersed to Avalon
  2 children (Ages 5 and 3) dispersed to Ephesus

- ➤ Esther Salome (Age 30) Number of children: 6
  1 child (Age 10) dispersed to Avalon,
  1 child (Age 12) dispersed to Fortingall
  1 child (Age 8) dispersed to France
  3 children (Ages 3-6) dispersed to Ephesus

- ➤ Matteas (Age 30) Number of children: 2
  1 child (Age 8) dispersed to Avalon
  1 child (Age 5) dispersed to Ephesus

Myriam of Tyana's (Age 62) children and grandchildren

- ➤ Joses Simeon (Age 42) Number of children: 6

2 children (Ages 18 and 14) dispersed to Fortingall
1 child (Age 12) dispersed to Avalon
1 child (Age 16) dispersed to France
2 children (Ages 10 and 7) dispersed to India.

➤ Jude (Age 38) Number of children: 4
1 child (Age 11) dispersed to Fortingall
1 child (Age 10) dispersed to Avalon
1 child (Age 8) dispersed to France
1 child (Age 6) dispersed to India

➤ Miriam (Age 39) Number of children: 4
1 child (Age 16) dispersed to France
1 child (Age 20) dispersed to India
2 children (Ages 12 and 8) dispersed to Fortingall

➤ Johannes (Age 31) Number of children: 5
1 child (Age 8) dispersed to France,
1 child (Age 7) dispersed to India
3 children (Ages 1-5) dispersed to Fortingall

Mary of Bethany's (Age 59) children

➤ Sar'h (Age 26) Number of children: 0 (no children yet) Sar'h goes to southern France
➤ Lizbett (Age 23) Number of children: 0 (no children yet) Lizbett remains in Avalon and Glamorgan, Wales
➤ Michel (Infant, born in 56 AD) goes to India

ANNA, THE VOICE OF THE MAGDALENES

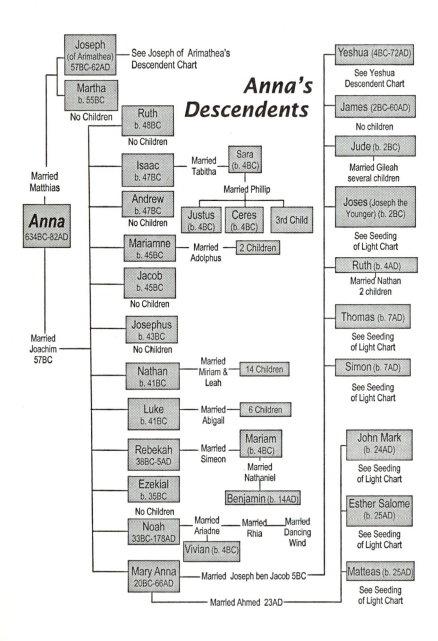

APPENDIX

Joseph of Arimathea's Descendents

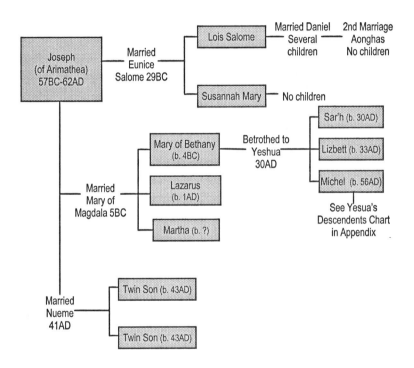

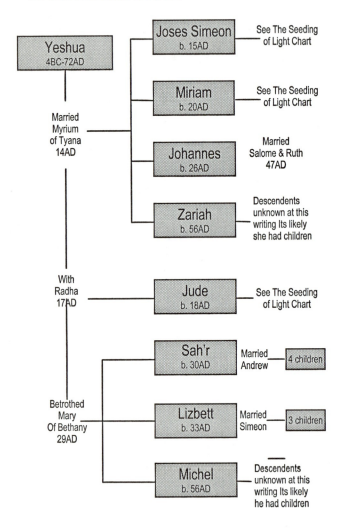

APPENDIX

BIBLIOGRAPHY

Cottrell, Leonard. *The Roman Invasion of Britain*. New York: Barnes & Noble Books and the Marboro Books Corp., 1992. (Originally published as *The Great Invasion*)

Jimenez, Ramon. *Caesar against the Celts*. New Jersey: Castle Books, 114 Northfield Avenue, Edison, New Jersey 08837. 1996.

Webster, Graham. *Rome Against Caratacus, The Roman Campaigns in Britain AD 48 – 58*. Barnes & Noble Books. 1982. (Copyright Graham Webster, 1981.)

CLAIRE'S ACKNOWLEDGEMENTS

My gratitude is eternally given to the Infinite One – the Beloved Friend, Councils of Light, Anna, Yeshua and the Magdalenes for enfolding me in your Grace, Wisdom and Love. My life is yours in Oneness, dedicated to the upliftment and liberation of all beings.

I wish to lovingly acknowledge my mother, Eileen; my brother, Harold; and my daughters; Susanne, Lara, Melinda and Heidi; and all my grandchildren, for all the ways your sweet presence enriches my life. My gratitude also extends to my spiritual family whose conscious dedication to awakening and devotion to love inspires me.

Birthing Anna's sequel onto the Earthplane could never have happened without the generous and patient collaborative presence of Catherine Ann Clemett and C. W. My appreciation and love for you, and all that you have given only deepens with time, as I realize the magnitude of our co-creation with Anna and the Councils. My gratitude also extends to J. K. for your financial generosity, which makes the production of this book possible. Thank you, dearest Virginia Essene, for passing the S.E.E. Publishing torch on to me. May this endeavor add to the light you have shown the world through your compassionate service and integrity over many years.

Special thanks go to my e-mail cheerleaders for your encouragement and to all of you who have so patiently held this amazing story in your hearts. Thank you, Catherine Ann, for your unwavering dedication to bringing forth the best possible interior layout design. And thank you, Shannon Bodie of Lightbourne for your sensitive artistry in creating our cover design. I also wish to acknowledge the R. R. Donnelley and Phoenix Color staff for your printing and production expertise.

I wish to acknowledge my beloved, Lorenzo, for believing in me; and for lovingly sharing each awakening step, which opens us to the joy and splendor of the Beloved's Infinite Heart.

May the Magdalenes inspire your way! Thanks to one and all!

APPENDIX

CATHERINE ANN'S ACKNOWLEDGEMENTS

I am most grateful to Anna, the Councils of Light, St. Germain, Yeshua, the Magdalene Order and all of the beings in the higher realms who had a part in opening this particular journey for me which my human understanding didn't even have a clue was a possibility at the outset. I am so glad I listened and was willing to follow my guidance.

I am immensely grateful to Claire Heartsong for her trust, her support, her belief in me and her willingness to have us join her in a collaborative way to bring forth this sequel. I also wish to thank my friend, C. W., who was not only instrumental in helping us lay the groundwork for the sequel, but was also the catalyst who got both of us to Utah to work with Claire in the first place.

There are several other people I wish to also acknowledge for their support, guidance, encouragement and assistance in various forms along the way including: Valerie Draves, Evelyn Ochoa, Virginia Essene, Vickie Moyle, Judith Rose Moore, Cynthia Slon, Suzanne Rollow and my mother, Evelyn Clemett. I am also grateful to Margaret Ruby for first mentioning Claire's book *Anna, Grandmother of Jesus* during a training of hers which I attended in 2004. This, as I've mentioned, was the start of a remarkable series of synchronistic events unfolding which led me to be in co-creation of this sequel with Claire.

And then there are all of you, who have felt deeply connected to the Anna book and Anna's messages of love and wisdom. I honor you for the space you have all held these many years in great anticipation of this sequel being birthed.

Claire Heartsong

Claire in a Dartmoor faerie glade, Devon, England

While raising a family, Claire received a Masters degree in fine art and art education. She taught art as an adjunctive faculty member of Boise State University until her spiritual path took her to Mount Shasta, California in 1989.

Her travels sharing Anna's message have taken her into the embrace of spiritual family world-wide.

She is presently enjoying living a quiet contemplative life with her spiritual partner, Lorenzo, in a remote and beautiful, wild mountain-river valley located in the Shasta-Trinity National Forest of northern California.

Now that the sequel is birthed, she is free to enter more deeply into meditation practices and conscious relationship as a path of spiritual awakening. This is embroidered with the delights of Nature and co-creating simple projects with Lorenzo. They enjoy combining their mutual love of inspiring prose with his passion for nature photography and her visionary art.

APPENDIX

Catherine Ann Clemett

Catherine Ann has been on a spiritual path her entire life although this did not come into the forefront for her until her late twenties. Her early life was devoted to training, performing, teaching and choreographing dance which culminated in her receiving a MFA in Dance, Drama and Theater from the University of Hawaii in 1978. Her professional dance career abruptly ended, however, as a result of injuries sustained in a car accident. Although devastated by this at the time, it opened the way for her to shift her focus to more spiritual endeavors studying with many teachers, channels, and healers over the years.

Catherine Ann has trained in many different light work and healing modalities as well as being certified as an Integrative Coach with Debbie Ford, training in past-life regression with Dolores Canon, and being certified in hypnotherapy through the National Association of Transpersonal Hypnotherapists. She started working for Claire Heartsong as her business manager in 2006.

As a free spirit, Catherine Ann's traveling, writing, developing seminars and workshops, and engaging in her passion, Argentine Tango, is where she focuses her attention these days.

Books by the Authors

Anna, the Voice of the Magdalenes
– By Claire Heartsong and Catherine Ann Clemett
www.annathevoiceofthemagdalenes.com
(*Available in paperback, eBook, and Kindle*)

Anna, Grandmother of Jesus
-By Claire Heartsong
www.annagrandmotherofjesus.com
(*Available in paperback, eBook and Kindle*)

Anna, Grandmother of Jesus (*French Version*)
-By Claire Heartsong
Ariane Editions Inc.
www.ariane.qc.ca

Understanding Twin Flame Union
-By Claire Heartsong
www.understandingtwinflameunion.com
(*Available in eBook*)

Twin Souls and Soulmates: The I AM Presence of St. Germain
-Channeled through Azena Ramanda and Claire Heartsong
Published by Triad Publishers, LTD, Australia, 1994
(*Currently only available through Internet search*)

Finding the One True Love: How Breaking the Rules Will Change Your Life
-By Angelina Heart and Catherine Ann Clemett
www.findingtheonetruelove.com
(*Available in eBook*)

Soul Weaving: Unlocking the Power of Your Twin Flame and the Treasure of Your Soul
-By Catherine Ann Clemett
www.soulweaving.net
(*Available in eBook, Kindle, and maybe later in paperback*)

www.claireheartsong.com

www.catherineannclemett.com

Also from S.E.E. Publishing Company:

Infinite Light
-By Lorenzo Dell'Anno
(*A book of inspirational quotes and nature photography*)
www.claireheartsong.com

Notes